IF WE
BURN

IF WE BURN

THE MASS PROTEST DECADE AND THE MISSING REVOLUTION

VINCENT BEVINS

PUBLICAFFAIRS

New York

PublicAffairs
Hachette Book Group
1290 Avenue of the Americas, New York, NY 10104
www.publicaffairsbooks.com
@Public_Affairs

Printed in the United States of America

First Edition: October 2023

Published by PublicAffairs, an imprint of Hachette Book Group, Inc. The PublicAffairs name and logo is a trademark of the Hachette Book Group.

The Hachette Speakers Bureau provides a wide range of authors for speaking events. To find out more, go to hachettespeakersbureau.com or email HachetteSpeakers@hbgusa.com.

PublicAffairs books may be purchased in bulk for business, educational, or promotional use. For more information, please contact your local bookseller or the Hachette Book Group Special Markets Department at special.markets@hbgusa.com.

The publisher is not responsible for websites (or their content) that are not owned by the publisher.

Print book interior design by Jeff Williams.

Library of Congress Cataloging-in-Publication Data
Names: Bevins, Vincent, author.
Title: If we burn : the mass protest decade and the missing revolution / Vincent Bevins.
Description: New York : PublicAffairs, 2023. | Includes bibliographical
   references and index. |
Identifiers: LCCN 2023011501 | ISBN 9781541788978 (hardcover) | ISBN
   9781541788961 (ebook)
Subjects: LCSH: Protest movements—History—21st century. | Government,
   Resistance to—History—21st century.
Classification: LCC HM883 .B488 2023 | DDC 303.48/40905—dc23/eng/20230510
LC record available at https://lccn.loc.gov/2023011501

ISBNs: 9781541788978 (hardcover), 9781541788961 (ebook)

LSC-C

Printing 1, 2023

For Mary Celeste and Bernadette,
for Rylee and Cecelia Dewi

Contents

Introduction 1

PART ONE

1 Learning to Protest 11
2 Mayara and Fernando 33
3 Pior que tá não fica 49
4 More Than an Uprising 55
5 Around the World 79
6 A Social Network 87
7 Cowboys and Indians 97
8 Minority Report 105
9 The Free Fare Movement 115
10 The Giant Awakens 127
11 Five Causes, Four Fingers 139

PART TWO

12 Eu Maidan 151
13 The Free Brazil Movement 171
14 Under My Umbrella 179
15 No Gods, No Representation 189
16 A Tale of Two Impeachments 203

17   I Was in the 212   217
18   O Mito   223
19   A Tale of Two Explosions   235
20   Reconstructing the Past   257
21   Building the Future   281

Acknowledgments   287
Notes   291
Index   321

Introduction

ON JUNE 13, 2013, THE military police attacked us. We were standing on a street named Consolação in the center of South America's largest city. The mass of people had come to a stop and was looking up a hill at heavily armored troops, deciding what to do next, when the cops decided for us. Without warning, they began shooting directly at the crowd—tear gas, shock bombs, maybe rubber bullets—it was hard to know in the moment. The point of this kind of repression is to force you to immediately seek shelter and stop thinking about anything but your own safety. The crowd stops being a crowd and is reduced to a set of individuals. You close your eyes and look down at the ground, sneaking peeks at your surroundings, seeking escape. We scattered through the night into whatever crevice we could find. It was dark, as winter was arriving, and about as cold as it ever gets in São Paulo. There are skyscrapers everywhere in this city, and I found a bit of refuge in the entrance of a residential building. It took me a few moments to regain my senses and realize where I was, after I had confirmed I could still breathe with some regularity.

I had been to a lot of protests in my life, around the world and in Brazil, and this was new. Usually the crackdown comes through waves of escalating, back-and-forth provocation and reaction between the cops and the demonstrators. There are several opportunities to leave if you don't want to stick around for the rough stuff, and you can often even understand why the police take the action they do. Not this time. This felt like an intentional assault carried out by the state.

I was not on the streets as a protester; I was working as a journalist, both as an international correspondent and one of a few people from the United States with some role in the Brazilian media. It feels a little silly to say that the police attacked "us," when the reporters were probably not the intended target of the offensive, and we were not the brave protagonists actually trying to take risks and make history that night. But the fact that journalists also suffered is, I believe, crucial for understanding how these events shaped history.

The police assault starts to become comprehensible if we analyze everything that led up to that night. But even more fascinating, even more puzzling, is what came next. How is it possible that the protests of June 2013 led to the country that existed by the end of the decade? This question is far from settled. When you pose it to the Brazilians who lived through all of this, you may be answered with careful (though usually varied and contradictory) analysis, or met with a flash of rage or a look of dejection, followed by an empty stare into the distance.

For now, we can briefly summarize the events that followed. The crackdown on June 13 led to an explosion of sympathy for demonstrations that had been organized by a small group of leftists and anarchists demanding cheaper public transportation. Millions of people took to the streets, shaking the Brazilian political system to its core. New demonstrators brought new demands—better schools and healthcare, less corruption and police violence—into the mass movement, which could be read as fundamentally progressive. Indeed, the leaders of the Workers' Party—which had been in power since 2003—interpreted the uprising in exactly this way.

At the beginning of 2013, it was possible to claim that Brazil's Partido dos Trabalhadores (PT), or Workers' Party, had carried out the most significant social democratic project in the history of the Global South. Outside the rich countries of the First World, a left-leaning government had managed to combine economic growth, within the capitalist world system, with social policies that meaningfully alleviated poverty, garnering widespread support within a liberal democracy. It appeared to Luiz Inácio "Lula" da Silva and his successor, Dilma Rousseff, that the people on the streets in June 2013 were simply asking for more. But just a few years later, the country would be ruled by the most radically right-wing elected leader in the world, a man who openly called for a return to dictatorship and mass violence. Public services would fall apart as poverty mounted and officials bragged about the state murder of Brazilian citizens.[1] In short—the Brazilian people got the exact opposite of what they appeared to ask for in June 2013.

IN THE PAST DECADE, FROM 2010 to 2020, this kind of story was far from unique. Around the world, humanity witnessed the explosion of mass protests that heralded profound changes. They were experienced as euphoric victory for their participants and met with adulation and optimism in the international press. But years later, after most of the foreign reporters were gone, we see that the uprisings preceded—if not necessarily caused—outcomes that were very different from the goals of the movements. Nowhere did things turn out as planned. In far too many cases, things got much worse, according to the standards articulated by the streets themselves.

Indeed, it might even be possible to tell the story of that decade as the story of mass protests and their unexpected consequences. At the risk of appearing over-ambitious, this book will attempt to do just that. What happens if we try to write the story of the world, from 2010 to 2020, guided by one puzzling question—how is it possible that so many mass protests apparently led to the opposite of what they asked for?

Beginning in Tunisia in 2010, protests rapidly escalated into something much larger, and qualitatively different, than what either participants or officials had initially expected. With one government overthrown, other movements erupted, either toppling leaders or leading to profound changes across the region, in a process the foreign press dubbed the "Arab Spring."

By 2013, the Brazilian people and media already had a ready-made set of concepts that could be used to interpret their incipient protest movement. Some outlets ended up calling the June demonstrations the "Brazilian Spring."[2] On the night of June 13, the crowd erupted into a chant as we were tear-gassed: "Love is over. Turkey is here!" They were referring to protests and repression going on at the same time in Istanbul. I put this on Twitter and—in one of my first experiences with the ups and downs of social media—it went viral. Over the next few weeks, I received photos and messages from people in Gezi Park, the site of the Turkish protest, holding signs saying things like "the whole world is São Paulo" and "Turkey and Brazil are one." By 2020, after street battles from Chile to Hong Kong, the world had experienced more mass protest in the previous decade than at any other point in human history, exceeding the famous global cycle of contention in the 1960s.[3]

But was that right? Was the whole world really São Paulo? Was it actually correct to affirm that "everywhere is Tahrir," as an Egyptian slogan had claimed earlier in the decade? I believe that in many places, certainly in Brazil, things would have gone differently if these connections had not been made. Did it make any sense at all to declare there was a "Spring" in Brazil, or even in the Arab world itself? Mass demonstrations in certain places had inspired uprisings elsewhere, both emotionally and in the tactics that were adopted. But local context differed wildly. By taking a truly global approach, we can begin to see which factors were common across many different locations, and which were crucially different. In order to understand what happened during that decade, and to learn from it, we need to pay attention to both.

Whether we recognize it or not, whether it appears clearly to the naked eye, we now live in a global system. Even back in 1789, the year of the revolution that would set the terms for so many political movements that came afterward, the rapid changes within France triggered reactions from the rest of the international community. And now, we are far more interdependent. Regardless of the format of this book that you are consuming—digital or physical or audio—it is the product of human labor and physical resources extracted all around the world, just like your clothing and almost everything else we own. There is no coherent way to discuss ambitious political movements without reference to this system.

Even before we look closely at this mass protest decade, it is possible to recognize that a certain set of approaches were morally and tactically privileged from 2010 to 2020. To varying degrees, you often heard that these were leaderless, "horizontally" organized, "spontaneous," digitally coordinated mass protests in city streets or public squares. They took forms that were said to "prefigure" the society they were meant to help bring about. For concepts that may appear unfamiliar, such as horizontalism and prefiguration—and for those that may not—I will attempt to explain how they emerged historically, and how those processes shaped what they mean today. Political struggle does not happen automatically. When human beings experience injustice, a surge of will and energy is required to make the jump to doing something about it; and it is another set of leaps entirely from making that choice to standing up, going outside, and taking a particular set of actions. The steps taken are the result, I believe, of drawing upon a range of things that have been seen or done before in one's own country—or, increasingly, somewhere else in the world, witnessed perhaps on the internet.[4]

And then after a set of actions is taken, it is a very different and quite treacherous journey entirely to correcting the injustice, or to improving society. That last part has been tricky to get right since 2010. It was my hope that by carefully analyzing that chain of human decisions and consequences, and by looking at the events of the decade in chronological order, some lessons might emerge. After working on this project for four years, I believe they have.

I AM NOT A HISTORIAN, and I have certainly never carried out a successful revolution. I'm just a journalist, and so I have no lessons to impart on my own. To the extent that I have any skills at all, I am able to recklessly throw myself around the world, tracking down the people that actually know things. I can sit down with them and ask them what they think.

For this book, I carried out over two hundred interviews in twelve countries, speaking with the people who created the street movements, many of the politicians who had to deal with them, and a lot of the people whose lives were affected.[5] Our conversations varied widely, but I attempted to orient them all around a few apparently naive, almost intentionally stupid questions: What led to the protest explosion? What were its goals? Were they achieved? If they weren't achieved, why not?

And then, instead of asking people what they did wrong or wished they would have done differently, I tried to approach follow-up questions in another way. I would often say something like: "What would you tell a teenager in Tanzania or Mexico or Kyrgyzstan, who may live through a political explosion, or might attempt to change life in her country? What lessons would you draw from your own experiences and impart to them?"

There is a reason for that framing, other than the desire to avoid retraumatizing or offending people who have made tragic sacrifices in the attempt to build a better world.

Looking at the years 2010 to 2020, it's clear that there was a huge amount of desire for changes to the structures that comprise our global system, and that this energy may very well be unleashed again soon. Like so many works of history, this one looks both forward and backward; given this orientation, people were far more willing to speak about the recent past.

And there is an especially good reason for privileging interviews here, for looking closely at these events, and understanding how participants felt as they unfolded. Some historians prefer to look at the *longue durée*, explaining social transformations through long-term changes in structures taking place below the surface, rather than individual choices. But revolutionary situations, especially of the type experienced since 2010, compress time and speed up the flow of history. They are "moments where the strangest improvisations can suddenly change the course of events," wrote Georgi M. Derluguian, a sociologist of Armenian, Russian, and Ukrainian descent.[6] A century ago, Russian revolutionary Vladimir Lenin apparently said that "there are decades when nothing happens; and there are weeks when decades happen."[7] But in cities in the twenty-first century, things move even more quickly than that, notes US political scientist Mark Beissinger, meaning there is little time to process what is happening and reflect on the next course of action.[8] Decisions are made instantly, often based on something already learned in the past, and these decisions really matter.[9] Within these moments of "thickened history," the short term can play the role of the long term.[10]

I was able to do research myself in English, Spanish, Portuguese, and Indonesian, and I relied on the help of partner researchers, journalists, and scholars to carry out interviews and investigations in Arabic, Russian, Ukrainian, Turkish, and Chinese as well. Over the same four years that I carried out interviews, I did my best to ingest the literature produced by scholars and participants. I combined these elements to create a narrative history, focusing on the period between January 1, 2010, and January 1, 2020.

Of course, decades are constructs, a convenience invented by humanity and imposed upon a far more complex reality. But that is true of language itself, and this particular trick is especially convenient for me because it limits the scope of the investigation, and that time period lines up quite nicely with a concrete set of events. The story begins in Sidi Bouzid, Tunisia, in 2010 and ends at the beginning of 2020 as world history entered a new phase, or at least adopted a different rhythm, due to the arrival of a virus. But I needed to limit myself even further if the project were to remain ambitious rather than fatally hubristic. We will only look closely at specific phenomena: protests that became so large they shook the foundations of a nation's political system, forcing it to be replaced or undergo rapid changes. Not all of them were failures, and even the failures contained small victories. For reasons that will become clear, all the cases chosen for serious analysis are outside the rich countries of the traditional First World. Since the legacies of 1789 and 1917 have served as reference points for so much revolutionary practice, it is important to trace the ways that intellectual history on the left has shaped contemporary protest, even if the desires expressed in recent episodes have fallen all over the political spectrum. In this book, I try to judge protest movements by their own goals. And inevitably, the story will be shaped by what I know best. I pay careful attention to the role of the international media and give special focus to events that I lived through. Whether I like it or not, it is true that I, along with many close friends, have been deeply transformed by the changes in Brazil, and I will have to appear briefly at times within the narrative for it to be honest.

Like many of my friends in the country, I have spent countless hours over the last decade trying to understand what happened to me in 2013, and what happened everywhere afterward. Unraveling this mystery, of how so many mass protests have led to the exact opposite of what they asked for, has been a personal quest of mine, too, and I must explain my relation to it. From 2010 to 2016, I was working as a correspondent for the *Los Angeles Times*, and I also ran a blog for *Folha de S.Paulo*, Brazil's most important newspaper. After I left, I covered Southeast Asia for the *Washington Post*, bringing me in contact with two other episodes that are relevant for this study. But the other characters in the story are far more important—and much more captivating.

Once we get to the end of the decade, we will return directly to the conversations I had with these actors, reflecting on the past and grasping at the future.

PART ONE

1

Learning to Protest

IN THE SECOND HALF OF the twentieth century, it came to be widely believed that the natural way to respond to social injustice was to take to the streets and protest—the more people the better. This historical development can only be understood in the context of the emergence of mass media.

In several of the world's most advanced capitalist countries, movements seeking political change found themselves overwhelmed by the power of radio, television, and newspaper coverage. Even when explicitly seeking to avoid mass demonstrations as their preferred tactic, they were swept up by the attention granted to them. Media coverage multiplied the effects of their actions in ways the activists had never imagined; moreover, it transformed the very structure of the movements themselves.

The inventions of writing, and then printing, and then the photograph—and finally the development of the ability to reproduce sound and moving images—were all technological leaps that profoundly transformed human society.[1] Indeed, it is likely that the idea of a "nation" itself was related to the ascendance of the printing press.[2] It is strange to remember this now, but for the vast majority of human history, we could only see what was directly in front of our faces, and the only language we could experience had to be produced by living vocal cords within a few meters of our ears. This is, strictly speaking, how our bodies developed to experience life. It made little sense to "demonstrate" to the entire country with a protest march if only a tiny percentage of the population was going to see it, and rulers could simply choose to ignore it.

Of course, people always had ways to react against ruling elites. These interventions were sometimes violent or imposed direct costs on the targets—people got killed, property got destroyed, grain was seized by the population, and so on. The academic terminology for the wide set of practices people used in these moments, from the ancient world to the twenty-first century, is "contention" or contentious politics.

The US sociologist Charles Tilly noticed that across history, when people protested, they tended to reproduce practices that already existed around them. They drew upon an existing "repertoire" of contention. That metaphor is fittingly theatrical and musical. There are a set of instruments and routines that a community has, a selection of performances everybody knows, and they use them in an improvised way.[3] In moments of rebellion, people turn to what is familiar, even if something unfamiliar might work much better. In sixteenth-century France, Tilly shows (through an analysis of early national media) that people would have never thought of demonstrating or organizing a rally or strike in the way we do today. They did, however, know how to run a tax collector out of town, force down the price of bread, or put on a *charivari*, the performance of a group belting offensive songs outside the home of a local offender, demanding retribution before they will shut up.[4] Over time, innovation occurs, and new routines of contention emerge as cultures change, but this process is relatively autonomous from the underlying causes of the revolts.

IN THE 1950S AND 1960S, a new repertoire of contention was forged through chaotic interactions with the firms that were charged with reporting the news and making profits.

In 1951, British pacifists inspired by the Indian revolutionary launched "Operation Gandhi." They sought the removal of the US military from their country, the end of nuclear weapons, and the withdrawal of the UK from NATO.[5] Like Black civil rights organizations in the USA, they were a highly disciplined, tightly organized group committed to nonviolence and willing to suffer personal consequences.[6] They underwent extensive training and made concerted attempts to present themselves as upstanding citizens rather than kooky vegetarian eccentrics (in the years just after World War II, pacifists often had that reputation). And, like Gandhi himself, they learned that actions unreported by the media would often amount to nothing.[7]

In the beginning, they considered two different approaches. The first was to launch a bold "umbrella" campaign in central London, with the umbrella symbolizing the futility and absurdity of trying to protect oneself from a nuclear explosion. They would parade with umbrellas in Grosvenor Square, suspend them from balloons over the capital, and carry them as they followed prominent figures from the US around the city. This was seen as too provocative. Instead, they chose to go out to military bases and atomic energy plants far from the city. Their activism took the form of a direct moral appeal to the people they hoped to convert. But out in the middle of nowhere, workers at the military-industrial complex simply ignored them, local farmers mocked them, and the media didn't send anyone to cover them. The pacifists found this embarrassing and ineffective. They realized they really needed to get people's attention. This may seem obvious to us now, but at the time they were learning by doing. One thing the pacifists figured out quickly was that they had to explain the meaning of their activities to passersby. They addressed this by making pamphlets.

Mass actions had never been on their agenda, both because they knew their causes were unpopular, and because absolute discipline was considered essential. But over the next few years, British dissidents—especially a group called the Committee of 100 led by philosopher Bertrand Russell—learned that assembling "very large numbers" in cities was the best way to make a splash. Shivering in a field somewhere was not. But the shift to mass protests created a troubling problem—how could you maintain strict discipline as numbers swelled?[8]

In 1960 in the United States of America, a group of young men founded Students for a Democratic Society (SDS), a left-wing association inspired by the heroic achievements of the Black civil rights movement in their country. The largely white students admired campaigns carried out by rock-solid organizations such as CORE (the Congress of Racial Equality), and they were horrified by the domestic social conditions that made them necessary. By this time, the United States—a Western European settler colony that rapidly expanded in size after its founding in 1789—had become by far the most powerful nation in the world, and it had never granted full citizenship to its nonwhite population.*

Students for a Democratic Society had its institutional roots in an old anti-Communist organization, but the members rejected anticommunism as a guiding philosophy for policy.[9] They fiercely opposed US foreign policy during the Cold War, especially the interventions that took the side of colonialism in the Third World. SDS supported civil rights and advocated for a more socialist economy, and it also took aim at an emerging process that affected students more directly. Advanced industrial society in both the capitalist West and the socialist bloc had undergone a profound bureaucratization that pushed individuals far away from the spaces where real decisions were made, and away from each other. In their influential 1962 "Port Huron Statement," SDS members proposed "participatory democracy," which would mean that individuals engage directly in decision-making, and a system in which "politics has the function of bringing people out of isolation and into community."[10]

Objectively speaking, these were some of the richest and most comfortable individuals that had ever lived on planet Earth. They spent their time learning so they could take important jobs in the most powerful nation in the world. But this generation of students often felt like they were little more than cogs in an educational machine that was increasingly integrated into the capitalist military-industrial complex. They were indeed important to the economy, which needed scientists and technicians, and their numbers were inflated by a demographic boom, meaning the balance of power shifted decisively to the young in the 1960s.[11]

SDS was not focused on large demonstrations, and had rarely thought about interacting with the media. It was a small group aiming to directly

---

* Even the limited successes of the Black civil rights movement must be understood in the context of the geopolitical situation abroad, and the putative commitment to democracy and equality at home. The Soviet Union accused the US of being a fundamentally racist society, and elites in Washington were increasingly embarrassed about proving them correct. Like the UK, the United States had some of the highest levels of media saturation in history. In a very different context, when people demonstrated in 1960 against another apartheid system in South Africa, a US Cold War ally, authorities simply gunned them down, killing or wounding 250 people in the township of Sharpeville.

organize students, without a mass communications strategy.[12] Its members were hesitant to create rigid structures or leadership positions with clear duties, which was a radical deviation from the way older organizations like unions and political parties had always operated. In the first half of the 1960s, SDS grew slowly through face-to-face outreach and personal connections as it experimented with new forms of political organization. But in 1965, an unexpected surge of attention engulfed the organization.

That fall, even though SDS had declined to lead a set of protests against the Vietnam War, the media chose to focus on the organization. SDS already had a bit of a reputation as an anti-war outfit, so perhaps reporters, always pressed for time, had seen the name somewhere and could use it to tell the story. Writing later, SDS president Todd Gitlin recalled that this pushed "a bewildered and incoherent SDS to the center of attention; SDS was suddenly outfitted with a reputation for activity that drastically outdistanced its political reality." The young leftists had always been skeptical of the corporate press as a matter of course, but they very quickly learned that mainstream journalism, embedded within a certain ideological framework and driven by the logic of capital accumulation, could rapidly reframe reality in deeply misleading ways. At the same time, some of them grasped the enormous power available here, if they could only counterattack in the press with an elegant set of "judo" techniques to finesse their own message into mass media channels. For example, one 1965 SDS statement pointed out that "we have seen antiwar leaflets photostated on the front page of newspapers with circulations in the millions. We could have been at the mimeograph for ten years, and not reached as many draftable young men as the press has reached for us in five days."[13]

All of this presented two problems. First, who was supposed to do this? SDS didn't have a press office, and its loose, quasi-leaderless structure made it difficult to decide who was supposed to speak for the organization. Rifts emerged as the media identified arbitrary spokesmen and celebrities. And secondly—paradoxically—the popularity bestowed on the group created an even bigger issue. SDS was flooded with new members, allowing it to grow at a rate of 300 percent in a single year. But these new arrivals did not want to join SDS—they wanted to join the organization they had read about in the newspaper, which didn't actually exist. They showed up with longer hair, less ideological commitments, and a strange set of assumptions about the organization.[14]

But because of the loose and "participatory" nature of SDS, there was no formal process for integrating and educating new members. They had paid intentionally little attention to organizational questions. In some cases, the new recruits (who were never actually recruited) simply set up their own new chapter somewhere, without ever speaking with the old guard. Gitlin came to the conclusion that both leaderlessness and unexpected, rapid growth spelled the end of the movement. By 1967, some protesters were complaining about "structure freaks," those who wanted to have any organization whatsoever.[15]

Gitlin eventually came to some conclusions about the way mass media worked and what constituted a story for the modern press. To qualify, the phenomenon at hand would have to be new—it was called the "news" after all—and it would have to arrive with intensity and surprise the audience. The media would inevitably choose from a huge assortment of existing facts and illuminate just one of many truths. Furthermore, any story had to be readily comprehensible to the general public. It had to fit into preexisting categories and correspond to the range of things that people already knew about and considered possible. In other words, it must be comparable to something that has already happened. It must be "old," at the same time.[16]

As the decade wore on, some members of this generation got caught in a perverse feedback loop. The individuals that quite liked media attention sought more of it, consciously or unconsciously adopting tactics that would provoke more coverage. But none of that changed the simple fact that the US government wanted to continue the war in Vietnam, and could afford to treat the demonstrators like a noisy minority (with frequent help from the press). As mass protest emerged as the predominant instrument of the anti-war movement, the original SDS leadership decided to retreat from the scene and go back to their roots. They had never wanted to privilege street demonstration, nor become a single-issue anti-war shop. They committed themselves to a new initiative called the Economic Research and Action Project (ERAP) and moved into the inner city to organize African American communities in the United States.

Inverting the Old Left

The "New Left," as SDS and associated groups often liked to call themselves, was formed as a reaction to the legacy of the Bolshevik Revolution. This, after all, had been the guiding star for the "Old Left," most specifically the Communist Party (which had been influential in the United States in the 1930s and 1940s).

But by the end of the 1950s, the Old Left did not really exist in the United States. It had been smashed by McCarthyism. Everyone who was insufficiently anticommunist was removed from public life in a top-down process led by the head of the FBI (the same man, J. Edgar Hoover, had also sought to crush Black political organizations in the country). The New Left in the US was more like a generation of ideological orphans raised on television in one of the most individualist societies on the planet than a reaction against any existing traditions. This certainly shaped the specific contours of their intellectual development, as did the context of the Cold War.[17] They were quick to assert that the dreams of the Old Left had been perverted by the leaders of the Soviet Union. In many ways the new organizational approach of this 1960s student left can be seen as a simple inversion of Leninism, the dominant revolutionary practice worldwide since 1917.

Writing as an underground dissident opposing the Russian Empire, Vladimir Ilyich Ulyanov had formulated a set of guidelines for organizing a revolutionary party. What we call Leninism also has robust ideological content—for example, he supported the seizure of the state and the replacement of bourgeois dictatorship with a "dictatorship of the proletariat," which would be more democratic than what came before it (since the working class is much bigger than the capitalist ruling class). This was understood to be an imperfect form, a transitional stage on the way to full communism.[18] The most fundamental difference between classical anarchism and this tradition is that anarchists reject this intermediate phase.[19] But as an organizational philosophy, "Leninism" can be adopted by groups of diverse ideological stripes. Lenin argued for a small vanguard of professional revolutionaries, strictly disciplined and hierarchically organized. "Democratic centralism" meant that decisions were made democratically, but once the Party had made one, everyone would adopt that line and work toward it collectively. If you didn't like it, that was fine, you didn't have to be in the Party.

There were a couple of reasons for this approach. First, the Russian social democrats were in a life-or-death struggle with the Tsar and his secret police. This requires a very particular set of skills that must be accumulated through experience and passed on to other trained and committed revolutionaries. And secondly, Lenin was engaged in a "desperate struggle against spontaneity," the competing revolutionary current that insisted workers would rise up and create socialism on their own. But for Lenin, socialism is not something that resides in the heart of every human being, only waiting to be discovered. It is the implementation of centuries of scientific advancement and theoretical elaboration. He argued that any purely spontaneous uprising, taking the path of least resistance, would simply adopt the ideology that is dominant in its society at the time. They will grasp at whatever is already in the air. Because the ruling class had a lot more means at its disposal to propagate its ideology, the revolutionary movement would need to be guided by a coherent ideology of its own.[20] Leninism insisted on subordinating means to ends, and individual to party. The goal was winning state power, and then starting the difficult transition to communism.

By the 1960s, SDS believed that the official Marxist-Leninist system of the Soviet Union had congealed into an undemocratic, centralized bureaucracy. The revolutionary means had become its ends. In the USSR, the hierarchical vanguard Party was now the state. SDS's approach—perhaps the thing that was truly "new" about the New Left—dictated that they should adopt organizational forms now that they would like to see in the world they wanted to create. The name given to this was "prefigurative politics"—what you are doing now will prefigure, or show a glimpse of, the world you want to live in tomorrow. Even ardent defenders of SDS recognized that this created a fundamental tension between organizational forms and the goals of political change. This meant experimenting with anti-hierarchical structures, and it opened them up to criticism that they didn't really care about their demands. Eloquent supporters of this approach admitted that this was somewhat true, that means were important, as well as the ends. But, they said, they refused to corrupt their movement, which was also about building community, for instrumental purposes. Looking back after the New Left failed in achieving most of its stated goals, sociologist Wini Breines wrote, "It is my conviction that the attempt to seek the 'salvation of the soul' *in* politics, to forge a new definition of politics in which violence, authority, and hierarchy did not reign supreme is the most unique and powerful legacy of the new left."[21]

Like almost everything in Western civilization, prefiguration has roots in the Christian intellectual tradition. Over 1,500 years ago, theologians like Tertullian and Saint Augustine looked at elements in the Old Testament that prefigured the arrival of Jesus in the New Testament. For example, Cain, who killed his brother Abel, the shepherd, prefigured the men who would kill Jesus, the shepherd of men, and so on. Over the centuries, the concept evolved (from a backward-looking, literary practice) and was reconfigured into forward-looking praxis, something that could be done now, to anticipate the End Times. In seventeenth-century England, the radical Diggers movement (which occupied land and organized strikes) justified its direct-action strategy with reference to biblical prophecy.[22]

Like the idea of socialism, the logic of prefiguration was the consequence of certain historical developments and intellectual institutions. Back in an imagined state of nature, if you wanted to build yourself a house, it didn't make sense to act, while you were cutting down the trees, as if you already lived in one. If marauders attack your village, you should probably not respond by acting the way you hope to live when they are gone. The New Left was not the first to rediscover prefiguration in the modern era. In the nineteenth century, anarchists active in the First International (Karl Marx was also a member) had asked, "How could one expect an egalitarian and free society to emerge out of an authoritarian organization! It is impossible."[23] Breines credited both anarchism and the Gandhian radical pacifists as "real forerunners" of the New Left.[24]

This ideological approach dovetailed with—or helped catalyze—a libertarian trend that was in the air in the North Atlantic in the 1960s. Many in the generation born after World War II did not want to be told what to do. As the decade wore on, new sets of practices made the structures developed by Black civil rights groups appear relatively authoritarian. It was not just within SDS that some of the original architects of contemporary contention found themselves attacked from below. Even Bertrand Russell, the founder of the Committee of 100, found himself besieged by a group of three young Londoners who baffled him by refusing to leave his flat, forcing the mathematician to call the police to remove them. In his autobiography, he notes that this earned the kids quite a bit of media attention, which may have been all they wanted.[25]

Under the Paving Stones

Outside of North America, the Old Left was very much alive. Marxist-Leninist parties comfortably governed most of the Eurasian continent. In the Third World, the official Communist organizational model offered the hope of catching up with the world's advanced First World nations and provided an excellent way to carry out the anti-colonial struggle against rapacious European powers. Even some countries that had suppressed local Communist parties, such as Egypt under Gamal Nasser, received support from the USSR and attempted to implement some parts of the Soviet model.[26]

Nasser had become a Third World hero after successfully clawing the Suez Canal back from the colonizers in 1956. By the 1960s, most of North Africa and the Middle East were living under some form of "Arab Socialism," with Nasser (in charge of by far the most populous country in the Arab world) inspiring widespread pride and hope in the region. He was never a communist, but in the 1960s Nasser relaxed the repression of the left and then created a Leninist group called the Vanguard Organization to defend his revolution.[27]

Meanwhile, Latin America was safely under the indirect control of the radically anticommunist United States government (with the CIA carrying out a military coup in Guatemala in 1954 and Washington offering tacit support for another a decade later in Brazil, rather than tolerate moderate liberal reformists in the hemisphere), but an unlikely 1959 revolution in Cuba had electrified leftists worldwide. In Western Europe, official Communist parties aligned with Moscow played major roles in national politics and intellectual life, coming close enough to forming governments after World War II that the CIA chose to intervene behind the scenes.[28] It was on that continent, especially in Germany and France, that "1968" would take on special meaning for the New Left outside the United States. But that was a year of uprisings that reverberated across a wide range of national systems.

In the history of revolutions, a couple of truisms had already emerged. One is that they are only successful when security forces defect or are defeated in violent conflict. Even if Mao Zedong was being a bit provocative when he said that "power grows out of the barrel of a gun," experts agree that he is not so far off. You can't run a country if the biggest army around wants to stop you.[29] Another is that revolutionary opportunities often arise when there are divisions in the ruling class—that is, when elites are fighting amongst themselves. And one more truism is that revolutions are contagious; at least, uprisings tend to cluster around certain moments in time. News of one success spreads to another country, where people try their luck too; or revolts happen in response to a major international event, like the end of a war or a financial crisis. The "Springtime of Nations" in 1848 was only one of the most famous revolutionary waves.[30] The ends of both world wars caused two more.

In France in the 1960s, the radical left-wing students were not orphans like their North American counterparts. They had grown up in dialogue with the powerful Parti Communiste Français (PCF). The young New Left there were often Leninists themselves, but of a different type. They were more likely to support Third World revolutionaries, whom they often viewed as the true subjects of world history, the heroic protagonists pushing human progress forward. Che Guevara and Ho Chi Minh's presence hung over their gatherings, on placards or in chants, while the established party, the pro-Soviet PCF, was more focused on the French working class organized in its unions.[31]

In West Germany the Communist Party was illegal, but the other half of the country was run by officials loyal to Moscow. Rudi Dutschke, one of the most prominent student leaders in the West, knew that system well, as he had grown up there. In 1967 the movement radicalized after its raucous demonstration in West Berlin against Shah Mohammad Reza Pahlavi, the man installed as leader of Iran after a 1953 CIA-led coup, was put down violently and one student was killed. Dutschke emerged as a prominent voice railing against capitalist government bureaucracy, drawing inspiration from protests in the United States (most famously erupting in Berkeley, California), and aligning his own struggle with the revolutionary leaders in the Third World.[32] In April 1968 a neo-Nazi, inspired by the assassination of Martin Luther King Jr. one week earlier in Tennessee, tried to kill Dutschke, sparking a new wave of protests and "sit-ins" often targeting symbols of US power.

Anti-American protests spread throughout France. European students mounted their own critique of the bureaucratization the US had pressured their countries to adopt, which slotted them into predetermined social functions. The media gave the French youth special attention, perhaps because they looked so similar to what already happened in Berkeley and Berlin.[33] Students at Nanterre demonstrating since March agitated over relatively quotidian concerns (or, rather, nocturnal ones—one demand was the freedom to sleep in one another's dormitory rooms), but it was the May invasion and police brutality at the elite Sorbonne university that really set things off. State violence had already spread to the metropole during an Arab-led demonstration earlier in the decade, when police massacred two hundred opponents of France's policy in Algeria.[34] The incursion into the Sorbonne, however, was a violation of middle-class values that shocked French society far more than the murder of large numbers of Arabs on the street.

The May explosion that followed combined some classic French revolutionary practices—barricades, throwing rocks at cops, strikes—with innovative routines and prefigurative practices. A "hard core" engaged in a cycle of intentional "escalation-provocation," in which committed militants would fight cops or fascists and invite spectacular repression, "immediately followed by a large and legal demonstration."[35] The "occupation" was one of the most important new forms of contention that spread in the 1960s, used in Paris as it was in California. Students took over campus facilities and elected leaders to an ad hoc Sorbonne "occupation committee." The PCF and unions joined the revolt, while new forms of life appeared to flower behind the barricades and in occupied spaces. Participants felt their assigned functions in capitalist society—students, workers, farmers—fall away, as human beings interacted directly as human beings. They lived in community and experimented with "direct democracy." When describing these days, French youths resorted to poetic language often reserved for romantic love or ecstatic spiritual or psychedelic experiences. Observers perceived echoes of older practices in the Western tradition, pointing to the late medieval Carnival, in which hierarchies were (temporarily) overturned in moments of euphoric liberation.[36]

Artists and bohemians, including members of a previously (and intentionally) obscure avant-garde group called the Situationist International, sprang into action and found their own revolutionary functions, covering the city in posters or libertarian slogans. "It is prohibited to prohibit," said one; "Be realistic, demand the impossible!" said another; while a famous slogan proclaimed that chaos could spontaneously generate utopia: *Sous les pavés, la plage.* "Under the paving stones, the beach."

Many of the French students praised Mao's Cultural Revolution, which was ongoing, whether they really understood the faraway events or not. Closer to home in Czechoslovakia, the "Prague Spring" also erupted in 1968. In both socialist countries, the dominant Marxist-Leninist parties were rocked by youth uprisings that challenged their bureaucratic structures. Even in the communist world, 1968 was a year of revolt against administered life and the conservatism of the Old Left.[37] Mao Zedong had instigated the chaos on purpose to destabilize the Party he had helped build. The leader of the People's Republic of China sought to ride the upsurge of energy with charismatic leadership and the elevation of a little red book of powerful but indeterminate aphorisms (without complete success). When things got too hot, Mao was able to rely on the military and reestablish control while maintaining his position as *éminence grise* in the Communist Party of China (CPC) for the rest of his life.[38] Things went rather differently for Alexander Dubček, the Communist leader of Czechoslovakia, who sought a liberal de-Stalinization of the national system in the Warsaw Pact country (Soviet leader Nikita Khrushchev had begun the de-Stalinization process in 1956, much to the chagrin of Mao himself). Leonid Brezhnev, the unimaginative and pliable leader imposed by the Soviet bureaucracy in 1964, chose to respond with force. He sent in the troops, and rather than addressing the inflexibility of the party model across the entire Soviet space, he doubled down. Thus began a long period of relative stability for the USSR, and of absolute comfort for the high-ranking *nomenklatura* (Party members with official titles).

Egypt had its own 1968, further driving home the extent to which that year unleashed a global wave of revolutionary contention. But circumstances there were very different. Students and workers in one of the cradles of human civilization were not responding to the horrors of US militarism in Vietnam or to Communist inflexibility. They were reacting to the shock of the loss to Israel in the "Six-Day" War, and the consequent crisis of legitimacy for the Nasser government.

Since the 1950s, the United States of America had cultivated both Saudi Arabia and Israel as regional counterweights to the strength of Arab Socialism and nationalism. At their most ambitious, those projects sought to bring all the peoples of the Arab world together into a single force, which would (like almost all of the Third World movement) oppose imperialism and seek to reshape the global capitalist order. Saudi Arabia, a reactionary monarchy founded in 1932 in the oil-rich Arabian Peninsula, stood in stark contrast to the secular republics in the region. And proud Nasserists naturally saw the Zionist project as an affront to Arab independence, the last gasp of a Western colonial phantom that had no place in a truly free region. Losing a war to the tiny Israel, whether it had the backing of the United States or not, was a profound blow. The Nasser government had combined domestic repression with full employment and soaring geopolitical ambitions. With the latter suddenly deflated, the system ran out of air too. Egyptians recalling that time report walking around dumbfounded, unsure of what they could believe anymore. After that war, both students and workers took aim at the other parts of the bargain. Twice in 1968, Egyptians confronted the military-police apparatus in the streets.[39]

But the 1968 constellation of uprisings did not topple governments, not even after Paris was brought to a standstill for weeks. The PCF used the leverage generated by the unrest to demand a significant wage increase for French workers, reflecting both the desires of the union rank-and-file and the limited ambitions of Moscow, which had no interest in provoking Washington by making a bid for revolution in Western Europe.[40] When the Old Left succeeded in getting the workers more money, this quickly took the steam out of the utopian student movement.[41] Supporters of Charles de Gaulle were able to put on demonstrations of their own on May 30. By June 30, moderate forces won an election comfortably, though de Gaulle ultimately resigned a year later. French-Austrian philosopher André Gorz asked, in a 1968 *New Left Review* essay, why the French people would award the revolutionaries with votes after they proved unable to assert their power to govern when they had the chance.[42] He had noticed that you could only surprise the ruling class with a spontaneous explosion once. Effective prefiguration, as he saw it, showed the masses that your concrete movement was worth buying into, and what it was capable of achieving. That did not happen. By November 1969, when leftists tried to organize a demonstration against Vietnam, the government simply forbade them. Dissidents reported a feeling of "asphyxia."[43]

Over the years that followed, many of the revolutionaries watched in horror as the events were redefined and reinterpreted until they were unrecognizable. No one had planned May 1968, and no one could credibly claim to speak for the uprising. Some of the class of 1968 had graduated to establishment positions in bourgeois Parisian society, and these voices tended to see May as a dream that had eventually come true, rather than a failed revolution. So when French television stations asked *soixante-huitards* (literally "68-ers") to explain what had happened, they called upon these respectable or eloquent figures who—whether this was intentional or not—reflected the dominant values in France in the 1970s and 1980s. The actual spark for the revolt had been the Vietnam War, and its initial targets were clear—capitalism, US imperialism, and Charles de Gaulle—but a narrative took shape that claimed the events were actually about individualism and self-expression, not collective action. They were about the liberation of desire, not humanity. Though almost no one had elected to identify as a student or "youth" back in 1968—as workers or Jews or militants or Maoists, yes—the story was now that the uprising was actually about affirming these identities. Some *soixante-huitards* watching the television, rather than appearing on it, fell into a deep depression. "How would I know, without my own evidence," one revolutionary asked, "that these years actually existed?"[44]

THROUGHOUT THE FIRST WORLD, ESPECIALLY the United States, the organizational approach developed by the New Left became more and more popular in progressive circles, most notably in those focusing on gender and minority identities. These experiments had their vocal detractors. In an iconoclastic 1972 essay, feminist activist and theorist Jo Freeman denounced the "Tyranny of Structurelessness"—that is, she claimed that when a movement insists it has no leaders, they emerge anyway; except, there are no fair and transparent mechanisms to select or remove those leaders. Often, a small clique of friends or the original members of a group end up exercising de facto power with no accountability. Freeman blames putative structurelessness for holding back the Women's Liberation movement in the 1970s, and making it impossible to achieve real wins.

Later in the decade, the battle over the "Old" left played out again, this time in the rapidly expanding field of consumer culture. This took place in a tiny corner of rock and roll, between two early punk bands managed by the same man. Malcolm McLaren, a British art school impresario influenced by the avant-garde (and the legacy of May 1968 in Paris), knew that he wanted his first group, the New York Dolls, to shock audiences. They already had a reputation for performing in drag, but he wanted to go further. So for a 1975 tour, he dressed them in red jumpsuits (designed by his partner, Vivienne Westwood) and had them perform in front of a big, Communist, hammer-and-sickle flag. This was too much. Guitarist Sylvain Sylvain reflected on the reaction: "In America you can be gay, you can be a drug addict but you cannot be a Communist," he said. "It kamikazed our whole thing. We'd crossed the line one too many times."[45] The New York Dolls had become his "prototype of testing public reaction."

For his next band, formed to promote the "Sex" clothing shop he ran with Westwood in London, McLaren picked out another radical political ideology from history. The Sex Pistols would be "anarchist," and so they would not be joining a movement with real armies, economies, and geopolitical power locked in conflict with the West. When McLaren drew on the ideology of the New Left as he understood it, and especially France's Situationist International, he found much to like in the elements that laughed at discipline and authority, were confrontationally anti-hierarchical, and refused to ever make concrete demands. The idea, instead, was a total "negation" of this society, a "voice that denied all social facts, and in that denial affirmed that everything was possible."[46]

The Myth of the Mauerfall

It would not be long before the hammer and sickle stopped representing real geopolitical power—across Europe, at least—when all those Communist countries simply disappeared. The fall of the Soviet Union stunned the world, and the rapid collapse of allied socialist states shaped the way a generation would approach the waves of history that would crash upon them afterward. All of it happened on TV—viewers in Los Angeles or London or Lima could watch crowds of protesters surge in Germany; they could see the hated *Berliner Mauer*, the Berlin Wall, torn to pieces; they could follow along as that country reunited and emerged triumphant at the 1990 FIFA World Cup in Rome.

Of course the North Atlantic powers, and the influential media outlets that broadly shared their worldview, had reason to feel triumphant, too. Suddenly and unexpectedly, they had won the Cold War. And the victory was delivered not by conflict, but by the apparently spontaneous uprising of the

people. As they framed and told the story, they privileged elements that confirmed some of their deepest assumptions. History might take a long time to
get there, but it was arriving at its natural destination. And indeed, Europe-
ans suffering under Communist rule had protested, demanding changes, and
Germany took its place once more as a global power. But quite a lot of other
things happened too.

Mikhail Gorbachev, a true believer in the socialist project, had risen to
leadership of the Soviet Union by winning at the game of Soviet bureaucracy.
During the long rule of Leonid Brezhnev (1964–1982), the *nomenklatura* had
cemented their power in the system. Very few people, not even convinced
anticommunists like Henry Kissinger and Francis Fukuyama, thought the
system was going to fall apart.[47] It is true that Washington became more confrontational in the 1980s, but things like Ronald Reagan's famous "Star Wars
program" had little to do with the end of the Bolshevik project.[48] Far more
important was that Gorbachev, a man who revered Lenin, also believed that
the fifteen Soviet republics and seven other Warsaw Pact member nations
could reintegrate with the West into a new global system.[49]

Historians are still working to explain why the Soviet Union collapsed
like it did. Global superpowers don't usually disappear overnight.[50] We
know that the economy was riven with contradictions and lagged behind
the world's most advanced countries; we know that the political system was
inflexible; and we know that the Party had used repression to construct and
maintain political power. But all three of these things were true, and remain
true, in many other countries that go right on existing. They might be true
for the vast majority of governments on the planet.

But we also know that the people who rushed into the streets in 1989–
1991 were not, as a rule, clamoring for the arrival of capitalism.[51] Even in East
Germany, many of them believed a reformed and improved socialism would
be on the way.[52] It is only partially true that this popular surge of energy contributed to the collapse of the system. And it is entirely wrong to claim that
the citizens of post-communist countries got the freedom and democracy
that was promised to them.[53]

The process that led to the end of the USSR started at the top, driven by
Gorbachev and a small group of elite reformers. *Perestroika*, or "reconstruction," was aimed at increasing industrial production and rooting out corruption, which necessarily entailed confronting the *nomenklatura*. But a "velvet
purge" (unlike the purges in the 1930s, no one was getting killed) put wily

mid-level bureaucrats on the defensive, and the collapse of the command economy structure cut off the flows of profits (and wages) sustaining the system. It was bureaucrats who really reacted to their change in fortunes, not the workers—who often kept going to work without getting paid. The *nomenklatura* at the national level seized the assets and territories they controlled, and Gorbachev refused to use force to stop them. As Russian historian Vladislav Zubok puts it, the USSR "met its end at the hand of its own leadership."[54]

At the beginning of the reform process, elites encouraged nationalist sentiment in order to undermine the *nomenklatura*. The former was far more successful than anyone planned, and the latter didn't happen at all. In many republics practically no popular demonstrations took place. The mass protests that did occur largely happened after the system was already falling apart, and Moscow could have easily put them down if it wished.[55] East German officials, who really believed in the socialist project they had spent four decades building, were horrified at the lack of leadership coming from Russia.[56] The transition after the Wall fell, after the *Mauerfall*, was bumpy for many East Germans, but they could rely on West Germany—one of the richest countries in human history—to spend two trillion euros to integrate them into its expanded state structures.[57] Much of the rest of the post-communist population got war or devastating poverty instead. In the first few years of the 1990s, violence broke out in Croatia, Chechnya, Moldova, Azerbaijan, Georgia, Tajikistan, Armenia, and Bosnia, killing hundreds of thousands of people.[58] There were going to be economic problems no matter what happened. But the leaders in Moscow, encouraged by Washington, embarked upon economic "shock therapy."

After elected lawmakers tried to stop him, President Boris Yeltsin, a close ally of Washington, illegally dissolved the Russian legislature and then sent tanks to shell the Parliament building. Russian elites rapidly privatized Soviet assets and removed controls on prices. This was the capitalist version of "under the stones, the beach"—once the command economy had been shocked to death, functioning markets would simply grow from the rubble.

This did not happen. Instead, Russia experienced a more severe rise in mortality than had ever been seen during peacetime in a modern society. Almost everywhere it was tried, shock therapy led to a deep and long recession, along with huge drops in indicators for education, poverty, and health.[59] By 1995, 45 percent of people in eighteen post-communist countries studied by the World Bank were living under the poverty line of four dollars a day, and the poverty hit children especially hard.[60] Before the transition, the poverty rate was 4 percent. As late as 2015, the average real income of 99 percent of Russians was lower than it had been in 1991.[61] Central Asia fared even worse. In countries like Kazakhstan, Uzbekistan, and Kyrgyzstan, the poverty rates jumped higher than 60 percent.[62] The collapse of the Soviet economic system vastly increased inequality and poverty, but it did not change who had the remaining assets. Those stayed with the former *nomenklatura* and their cronies, who quickly became a new class now called "oligarchs."

The name given to the process that emerged in the 1990s, by which the entire world seemed to be integrating into a single capitalist system, was "globalization." Harvard historian Odd Arne Westad has claimed that a better name for what really happened is "Americanization"—the United States had succeeded in shaping a global economic system and establishing itself as its hegemon.[63] Americanization could be felt in the political-economic sphere as well as the cultural. The production of entertainment and knowledge that took place in Hollywood studios or New York newsrooms became influential for an unprecedented number of global consumers. For sociologist Georgi M. Derluguian, who watched carefully as the old system fell apart in his native Caucasus region, globalization signified the revival of an old idea about automatic human progress, in liberal capitalist form. It was "the latest technological embodiment of the Hegelian universal spirit pursuing its self-realizing plan." Concretely, globalization was simply "the inter-related consequences of the collapse of the former developmentalist states."[64]

Neo

Decades before the Soviet Union crumbled, the Third World movement had fallen apart. Nasser died unexpectedly in 1970, and his successor, Anwar Sadat, soon found it served his purposes to abandon anti-imperialism for an alliance of convenience with the world's richest country. Earlier, in Indonesia, one of its founding fathers and leading lights, President Sukarno, was shunted aside as the United States assisted the military in seizing power and carrying out the intentional murder of approximately one million people. Indonesia's capital, Jakarta, became shorthand for slaughters carried out by anti-leftist regimes across the world, especially in Latin America.[65]

But the Third World movement was always a forward-looking, optimistic project that sought to effect true decolonization across the international system and allow the vast majority of the world's population to take its rightful place alongside the rich countries, rather than perpetually "developing" behind them. So in the early 1970s, these countries tried to wield the tools of the global system against itself. The New International Economic Order (NIEO) was an attempt to use the UN—where Third World countries clearly had a majority—to redress economic injustices and level the playing field. First World leaders reacted with horror to the idea of the end of North Atlantic dominance of the global system.[66] They found ways to stop NIEO in its tracks—signifying the wane of Third Worldism—by ensuring that the UN (where every country has a vote) remained largely powerless when it came to governing the global economy. Instead, organs like the International Monetary Fund (IMF) and the World Bank, which were controlled by rich countries, would have the power that mattered. The reaction to the NIEO helped set the stage for the neoliberal era.[67]

The use of that word, neoliberalism, is contested now in the English language. In recent times, it is most often used by a left wing that is openly opposed to neoliberalism, so it can be perceived as an insult despite the fact that the word was coined in 1938 by proponents of the neoliberal project.[68] Critics of the term have a point, however, when they claim that it can refer to many things at the same time. But the word must be used in this book, since so many protests around the world over the past few decades self-consciously took aim at "neoliberal" policies. So it is crucial to break down what we mean when we do so.

Neoliberalism operates at several levels, and the first is global. Its early proponents, especially the "Geneva School"—theorists like Ludwig von Mises, Friedrich Hayek, and others who did important work in the Swiss city—had a deep appreciation for how the first liberal era had created a worldwide capitalist economy, and they also harbored deep anxieties that the era of mass democracy and decolonization would get in its way. They wanted to impose limits on what national states could do to govern their own resources and economies—it was more important to ensure that an investor in London or New York could buy and sell copper mines in the Congo, for example, than to grant the Congolese people the full power to determine their ownership. Recently, Canadian historian Quinn Slobodian has employed the metaphor of a global "encasement" of the world's countries—the way the slices of an orange are encased by its peel—to describe these intentional limits on national sovereignty.[69]

Secondly, neoliberalism works at the national level, with policies that reduce the size of the welfare state and privilege the ability of markets to set prices above all other economic goals, while assuring everyone that increased growth will make all of this worthwhile.[70] The "shock therapy" of following the Soviet Union could be seen as a "quintessentially neoliberal policy prescript," according to German economist Isabella Weber, although the first experiment with the implementation of radical neoliberal prescriptions came in Chile after a US-backed coup that ended the presidency (and life) of democratically elected socialist President Salvador Allende in 1973.* Crucially, all of this worked out quite well for those same investors in London or New York.

And finally, many theorists assert that neoliberalism works at the level of the individual—shaping human beings who think of themselves as autonomous individual firms whose success must be prioritized above all else—maximizing, optimizing, hustling, and striving rather than existing as part of any community.[71]

For the countries of the former Third World movement, globalization was the end of their attempt to catch up with the First World through intentional economic upgrading. Those words themselves, "Third World," had been transformed (in English and French at least) from a thoroughly positive term signifying the subjects of history—the true revolutionaries who inspired the students on the streets in 1968—to objects of pity and derision.[72] Meanwhile, far more post-communist citizens fell into "Third World" conditions than entered the First.

---

* The Brazilian dictatorship, despite the best efforts of some neoliberals in both Washington, DC, and Rio de Janeiro, remained committed to an earlier "development" model. The state born out of the US-backed military coup in 1964 was active in managing the economy, with the goal of producing advanced goods at home rather than importing them from rich countries. The center of this push was the industrial base in the state of São Paulo, where metal worker Luiz Inácio "Lula" da Silva rose to the leadership of the proletariat created by this drive for modernization.

2

Mayara and Fernando

MAYARA VIVIAN WAS BORN IN São Paulo in 1990, as the new global order was taking shape. She grew up in Jardim Celeste, a working-class neighborhood on the outskirts of the megalopolis, not far from the city zoo. Like millions of other Paulistanos, she lived in a big, dirty, white building, surrounded by other tower blocks, in a rough neighborhood.

Her mother, and her grandmother, made ends meet working odd jobs—selling soap, bedding, and cosmetics door-to-door—and things got especially bad after her uncle got laid off from a big printer downtown. But a lot of people had it worse, she knew that. There was always enough to eat, but not by much; once, she ran away to live with an aunt, mostly because she could afford to buy cream cheese. Outside on the streets there were nice punks and the bad punks—the skinheads and the gangsters—and Mayara, always a rowdy and gregarious kid, spent a lot of time outside on the streets.[1]

In the 1990s, Brazilian democracy was finding its feet once more after decades of military dictatorship. The country was not poor by global standards—but it remained far behind rich countries. And it was one of the world's most unequal societies. Many white, middle-class Brazilians would never dream of cleaning their own homes or cooking their own food. That was done by struggling women, almost always with darker skin than their employers. Truly wealthy people in São Paulo would avoid the streets entirely, cruising around in bulletproof cars or taking helicopters from the top of one of the city's skyscrapers to another, avoiding the traffic and crime below. All of this gave the city a decidedly post-apocalyptic aura, which shocks foreigners and reminds them more of *Blade Runner* than *The Girl from Ipanema*. From the top of the tall Edifício Itália downtown (named after the country that gave the city a big chunk of its immigrant population), high-rises like Mayara's extend literally as far as the eye can see. In every direction.

Mayara got into music, and politics, very early. In 2003 she attended her first protest, on the city's main thoroughfare, Avenida Paulista. They were trying to stop George Bush's war against Iraq. President Luiz Inácio "Lula" da Silva had just taken over as the country's president and declined to help the US president with the invasion. As Lula tells the story, he told George W. Bush: "My only war is on hunger." A former metalworker and union man, his Partido dos Trabalhadores (PT) had built roots in Brazilian society, embraced ideological pluralism and "participatory democracy," and was proudly left-wing. But Lula was not going to start an open fight with the United States, either. Over the previous century of intervention, most Latin American leaders had learned to avoid those conflicts if they could. It was only after the US-backed coup d'état against Hugo Chávez in late 2002 that the Venezuelan president became the rare South American leader to take a consistently adversarial stance toward Washington. So it fell on a wider group of protesters in Brazil, mostly on the left, to make the case more forcefully against the invasion. They were not alone, of course. This may have been one of the largest street actions in human history. Over ten million people protested, from Berlin to Tokyo to Cairo to California. I joined in, as a university student, and my roommate got arrested, ending up on the front page of the *San Francisco Chronicle*.

On the street in São Paulo, Mayara noticed that there was a kind of split among the protesters that were blocking two lanes on Avenida Paulista. On one hand, there were the more organized and traditional left-wing groups—"bureaucratic," she called them—and on the other was a group of more raucous and freewheeling kids. She knew which she identified with more. But she wasn't going to be joining in any disputes that year. She was only thirteen. It was remarkable she was there in the first place.

Two interrelated historical currents helped pull Mayara onto the streets that day—the "anti-globalization" movement and Brazilian anarcho-punk. The fall of the Soviet Union had devastated the Old Left, and in the 1990s the target of the most visible contentious politics shifted from national governments to international organizations. An assorted group of anarchists, environmentalists, Trotskyists, labor groups, and anti-establishment subcultures came together and took aim at entities like the World Bank, the IMF, and the World Trade Organization.[2] The activists often preferred to be called the "alter-globalization" movement, since they were not against the idea of a world united. They took issue with the particular way that globalization was taking shape after the end of the Cold War. They wanted a different type of globalization that did not privilege corporate profits and international investors while crushing labor and restricting the sovereignty of countries in the Global South. Books like *No Logo* by Canadian author Naomi Klein (helpfully promoted by the band Radiohead) and magazines like *Adbusters* (which sought to use the tools of corporate marketing against itself) provided the anglophone intellectual framework through which a lot of young people understood alter-globalization.[3] Their weapon was confrontational mass protest, aimed at stopping the roving meetings of those international organizations. They shocked the world in 1999, when tens of thousands of people took to the streets in Seattle to disrupt a meeting of the World Trade Organization. Alongside the loose and diverse coalition of forces, anarchists adopted the "black bloc" style—wearing dark clothing, covering their faces, and destroying private property. The protesters overwhelmed local police, who responded with tear gas.

During the eruption in Seattle, millions of people relied on Indymedia, a website founded by activists a few weeks prior. Indymedia reflected a radical anti-authoritarian ethos, built between the neo-anarchist movement and the libertarian ideals of the early internet. Its goal was to allow readers to bypass corporate media, and anyone could publish on the site. The idea of an editor even choosing to accept, reject, or edit anything it published flew in the face of what it stood for. For a generation of curious young people (myself included), Indymedia is the place where we came of age online.

Indymedia spread quickly around the world and arrived in Brazil in 2000 with its name translated as the Centro de Mídia Independente (CMI). A small group of volunteers (no one got paid at Indymedia) would meet at a little office in downtown São Paulo and bang out articles on dirty old desktop computers. They had cells all around the vast country, from the chilly southern capital of Porto Alegre to the middle of the Amazon.[4] The "antiglobalization" movement first exploded onto Avenida Paulista in 2001, with the "A-20" (April 20) protest against George Bush's Free Trade Area for the Americas. Mayara was inspired. She wanted to go, but eleven was too young for even her to hit the streets. Her forays from home in those days were limited to punk shows.

Brazilian punk rock music took off in São Paulo in the 1980s, and it was dangerous. They sang in Portuguese, and the fans formed gangs. Bands like Ratos de Porão, Olho Seco, and Cólera (Basement Rats, Dry Eye, and Cholera) reflected the chaos of Brazil in the last decade of the dictatorship. The violence they were singing about was very real, and it ground down the community. Death and drugs made for shocking content but began to appear to some Paulistanos as a dead end. By the 1990s, a second punk wave arrived—and these younger bands were more likely to reject violence, sing in English, and get actively involved in left-wing politics. There had always been a vague association with anarchism in the Brazilian punk scene, remembers Frederico Freitas, singer in the straight-edge, Third Worldist vegan hardcore band Point of No Return.[5] But this second wave was more likely to actually start reading about the stuff, collecting books by nineteenth-century thinkers like Proudhon, Kropotkin, and Bakunin. Punk music was left-wing and anti-nationalist in Brazil, and it played a major role in bringing anarchism back in the country.[6] Freitas helped found the recurring Verdurada—loosely translated: Veggiefest—party, which was a mix of punk shows and political discussions. Bands would play and then stop for everyone to listen to a feminist speak or someone from Brazil's monumental Movimento Sem Terra (MST), the left-wing Landless Workers' Movement that invaded large properties around the country and pushed for radical land reform. The extra (vegetarian) food would be donated to São Paulo's ample homeless population. Everything at the Verdurada was structured horizontally—no authority, no leaders—and the organizational model was not so different from that of a mosh pit, the kind where the band plays right in front of the churning crowd.

Mayara liked bands of both types, and she especially loved Cólera, Invasores de Cérebros (Brain Invaders), and the all-woman outfit Menstruação Anarquika (Anarchic Menstruation). The second wave had too many clueless rich kids for her liking, but that could be ignored as long as the music (and the politics) were good. For her the world of punk, and the associated universe of activist causes, offered a kind of second family. To find out what was going on in the scene, she would ask the kids in her neighborhood, or head down to the Galeria do Rock alternative shopping mall and check out the flyers posted on the walls. Her uncle had a crappy old computer at the house, but to use the internet she had to wait past midnight when the connection got a bit cheaper. She read Indymedia, of course, when she went online.

THE ALTER-GLOBALIZATION GENERATION WAS EVEN more anti-authoritarian, even more apparently structureless, and even more anarchist than any of the dominant protest movements in the twentieth century. In the 1960s, the New Left had insisted that means also mattered in addition to the ends. David Graeber, the anarchist and anthropologist from the United States who was active in the new protest movement, went even further. In a 2002 essay for *New Left Review*, he explained that for them, the means were the ends. They were not doing something in order to get something else. The point was what they were doing. He wrote, "This is a movement about reinventing democracy. It is not opposed to organization. It is about creating new forms of organization. It is not lacking in ideology. Those new forms of organization *are* its ideology. It is about creating and enacting horizontal networks instead of top-down structures like states, parties or corporations." He defended "pre-figurative politics" and celebrated a "rich and growing panoply of organizational instruments...all aimed at creating forms of democratic process that allow initiatives to rise from below and attain maximum effective solidarity without stifling dissenting voices, creating leadership positions, or compelling anyone to do anything which they have not freely agreed to do."

Like many other people in the movement, Graeber complained that "anti-globalization" was an entirely inaccurate label imposed by capitalist media. In reality, they were pro-globalization but anti-neoliberal. He wrote, "In Argentina, or Estonia, or Taiwan, it would be possible to say this straight out: 'We are a movement against neoliberalism.' But in the US, language is always a problem. The corporate media here is probably the most politically monolithic on the planet: neoliberalism is all there is to see—the background reality; as a result, the word cannot be used." In Graeber's essay, he offered a novel explanation for the resurgence of anarchist politics. It was the end of the Soviet Union, yes—but not the collapse of the officially Marxist-Leninist states. Anarchists could never be very good at war, he said, but they could flourish in peace: "The moment the Cold War ended, and war between industrialized powers once again became unthinkable, anarchism reappeared just where it had been at the end of the nineteenth century, as an international movement at the very center of the revolutionary left."[7]

In Brazil under Lula, anarchism was far from the center of national politics, but a small group of alter-globalization activists and Indymedia journalists took part in digitally coordinated global events and reproduced the "new language" of civil disobedience that Graeber elevated, "combining elements of street theater, festival, and what can only be called non-violent warfare." At the World Social Forum in Porto Alegre, young Brazilian activist Rodrigo Nunes found space for a school—training grounds for a carnival of protest—conducted by London's Clandestine Insurgent Rebel Clown Army.[8]

AT THE TURN OF THE millennium, a different Paulistano developed another critical—but slightly different—approach to the age of globalization. Fernando Haddad, a cocksure and handsome young leftist hailing from Brazil's sizable Lebanese community, was working at USP (the University of São Paulo, the best college in Latin America).[9]

Fernando's grandfather, Habib, was a Greek Orthodox priest who had a reputation for standing up to French colonial authorities.[10] Just after World War II, he decided to take his family on the same path that had been forged by so many (mostly Christian) Arabs over the previous seventy years. He made his way to Brazil and started selling fabrics in downtown São Paulo. Like so much of this community, young Fernando excelled at the country's best schools, and he chose to study law, he remembers, after watching his father lose a house in a legal battle. But at university he gravitated toward politics and student organizations. He wound up part of a weekly Marxist pizza party and discussion group in the hip Pinheiros neighborhood.[11] Haddad found himself on the anti-Stalinist left, but he was never attracted to libertarian opposition to state power in general. Fernando joined the Partido dos Trabalhadores (PT), the Workers' Party, while the country was still under its military dictatorship, then pursued advanced degrees in economics and philosophy.

At just thirty-five years old, he sought to update Marx's class analysis for the era of planetary neoliberalism, writing *Em defesa do socialismo* on the 150th anniversary of *The Communist Manifesto*. As he saw it, the collapse of the welfare state and the arrival of neoliberalism meant that leftists in the Global South would face serious challenges. But they must not abandon the socialist project—thus the title, *In Defense of Socialism*. He claimed that social democracy outside of the rich First World was impossible—that the modest gains made by workers in North America and Europe in the twentieth century were dependent on "extraordinary profits" flowing to those countries from the Global South. Any attempt to create global social democracy would be riven with contradictions and end in one of two ways. If it did not turn to explicit socialism, it would fall prey to neoliberalism.[12]

The PT came into life in 1980 when industrial workers, along with progressive forces in the Catholic Church, veterans of the (Marxist-Leninist) armed guerrilla struggle against the dictatorship, and dissident intellectuals, founded a new mass party.* Over the next two decades, the Workers' Party built up a base of active members who took part in internal decisions.[13] At the same time, changes in the global economy undermined the industrial base that had created Lula's union movement in the first place. After the US government raised interest rates under Federal Reserve Chairman Paul Volcker, many Latin American countries were plunged into debt crisis, and consequently the Reagan years were sometimes called a "lost decade" in which catch-up with the First World was reversed and factories began to close.[14]

When PT candidates made it into government office, they found they had to govern in concert with the local elites who held the real power. The end of the dictatorship had changed the political system; but the economic structure of society remained largely the same as before the 1964 coup. The most ambitious reforms proposed back then were stuck in their tracks by the military takeover, and the new global system made projects like land reform or radical redistribution very hard to imagine.

In his book Haddad wrote that in the neoliberal age, politics would take one of three forms: technocracy devoid of political content, authoritarianism, or outright fascism. Representative democracy was obviously in crisis, he recognized, but he insisted that the form must be protected, as it was the "best way to defend classes without property." Unlike the younger anarchist left, who wanted to rush forward and get rid of the state entirely, he insisted on a defensive posture. This dying form, the democratic government, must somehow weather the neoliberal storm and, if at all possible, be revitalized.

Haddad was deeply worried about the power that media have in bourgeois democracy. It was not only that a particular class of rich people ran the public sphere and chose which topics would be discussed. Market logic

---

* Unlike his brother Frei Chico—tortured by the secret police in 1975—Lula was never in the powerful Brazilian Communist Party (something that made his union leadership slightly more palatable to the government), but his movement was always proudly left-wing.

also meant a cheapening of information and the impossibility of critical engagement. Capitalist media expels an endless stream of undifferentiated facts. Television was the worst offender. Its content took the same form as the advertisements that made the whole game possible, which sought to provoke "the greatest psychological effect in the shortest amount of time." Politics, he lamented, had become *marketing*.[15]

Members of the PT had good reason to be suspicious of media power in general, and in Brazil in particular. The first time that Lula ran for the presidency, in 1989, he faced a small-scale information war. It was the first time Brazilians were directly choosing their president since 1960, and Lula seemed to be doing fairly well against playboy maverick Fernando Collor. As the election progressed, delivery companies boycotted the distribution of Workers' Party materials, meaning the PT had to take their own publications around the country on buses. Rede Globo, the flagship of the media super-conglomerate owned by the billionaire Marinho family—and by far the most important TV channel in the country, where you watch the football and the *novela*—edited the final debate selectively, to the obvious detriment of the leftist. Collor won and was rapidly impeached for corruption.

In 1994 and 1998 Lula lost (fair and square) to Fernando Henrique Cardoso (or FHC, as everyone calls him). FHC is a genteel academic, the kind of guy who speaks French and wears tweed and is anything but a reactionary. As a sociologist, he worked within the field of "dependency theory," which operated from an understanding that rich countries exploit poor countries.[16] But as president he oversaw a wave of privatizations and the institutionalization of macroeconomic policies that left Brazil's assorted neoliberal think tanks (in the country since the early 1980s) with little to complain about.[17] Relations with the United States were good under FHC, with the notable exception of a Commerce Department report, accidentally published just before President Bill Clinton came to visit, that said corruption was "endemic" in Brazil.[18]

In 2001 Fernando Haddad put academic theory aside to join the world of concrete Brazilian politics. He took a job at City Hall, working for São Paulo mayor Marta Suplicy (her family is especially legendary in the city—her ex-husband, Eduardo Suplicy, is a beloved elder statesman of the left, and her son, Supla, is a punk rock singer who sports a halo of yellow spiked hair). Haddad had matured into something of a Gen X hipster: professorial but well-connected to the worlds of music and culture, with a bit of a nonchalant

and slightly ironic air. As a young government employee, he took a helicopter ride over the poor *periferia* of the city and was shocked by the sight—a
"monster: a sea of cement with the state nowhere to be seen"—a harsh reality
that his middle-class upbringing had never forced him to face. But within
the PT, he impressed colleagues with his intelligence, loyalty, and concern
for expanding educational opportunities. In 2003, Lula finally entered office
as president, and Haddad soon joined the federal administration, leaving
bread-and-butter city issues behind.

LATER THAT YEAR MUNICIPAL ISSUES rocked the country, but far from both
Mayara and Fernando, in the city of Salvador. The capital of Bahia, the state
most famously associated with Afro-Brazilian culture, raised the price of a
ride on the bus. A small number of students protested in response. But then
more and more young people joined, until thousands of them were blocking
the streets, occupying public vehicles, and apparently getting the support
of the public while doing so. Commuters would honk in solidarity, give the
kids a thumbs-up, or tell the media that the disruption was all worth it. In
Salvador, like the rest of Brazil, working-class people put a big chunk of their
income toward getting to their jobs and back. And in Bahia—like the rest
of the world—the daily grind of braving traffic and cramming into uncom-
fortable spaces, only to go work all day and then come home again, was one
of the worst parts of contemporary urban life. Indymedia Brasil paid close
attention to the little uprising and covered it for the rest of the country.

The student union in Salvador—strongly linked to the Partido Comunista do Brasil (PCdoB)—had played a role in starting the wave of protests,
but it grew far too large for them to control. In some cases, protesters insisted
on keeping party political flags out of the demonstrations, declaring that the
movement should be *apartidário*—or without a party, nonpartisan. But the
mayor, who now understood that he had to solve this problem, could hardly
negotiate with the sudden, leaderless explosion—so he called in the student
leaders. After negotiations, they got nine out of the ten things they asked
for—but they didn't stop the bus rate hike.[19]

This opened a split on the young left in Brazil. For the student leaders
and the PCdoB, the movement had used their leverage to get as much as they
could, and this was a victory. For the autonomist left, the more anarchist
and anti-bureaucratic youth, the Communists had done what Stalinists and
hierarchical political parties always do—they had spoken for people they had

no right to speak for, and they had sold out the street movement in service of maintaining a cozy relationship with politicians. The PCdoB was a Marxist-Leninist party, practicing democratic centralism and tracing its roots back to the Communist Party founded in 1922. And they were loyal members of Lula's ruling coalition, believing their job was to defend this new government, so it is probably true that they were never going to bet on a general insurrection in the first year of left-of-center rule since the 1960s.

The local man with a camera who always showed up at these sort of things, Carlos Pronzato, made a wobbly little documentary about the Salvador protests called *A Revolta do Buzu*. After it was shown in the glitzy beach city of Florianópolis, local youth got excited and formed the Campanha Pelo Passe Livre—the Free Fare Campaign. Except when these kids took to the streets, they actually pulled it off. After intense street contention starting in 2004, they got the city government to give up on raising the bus fare. Across the country, the alter-globalization generation was inspired.

In January 2005, at the meeting of the World Social Forum in Porto Alegre, a group of activists created the Movimento Passe Livre—The Free Fare Movement—or MPL. Many of its founders came from Indymedia. Their goal, the crusade that gave the group its name, was for a Brazil in which no one would ever have to pay for transportation at all. And of course, their method was direct action.

Now fifteen years old, Mayara became a founding member of the MPL. She made the long trip down to the southern tip of the country to help plan and prepare food. The average age in the group was not much higher than hers. Lucas "Legume" Monteiro, whose nickname translates to "Vegetable," was a few years older. Lucas was from a comfortably middle-class family in São Paulo, and despite appearances, Vegetable didn't get the nickname from the vegan punk milieu in which so much of the group mixed socially.[20] He got it playing Magic: The Gathering at school, but his family had other links to the punk world. His father was a successful musician, and his stepfather was an old punk, featured on the back cover of the album for a 1982 festival in São Paulo: "The Beginning of the End of the World." At twenty-one years old in 2005, Vegetable was basically an elder as far as Mayara was concerned.

In its founding "charter of principles," the MPL declared that it would be a fully independent, "autonomous," and "horizontal" organization. There would be no leaders or specialized roles, and decisions would be made by consensus. Every single member should agree on any course of action. This was definitely not Leninism. In this model, the majority should not be able to force any individual to do something they didn't agree with. This approach was partially inspired by some of their neighbors in South America.

IN DECEMBER 2001, THE GOVERNMENT of Argentina froze the bank accounts of its citizens after the International Monetary Fund halted loans to the country. In response people banged pots and pans, went on strike, ransacked private businesses, and blocked major roads across the country. After President Fernando de la Rúa resigned, Argentines (many made unemployed by the crisis) formed hundreds of neighborhood assemblies, filling the vacuum created by state collapse, discussing day-to-day problems, and occupying factories.

The assemblies adopted *horizontalidad*, or horizontality (a word that had only recently entered the nation's political vocabulary), for a couple of reasons, according to Argentine historian Ezequiel Adamovsky, who proudly took part in the same bank occupation that served as the ad hoc offices for Indymedia. First, the country's traditional—and hierarchical—structures had failed the people or disappeared, and neither the state nor private companies, nor even the old left-wing parties and unions, could offer a way out of the crisis. Argentina faced a "rift in the system of representation," he said. And secondly—paradoxically—the anti-neoliberal movement might have been influenced by anti-state and anti-political discourse since the 1980s in the mainstream press as elites pushed for neoliberal privatization. In practice, the *asambleas* employed "horizontality" because everyone was at the same level, and no one could decide anything for anyone else.[21]

"Horizontalism" as a word and as an operating principle took off globally after a book of the same name by US anarchist theorist Marina Sitrin was published in 2006, and it names an ideology that privileges fully horizontal organizations as a moral and political imperative.[22] This ideal had existed in the left-libertarian and anarchist traditions under different names for years. In Chile, for example, this might be called *asambleísmo* or assembly-ism. But "horizontalism" repackaged them in a certain way for the digital age. Many people in this world were influenced by the Italian *autonomistas*, leftist groups that worked outside the bounds set by the Italian Communist Party after 1968 and developed innovative forms of direct action. But for the members of the Movimento Passe Livre who often watched documentaries about the radical contention in neighboring Argentina, "autonomy" meant full independence and self-governance. No funding or direction coming from the outside.

The MPL charter proclaimed that "it can be said that a horizontal movement is a movement in which everyone is a leader, or where leaders do not exist." For Mayara, all of these principles, as well as their role in creating a better society, were self-evident. She said, "It's fundamental. If we are fighting to build a democratic city, we need to have a democratic movement and struggle in a democratic way."

This Is the End

The discourse in the rich anglophone world, taking place in the halls of power and on slick corporate media, was very different from the conversations happening on slow-loading websites and in grimy São Paulo bars. The first years of Mayara's life—the moment in which Fernando Haddad entered formal politics, the new era born with the death of the Soviet Union—were not experienced as struggle, but as triumph and opportunity.

During the twentieth century, both major schools of post-Enlightenment thought—Marxism and liberalism—had professed that history was going somewhere. They disagreed on the destination, of course. When the "Second World" led by Moscow fell to pieces in the 1990s, liberal democracy appeared to be the only coherent ideological project that resonated across the entire planet.[23] (When we talk of "liberalism" here, and throughout the book, we mean the broader philosophical tradition that prioritizes property rights and individual freedoms, not the US meaning that indicates something like "progressive," or "center-left.") The idea that history is moving toward something, that it has an ultimate end, can be called teleological—from the Greek word *telos*, or "end." Put simply, the end of the Cold War gave birth to the era of liberal teleology.

A political scientist and employee of the US State Department, Francis Fukuyama, asked if we had reached the "End of History" and grounded his analysis in Hegelian philosophy and an analysis of recent events.[24] But in the English-speaking world, more broadly, a vulgar version of teleological thinking simply assumed that things were going to work out. The West won and would continue to win because it was superior—more powerful and morally privileged. From now on, things would keep getting better (according to the standards of a liberal, capitalist democrat), and one had to simply accept the flow of history rather than fight against it.

Back in the 1960s, Martin Luther King Jr. had criticized this type of lazy thinking in his *Letter from Birmingham Jail*. Taking aim at the white liberals who seemed to believe that things would simply improve on their own, he attacked the "strangely irrational notion that there is something in the very flow of time that will inevitably cure all ills. Actually, time is neutral. It can be used either destructively or constructively," he wrote. "We must come to see that human progress never rolls in on wheels of inevitability. It comes through the tireless efforts and persistent work of men willing to be cowork-ers with God."

Nevertheless I feel that, during my childhood in California at the end of the twentieth century, those assumptions undergirded much of what I learned. Liberal teleology is closely related to something else we might call the "ideology of progress." People on television would say "this is the nine-ties," as if that automatically implied more freedom, progress, feminism, and fun, simply by virtue of being a bigger number than "eighties." I can't even count how many times I watched some special about the end of the Cold War that presented events like this: Ronald Reagan said, "Mr. Gorbachev, tear down this wall!"; crowds rushed into the streets and overwhelmed Commu-nist elites; David Hasselhoff sang to the people; and everyone lived happily ever after. As I entered university and studied political economy, we began with literature in the field—modernization theory—that assumed global societies would progress through stages on the way to becoming more like the United States. There was no more Third World, but rather "emerging markets"—a term coined at the World Bank in the 1980s—which implies automatic motion at the same time as it places these markets squarely, per-manently, in a position of catch-up relative to the rich West.

Like almost everything in Western civilization, the concept of historical teleology has its roots in the Christian intellectual tradition. Aristotle dis-cussed teleology, but he was speaking about the purposes of things; it would have not made sense to him to claim that history had an endpoint. For the ancient Greeks, time was not linear; history was cyclical. But in the Abra-hamic tradition, history would come to an end with Salvation. Indeed, the meaning of everything that had ever happened previously would be resolved and defined by that final moment. For those of us who live in the wake of this tradition, time is a line, an arrow pointing to the End Times. As European intellectuals began to question their absolute fealty to Christian faith, this understanding of time was transformed, but never discarded.

Throughout the age of rationalization and industrialization, the notion of progress took the place of Providence, the hand of God. Hegel and Marx provided the most robust (and influential) accounts of the ways in which history might be understood to move forward through stages without the guiding hand of the Lord. For Marx, class struggle is the engine of History, and the process that pushes humanity through stages.

To identify theology as the deep root of all of these systems (and most everything else) is not to discredit them; every idea has its own history. And there is nothing suspect about movements that seek to give life and its tribulations meaning through their relationship to a higher, noble purpose. But as noted by Karl Löwith, the German philosopher who traced these intellectual developments back to Saint Augustine, we began to assume that progress marches on without having a conscious understanding of why it would do so.[25]

In the 1990s, the skies were clear and blue for true believers in the universal liberal project. Everything would be coming up democratic and capitalist. Some analysts began to speak about the reasons for the "exceptions" to the global democratic trend, such as in the Middle East—turning to some kind of religious or cultural explanations, such as the "obedience to authority" inherent to the Arab mind. The solution, of course, was that the adoption of neoliberal reforms, which would lead to economic growth, would carry all the world's nations to the promised land.[26]

The end of the Cold War also changed the way the United States government approached protests and even revolution. While the Soviet Union was around, Washington often acted as a fundamentally counterrevolutionary power—afraid that any instability would open the door to communism. But in the 1990s after Russian chaos led to capitalism, the US launched major efforts to remake the world in its own image. By the turn of the millennium, over $700 million a year was spent on democracy promotion, and in 2000 the US government directed a lot of money—not in North American terms, but enough to tip the scales in Serbia—to Otpor, or "Resistance," the group that led the successful "Bulldozer Revolution" against Slobodan Milošević that year. Nongovernmental organizations (NGOs) made a difference too—in the former Soviet republic of Georgia, the Soros Foundation, named after the Hungarian American liberal philanthropist George Soros, helped support *Kmara* (the local version of *Otpor*), as did the National Endowment for Democracy. In November 2003, protesters there brought down President Eduard Shevardnadze, the man who had first run the country in 1972. As a result, Georgia turned West and away from Russia, and the "Rose Revolution" became the first of many in the region this century to be named after a color.[27]

In the years leading up to a terrorist attack on New York City in September 2001, founding neoconservative members of the Project for the New American Century insisted the US could also use its military force to spread democracy; guns and bombs could be used to give History a little push in the right direction. Many of these men had influential positions in the George W. Bush administration, and when—after the 2003 invasion of Iraq—regular people toppled a statue of the brutal Saddam Hussein, this was sold to viewers back home as another *Mauerfall* moment, as the obvious continuation of the legacy of the falling of Communist regimes. As it turns out, the US military had actually pulled it down for them.[28] That did not stop Fox News and CNN from playing a clip of the statue falling down, every 4.4 and 7.5 minutes respectively, on that day. It would take years for the political elites in the US to recognize that the invasion had not been a success for liberalism and democracy—or to consider, even, that Mayara and all those protesters on the streets around the world had been right all along.

Learning to Report

At the beginning of the twenty-first century, Jim O'Neill of the Goldman Sachs investment bank in the United States came up with the term BRIC— that is, Brazil, Russia, India, and China—to name four up-and-coming emerging market economies. They were each great places to put your money.

But the term really took off after the irruption of a global financial crisis in 2008. The rich, freewheeling capitalist countries like the US and the UK had seemingly discredited themselves by tanking the global economy in 2008, and the so-called BRICs were taking their place on the world stage. They created a formal organization in 2009 (adding South Africa to round out the acronym to BRICS a year later). As President Lula hosted the second summit in Brasília in 2010, his country turned a lot of heads around the world. Gross Domestic Product (GDP) growth that year in Brazil was 7.6 percent, as the US economy shrank by 2.5 percent.

I was working at the *Financial Times* in London and paying close attention. I had accidentally become a journalist back in 2007 in Venezuela (I was looking for any work I could get), and I was one of a few people in the newsroom with language skills and experience in South America. My editor, like many of the bigwigs in English-language journalism at the time, had cut his teeth covering the fall of Communism. In the world's most important outlets, the "developing world" or the "emerging markets" were often interpreted by men who had more experience in North America or Europe, and whose education (like mine) had been deeply shaped by liberal assumptions. The BRICS appeared to be a set of powers rising on the new tides of truly global capitalism. And while they were not all as democratic as Brazil, all of them (including Russia and China) had become a lot more liberal than they used to be.

3

Pior que tá não fica

I ARRIVED IN SÃO PAULO at the end of 2010. The *Financial Times* had decided that they needed a second correspondent to beef up their Brazil coverage. The booming country was set to host the 2014 FIFA World Cup and had just won the right to host the 2016 Summer Olympics in Rio de Janeiro. I came to write about the rise of a new global power, a democratic Brazil that was growing and thriving under Lula.

The ascent was not perfectly smooth. Just after Rio won the right to host the Olympics, drug traffickers in one of the city's famous *favela* communities shot down a police helicopter.[1] I knew that as a correspondent I would be tasked with answering embarrassingly gringo-centric questions like: "Is Brazil ready to host the World Cup?" and "Can Rio really put on the Olympics?" That was part of the job. The reality was that Brazil remained one of the world's most unequal societies—nearly as bad as South Africa had been under apartheid—and the vast chasm separating the rich and the poor was so obvious that no one ever mentioned it. Indeed, that seemed prohibited in polite society. Working people suffered from violence and relied on woefully inadequate public services.

But the gains since Lula took over in 2003 had been tremendous. Tens of millions of people had risen out of poverty, even as rich people fared incredibly well too. For a decade, a construction boom in China had meant robust demand for Latin American commodities. With this money coming in, Lula expanded a set of modest but efficient social programs that distributed more gains to the working class. The most famous was Bolsa Familia, a welfare program for poor families that kept their kids vaccinated and in schools. Fernando Haddad continued his ascent in formal politics, becoming Lula's minister of education in 2005. Together they created Pro-Uni, a program that put a generation of working-class kids in university. Brazil enjoyed significant global prestige. Lula especially gained favor as the poor kid who made good, won power playing by the rules, and developed friendships all around the world. Brazilian elites (and the media they own) certainly noticed when Barack Obama famously called him "my man" and "one of the most popular politicians on Earth" in 2009.[2] Yet this was not the realization of the socialist revolution. It was not even the industrial "upgrading" policy that had guided so many development projects in the twentieth century. It was built on the classic Third World practice of extracting the land's raw materials and shipping them off to other countries. But here, it seemed to be working. Inequality was falling, and things were getting better. As his second term came to an end, Lula enjoyed a ludicrously high approval rating—83 percent of Brazilians supported the president.[3]

Not many people had expected this. Progressive reform in the world's fifth-largest country by population had been violently halted in 1964, with the US-backed military coup, and no leftist had come close to the presidency since. As Lula finally closed in on electoral victory in 2002, the "markets" appeared unhappy with the prospect. Every time a poll showed him in the lead, the price of the Brazilian currency, the *real*, and the value of Brazilian bonds would drop rapidly. Lula wrote a "letter to the Brazilian people" (even though he was really writing to the representatives of global capital) declaring that he would maintain the basic economic structure established under President FHC, but the investor class was very wary of the Workers' Party. Eight years later, almost everyone in that class was much richer, and the Lulista approach—more stuff for everyone—was looking very good.

With a center-left party in power in Brasília, the countries of South America had made a renewed push for regional integration, and Lula tried to build Brazilian influence in Africa, especially through a set of huge, nationally strategic construction companies. Lula's two terms were a major part of the "pink tide," a term favored by international journalists to name the arrival of several left-of-center governments in Latin America. A generation after the fall of authoritarian capitalist military regimes, social democrats or socialists took power in Venezuela, Argentina, Bolivia, Uruguay, Chile, Ecuador, and Paraguay. It was no surprise that democracy would cause such a tide to rise; the era of US-backed coups repressed a genuine desire for reform in Latin America, and—since they fought and died to fight illegitimate power, rather than exercising it themselves—the left often had moral and intellectual authority.

To begin my career as a Brazil correspondent, I applied a technique I had perfected in Venezuela. I gave myself a crash course in its language and culture by getting into the local music scene and going out as often as I could.

São Paulo is a truly international city. It quickly stops mattering if you come from somewhere else. Of course, as a citizen of the world's richest country and a writer for some fancy publications, I got a very different welcome than would be offered to immigrants from Bolivia or Senegal (just as it is a lot easier to be British in Manhattan than it is to be Nicaraguan). But like in New York, after you've lived in the place for a year or two and speak the language, you are basically just another Paulistano. As strange as it may seem, I felt at home very quickly.

But my future as a journalist was far from certain. The age of reporters with job security—especially international journalists—was over. The arrival of online advertising and the consequent decimation of newspapers meant that shrinking budgets were increasingly directed to the kinds of activities that generated lots of clicks online. Nuanced global journalism might draw in some readers, but it was simply less cost-efficient than the kind of opinion piece, aggregated blog, or listicle that someone could bang out from a desk. This meant that my field was increasingly dominated by the kinds of young people who would take the plunge and just move somewhere, hoping for things to work out. The work of foreign correspondence always had a tendency to reproduce neocolonial dynamics, but this made it worse, because it is only a certain kind of young person that can afford to move abroad on a lark. My job, as I understood it, comprised three interrelated, but certainly distinct, goals: tell the Brazilian story while remaining faithful to the truth; attempt to build a life in the country, where I would remain for many years; and try to somehow construct the kind of long-term career that could support an adult life. If I was lucky, if I could make a splash and get noticed, I had a shot at getting another job when I was done here.

As you would expect for a young correspondent, I was tasked with covering the 2010 elections. Lula was done; Brazilian presidents cannot serve more than two consecutive terms. The next Workers' Party candidate, Dilma Rousseff, had a long and impressive story of her own. Born to a Bulgarian immigrant father and a schoolteacher in the state of Minas Gerais, the young Dilma became a Marxist guerrilla seeking to overthrow Brazil's military dictatorship. She was arrested and subjected to horrifying torture. Afterward, she became an economist, served as an administrator in various government positions, and sat on the board of Petrobras—the state-run oil company. She had a reputation as a gruff and competent technocrat. Dilma, as she was referred to, would be Brazil's first woman president.

But all that really mattered, as far as the election analysts were concerned, was that Lula was telling the country to vote for her. After his performance, people would vote for whomever he chose as a successor. The election was never even close. The most interesting and unexpected story I did in 2010 was about a clown.

Since I didn't grow up there, I didn't know much about the famous performer known as Tiririca. He is the kind of intentionally absurd Latin American television character that was lampooned on *The Simpsons*, except unlike the "Bumblebee Man," Francisco Everardo Oliveira Silva is fully self-aware and a truly brilliant performer. He had made his name in the 1990s. He claimed to be illiterate. And now he was running for Congress. The campaign was based on a set of flawlessly executed television spots that, of course, went viral online. In one clip he is a plump, middle-aged man wearing a bright wig, a red hat, colorful trousers, and a bizarre graphic top. He spins around, grinning. He overpronounces and mispronounces his words. "I want to be a Congressman, to help the people that are most in need, especially my own family," he says. "What does a Congressman do? In reality, I don't know. But vote for me, and I'll tell you." And then he dropped his famous campaign slogan.

Vote no Tiririca! Pior que tá não fica. Although it lacks the comedic rhyme of the original Portuguese, the translation is simple: "Vote for Tiririca! It can't get any worse."

I cannot overemphasize how genuinely funny all of this was. His target was clear, and his aim—perfect. He was calling the system absurd and corrupt, saying that an idiot from television would do a better job than the people already in Congress. Voting for Tiririca was a way to give the finger to the political establishment.

In an interview with *Folha de S.Paulo*, he said that he really wanted to improve Brazil. He also said that he meant what he said—he really didn't know what happens in Congress. And, he said, he really believed that things in Brazilian politics could not get any worse.

Tiririca received far more votes than any other congressional candidate in the history of Brazil. He got twice as many votes as the second-most-popular candidate for the legislature that year; he got double the amount that any "real" politician received. He entered Congress on January 1, 2011.

Dilma took office on that day, too. Like every other Brazilian president, she would have to deal with an unwieldy and unruly coalition in Congress (there were over twenty parties in the legislature) in order to actually govern, so having one former clown in there didn't change her job too much. One of the most significant moves of her early administration was an attempt to "sweep" away corruption without hesitation.[4] When allegations surfaced against some members of her own cabinet, she got rid of them immediately. A number of scandals had dogged Lula's government (and indirectly helped both Haddad and Dilma to rise, as they took the places of men who fell to accusations), but they'd never really reached the president himself. At the beginning of her term, Dilma's approval ratings hovered around the 70s.

In January in São Paulo, Mayor Gilberto Kassab (also a Lebanese-Brazilian) raised the price of a bus ride. The Movimento Passe Livre sprang into action, yet again. Six years into the existence of the group, there were less than fifty dedicated militants in the MPL, including Mayara, but they managed to get a bunch of kids and punks together, cause some trouble, and get noticed.[5] Over three months, crowds of them marched on or invaded bus stations. They organized *catracaços*—mass fare evasion, carried out by jumping or breaking the *catracas*, or turnstiles—and faced down waves of repression from the police, though they failed to stop the price hike.[6] As they often had in the years since their founding, they would encourage kids to go rip down any flags that anyone brought to the streets because of their fundamental opposition to parties and hierarchical organizations. Theirs was an *apartidário*, or "a-party" *movimento*, after all. *Vice* magazine would soon make a punchy little documentary about the group.[7] But at the beginning of 2011, Brazil was not the site of the uprising that the whole world was watching.

4

More Than an Uprising

JUST BEFORE NOON ON DECEMBER 17, 2010, Mohamed Bouazizi walked to the local government building in Sidi Bouzid, Tunisia, poured paint thinner all over his body, and lit it on fire. It was suicide, and it was an act of protest against a specific official. But even his relatives do not agree on what Mohamed really wanted to say, or what he expected to happen next. A scene like that—so horrifying, and so moving, and so troubling—must be interpreted by the people that it leaves behind. And over the days and weeks that followed, his death would not only take the form of a brazen political statement, but become one of the most important events of contemporary Arab history.

Mohamed was twenty-six and sold fruits and vegetables at the market just a little bit outside the dusty city center. He didn't have a permit, so he was constantly fighting with local authorities. This kind of thing was very common in Sidi Bouzid, a town about 150 miles south of the Mediterranean coast and the capital city, Tunis, which sits on the same beautiful strip of land as the ancient city of Carthage. Since the end of Arab Socialism and especially since the 2008 financial crisis, unemployment had been widespread throughout North Africa. His region had a proud reputation for being tough and rebellious since the days when Tunisia was a French colony. The Bouazizi family was known for being tough too.[1]

As they tell it, Mohamed was the victim of constant harassment. But one inspector, a woman, went too far. She confiscated his scale, which he needed to sell his wares. There was no way he could afford a new one. This led to a fight, and she struck him. In response, he escalated the situation, as high as anyone could go. This tactic, self-immolation, was not unknown in the Tunisian repertoire. A few months earlier in the breezy seaside town of Monastir, another street food vendor had set himself on fire. But there, nothing happened. His death had occurred in a different place within the very specific structure of this society.[2]

TUNISIA, A COUNTRY OF AROUND ten million people nestled between Algeria and Libya, won its independence from Paris in 1956. The young nation's first leader, Habib Borguiba, was relatively liberal, and women enjoyed more rights there than in most of the region. He did not take the bold anti-imperialist positions that Nasser did. Borguiba was running a small country, and he kept his head down on the international front. But as Egypt gained prestige throughout the region, Tunisia—like many Arab countries—took on elements of Nasser's socialist model.

The country remained intellectually intertwined with France. French philosopher Michel Foucault taught at the University of Tunis in the late '60s (where he gained a reputation for sexually abusing underage locals). In 1963, Tunisian leftists living in Paris founded the Marxist-Leninist journal *Perspectives*. The events of May 1968 radicalized this group even further, and they launched an Arabic journal aimed at the working class back home. *Perspectives* gave birth to both a Maoist party and one that was aligned with Albania's resolutely Stalinist leader, Enver Hoxha (for a while, Brazil's PCdoB had the same orientation). As Tunisia abandoned socialism in favor of free-market capitalism starting in the 1970s, leftists and workers responded with a wave of strikes and contentious politics. The army deployed US-supplied helicopters to quell them. Activists reported that the bloody crackdown, which took up to three hundred lives, was led by Director of National Security Zine El Abidine Ben Ali. In 1987, the same Ben Ali seized power by declaring Bourguiba medically incapacitated; he then immediately implemented a neoliberal structural adjustment program.[3]

For a North African country in the age of neoliberalism and brutal dictatorships, Tunisia had a robust and autonomous set of labor unions in 2010. Unlike the Egyptian Trade Union Federation (ETUF), which had been fully integrated with the state since the time of Nasser, the more independent Tunisian umbrella union (UGTT) still had some bite. The men at the very top got along with the government, but below that level, many union members were radical leftists. Tunisia even had a union of Unemployed Graduates, the kind of group that had only time on its hands and several bones to pick with the ruling class.

A 2008 rebellion in the Gafsa mining region—with the slogan "a job is a right, you pack of thieves!"—had grown outside the control of police and labor officials alike, with the assistance of organized leftists.[4] Though neither organization was large in absolute terms, the illegal communist parties that emerged from *Perspectives*—both Watad (Struggle) and the Tunisian Communist Workers' Party (PCOT)—believed that revolution was necessary, if not necessarily imminent, and they had trained their highly disciplined members to prepare for it.

Jawaher Channa, the daughter of a teacher in the countryside, joined the PCOT while attending university in the capital—they were the group most resolutely opposed to Ben Ali, she remembers—and then immediately got kicked out of school. When the Gafsa rebellion erupted, she was studying in the beach city of Sousse and she—like her comrades around the country—got directions from the Party that they should drop everything and spread the word about the uprising. She had been schooled in how to rally fellow students, how to be arrested, and how to withstand torture. Party members were always at the front of demonstrations, whether they were against Israeli policies in Palestine, their own government, or the capitalist system more generally. They were "the kings and queens of the streets," she liked to boast at the time.[5]

But Ennahda, the relatively moderate Islamist party, was a lot more popular, and its leaders were living in exile in London. Center-left secular parties like the opposition Parti Démocratique Progressiste (PDP) also had a significant role in civil society in the years leading up to December 2010.

One of Mohamed Bouazizi's cousins, Ali, was a member of the PDP. He posted a video of his cousin's death online and began agitating for more protests in the region.[6] Very quickly, another relative informed local media and Al Jazeera, the well-funded Qatari outlet that had been paying high salaries to experienced journalists and putting together a world-class news operation over the previous few years. Watad and the PCOT once more activated their Leninist cadres, most crucially the youngest ones. Students got up on the tables during lunch break, telling their classmates that it was time to rise up. They began to graffiti walls across Tunisia with old leftist slogans, like "Work, freedom, and national dignity!" or "Water and Bread Yes! Ben Ali No!" They had some help from leftist teachers, who were active in schools around the country.[7]

Tunisia's small community of bloggers, as well as a new set of people using Facebook, a social network from the United States, spread news of the ongoing clashes in Sidi Bouzid and the surrounding area that, along with Al Jazeera, helped break the official media silence. Ali may have embellished his cousin's story a bit, saying that he was a college graduate, and adding the humiliating "slap" from a female police officer, which probably made Mohamed Bouazizi a more sympathetic martyr.[8] This story spread far and wide.[9] Vast networks of Tunisians, unemployed or under-served and formally "unorganized," took action on their own terms.[10] All of the above meant that—unlike most uprisings in this part of the world—the protest wave actually reached the capital, a week later, on Christmas Day.[11]

In Tunis, one youth group unfurled a large red banner, reproducing a play on the original French phrase from 1968. It read: "Under the paving stones, the rage."[12]

Ben Ali's forces cracked down on union members and protesters in the capital, while the government accused Al Jazeera of biased reporting intended to undermine the country.[13] On December 28 a group of Tunisian attorneys gathered in front of the National Palace of Justice. Lawyers had already protested in the city of Kasserine, but the arrival of this distinguished professional group onto the scene standing tall outside the center of judicial power in Tunis changed the dimensions of the wave of contention. By the final days of 2010, lawyers were protesting in almost a dozen more cities. The organized bourgeoisie was starting to join the revolt.[14]

Mohamed Bouazizi's funeral, on January 5, attracted thousands of people, and thousands more protested throughout the country. Jawaher did too. She had been doing this for five years now, but this crowd was imbued with a special energy. It felt as if they were making history, and they were not backing down.

She was at the front, naturally. The police walked up to them and called her out, along with her seasoned activist friends, by name. They said it was time to go home. "We are demonstrating peacefully!" Jawaher responded, knowing very well that this would be read as a refusal and a provocation. But she wanted to show the people behind her that they were not giving in. The police grabbed her and dragged her across the street until she passed out. She woke up in the police station.

They tortured her. They subjected her to the "rotisserie chicken," in which you are bound to a wooden pole, hung upside down, and then beaten. It's the exact same thing that the military dictatorship did to Dilma Rousseff in the 1970s. Except in Brazil they call it the *pau de arara*: the "parrot's perch." The overlap in tactics is probably no coincidence. After the US-backed military coup in 1964, the Brazilian generals learned dirty tricks from their allies in Washington. But they also closely studied methods developed by the French during counterinsurgency operations in North Africa.[15] The cops started to rip Jawaher's clothes off, but she said she would jump out the window and commit suicide rather than let them touch her.

While Jawaher was still in jail, on January 11, the UGTT mega-union announced that all of its members could join a general strike. Ben Ali had now lost organized labor, including the normally pliant leadership at the top. The US ambassador, reporting to President Barack Obama, and the foreign policy chief of the European Union both expressed concern.[16] This was a very big deal, since support from the West had been crucial for maintaining the assorted set of neoliberal-authoritarian regimes in place in the Arab world. Amnesty International soon announced that at least twenty-three people had been killed in the recent uprising.[17] The world was paying attention, and the message being transmitted to most people was that a dictator was cracking down on a diverse set of civilian protesters with a legitimate set of demands. All of this was true. But it's not like it was the first time something like that had ever happened in North Africa, or indeed in Tunisia. No one knew quite how this was going to end.

Jawaher got out of jail much earlier than she expected—someone from the UGTT intervened and pressured the police to release her. This was a strange moment. The dictatorship could no longer keep even card-carrying Communist feminists in jail after they had clearly broken the law in public? She feared that Ben Ali would soon have his revenge, after reconsolidating power, unless people stayed in the streets. She knew how every other uprising in her life had ended. But she began to hope that this time, they really had a chance.

Next, another set of Tunisian organizations, including the Human Rights League, the Association of Democratic Women, and the Anti-Torture

Association, called for an end to violence against the protesters. Ben Ali blamed masked saboteurs for the bloodshed. At the same time, he promised to employ three hundred thousand university graduates by the end of 2012. This did not work. Protests continued into the night of January 11, and schools were suspended throughout the country. Tunisians around the world staged another set of demonstrations in support of the revolt back home. On January 12, the government instituted a night curfew in the capital, and the next day Ben Ali called for an end to violence against the protesters and promised not to seek another term as president. This did not work. On January 14, a group marched from the headquarters of the UGTT to the Ministry of the Interior, and the crowd swelled as it moved through the city. Into the night, people clashed with police directly in front of the Presidential Palace. The army refused to open fire on the protesters.[18] Ben Ali gathered his family and fled to Saudi Arabia.

The president had fallen, after twenty-three years in power. News spread quickly throughout the world. One thousand and five hundred miles to the east in Alexandria, Egypt—the Mediterranean city built by Alexander the Great 2,300 years earlier—Hossam el-Hamalawy was sitting in a small café near the sea.[19] Hossam had been a dedicated activist and labor organizer for years, and he was smoking shisha with his friend, a diving instructor. Online, he was known as 3arabawy, the transcribed version of the Arabic for "The Bedouin." He was not actually a nomad from the desert—he was from Cairo—but this handle gave him an easy way to assert his proud Arab identity. Hossam was trying to convince his friend, in vain, to form a diving instructors' union. He wasn't buying it. A noise erupted in the coffee shop, and everyone's eyes turned to the TV. The journalist announced that President Ben Ali had fallen. The place burst into applause, and people began shouting. One man yelled, "Mubarak is next!"

Eighteen Days Later

Protests had been staged in Tahrir Square, in the center of Cairo, for years. But they were never aimed at President Hosni Mubarak, the man in power since 1981—at least not directly. In 2000, Palestinians began the Second Intifada, or uprising, against Israeli control over their lives, and supporters in

Egypt filled the square in solidarity. The Gaza Strip is just a few hours' drive from the capital, and Israel has been a deeply important issue for Egyptians since the country was founded. As a result of the 1978 Camp David Accords, and the Egyptian government's permanent reorientation toward the West, Egypt had been helping the Zionist state to enforce the impenetrable border enclosing the Gaza Strip. Then in 2003, protesters filled Tahrir in a failed attempt to stop the invasion and destruction of Iraq.[20]

Gehad, a listless young woman from the capital, grew up identifying the very idea of protest with the Palestinian cause and opposition to Western imperialism. Her mother was a doctor, and her father was in the country's expansive armed forces—well, he really worked in oil exploration, but the army controlled that sector, along with many more—and Gehad had a relatively comfortable upbringing. For a time she was quite devout, donning the headscarf and living as a *hijabi*; then she took it off and became more liberal and secular, angering her mother even as she still valued her faith and considered herself a Muslim. She was a precocious, weird teenager, reading too many fantasy novels and preferring to listen to old Lebanese music, rather than the rock or pop most of her friends favored, as she whiled away her hours on the internet.[21]

Gehad felt that support for their more oppressed neighbors brought her entire generation together. She used to sit around all day, hanging out in Free Palestine chat rooms, which is where she learned about politics. At the age of thirteen she ditched school to go support the Second Intifada, and then she protested the Iraq War in 2003. In the Egyptian repertoire, these were the causes that gave rise to the occupation of Tahrir as the natural performance. Then in 2004, a new organization emerged. It was called Kefaya, or "Enough," and owed its existence to rumblings within the Egyptian elite, as well as vibrations unleashed from the West.

WHEN NASSER'S SUCCESSOR, ANWAR SADAT, sought rapprochement with the West, it shocked Moscow. The Communist method for maintaining Arab allies (Syria was another) essentially consisted of shoveling money and assistance at them without ever exercising any real control over their states. When Sadat evicted more than fifteen thousand Soviet advisers, the Egyptian military high command was flabbergasted—those were the guys supplying all their arms in an ongoing conflict with Israel. In 1973, Sadat tried to take back the Sinai Peninsula, which Egypt had lost to Israel in the

1967 conflict, leading to another full-on war with the Jewish state. Throughout the war, he told US secretary of state Henry Kissinger his plans, hoping to curry favor with the Americans. Kissinger simply passed the information on to the Israelis. Many in the military believed that Sadat threw away the campaign, and after the war—which the government called a win, but many considered a set of lost opportunities—the armed forces felt deeply alienated by the leader (except for the weak air force, led by a loyal man named Hosni Mubarak). Sadat cracked down hard on the left and reversed the land reform that had undergirded Nasser's revolution, handing a lot of property back to the country's feudal class, and began an *infitah*, or "opening," that commenced with the deconstruction of Arab Socialism in the region's most populous country. The Egyptian people responded with bread riots across the nation in 1977.[22]

The Muslim Brotherhood, one of the most important Islamist groups in the modern world, had been around since 1928 and was therefore older than the Egyptian republic itself. The Egyptian government had, variously, subjected the group to intense repression or used it as a counterweight against the left. But there were smaller, more radical and jihadist groups in the country too. In 1981 one of them murdered Anwar Sadat in front of the whole country, and not too many people cared.[23] Under the country's next president, Hosni Mubarak, the army remained sidelined, and the police (always important in the Egyptian republic) took on increasing power. Of course, Mubarak maintained the country's pro-Western orientation.

The global debt shock in the 1980s caused by the surprise increase in US Federal Reserve interest rates hit the region particularly hard. By the middle of the 1980s, Algeria, Jordan, Tunisia, and Egypt were paying 30–60 percent of their export earnings to service debts to rich countries.[24] The IMF of course was there to bail them out and push the countries toward free-market reform at the same time. The United States and its National Endowment for Democracy (NED)—which had also taken on some of the activities pioneered by the CIA—were now promoting more robust capitalism as a force that would bring about democracy in the country.[25] And in 1991, Egypt earned a huge chunk of debt relief in exchange for supporting George H. W. Bush's invasion of Iraq. By the first years of the new millennium, Egypt had privatized billions in assets, which landed in the hands of a new, super-wealthy capitalist class. But neoliberal reforms did not magically deliver democratization as liberal teleologists would have assumed; to the contrary, they required the repression of dissent to be implemented, just as they had in Chile in the 1970s. Unemployment shot up, while the economy was powered more by real estate speculation, remittances from laborers in rich Gulf states (like Saudi Arabia, Kuwait, and Bahrain), and the construction of shopping malls than any really productive activity. There was certainly no longer any push to change the very shape of the global economy.[26]

As part of his campaign to democratize the Middle East, George W. Bush had been pressing Egypt to show some progress in creating more democratic processes. In response, Mubarak apparently let the Muslim Brotherhood win seats in the next election, with the goal of scaring the Americans into backing off.[27] Kefaya—Enough!—flowered into this small space Mubarak opened for legitimate civil society, as well.

When Mubarak indicated he might hand the country over to his son Gamal, it was too much for many people in the establishment. Liberals, Nasserists, secular reformers, Islamists, and Marxists alike united in their opposition to a hereditary Mubarak regime. Gamal, the son of the dictator, was a creature of the elite, global business world. He had run a private equity fund in London, he surrounded himself with a close group of his cronies, and he had no links to the revolutionary struggles that had built and fought for Egypt—a quality that especially irritated the military.

Reflecting global trends at the time, the new Kefaya was "non-hierarchical" and "cross-ideological."[28] Its members published articles and organized rallies, but they never seemed to put real pressure on the government. Mubarak carried on as usual. But then, a wave of wildcat strikes began to take off outside the capital. Inspired by the industrial action, one group of activists based in Cairo attempted to drum up support for a national strike on April 6, 2008, in solidarity with workers in the Nile Delta. They didn't pull it off—that was beyond their organizational capacity—but the group stayed together.[29] The small "April 6 Youth Movement" got some attention and some support from US-based NGO Freedom House, in addition to receiving some training in a very different tradition than that of revolutionary socialist Hossam "3arabawy" el-Hamalawy and the leftists in Tunisia.[30*]

---

* The April 6 Movement spoke with *Otpor,* the Western-backed Serbian group that worked to bring down Slobodan Milosevic in 2000 and adopted the same raised fist as the group's logo. The support from Freedom House, however, caused controversy within the group.

But these groups failed to create any major bouts of contention in 2008 or 2009. Then the police killed Khaled Said.

The nation found out that Khaled Said, a regular guy from Alexandria, was dragged from an internet café in June 2010 and beaten to death by the police. Citizens across the nation were shocked at the image of his disfigured body, going viral online, and he became a symbol of the expansion of brutal police repression to regular people. As a public figure and a martyr from the quiet Cleopatra suburb, he became more innocent, and heroic, than the real individual had ever been.[31] He was no leftist, nor was he an Islamist radical— and his death incensed liberal and conservative Egyptians alike, who knew very well that Mubarak's police were a threat to almost anyone. Most people had stories of state violence; they had either seen something or had a family member suffer grave injustice. What was new, in 2010, was that images of the repression were available for immediate viewing by tens of millions of people, and that they could soon join a page on Facebook to share their collective outrage.

Facebook had launched in Arabic in 2009, and by 2010 around a quarter of Egyptians used the internet regularly (especially young people in cities).[32] Wael Ghonim, a marketing executive at Google, set up the page "We Are All Khaled Said," and Abdelrahman Mansour, a former Muslim Brotherhood member who had trained a bit as an activist with Hossam "3arabawy," helped him run it. The group grew in members and activity throughout the beginnings of the Tunisian uprising. It was the We Are All Khaled Said page that called for a protest on January 25, just eleven days after President Ben Ali fell in Tunisia. But once more, the protest would not be directed at the Egyptian president. They would call for the removal of the interior minister.

The date was the national celebration of Egyptian "Police Day," which could allow the rally to emphasize its focus on police brutality, and to recall a time when cops had played a far more heroic role in Egyptian history than they did now. Tahrir means "liberation" in Arabic, and the square was renamed after Egyptians won formal independence. But informal control persisted, and in 1952 fifty police officers died fighting British troops and defending national dignity near the Suez Canal. The contrast with the way the police were acting now was clear.

At the planning meetings, Hossam and other activists laid out the routes and made preparations. Someone asked, "What will we do after we reach Tahrir Square?" Everyone burst into laughter. That was not going to happen.

On the morning of January 25, the uprising back in Tunisia was far from finished. When Ben Ali fled, it was not clear what was supposed to happen. Politicians invoked an article of the constitution allowing them to appoint one of his allies as president, but this generated more protest. What was left of the government found another article to invoke and appointed the same man as prime minister, and he sought to form a national unity government. Elites were divided on the next steps. A new set of demonstrations demanded that no one from the previous regime remain in power, and since January 23 they had been occupying the Kasbah—the government square—in Tunis.

On the afternoon of January 25 in Cairo, far more people showed up to the Police Day protest than anyone expected. Marches broke through the lines of cops, who responded with the repression they had been trained to unleash. But they were unprepared for the number of people who came out that day. The protesters charged past them to the square. Hossam was in the back, and he got a call from a comrade up front. "There are like a million people here," she said. "What are you smoking!" Hossam replied, until he checked videos now circulating on the internet. This was bigger than anything he had ever seen in his life. Gehad had stayed home—not out of fear, but because she didn't think much was going to happen that day. Protests like this at Tahrir had been happening for years, and despite the events in Tunisia, she figured this one would peter out like all the rest. But then she saw the image of a man facing down a police vehicle, impervious to the blast of its water cannon, and something stirred inside her. She knew she was going to join this revolt. She had been drifting for months, unsure what to do with her life after a teaching job that didn't work out. Now, she had a mission. The protest on January 25 finally fizzled out, and the demonstrators went home. But Gehad had plans for Friday. She would be going to the next protest, marked for three days later.

Friday is prayer day. As waves of young people and activists made their way toward Tahrir Square on the twenty-eighth, they were astounded to see new streams of people coming out of the mosque after ceremonies. Together now, they chanted, "Bread, Freedom, Social Justice!" and "The people want the fall of the regime"—a demand that not even the seasoned activists had planned to make three days earlier. Some preachers had come out in support of the revolt during Friday prayers. And then, a huge procession emerged from Imbaba, the poor neighborhood that looks much like a Brazilian *favela*, and stomped onto the bridge over the Nile to add their numbers to the movement. As protesters from all over Egypt pushed forward, now part of a far larger mass than anyone could have imagined, it felt like something had shifted in the nature of time itself. They had cracked open the structure of reality, and with each step, with each victory against police defenses, with every movement, it felt as if they were literally moving history forward. "A weird distortion in the air"—or the feeling of "magic"—this was the kind of language that participants grasped for to describe the sensation. Everything was possible.[33]

The armed forces—not the target of the demonstrations—stayed out of the clashes. Some soldiers were seen smiling and hugging demonstrators. Some protesters chanted, "The people and the army are one hand."

Hossam marched toward the center of town because today, he was on the front line. He had no sense of how many people were behind him, and so, when they approached a pedestrian bridge looming above, he ran ahead and scurried up, so he could look back. He immediately burst into tears. It was a sea of people, and he couldn't even see where it began. He began to exclaim to himself, "It is happening, it is happening. It is happening!" A few minutes later he ran into a longtime friend of his, an engineer who had always laughed at Hossam's political engagements. For years, he had worked on a strategy called "visualization of dissent"—coordinating with striking workers, and distributing images of uprisings as widely as possible, so that regular people might see themselves in them and imagine they could change the world. Now, he could see them participating in front of his eyes. People had called him a clown for believing in revolution, and yet, they were there with him. He ran into an Islamist friend who always disliked Hossam's political commitments. Then he ran into this man's sister, and his mother! He knew he had been right all along.

January 28 was relatively spontaneous in that it came together very quickly, and it was indeed leaderless, horizontally structured, and ideologically diverse. But it was not nonviolent, and this was no longer a protest. A huge mass of Egyptians went to battle with the police that day, and the police lost. Some ripped off their uniforms and scattered into the wind. Protesters burned down over ninety police stations that night. One wave of Egyptians battled cops on the Qasr al-Nil bridge, holding their ground while suspended over the Nile, pushing back, taking losses, and then advancing again until the police simply retreated. At that point, the revolutionaries could have taken anything. They chose to stay in Tahrir Square, the default destination for many in the crowd; it was an empty piece of land, and its conquest offered no strategic value, except for its visibility.[34]

This had not been planned, and some participants soon questioned why it happened. Would it not have made more sense to actually charge the halls of power and take control? Should a revolutionary movement not seize the television and radio stations so it can stop the regime from broadcasting its propaganda? It was all right there for the taking. But if they did that, who would have been in charge of deciding what to do with them? This was not a movement led by a revolutionary vanguard; it was a huge mass of individuals that, just days ago, were little more than an event on a Facebook page. In any case, that is not what they did. They took the Square. And they stayed there.[35]

It was packed with people. The government had shut down telecommunications that day in the hopes of cutting the legs out from under the marchers. This was a mistake. Cairo is a dense, tightly knit city. For millions of people, Tahrir Square is basically just down the road. If you want to know what is going on with that protest, or your son or daughter, you can just walk over. Lots of people did exactly this. After decades of dictatorship, there were very few formal structures in civil society. But there were surely informal structures. The people, or "the street," kept everyone abreast of what was going on.[36] Over the next eighteen days, Tahrir Square became a carnival of prefiguration and structurelessness, the symbol of the world of Egyptian resistance.

Communists and tattooed lesbians broke bread with pious Islamists and children who lived on the street nearby, all of them united in opposition to Mubarak. Laughing, smiling, suffering, sacrificing, and working together, these people created a new mini-society—keeping everyone fed, safe, and healthy. Gehad had never felt more alive in her life. As soon as she arrived, she saw a simple woman in *hijab*, appearing neither rich nor poor, holding a sign that simply read "Hope." In a few days, Gehad had gone from a state of depression to the experience of the sublime. Like many other people, she went back and forth between her home and the Square. Life there felt "legendary," it felt "mythical," and it felt as if it belonged to a different universe, one that was unforgettable yet hard to truly believe. One that was profoundly, unimaginably beautiful.

Governments in the West didn't know how to respond to all of this. In early February, with Tahrir still packed to the brim, former UK prime minister Tony Blair came out to publicly defend longtime ally Hosni Mubarak as "immensely courageous and a force for good," mostly because of his friendship with Israel. US president Barack Obama sent veteran diplomat Frank Wisner Jr.—the son of Frank Wisner, the man who pioneered the use of covert operations at the CIA in the 1950s—to Cairo to represent the State Department and assist with negotiations.[37]

Global media, however, did know how to respond. They turned their cameras to Tahrir Square and sent their reporters to Cairo. One reference point appeared immediately: this was 1989, but this time in the Middle East. The images certainly looked very similar. *Radio Free Europe*, the US-funded outlet that had been intentionally trying to bring down that wall in the Cold War, reported, "Not since the fall of the Berlin Wall in November 1989, and the jubilant scenes of East Germans rushing across to the West, has the world witnessed such a tidal wave of humanity on the march."[38] The contradictions of the Arab "exception" were finally working themselves out, and History was finally pushing these countries into the liberal democratic order.

But who could Western outlets get on TV to explain what was happening and what the movement wanted to achieve? This mass of people had no official representatives. So the journalists chose the people who could explain— ideally in English, and ideally in a vocabulary their viewers would appreciate. They were not likely to grab a teenager who lived on the street, addicted to cheap drugs, and put them on *The Daily Show*, even though some of these kids had fought most bravely against the cops. And they probably were not going to interview a fervent Islamist on CNN, even though the Muslim Brotherhood—which joined late, but certainly participated in the revolt— was the largest organized group in the square.

There was an elective affinity between media coverage and revolutionary elements with a liberal, pro-Western orientation. The term "Arab Spring," applied in January by a US political scientist in *Foreign Policy* magazine, was widely adopted by the global press, despite the fact that spring has very different connotations on the northern edge of the Sahara Desert, and none of the original protesters used it. It was actually winter, but the concept harkened back to the "Prague Spring" in Communist Czechoslovakia and before that to the 1848 "Springtime of the Peoples" across Europe. On *Democracy Now*, Amy Goodman spoke with columnist Mona Eltahawy, who called Mubarak himself the "Berlin Wall." On CNN, Anderson Cooper spoke with

Wael Ghonim from Google, who said that the leaders were "every single person there." The network then cut to US president Barack Obama, who said that it was nonviolence and moral force that "bent the arc of history towards justice once more."[39] Later, the US president offered Poland as a transition model for the Arab world.[40]

Commentators were dazzled by the fact that the internet, US-based social media especially, seemed to have made this all happen. The Western media gave special attention to the euphoric, prefigurative, and ultra-democratic elements within the revolt.[41]

Jack Shenker, a *Guardian* correspondent who lived in the country and knew many revolutionaries well, put it this way: "Egyptians built something different from Mubarak Country: a different set of borders, a different set of social relations, a different narrative about who they were and what they could do. Everyone, including me, wrote about the inventive food supplies and toilet systems, the hijacked power cables and tented schools, the in-house hairdresser and exuberant street weddings." For anglophone readers, all of this appeared as the kind of decentralized and anti-hierarchical movement that could herald open progress, rather than the kinds of dedicated (or Leninist) revolution that insisted on a given path. No, this was aimed at transforming power, rather than seizing the state. Shenker continues, writing that Egyptian revolutionaries had not "viewed power as something just 'out there' to be captured; they've understood it as something diffuse, scattered across complex domestic, regional and global nodes.... It means a reimagination of how power functions, and the opening up of a space in which that reimagination can take place. It means a rejection of rigid hierarchies and ideological blueprints, of charismatic leaders and the obedience they crave.... Inspired by the *horizontalidad* movements of Latin America over the last two decades, this sort of rhizomatic organization," he said, "was the natural outcome of the oppositional activity that had taken place during the Mubarak era."[42]

Mahmoud Salem—who had been blogging as "Sandmonkey" since 2004 and therefore quickly became an accidental and unofficial spokesman for the explosion—put it a different way: "We were anarchists, without knowing we were anarchists."[43] Mahmoud went to battle at the keyboard and in the streets. He was often on the front lines, intercepting tear gas canisters and throwing them back at the police. He and two friends grabbed a boat and crossed the Nile River to occupy Tahrir Square.[44]

And in the end, all of this worked. Of course, the military provided a major assist. A day of savage repression on February 2, in which plainclothes thugs rode into the square on camels, convinced many of the country's most important men that Mubarak had to go. On February 11, the generals refused an order to fire on the people. Mubarak was done. Gehad woke up to the news of a new country being born; after a long night in the square, she had been napping at home. When Egypt found out that the dictator was gone, a roar erupted through the neighborhoods of the capital—the kind of screaming you only heard when the national football team scored a goal. Hossam "3arabawy" heard the same thing all the way across town, and he couldn't believe it. Everyone was jumping and yelling with joy, together. The country was now controlled by SCAF, the Supreme Council of the Armed Forces, which promised to hold democratic elections soon.

This Is War

Although they are both grouped into the so-called Arab Spring, things in Libya and Syria went differently. They did not live through demonstrations that grew so large that they forced a transformation of power. Unlike the cases we analyze more closely in this book, protest movements in Libya and Syria did not experience that strange shift, from quantitative to qualitative change, from numerical growth to full transformation, on their own. In both countries, the outcome had little to do with the tactics and ideology of contemporary street contention. Something else happened, something much more familiar to students of history. But the outcomes there profoundly changed the future of mass uprisings—both those already underway and those yet to be born—and so we must explain that distinction.

In Tunisia, the first "Kasbah" protests at the government square ended without complete success. But in February they returned, and the "Kasbah II" occupation forced the resignation of Ben Ali's old prime minister, and the interim president announced a National Constituent Assembly to write a new constitution.[45]

In Egypt, the sudden fall of Mubarak appeared as a lightning bolt from heaven. As would become increasingly common throughout the decade,

Mahmoud "Sandmonkey" Salem turned to pop culture to explain how many people viewed the possible fall of the leader. "It was like *The Lord of the Rings*," he said, referring to the Hollywood adaptation of the J. R. R. Tolkien story. "If you take Tahrir, that is Mordor, and then you automatically bring down Sauron [that is Mubarak]." In the movie, once Sauron falls, all the dark magic in the universe simply dissipates, and all the forces of evil disappear. That is not what happened.

All the same people and all the same structures remained in place, except now, SCAF was in power at the top. Domestically, the military faced a chaotic and mind-bogglingly complex political scene—who were they supposed to talk to in order to make sure they could keep "the revolution" happy?[46] How many people were ever actually in the square anyway, and whom did they represent? Empirical analysis of the biggest crowds, which came out later, indicated that participation was more complex than initial narratives would have suggested—most people cited economic concerns as their primary motivation, far ahead of democracy; around 25 percent of people in the Square supported the Muslim Brotherhood; more were middle-class, rather than poor and unemployed, and a majority got their primary information from television (especially Al Jazeera), rather than the internet.[47] But how much did that actually matter now to the real configuration of power across the country? Most urgently, the government wanted to be able to stop another flood of anarchy from breaking through. It was just over the border that the dam broke first.

Since 1969, Libya had been governed by Muammar Gaddafi, a mercurial pan-Africanist revolutionary that spent some time as one of the West's most infamous enemies. More recently he had made peace with the North Atlantic powers, giving up his weapons of mass destruction and reestablishing relations during the years of the Global War on Terror. The state he had constructed was fundamentally authoritarian, and it also distributed material benefits to much of the population. In the 2010 United Nations Human Development Index, Libya scored higher than any other African country.[48]

Starting in February 2011, some of his longtime opponents in the east of the country began protests, and then an armed uprising. Largely led by tribal, regional, and Islamist forces, rebels seized a number of cities quickly, but government forces began a brutally effective counterattack. The North Atlantic Treaty Organization (NATO), a security alliance created to counter

Soviet influence during the Cold War, elected to implement a "no-fly zone" to stop Gaddafi from massacring his own people.

Gaddafi surely had domestic enemies with very good reasons to want him out of power. He had surely employed systematic repression as he reproduced state power, and he had surely committed crimes against humanity. All of the same was also true for Saddam Hussein, another leader marked for removal by Western forces. Despite its stated intention, the NATO attack in Libya was a regime change operation. Without outside interference, Gaddafi could have easily kept control of the country.[49] To justify military action and the violation of Libyan national sovereignty, the international forces invoked the "responsibility to protect," a doctrine developed in the wake of tragedies in Rwanda and Kosovo in the 1990s, with the aim of protecting civilians from things like genocide.[50] But the targets chosen by NATO revealed that the real goal was to overthrow the government. A layperson would have never guessed it, but a "no-fly zone" actually meant bombing quite a lot of Libya. Fighter jets carried out thousands of airstrikes, killing scores of civilians, and they bombarded Gaddafi's hometown, even though no one in the loyal region needed any protection from the government. NATO simply wanted the leader of the country to fall.[51] And he most certainly did, in dramatic, terrifying fashion. Rebels sodomized Gaddafi with a knife and then uploaded the video to the internet. Anyone in the world could watch the Libyan leader being tortured to death.

For many other world leaders, especially but not only the autocrats, these shocking images offered a few lessons. First, if you have weapons of mass destruction—don't give them up.[52] Second, foreign powers will use legitimate or apparently legitimate uprisings as an excuse to push their own agendas. And finally, whatever you do, don't let this kind of uprising win—unless you want to end up like Gaddafi.

Hillary Clinton, serving as secretary of state in the United States, left the world with no doubt as to what had happened. Speaking later to a television reporter, she paraphrased Caesar (who, as it happened, also attacked North Africa). She said, "We came, we saw, he died," and laughed.[53]

Neither rising power China nor decadent power Russia liked any of this one bit. Along with Brazil, they had not voted for UN Security Council Resolution 1973, which authorized the "no-fly zone." Hu Jintao, leader of the People's Republic of China, called for a cease-fire and said, "If military action brings disaster to civilians and causes a humanitarian crisis, then it runs counter to the purpose of the UN resolution."[54] As a result of the NATO operation in Libya, former Russian president Vladimir Putin—who had stepped aside in 2008 to let Dmitry Medvedev run things—decided he must return to the presidency.[55] Previously one of the most eagerly pro-Western leaders in Russian history (he supported Bush's War on Terror in the early 2000s and sought to align with the EU and NATO), he was now developing a new security doctrine based on the idea that the West was not accepting the world as created by the end of the Cold War and was instead using destabilization and illegal invasions to push for wider and wider influence.[56] In 2011, Dilma Rousseff became the first woman to ever open the UN General Assembly (Brazil always goes first) and used the speech to take aim at problems with the "responsibility to protect" doctrine, insisting that the use of force should be a last resort.[57]

In March 2011, just before the NATO attacks, citizens in Syria began to rise up in protest against President Bashar al-Assad, who had been in power since 2000. Originally trained as an ophthalmologist in London, he took over for his father, Hafez, after his older brother died in a car crash. This kind of hereditary succession was a betrayal of the original republican ideals of the Ba'ath Party—as was the abandonment of socialism for neoliberalism and the government's close identification with certain ethnicities, rather than all Arabs—but under Bashar the country remained, in rhetoric at least, opposed to the foreign policy of the West. Syria was friendly with Iran, and Bashar al-Assad had let *jihadis* go to Iraq to fight against the US and British invading forces.[58]

Small protests started in Daraa in the south, and they were initially peaceful. The demonstrations were obviously inspired by the events in North Africa, and some Syrians came to believe that Western forces would intervene, as they had in Libya.[59] But unlike the situations in Egypt and Tunisia, loyalties in Syria were divided along sectarian lines, and minorities like the Alawites (who made up much of the army high command) and the Shia often felt that their interests were better served by the government than by the alternative. As the protests began to spread, violent elements appeared alongside peaceful demonstrations; some Syrian minorities feared that Sunni militants might impose a totalitarian religious regime if they won or massacre Alawites as they had in the 1970s. Bashar al-Assad was able to convince his security forces to stick with him, as he opted for brutal repression. They did not identify the uprising as "the people," spontaneously clamoring for the extension of universal rights, but instead viewed these Syrians as representatives of specific, opposing interests. The bloody suppression of the demonstrations led to further radicalization on the part of the rebels. Meanwhile, the leadership in Saudi Arabia, Washington's most important ally in the Arab world, came to the conclusion that it was in its own interest to back Sunni rebels in Syria.

Painted on the walls of the ancient nation, regime loyalists delivered a very simple message: "It is either Assad, or we will burn the country."

Sealed with a Kiss

No country had more reason to pray for the arrival of a metaphorical "spring" than Bahrain, the island nation in the Gulf of Arabia. This is a very hot part of the world, but there is more coastline here than dry sand, more beach than desert, and for centuries locals were renowned as skilled pearl divers. In 1783 the country was conquered by Sunni Arabs from the peninsula to the west, and the House of Khalifa has ruled Bahrain ever since. As 2011 began, Hamad bin Isa Al Khalifa, a close ally of the House of Saud, ruled as king. Bahrain is majority Shia, and the royal family systematically privileges the Sunni minority and excludes the Shia from the benefits of full citizenship.

In Gulf economies shaped by oil exploration (Bahrain was the first country to discover the stuff in the region, and will soon be the first to run out), jobs in state-run companies are all-important. The Shia majority is denied positions with strategic value. Rather than allow them to serve in the security services, the ruling family invites people from Sunni countries like Pakistan, Yemen, and Syria to staff the repressive apparatus. As uprisings spread throughout the Arab world, Bahrainis did not just have complaints about economic policy and police brutality, or the current leader—the complaints of subjects in young republics like Egypt and Tunisia—they were dealing with the kinds of issues that most European countries had resolved in the days of the original "spring," back in 1848. An unaccountable monarchy brazenly stepping on the rights of the oppressed majority. The National Assembly, the body created to give some representation to the people, was scrapped in 1975 after Marxists and Islamists formed an alliance to oppose a draconian national security law.[60]

Ebrahim Sharif is the unassuming, cheerful leader of Wa'ad or "Promise," a Bahranian political party born dedicated to the dream of socialist revolution. Historically, Bahrain had one of the strongest left-wing movements in the Gulf, and Sharif is well-steeped in the history of global revolution from reading a lot and hanging out with aging veterans of the Dhofar Rebellion, a failed bid to overthrow the Sultanate of Oman with a long, Che Guevara-style guerrilla war. But in the past few decades, the goals of the Promise party have been much more modest. Overturning the monarchy and instituting a republic would be far too provocative to next-door powerhouse Saudi Arabia, the thinking went, so the left-of-center opposition had limited itself to calling for a democratic constitutional monarchy—the royal family would stay, but the people would be granted some basic rights.[61]

All of this seemed possible in 2001 when the young, then sheikh Hamad submitted a National Action Charter, outlining a set of moderate reforms, for referendum. It was approved by 98 percent of the population. But Sheikh Hamad decided to interpret this as a mandate to subsequently write an entirely new constitution and keep power for himself. The opposition—leftists like Sharif, the Shia parties, democrats, anyone who opposed absolute monarchy—was floored. They had been played.

February 14, 2011, was the ten-year anniversary of this referendum, the last time the people had been able to articulate their will as a nation, and so it was the perfect day for the wave of Arab uprisings to crash onto Bahraini shores. Ebrahim Sharif attended the protest. Usually it is mostly the Shia who demonstrate, but Wa'ad is a cross-sectarian opposition party, and its Sunni (and secular) members traditionally join in too.[62] So he headed, a bit unprepared, to Pearl Roundabout—the closest thing to a Tahrir Square that the country had. He was immediately called upon to give a speech, which he did. But it all happened so fast that he barely had time to decide on his message. "I don't know what I said—something like 'we need to do whatever they did in Egypt.'" That's the way he remembered it afterward, but the full thing made it onto YouTube, the video aggregation website hosted by the California technology company Google.

Soon after, the leader of the largest Shia party got in touch with him. He planned to go speak with Crown Prince Salman bin Hamad Al Khalifa, but he didn't want to let anyone claim that this was a sectarian uprising. That was a favorite tactic of Sunni elites in the region to dismiss opposition concerns—especially effective when paired with the claim, almost always baseless, that Iran was behind whatever the population was asking for. The Shia wanted to present a united, cross-sectarian front, and they wanted Sunni leftists like Ebrahim Sharif to be a visible part of it. Sharif called a meeting of the entire opposition, and they assembled in his quiet, suburban home. This uprising, however, would not end with negotiations.

Member countries of the Gulf Cooperation Council (GCC)—Saudi Arabia, the United Arab Emirates, and Kuwait—sent their forces over the bridge into Bahrain on March 14 and surrounded the small island, helping the crown prince to crush the protests and annihilate the opposition. There were far more troops roaming the streets than necessary, and they were terrifying. The opposition was rounded up, and authorities cracked down especially hard on Sunnis like Ebrahim Sharif who had "broken ranks" and betrayed their putative allies in the ruling Sunni minority. They obliterated the Pearl Roundabout—paving over it in such a way that you can't even find where it used to be—and named the new construction after a historical figure hated by the Shia, a clear slap in the face to the majority.[63]

And that was it. There was little outcry in the West, and Arab media largely ignored the crackdown. There was no talk of "responsibility to protect" or even any real hiccup in relations between the United States and Saudi Arabia or Bahrain. A few things may help explain this. First, Bahrain is the home of the Fifth Fleet—the island hosts a huge US naval base. Washington was not going to countenance the "loss" of Bahrain to a Shia government (representing the majority of the people) that might be friendly with Iran. The foreign policy establishment had already "lost" Iraq to the Shia after the invasion of that country did not go as planned. Washington's partnership with Saudi Arabia, forged back in the days when both Wahhabism and Zionism were cultivated as the best ways to counter the appeal of secular nationalism and Arab Socialism, was too important to let human rights and democracy get in the way.[64] There may have been a deal struck—Washington will keep quiet on Bahrain if the Arab league backs the invasion of Libya.[65] These were the things that Ebrahim Sharif was left to ponder as he was tortured, over and over.

It didn't make sense, what they were doing. They already knew everything. His speech was on the internet. Why were they torturing him? They would ask him, "Did you say this or not?" and he would say, "Yes! You have the video!" He had been in the respectable opposition for decades. He didn't have any secrets. But the assaults continued. And the punishment was not only physical. Every morning the captives would wake up with a portrait of Saudi king Abdullah facing them, and they would be tortured if they didn't kiss it.

5

Around the World

THE INSPIRATIONAL EXAMPLE OF THE so-called Arab Spring, and especially the fantastically well-illuminated scenes of the prefigurative carnival in Cairo, was only the beginning of a year of global movements that sought to transform society.

In the United States, the world's most powerful nation and the place where many people learned the meaning of "protest" back in the era of television, demonstrators took aim at Wall Street. The magazine *Adbusters* called for a Tahrir Square moment in the US, and soon thousands of people would horizontally encamp outside the center of the global financial system. This would have a profound impact on political culture in the country, largely through its interaction with the media. Todd Gitlin, the early president of SDS and prescient critic of corporate journalism, was there, and David Graeber became one of its most recognizable public intellectuals.

But before that, millions of people took to the streets (or took over the streets) in Southern Europe. The still-unfolding global financial crisis hit these countries especially hard, due to the structure of North Atlantic capitalism and the configuration of the European Union. For regular people this took the form of austerity and rising unemployment, and young people were shut out of the economy, with Greek and Spanish people taking the worst blows of all. Protests had already erupted in Athens a year earlier, and three people lost their lives. But on May 15, the newly formed group ¡Democracia Real Ya! or "Real Democracy Now!" occupied the Plaza del Sol in Madrid. This was the arrival of the "Tahrir model" in the West, and the press called them the *indignados*—those furious at banks, politicians, and the real-life devastation they had wrought. Over a hundred protest camps sprung up across the country, and Spanish protesters called on more of their Greek brothers and sisters to join the struggle.[1]

And they did. A teenager set up a Facebook page to organize a protest at Syntagma Square in downtown Athens, which remained occupied until the summer. Invoking the spirit of Athenian democracy, assemblies sprang up around the country. These groups, especially those affiliated with ¡Democracia Real Ya!, were committed to horizontalism and radical participatory democracy. Throughout Spain, protesters set up "people's assemblies" that sought to come to decisions through full consensus. Anybody was free to join.[2]

The contention was not limited to the permanent settlements. During these months, it's possible that up to three million Greeks, a third of the population, and six million Spaniards out of around forty-five million total participated in a wider set of marches and demonstrations. A vast majority of people in both countries said they agreed with the wider goals of the protest movements. In Spain and Greece, demonstrations pushed the governments to the brink of collapse. But it did not come to that.[3]

This was the West, where life is different from Yemen or Egypt. European nations have a different place in the global system, and institutions in these countries were stable enough that a systemic rupture did not occur. The armed forces in NATO countries were certainly not going to abandon the state (however weakened) as the legitimate democratic authority in favor of an amorphous, left-leaning movement, and NATO certainly wasn't going to bomb itself. Life was very difficult for young people in Southern Europe after 2008, but few protesters were ready to take up arms, fight, and die for the rejection of EU-style capitalism. The continent's repressive forces—and they certainly exist—had the confidence to allow legal protests to flourish, and the confidence that they could do their job and violently repress the lawbreakers without inviting condemnation from the international community. Unless society actually ground to a halt, and the reproduction of the economic system became impossible, the institutions could survive. And they did.[4]

The demonstrations got big, very big, but they remained demonstrations. After the summer, the assemblies shrank, and then they shrank further. Only unemployed people or students could spend all their time there (which dictated, to some extent, the demographics of the long-term occupations), and even they found their energy sapped eventually.

Within this wave of First World occupiers, there was a fundamental split over the meaning of the protest camps. For anarchists, they were self-governed communities operating autonomously from society, a seed that could grow into a world of its own; for others, they were a temporary rallying point, a stage from which to blast out their claims.[5] At Occupy Wall Street (OWS), which began that fall, many aspects of the former didn't really work out, while the latter did.

Occupy Wall Street (OWS) insisted that all decisions be reached through consensus. At its most extreme, this led to outcomes in which a tiny number of people could block the will of the majority. One day, civil rights pioneer John Lewis arrived, signaling he supported the movement. A congressman in the United States government, this man had marched with Martin Luther King Jr. and helped forge the modern repertoire of contention with his own body back in the 1960s. Most people in the ad hoc assembly wanted to let him speak. Two did not. "No particular human being is inherently more valuable than any other," one of them—a white graduate student—said. Lewis was not allowed to speak.[6] And then in New York, there were fights over who controlled the all-important social media accounts. The same thing had happened in Spain. Facebook and Twitter were the sites where the demonstrations were defining what they were meant to demonstrate.[7]

Occupy Wall Street was tiny compared to other uprisings in the decade.[8] It most definitely was not about to force the end of the First Republic of the United States; life barely changed for people who went to work every day in downtown Manhattan. But it took place just a short walk from the most powerful media institutions in world history, and (after some initial hesitation on the part of papers like the *New York Times*) they were able to get their message out.[9] A generation that had very rarely heard any left-wing positions articulated suddenly saw them embodied in the real world, and some participants went on to influential media careers. OWS engendered a real discursive shift in the country, but the physical occupation ended with a whimper.

I WATCHED ALL OF THIS from Brazil. I had Facebook and (still, I think) Myspace, but those were for keeping tabs on friends from university or high school. For news, I would open my web browser and read the *Financial Times*, Brazil's *Folha de S.Paulo*, or my new employer (and, coincidentally, my hometown publication), the *Los Angeles Times*. Our audience was principally the one million print subscribers in California, but the internet was rapidly changing the way we worked.

During Dilma's first year in office, we had no earth-shaking uprising in Brazil. But near my home in downtown São Paulo, on the same road as the old offices of Indymedia Brasil, I could feel the light tremors that connected the streets below me to the spirit of the age. The Movimento Passe Livre protests had taken place earlier that year, though they did nothing to stop the rise in bus fare. In June there was the Parada Gay, which entirely overwhelmed my block. Globally speaking, São Paulo is a quite tolerant place, and the Gay Parade was always large. But this year, four million people rushed the street. And there was the Marcha da Maconha, or the Marijuana March, which brought together a very diverse group. Mayara was there, of course. Though it wasn't the kind of raucous, directly confrontational event that her MPL organized, there were a lot of people from the autonomous movement on the streets, and the day ended in clashes with cops. Brazil's very small but very well-organized right-libertarian movement also put people into the streets that day—but they were not the ones who faced off with the police.

Then in October, Ocupa Sampa—that is, "Occupy São Paulo"—popped up beneath a bridge near City Hall. It was directly inspired by Occupy Wall Street (which was inspired by Tahrir Square, which was inspired by the uprising in Tunisia), and it was more visible than it was well-attended. I walked by this part of town all the time, and the tents were always present even if they were fairly empty. In this part of the world—and that part of the city especially—street life is dominated by crime and violence that far exceed anything in New York or Cairo. This scared away some potential sympathizers.[10]

The organizers called themselves *indignados* and said that the movement was about direct democracy, as well as the environment. To explain the encampment, the media turned to "Anonymous," the decentralized "hacktivist" collective famous for subversive action and for wearing the mask from *V for Vendetta*, a revolutionary British graphic novel made into a 2005 film in the United States.[11] Under the bridge downtown, however, things looked desolate. The movement did not "occupy" São Paulo at all; something like the opposite happened. Ocupa Sampa was swallowed up by the darkness of the city center. It was on the other end of the continent, way over on the coast of the Pacific Ocean, that South America was most visibly rocked by the spirit of 2011.

The leaders of Chile's student protests disagree on the extent to which the events of that winter were inspired by the so-called Arab Spring. They had originally planned their action for 2010, but it was delayed when an earthquake devastated the country that year.[12] And crucially, these leaders were from organized, long-standing, and intentional student associations. Their contention was planned well in advance; they were not a "spontaneous" reaction to an episode of police abuse or war or revolution in the region. But they were certainly carried out by student leaders who had been paying attention to the events of 2011, and they were reinterpreted and reproduced by a global media that had gotten used to covering large explosions of progressive, youthful energy.

THE PINOCHET DICTATORSHIP, WHICH TOOK shape after the US-backed coup that ended the presidency and life of socialist president Salvador Allende, made life very difficult for students whose parents were not members of the upper crust. True to the spirit of primordial neoliberalism, Pinochet privatized and financialized everything he could, which meant that a lot of families went broke, or took on serious debt, trying to make it through the educational system. This affected even the comfortable middle classes.

The terror unleashed by the *junta* was effective; there was comparatively little protest in Chile under the dictatorship. One small exception came in 1983–1985 when a global economic crisis (the same that affected North Africa so severely) led to a wave of protests. After the vote that ousted Pinochet in 1990, the center-left Concertación, or Coalition of Parties for Democracy, discouraged rowdy activism, afraid that too much trouble could lead to another military coup. So Chile became famous for a "conspicuous absence of contentious politics" in the years when the rest of Latin America was rocked by rolling waves of anti-neoliberal protests.[13] This changed in 2006 with the Penguin Revolution.

A new student association, "more democratic, and horizontal" than its predecessors, but still formally structured, submitted a set of proposals to the government that would increase public funding and reduce inequality in education. After this was ignored, the students launched a set of confrontational street protests, and then got hundreds of thousands to take part in a sit-in in Santiago. Chile is a neat and tidy country, visibly influenced by the legacy of the English capital that flowed into the country after it won independence from Spain. High school students dress very formally, in black-and-white uniforms that have earned them the nickname of *pingüinos*. During the demonstrations, public support for the little penguins reached as high as 87 percent, and socialist president Michelle Bachelet formed an advisory commission, which came up with a package of reforms that she took to Congress. But lawmakers would not pass them. Many students learned a lesson that year—you have to negotiate while the movement is still alive. If the energy has already dissipated, elites have no reason to do anything they don't want to do.[14]

Five years later in 2011, the same generation launched an altogether more spectacular set of demonstrations. A conservative was now in power, the billionaire businessman Sebastián Piñera, which meant that progressives didn't have to worry if a bit of contention might be bad for the executive. The protests were organized by elected student leaders at the country's most important universities, and they were aimed at the for-profit, neoliberal education model. They had formal associations, they had resources (often money raised from their families or professors), and they had the attention of a sympathetic media. The country's Mapuche indigenous people also began to embark on a set of active protests in defense of their rights in the same years, but social scientists find that they received far less attention than student actions that took place in the capital. The student leaders disavowed the destruction of property, caused by some protesters in hoods, and instead generated the kinds of images that for-profit media love to reproduce. They employed carnivalesque or even affective tactics, staging parades in their underwear, or putting on "kiss-ins."[15]

Media in the country, and around the world, would often highlight that the movement was not affiliated with any party. But there were big exceptions. It was true that Giorgio Jackson, a student leader at the Pontifical Catholic University of Chile, and Gabriel Boric, a rising star at the University of Chile, were not in any of the Old Left parties. Boric was an indie rock kid with messy hair from the freezing-cold far-south of the country who helped build an "Autonomist Left" non-party group in college. But Camila Vallejo, the president of the student union at the University of Chile, was a member of

Chile's communist party, the Partido Comunista de Chile (PCCh). Vallejo was a talented communicator who had been shaped by the Party's internal education system. The PCCh had been around since 1912, having survived two right-wing dictatorships. It was tightly structured, and its young members get an education in both Marxism-Leninism and practical activism. Camila Vallejo got special attention from international media for other reasons. The *New York Times* gave her a big spread, with the slightly confusing headline "The World's Most Glamorous Revolutionary." Camila certainly dresses well, but she looked a lot more like a leftist college student than anyone who spent a lot of money on clothes. But the article got to its real point with a quote at the end of the first paragraph: "She's hot."[16] The students managed to win very wide support from the broader population. But when it came to translating their leverage into policy outcomes, they kept hitting the same wall, said Giorgio Jackson.[17] It was the constitution put into place under Pinochet and still in effect. The Chilean redemocratization movement had never overcome that major hurdle. By contrast, Brazil adopted a new, relatively progressive constitution in 1988 after the fall of its dictatorship, offering many rights to the population including free medical care and free public universities (though real-life inequality has often gotten in the way of its more ambitious promises).

The 2011 student movement forced Piñera to replace the education minister three different times. He eventually agreed to meet some of their demands. Most importantly, he lowered the interest rates on student loans. But the big structural questions were off the table. There was a split within the movement on how to deal with this—on whether the point was to extract concessions by playing politics (largely favored by party members) or whether the correct move was to expand street actions and radicalize.

Back in Brazil, members of the Movimento Passe Livre paid close attention to their comrades in Chile, and they naturally sympathized with the latter group. They favored the more "autonomous" forces that gained influence as the year wore on. Several members of the MPL went to meet with protesters in Santiago and came back to São Paulo with a manual for training students in the art of contention. But Piñera and the rest of the Chilean state stood stubbornly in the way of radical change. As the demonstrations dragged well into 2012, it became clear that despite the largest protests since the fall of the dictatorship, no major victories were imminent.

6

A Social Network

IN JULY 2012, I GOT an email from another journalist in São Paulo. "We should go have dinner with a couple big shot reporters from New York," he wrote. "They're here looking to meet people." I didn't know who they were, but it was easy to read up on them. David Carr was a media correspondent for the *New York Times* who commanded a large following online. Andy Carvin was a journalist at NPR who had just written a book called *Distant Witness* about his experience using Twitter to report on—and to some extent participate in—the events of the so-called Arab Spring.

A few months prior, I had started working in the newsroom of *Folha de S.Paulo*, Brazil's prominent mainstream newspaper, which was organizing their talk. I was now the Brazil correspondent for the *LA Times*, but that was no longer the kind of gig that was going to get you an office.* I worked out a deal with *Folha* that I would maintain an English-language blog on their website, called *From Brazil*, primarily so I could have a place to work that wasn't my little bedroom.[1]

---

* Despite the historical importance of the *LA Times* Brazil correspondent position—my predecessor had played a key role before the US-backed 1964 coup—the newspaper was just barely able to keep it alive for me. To fund my work, they partially relied upon a grant from the Ford Foundation—an organization that also had a long relationship to authoritarian regimes in Latin America.

At dinner, Carr and I got along very well, and I soon felt that he had taken me under his wing. He asked if I had Twitter. He wanted to tag me in a post. No, I said. Well, I had created an account, but never put my name on it. Frankly that seemed like a strange existence—in which your popularity was quantified in real time in front of the entire world. That was very different from the social networks I had been on since 2002: Friendster, then Myspace, and Facebook, where you "connected" with your friends, rather than seeking *followers*. Until that point, social media had played precisely zero role in my professional life. I only dealt with editors, trying my best to show I could cover politics in Brazil (which was never going to be a huge crowd-pleaser) well enough to stay in the game. But it made sense that a boost from Carr might be a good place to start. I created a public Twitter profile. He was the expert, after all.

Their talk for *Folha* was to be about the power of social media. This made sense for a couple reasons. First, Brazilian corporate media is in almost universal agreement with US media on big geopolitical issues. In countries like Argentina or Mexico, various media platforms view the US as a meddling imperialist power, or at least a very unreliable ally. At *Folha*, journalists liked to tell foreigners that they were the "*New York Times* of Brazil." It made perfect sense that *Folha* would want to hear from Carr and Carvin.

And second, social media was a very important emerging issue—for Western media, the US government, and a wide range of civil society groups around the world. Among these, there was near-universal agreement that technology in general, and social networks like Facebook and Twitter specifically, were going to make the world a better place. More free and more democratic.

Of course they would—technological advances had driven human progress since the time of the Enlightenment. Indeed, the leaps and bounds in technical capacity helped give rise to our idea of "progress" in the first place.

It was only a tiny minority of people, mostly drowned out by cheerleaders for these companies or ignored by well-funded government and nongovernment organizations, who pointed out that we were not dealing with *pure* technology; that these were a set of tools, and a set of powerful for-profit firms, that had taken shape in very particular historical circumstances.

The internet as we now know it today was created by the United States Armed Forces during the Cold War. The agencies that built its core structures were responsible for keeping groups like Students for a Democratic

Society under surveillance and assisting counterinsurgency efforts in places like Vietnam. Domestically, the computers gave rise to a network allowing communications between researchers in the private and public sectors. Perhaps even more important than its roots in the US military-industrial complex, however, was the time and place that regular people began to move parts of their lives online.

The Ronald Reagan, George H. W. Bush, and Bill Clinton administrations privatized the machine world into corporate America. Nothing was more natural for the politicians of this era—public ownership was seen as barbaric, if not outright un-American.[2] So for-profit firms would control the computers and the built environment of the online experience. One could very easily imagine a different internet if it had been built by a different country—France? Vietnam? Iraq?—or even at a different moment in US history.[3]

But in the first two decades of the twenty-first century, the vast majority of the digital experience took place in spaces engineered and controlled by US corporations. As more and more of the world gained access to the network of machines—starting, of course, with the wealthy and especially young segments of the world population—North American users became a minority, but the entire ecosystem remained profoundly shaped by these firms.[4]

The companies often arose in Silicon Valley, a region of California where government contracts and good universities allowed for physical infrastructure to flourish in suburbs in the San Francisco Bay Area. Culturally, this new corner of US capitalism was shaped by free-market libertarian ideals, as well as a version of new-age individualist utopianism that had some roots in the New Left. According to one prominent strain of thought, decentralization and the destruction of all hierarchies that accompanied the advance of network technology would distribute power, and it would mean democratization. Some took this very literally—at the Synergia Ranch commune, run on a cybernetic notion called "ecotechnics," both organization and collective action were strictly forbidden. In practice, dark versions of abusive authority quickly emerged.[5]

The founders of the Silicon Valley companies, enthusiastic publications like *Wired*, and the US government itself all routinely professed—and seemed to believe—they were "changing the world." For the better, of course. But they also needed to make money. And for many of them, the solution to that problem was advertising. I, myself, remember being delighted when I could begin using Gmail, the robust email service from Google. You had to get an invitation back in 2004. I never really thought to ask what paid for it. The answer came out eventually, which is that Google searched all of your communications in order to understand you better, so that other companies could sell you more things.

Facebook, a company founded by an undergraduate at Harvard, also began as a service restricted to a small elite. The "social network" expanded to Columbia and Stanford, and then to other prestigious colleges, then to wider sections of the population, until everyone was invited. Its founder, Mark Zuckerberg, certainly didn't invent the social network—many others came first. But in terms of an advertising-based, moneymaking operation, men like Zuckerberg took a huge leap forward from the television model that Fernando Haddad had described at the beginning of the millennium. Social media barons didn't have to make the shows. Instead of producing content to attract eyeballs, they simply had the users do that themselves. Their communications with their loved ones, the photographs of their lives, their public discussions about culture and politics—all of that would be content now that could be used to help other corporations sell things. Regardless of original intentions, the logic of this dynamic drove a number of innovations designed to keep the user glued to the website as long as possible. I distinctly remember the day that Facebook added the "like" button to its user experience. My network (it must be admitted, friends from a good California university, many of whom ended up working in "technology" firms after the 2008 crash dashed their other hopes) reacted with shock and disgust. Allowing everyone to affirm (but not critique) and quantify each other with a click seemed like a cheap engagement trick—which it was, and it worked.[6] But even as they emerged as wildly profitable entities in the business world, these technology companies retained the sheen of anti-systemic, vaguely countercultural quests to save the world. For some of these firms, that reputation was not just marketing.

TWITTER HAD ROOTS IN THE alter-globalization movement. The anarchist Evan Henshaw-Plath, one of the engineers who created the "micro-blogging" social network, had been a software developer for Indymedia. Back in the late 1990s, he helped build a "status update" newswire on the top of Indymedia's web page in order to keep readers abreast of what was going on—mostly where the cops were and what they were doing—during protests. Then they developed a way to send these out en masse via text message. This eventually grew into Twitter, launched in 2006. With major investment flowing into the company, and the arrival of founder Jack Dorsey (who was certainly into a kind of radical politics, but more business-driven, Henshaw-Plath remembers), the company began to look for ways to make money.[7] Anyone could send the little "tweets" and choose whom to "follow." Quickly the service moved onto the internet exclusively and became something very similar to Facebook, except that you had a much smaller profile and could only post short dispatches.

During the George W. Bush administration, the US State Department began training movements in Asia, Latin America, and the Middle East in the use of digital tools.[8] It became state policy to push for global democratization using technology and social media. In 2009, thousands of Iranians took to the streets to protest what they believed to be a fraudulent election. Some of them were using Twitter, and this seemed to confirm that social media could push the world toward the end of history. Andrew Sullivan, for *The Atlantic*, published a piece titled "The Revolution Will Be Twittered." In the *New York Times*, Nicholas Kristof claimed that "in the quintessential 21st-century conflict...on the one side are government thugs firing bullets... on the other side are young protesters firing 'tweets.'"[9] It did not change the mainstream narrative much when this round of contention in Iran achieved very little, and the Iranian government actually used social media to identify and promptly arrest many of the dissidents. Mark Pfeifle, a former deputy national security adviser in the George W. Bush administration, tried to give the Nobel Peace Prize to Twitter.[10]

Gordon Brown, the prime minister of the United Kingdom, went even further. Referring to the 1994 genocide in central Africa, he said, "You cannot have Rwanda again because information would come out far more quickly about what is actually going on, and the public opinion would grow to the point where action would need to be taken."[11]

In 2010, Secretary of State Hillary Clinton, under President Barack Obama, likened the promotion of internet freedom to support for dissidents in the USSR during the Cold War: "As networks spread to nations around the globe, virtual walls are cropping up in place of visible walls." In the *International Herald Tribune*, Roger Cohen wrote that while "Tear down this wall!" was a twentieth-century slogan, the same demand for the twenty-first was

"Tear down this firewall!" Eli Lake, writing in the *New Republic*, made the same comparison.

Belarusian theorist Evgeny Morozov—who knew very well that the end of communism did not go the way most people in Washington, DC, and California thought it had (Aleksandr Lukashenko has been entrenched in power in Belarus since 1994)—tried to push back against this wave of uncritical boosterism for California businesses. These people had their Cold War history very wrong, he said. Authoritarian governments are not passive simpletons waiting to be overthrown, and they could learn to use the internet themselves, he pointed out. Whether rich Westerners realized it or not, situations even worse than the governance of a stable authoritarian state were possible, including civil war or failed states. But if he was given any attention within what became a tsunami of praise for the technology sector, it was so he could be attacked with reckless abandon. In the mainstream press, the internet guys were almost always the good guys.[12]

Confidence in this perception was so deeply internalized that these capitalists spoke of "disruption" in society without feeling the need to demonstrate that aggressively shaking things up would lead to improvements. This was not far off the logic of "beneath the stones, the beach," or Tiririca's "it can't get any worse." Smash things up, and something better will emerge from the wreckage. This assumption seemed widespread. In the 2008 election campaign, a young senator named Barack Obama had plastered his face over the unaccompanied word "CHANGE," and few people stopped to recognize that everything bad that happens is change, too.

The events of the so-called Arab Spring only reaffirmed the faith of the liberal techno-optimists. It was undeniable that Facebook had played some role in the events of January 2011, and many of those who became unofficial spokespeople for "the Square" also became such on Twitter. Over the following ten years, media companies, brands, and all kinds of corporations would spend ungodly sums of money trying to figure out which kinds of things generate engagement on corporate social media. But for whatever reason, some people—whether it was because they were articulate, loud, interesting, or shocking—rose to prominence on these networks (often to the chagrin of others who had more influence on the ground or had gained a following in the older world of long-form blogs).

"The Che Guevara of the 21st Century is the network," wrote Alec Ross, the officer in charge of digital policy in Hillary Clinton's State Department, in 2011 in *NATO Review*. In the Brazilian press, the coverage was not so different: "In North Africa, a new form of popular mobilization is trading in weapons for cellular phones," declared a report broadcast that year by the Globo network. "The Facebook Revolution allows individuals to construct the very facts that they are narrating. Nothing will stop it."[13]

But for the real people this term, the Square, usually named—the progressive, secular revolutionaries in North Africa who had inspired so many others around the world—things were far from perfect, even in the wake of the most successful uprisings. Tunisia was locked in torturous negotiations to shape its future. And in Egypt, though some demonstrators had chanted that "the people and the army are one hand," faith in the Supreme Council of the Armed Forces (SCAF) had dissipated after Mubarak's departure. SCAF put forward a set of constitutional amendments, but many revolutionaries opposed quick and easy changes to Mubarak's constitution, saying that they were "rushing the process of transition to benefit conservative political forces that are already well organized, such as the Muslim Brotherhood."[14]

Then in October, a crowd of people from Egypt's Coptic Christian minority gathered in front of the Maspero television building in downtown Cairo to protest the destruction of a church in Upper Egypt. SCAF forces crushed the demonstrators, killing at least twenty-four people. Government tanks rolled over their bodies, while state media blamed the protesters for inciting violence. This was the exact same type of brutality that had inspired the uprising in the first place. But the Egyptian revolutionaries only really had one arrow in their quiver: they could try to take Tahrir Square again. All types of protests took place in 2011 and 2012, but unless they forced the country to a halt, again, they remained demonstrations. Unless they could oust SCAF and replace it with a new revolutionary government, they would have to rely on negotiations and conversations until the planned elections. But the Square was splintered into a number of small groups, which made them easy to ignore. If SCAF wanted to dialogue with civil society, the Muslim Brotherhood stood out as a single coherent organization with a reliable base of support.

New elections did go ahead in May 2012. The Muslim Brotherhood would be represented by Mohamed Morsi, who was rigid and conservative by the previous standards of the Islamist group. Candidate Ahmed Shafik represented a continuation of the Mubarak approach to governing. Hamdeen Sabahi, a Nasserist social democrat and one of the founders of the Kefaya coalition back in 2004, promised a fairer economy and full democratization. In interviews and private conversations, he sometimes pointed to a development path forged far outside the Arab world—he was inspired by Brazilian president Lula, who had governed democratically and improved the lives of the poor without breaking with the global system.[15]

Gehad chose to vote for Hamdeen Sabahi—she thought he was the candidate who most stood for "bread, freedom, and social justice," that original revolutionary slogan. Some other young secular revolutionaries, like Gehad's future husband, Ahmed, chose to back Abdel Fotouh, a former member of the Muslim Brotherhood seen as progressive compared to most Islamists. That seemed like a good tactical choice, Ahmed figured, given that Fotouh could both represent the revolution and appeal to the country's large religious bloc. Ahmed would have been very happy to see Hamdeen Sabahi win too.

Other revolutionaries called for a boycott of the vote. For some, the point was never to "represent" the people with new repressive structures at all. Hossam "3arabawy" el-Hamalawy, the revolutionary socialist, believed in seizing state power, but he thought that the uprising was still underway, and the priority was to remove SCAF, not legitimize their rule by taking part in their elections. They had been successful in organizing strikes since the fall of Mubarak, and it was obvious to him that the revolution still controlled the streets. The blogger Mahmoud "Sandmonkey" Salem came out in support of spoiling ballots. He said that the real point was to say "fuck you to the Supreme Council of the Muslim Brotherhood." He rejected the interim military government that was clearly in dialogue with the Islamists, and he did not trust SCAF to put on fair elections.

But quite a lot of people voted, and the election seemed legitimate. In the first round Morsi got 25 percent, Shafik received 24 percent, and Sabahi and Fotouh took 21 and 17 percent, respectively. The secular revolutionaries were horrified. The election would come down to a runoff between the Muslim Brotherhood and the old regime. If they had been able to organize a united front, the combined votes for Sabahi and Fotouh would have easily surpassed the numbers earned by Mubarak's man. In the second round, Morsi won. After eighty-four years, the Muslim Brotherhood would be in charge of running the country. This was good news for Turkey, while Saudi Arabia, despite its religious extremism, had long viewed the Brotherhood as its rival. To some extent, Morsi's arrival seemed to be a victory for Qatar, the small Gulf monarchy that had played an outsize role in regional politics since founding Al Jazeera, and whose leaders were more friendly with the Muslim Brotherhood than the monarchy in Riyadh. It was not clear what it would mean for Egyptians. But still, Gehad thought, at least the country now had a democracy, and after Morsi took over, the forces of civil society would be able to protest, or regroup, to win the next election.

Meanwhile in Syria, the uprising had turned into a fully fledged war. The Obama administration took the same position as its Saudi ally and began providing secret support to the Free Syrian Army in 2012. Early in that conflict, international support for the Syrian opposition was driven by a very prominent online personality. A young and beautiful woman, posting as "Gay Girl in Damascus," regaled Western followers with tales of resistance to the brutal Assad regime. They were shocked when she was abducted by the Syrian government. Supporters launched a campaign to find her and save her life. Journalists (including Andy Carvin at NPR) began to look into her story. It turned out that she was a fiction made up by a bored graduate student from the United States.[16]

In Yemen, the eruption of mass protests starting in 2011 had forced Ali Abdullah Saleh to step down after thirty-three years in power. But Saudi Arabia, the powerful country to the north of the border, brokered a deal that allowed his deputy, Abdrabbuh Mansour Hadi, to take over. In early 2012 he ran unopposed for president, and protests started again as rebels in the north and south of the country boycotted the vote.[17]

Tunisia, the country that had started it all, struggled through the difficult process of drafting a new constitution. Preexisting parties—the Islamists and the leftists and the liberals—tried to hammer out a document that would bring the country into the democratic world, reflect the interests of the people, and deliver on the spirit of January 2011. But Maya Jribi, the secretary general of the Parti Démocrate Progressiste (PDP), noted that the uprising had not provided the country with a concrete political direction. They were using the institutions that were there before, rather than building truly new ones. There was no major change to economic conditions in the country.

"What happened," she said, "is more than an uprising, but less than a revolution."[18]

7

Cowboys and Indians

I LIVED A BLESSED LIFE as a correspondent in Brazil. The task I was given, to attempt to understand the country, was endlessly fascinating. As a journalist, your only real value is that you can get very smart, or very interesting, or very important people to speak with you because they want to be in the paper, or because it is their job. This was an immensely enjoyable endeavor during a great time to be alive in São Paulo. And considering I had a (relatively) full-time job, paid in US dollars, I lived a much more comfortable life than the vast majority of Brazilians. There is no way you can do this job properly without correctly identifying your own objective relationship to the subject matter, and the vast majority of citizens of the United States of America are in the top 10 percent of earners in the global population.[1] University-educated professionals in exclusive fields like media breathe even more rarefied air. In Brazil, just as in the United States, having light skin makes your life a lot easier. In the thirteen years since I moved to Brazil, not a single cop has ever said a word to me on the street. Their job is the repression of a different population.

Every day, I walked from my apartment downtown in the Praça da República to the offices of *Folha de S.Paulo*, where I had my desk space. I would pass through parts of Cracolândia, or "Crack Land," the sprawling community of street residents and drug users in the city. But this is not a poor country; it's an unequal country. No matter how plush my life was in São Paulo, I was still often shocked to hear about how some colleagues in the Brazilian media lived: single people in their twenties who had a maid come to clean their apartments three or more times a week; highly educated, cosmopolitan intellectuals who hadn't the slightest clue how to do the dishes. The journalists at *Folha* were not highly paid, but almost all of them came from families of European descent and attended elite, private educational institutions. Less than half of Brazilians identify as white. Looking around the newsroom in 2012 (several times), I never saw a single Black reporter.

As it happens, Brazil was not cheap at all when I arrived. In some ways, it was more expensive than London, where I lived until 2010. Some of the hype surrounding Brazil was the result of a coincidental global imbalance that emerged in the wake of the 2008 financial crisis. As part of the response to an inflation crisis in the 1980s (caused by the debt crisis initiated by the US Federal Reserve's interest rate increase under Chairman Paul Volcker), the government had saddled Brazilians with some of the highest real interest rates in the world. This worked to stabilize the currency, but it also meant that even if regular people could buy their first washing machine under Lula, they paid exorbitant (and hidden) fees to finance them.

After the 2008 financial crisis, the United States government failed to construct a fiscal response (for example, boosting the economy by spending money on things like infrastructure and public services) and instead relied on the Federal Reserve to slash its rates to historic lows. This unleashed a wave of capital into the world (and especially into the tech sector) seeking returns. When it came to Brazil, the "carry trade" strategy—simply take out money with low interest rates and put it in a place with high ones—served to inflate the value of the *real*. This made it a bit cheaper for normal people to buy foreign goods or travel abroad for the first time; it also meant the deindustrialization of the economy, and it allowed Brazil to become the world's sixth-largest economy.[2]

But on the ground, and in the data, it was undeniable that something real was happening. Many people you met, rich or poor, were doing things they had never done before. Poor people got full-time jobs with benefits, or took their first flight. Middle-class kids got to vacation in Paris or Tokyo or Mexico City. Throughout 2012, Dilma's approval rating hovered around 65 percent. Conservative forces were muted. Analysts called this phenomenon the *direita envergonhada*, or "embarrassed right," a legacy of the fact that almost everyone agreed that during the military regime, the left had fought for democracy, and the right had defended dictatorship. A colleague at *The Economist* (who grew up in Poland, where they had a different historical memory of the left) wrote a bemused column during Rousseff's first term, noting that out of thirty-two registered parties, twenty-six had names that suggested progressive values. The Brazilian political terrain comprised "fifty shades of pink," someone told the magazine.[3]

Much of my work as a reporter was focused on the ways in which the social revolution was still incomplete. I went out and spoke to teachers worried about abysmal educational conditions for poor children—these had improved under Education Minister Haddad, but there was a very long way to go. There was the obvious, and persistent, problem of crime that had made Rio's *favelas* infamous. I attended parties organized by drug traffickers as research—yes, journalism—in municipal territory controlled by organizations such as Comando Vermelho (Red Command) or Amigos dos Amigos (Friends of Friends), where I spoke with some of their leaders. Cops were not allowed anywhere inside their turf. Teenagers wearing nothing but sandals, surfing boardshorts, and huge assault rifles handled their security.

I especially loved getting out of the cities; I was lucky enough to report from every one of the twenty-six states, often crossing the whole country by bus.

The Amazon basin covers 2.5 million square miles, roughly equivalent to the area covered by the European Union and India combined. Brazil governs the lion's share of the rainforest, which is home to much of the planet's biodiversity and so crucial for the globe's oxygen production. Once you get out there, you realize that much of this biodiversity is bacteria, viruses, or animals that are trying to kill you, but that doesn't make them less beautiful, or less important. I spent a lot of time in the jungle, attempting to explain why so much of it was going away. The battle over land has been at the center of Brazilian politics since the country's birth, and it is relevant to the future of humanity. I became close to a group of scientists who operate as an environmental protection force for the federal government. My main contact in this world was a federal agent in Brazil's Institute of Environment and Renewable Natural Resources (IBAMA) named Olavo Perin Galvão, a kind man who patiently explained to me the diversity of the forestry and the nature of the work done by his team. Armed and highly trained, they scanned the vast region for potential deforestation sites using satellite data to find suspicious holes in the forest followed by flyovers in small planes. Finally, when there was a clear target, they would touch down in a helicopter to investigate. Often, they would find telltale equipment or land converted into pasture for cows. Sometimes there were people on the sites, shooting at the helicopter as it got closer to the ground. I touched down with them many times. They would fan out, searching for clues, and immediately determine what kind of operation was underway. Olavo would examine the soil and track down any supplies or equipment. Many times, as the day ended, I would stand back and watch as they torched everything they found.[4]

The IBAMA had the authority to fine ranchers with the backing of the federal government. But they also ran up against the other concrete power structures in Brazil's political economy. The president governing from Brazil's capital, Brasília, does not control every aspect of life on the ground any more than politicians in Washington, DC, could micromanage frontier law in the Wild West. If you worked the courts right or put operations in the name of some low-level criminal, the benefit of the deforestation could outweigh any fines incurred. That is, given the real set of regulations and punishments within the Amazon, it is economically rational to cut it down. Indeed, the local political structures were often highly sympathetic to the deforestation economy, if not entirely dependent upon it. Olavo told me, one day in the truck as we rolled through the wasteland, how many serious threats they received.

Many people understand that the forest is shrinking. Few realize what takes its place. The communities that exist in between the thick, dark green foliage, are primarily cowboy outposts, in every sense that the word connotes. Men wear big belt buckles, cowboy boots, and big cowboy hats. They amble into watering holes to get drunk and listen to country music without bothering to hide the pistols on their hips. Cattle, which transform the soil and help destroy the jungle, are their source of income. At one bar, I stood out like a sore urban thumb and told the locals unconvincingly (but accurately, technically) that I was going to write about country music and culture. Residents look on city folk that come out there as empty-headed do-gooders trying to destroy their livelihoods. This scene attracts outlaws who can cross state lines and start a new life to evade the police. After that night in the cantina, I went to watch a local motocross show on a deforested piece of dirt nearby with a young woman I met.

"We have to leave," she said, as soon as we arrived. Her ex-boyfriend was there. Oh, it's no big deal, I said, it's not like we are on a date. I'm just a clueless gringo journalist, we can tell him that. "Oh no, you don't understand," she said. "He moved out here because he is wanted for murder in several states." I skipped the race.

RELATIONS WITH THE UNITED STATES had improved under Dilma, after Washington was displeased with President Lula's attempt (together with Turkish president Tayyip Erdoğan) to organize an Iran nuclear deal in 2010. The US consistently pushed Brazil to adopt its oppositional stance toward the Hugo Chávez government in Venezuela. For her part, Dilma enthusiastically supported the BRICS and was committed to building networks of "South-South cooperation."[5] In 2010, when Brazil began development of its massive offshore oil reserves—accompanied by the largest stock offering in the history of the world—experts in the North Atlantic issued concerned warnings that the "developmentalist" provision to reinvest the profits in local industry would be unfair to international companies.[6]

At home, Dilma oversaw the launch of a Truth Commission that investigated the crimes committed by the military dictatorship. It was the reproduction of a successful model developed in places like Argentina, Chile, and South Africa. It had no teeth, but behind the scenes at the armed forces, the top brass did not like this one bit. The armed forces had been re-empowered starting in 2004, when the Brazilian military went to Haiti as part of the United Nations Stabilization Mission in Haiti (MINUSTAH) and reportedly committed egregious abuses against the local population, especially Haitian women. And if you listened carefully, you could hear wealthy Brazilians start to complain that the poor seemed to be doing a little too well.* But all of this felt like background noise—the quiet mutterings of a ruling class that was

---

* A recurring complaint, during Dilma's first term, was that domestic workers were becoming too expensive. The other side of this story, of course, was that working-class women could demand good wages and benefits for the first time. For my story, see the *Los Angeles Times*, "In Brazil, changing times usher in 'servant problem.'" A more blatant case of class hatred came when one Facebook user in Rio famously complained that poor Brazilians could now be seen aboard airplanes.

getting used to a new reality. Nothing served to reinforce the idea that this moderate social revolution was here to stay more than the new man in charge of São Paulo.

2013 Begins

Fernando Haddad took office as mayor on January 1, 2013. This was a surprise achievement for São Paulo progressives, both culturally and politically. The country's economic powerhouse had elected center-right candidates in the past two contests. But now, after a full decade of Workers' Party rule at the federal level, voters handed city hall to a socialist intellectual who had matured under one of Lula's large wings. He was also a man who played guitar onstage alongside US rap group Public Enemy, proposed an urban model with less cars and pollution, and promised to revitalize the historic city center.[7] As he set up the office of his secretary of culture, he established links with some of the young people organizing street festivals and protest events since 2011, including some of those who had ties to the alter-globalization movement. By the numbers, his victory was driven by votes in the city's poor *periferia*, but it also delighted a lot of people in the left-leaning world of university-educated artists, musicians, and writers—speaking frankly, for the social groups I had joined.

The short campaign had provided a little bit of drama. For a while, media personality Celso Russomanno dominated headlines. He was a man permanently in TV makeup—a gifted showman who had made his name giving tips to consumers and defending the rights of the customer. Whether this was celebrated or derided, it was a fact that the Lulista model of development meant incorporating the poor into full citizenship through participation in consumer society, and these were popular themes.[8] The country, like so many in the Global South, was living through a boom in shopping mall construction.[9] Even more newsworthy was the fact that Russomanno raised eyebrows by appealing directly to the country's growing evangelical Christian population. This group's power and influence were on the rise, but it had never been so clearly in the spotlight. I went to spend time in the churches, where two things became clear.

First, they provided a truly meaningful space for regular people. Protestant pastors engaged directly with working Brazilians (almost all of whom used to be Roman Catholic), and many reported turning their lives around after finding Jesus in these new churches. Second, pastors often presented donations to the churches not so much as good works done in service of the Lord, but as a kind of investment. If you did what the church asked, you were going to get rich; you were going to eventually get more money out of this whole scheme than you put in. That explained why so many founders of the megachurches were mega-rich, and why countries in Africa, like Angola and Madagascar, actually shut down their churches.[10]

AS SOON AS HE TOOK power, Haddad felt that he was fighting a rear-guard battle against the city's conservative elites and the media they owned. Fights over politics, playing out in media both social and traditional, often revolved around his flagship programs to expand bike lanes in the city and spend money treating drug addicts living on the streets downtown. Fights over control of the streets got particularly nasty, with motorists insisting that São Paulo was not Amsterdam or Berlin and that trying to push cycling culture was left-wing social engineering. A columnist at *Veja* went as far as to question why the *ciclovías* were painted red—was that propaganda meant to spread the color of socialism and the Workers' Party? Even more outlandish was the claim made later in the magazine—the kind of thing that would go viral online—that Haddad was the "Taliban of the bicycle; ISIS on two wheels."[11]

Influential sectors felt that all of this progressive stuff had gone too far. The new mayor became deeply frustrated with the media coverage; he felt he was always playing defense, facing off with the right.

In March 2013, I wrote an article about media culture in Brazil and focused on national politics. The story sought to situate and explicate a puzzling phenomenon: How was it that Dilma Rousseff now enjoyed approval ratings as high as the 70s, but not a single major publication, television station, or online outlet supported her administration? Coverage was universally critical. Almost all of the major media in the country had also supported the coup back in 1964, and I noted that it was the exact same outlets—and the same families controlling them—that dominated the landscape in 2013. I was working inside one of these, and I think that emphasizing this point may have caused a little bit of discomfort in the newsroom. My colleagues there stressed it was also important to recognize that their bosses weren't the only ones who had class interests—much of the best media in the country was aimed at the audience who drove subscription and advertising revenue. "Think of a lawyer in São Paulo," one editor said. And this class especially, like the economists they consulted, believed that Dilma's economic policies were dangerously wrongheaded.[12]

But in May 2013, it was neither municipal concerns nor macroeconomics that held my attention. A sadly familiar story—in the state of Mato Grosso do Sul, local ranchers had apparently hired *pistoleros*, local gunmen, to murder members of the Terena tribe. Of course, it was a fight over land. In disputed territories, indigenous people sometimes fight with bows and arrows, or clubs. The cowboys always use bullets. They may not have the federal government on their side, but they have enough to get the job done. In the Guarani-Kaiowá community, this dynamic had led indigenous people to slowly kill themselves. Over the previous three decades, members of this tribe had committed suicide at sixty times the national average. As June 2013 began, I was sitting in a hut with Alda Silva Kunha Tupa Rendyi, listening to her explain why they no longer wanted to live.

8

Minority Report

ISTIKLAL AVENUE RUNS THROUGH THE center of Istanbul, on the European side of the ancient city. There are no cars here, just endless street cafés and vendors selling ice cream in the summer or roasted chestnuts in the winter. You can pop down a tiny side street, perhaps built when this was still the capital of the Byzantine Empire, and have grilled lamb and fresh vegetables, or a bottle of Efes beer, brewed and bottled in Turkey. Just a few blocks east is the water of the Bosporus Strait, which you can jump on, via ferry, to the more conservative and religious Asian side of the city. Istiklal, on the other hand, has been the traditional heart of secular elite culture, the stomping ground of the urban bourgeoisie and its fun-loving children, many of whom fared well under the modernizing regime of Mustafa Kemal Atatürk. If you walk up to the end of Istiklal Avenue, you will find a big open space, Taksim Square, and then a humble patch of trees and grass, called Gezi Park. It is not a particularly special or beloved park, but it is in the middle of everything.

In the beginning of 2013, activists staged a set of interventions in defense of the environment, public space, and the secular lifestyle in general. There was nothing very surprising about this. This was a democracy, and the city was going through a number of transformations that were always going to be subject to discussion and contestation. That is how the game is supposed to work in the era of liberal globalization. For many years, Turkey had often been held up, especially by Westerners, as a model for the rest of the Muslim world. Under Recep Tayyip Erdoğan, first elected prime minister in 2002, the European Union began to seriously consider (or at least discuss) the possibility of admitting the country as a member. Erdoğan had incorporated its Muslim majority more fully into the body politic, while remaining ardently pro-Western and bringing the country in line with the rules of the global capitalist economy. The Turkish left, historically strong enough that the military felt the need to take power in a violent 1980 coup, denounced this as neoliberal capitulation and pointed to widening inequality. But Erdoğan had established a broad coalition of supporters, and his project—moderate Islamism, pro-business, and pro-Western, contesting elections—appeared hegemonic. In March 2013, his approval rating hovered around 60 percent, though it was only 46 percent in Istanbul.[1]

Protests began when intellectuals and artists in that city mobilized against the demolition of a beloved downtown café and then a historic movie theater, which were to be cast into the dustbin of history to make way for a new shopping mall.[2] The activists failed, and the mall went forward. A group of environmentalists made contact on social media so that they could do something to protect the city's remaining green spaces from rapacious development. Furkan, a college student from Istanbul, joined the loose network and started planning. Like many of his friends, he looked more to Europe than to the Arab world for inspiration. They were moved more by the ways that environmentalists organized in the West, and the way that leftists had taken to the streets in nearby Greece in 2011, than the example of Tahrir Square. In any case, he didn't have much hope his little group of tree huggers would accomplish much, aside from slowing down the ongoing commodification of Istanbul.[3]

On Twitter, he discovered that the city planned to bulldoze trees in Gezi Park on the night of May 27. In addition to destroying a bit of nature, the president wanted to build a large mosque, which would celebrate the Ottoman period. Furkan and a few dozen comrades went to the park. A group totaling perhaps eighty-five activists, fifteen journalists, and one member of parliament from the pro-Kurdish party managed to stop the bulldozers. But those big machines were going to come back. The protesters spread the word, and a thousand people came out the next night. Most were committed environmentalist types, with a smattering of different political viewpoints represented—but the one commonality was that nobody was pro-Erdoğan. On a whim, some of them dragged out tents so there would always be someone there to protect the park. In the middle of the night on May 29, the government arrived, this time to clear out people instead of trees. As the cops began to tear gas the settlement and torch the tents, Furkan scrambled in panic across the square. Desperate to escape, dozens of people tried to rush down the same small set of stairs at the same time, and they crashed to the ground. The whole thing was filmed on camera phones.[4]

On May 30, the entire country woke up to the shocking images of a crackdown on nonviolent environmental protesters, in the middle of Istanbul, with Taksim Square on fire. Except, that is, for those who tuned in to state media, which wasn't talking about this at all. But social media—Twitter especially—and international coverage made it easy for well-connected Turks to see past the censorship. And so citizens poured into the square in solidarity with the victimized demonstrators and in protest of police brutality. Then, photographer Osman Orsal produced an even more scandalous image. A young woman, elegantly poised and wearing a flowing red dress, was pepper sprayed at close range by the Turkish police. After seeing this on Twitter, a lot of people felt like Hazar, a shopkeeper in the bazaar from a middle-class family. He said: "A sandstorm is erupting, and I want to be one of the pieces of sand. I just want to support the people." The square was entirely packed now, twenty-four hours a day, and the whole world was watching.[5]

The Turkish Model

In 1922, the mighty Ottoman Empire finally collapsed, after more than six hundred years. After Mehmed the Conqueror took Byzantium in 1453, the sultans embarked on a conquest that eventually gave them control over a huge swathe of land stretching from modern-day Algeria in the west, deep into the Arab Peninsula in the southeast, and up to what is now Hungary and Ukraine in the north. They did not force their subjects to learn Turkish, but maintained a network of local rulers who were loyal to Istanbul. They traded in both African and European slaves—the Cossack people, from the steppes of modern-day Ukraine, acquired a heroic reputation (among Slavs, at least) for liberating prisoners in horseback raids before they could be sold at Crimean ports. But as the world was increasingly transformed by European imperialism and the attendant rise of capitalism, the Ottomans were dragged through slow decline.[6] The Republic of Turkey was born in 1923, and President Mustafa Kemal Atatürk pushed through a set of modernizing, Westernizing reforms. These "Kemalist" measures abolished the Ottoman caliphate, instituted the use of the Roman alphabet, declared the state to be fully secular, and banned the use of Muslim headscarves in any public institution. Many Turkish women remained *hijabi*, but not if they were serving in government or teaching at a public school. Atatürk suppressed local efforts to reproduce the Bolshevik revolution, but he also learned lessons from the Soviet Union. Turkey used central planning, but to build a national bourgeoisie and capitalist economy, rather than the proletarian-led industrialization favored by the USSR. Nasser's system in Egypt was not wildly different from Atatürk's creation, economically speaking, but Nasserism was more leftist, and more committed to the cause of the Third World, than Kemalism had been.[7] And modern Turkey, unlike Egypt, did not cover a territory that had been a coherent nation for thousands of years. Its version of nationalism relied on exclusionary and destructive violence. Late Ottoman leaders carried out a genocide against the Armenian people, and the republic was locked in eternal conflict with the Kurdish people, unhappy to be locked within Turkey's new borders.

After World War II, Stalin thought he might be able to establish naval bases in Turkey, but the government in Ankara ultimately chose to side with the West in the Cold War, joining NATO in 1952.[8] As the organized left grew in power and influence in the 1970s, the state backed far-right nationalists as well as Islamists as counterweights until, in 1980, the military seized power, ending parliamentary democracy, banning all unions, and annihilating the socialist movement with a series of executions, imprisonment, and the use of torture. The coup led to a "controlled opening" for Turkey's religious groups, and it meant the beginning of neoliberalization in the country. Prime Minister Erdoğan's party, the Justice and Development Party (AKP), grew out of the pro-business, pro-American wing of an Islamist party founded in 1983. The former mayor of Istanbul (1994–1998) took power in 2003 and proved to be a valuable US ally in the Global War on Terror, all while maintaining a wide base of support at home. The AKP movement embraced people who were truly marginalized by the old development model—like more conservative Muslims and small business owners (as long as they were ethnic Turks)—though these groups had not been as excluded from the political system as ethnic minorities or the organized working class.[9] Some leftists backed Erdoğan, seeing him as a truly populist figure, elected in a democracy that was preferable to authoritarian secularism and far-right nationalism.[10]

In 2010, Erdoğan successfully passed a constitutional reform that further sidelined the military, established the rule of law in line with European Union standards, and also made it easier for police to crack down on activists.[11] With Erdoğan approaching a decade in power, the groups that his movement had been championing since the 1990s no longer seemed so marginal. And a lot of people in downtown Istanbul (often, it must be said, the direct beneficiaries of secular Kemalist modernization) didn't like what was happening to their city.

Erdoğan found himself in a complicated position as a result of the so-called Arab Spring. Or, that is, he put himself in one. On the one hand, the fall of Ben Ali and Mubarak seemed to offer a chance for the real expansion of Turkish influence—and the AKP model. Then there was the problem of Syria. At first, Erdoğan wanted to position himself as a mediator between Assad and the opposition, while the Kingdom of Saudi Arabia wanted regime change. But as the Saudi position gained traction in Washington, Turkey changed its orientation too. The Free Syrian Army, the armed rebel group originally formed of defectors from the Syrian Army committed to overthrowing Assad (that received Saudi funding and later, US support), was founded on Turkish soil in July 2011. Turkey had provided active assistance to the NATO operation against Gaddafi in Libya, after a lot of hand-wringing and indecision. And closer to home, the Turkish government was wary of any developments that would prove advantageous to the Kurdish movement in general, or more specifically to the militant Kurdistan Workers' Party (PKK) that Ankara considered its mortal enemy.

Erdoğan had both ideological and geopolitical incentives to pull for Islamist movements in North Africa, and he did. The Turkish president supported Ennahda in Tunisia and was close to the Egyptian Muslim Brotherhood after the victory of Mohamed Morsi. These were the movements that might re-create the "Turkish Model"—in other words, the pro-Western, neoliberalized, moderately Islamist—mode of governmentality he had developed over the previous two decades. But this isolated him in the region. Saudi Arabia did not like the Muslim Brotherhood government one bit. And putting the pro-Western Turkish Model aside, it was obvious that any successful democratic or social revolution in the most populous and influential Arab country would call into question the point of the Kingdom—why would anyone need a repressive, murderous monarchy if the Arab world can come together behind a prospering, progressive Egypt, or a new version of Nasserism or Pan-Arabism, or even a relatively stable Islamist democracy?

In April 2013, a movement called Tamarod—"Rebellion"—appeared in Egypt, collecting signatures to call for the end of the Mohamed Morsi presidency. They were clearly drawing on the repertoire of revolutionary associations developed in 2011—they presented themselves as a youth-led, grassroots, digitally coordinated uprising—and they collected a whole lot of signatures, very fast. With an official spokesman in Mahmoud Badr, an activist since the days of Kefaya, or "Enough," they appealed to revolutionaries as well as secular elites, and charged Morsi with overstepping his power to impose conservative religion on the country. Erdoğan quickly took Morsi's side.

Resista Brasil!

After the woman in the red dress went viral, the world was served with images of supporters of the park and opponents of Erdoğan packing Gezi to the brim. In the beginning of June, Taksim Square was home to a permanent settlement of demonstrators. At the same time, Gezi Park welcomed protesters who could come by every day in the evening after work. Turks living abroad spent days glued to Facebook, and some of them with the means and inclination jumped on planes to join the movement.[12] More demonstrations erupted in Izmir, Ankara, and a dozen other cities. But in the first days of June 2013, Gezi Park became the national platform for a range of political causes, a site for clashes with the police, and a space for a radically different type of communal experience.

None of this had been planned. And there was no obvious demand for them to make, no stupidly clear target to match their escalated sense of purpose—no dictator that had been in power for decades, for example—and so, the causes remained nearly as diffuse as the participants. In the Turkish context, getting the military to defy the president (as had happened in

Egypt and Tunisia) would certainly not be a revolution—it would just be another coup. Gezi was not as "leaderless" and horizontal as Tahrir, Plaza del Sol, and Occupy Wall Street, since the Taksim Solidarity umbrella organization quickly formed in an attempt to give some direction to the revolt.[13] But this didn't always work out in practice, as it wasn't exactly clear who was under that umbrella. Anyone could come to the park, and participation was diverse. The environmentalists had started the movement, and from the beginning there had been representatives from the Peoples' Democratic Party (HDP), a progressive party that routinely defends Kurdish interests. The organized left, including the Turkish Communist Party (TKP), was there. Unlike most of the crowd, the TKP had been fighting with cops here ever since they threw their bodies against the 2003 attack on Iraq, as US fighter planes used Turkish airspace for the invasion. Feminist and LGBT groups quickly made their presence known. There were Kemalists of different stripes: secular social democrats, as well as the ultra-nationalist (anti-Kurdish) wing.[14] Disconcertingly, the Square also attracted the support of some Grey Wolves, the far-right nationalists who had been responsible for part of the wave of terror against the left before the 1980 military coup.[15] But they were resolutely opposed to Erdoğan, so the progressives understood why they would be there. Some people on the front lines were wearing those masks from *V for Vendetta*. And there were a whole lot of normal, mostly middle-class citizens without explicit political identities or experience.

Surveys indicated that most people in the square were far more educated than Turks as a whole and came from well-off neighborhoods nearby (while farmers, housewives, and shopkeepers were less likely to support the occupation).[16] The professionals were united, very loosely, in defense of secular values, in opposition to the commodification of public space, and in solidarity against police violence. And then there were the football hooligans.

In English, "hooligan" implies a quite unsavory type of violent character, but outside of Britain, the better word is usually *ultras*, designating groups of tight-knit superfans that may or may not have an explicit political ideology. In many places—and certainly in Istanbul—there are leftist *ultras*. A group of fans of the local Fenerbahçe club, calling themselves "Vamos Bien," a phrase they took from Fidel Castro, is an anti-fascist, feminist, and socialist *ultra* group in Istanbul, and they were there from the first day. *Ultras* are well-organized, and they have a lot of experience fighting, and with repression. Fans who were in the Fenerbahçe stadium on May 12 of the previous year, for example, remember when police helicopters bombed the stadium with tear gas. The members of Vamos Bien called the middle-class, more celebratory protesters "the flower people," and they weren't exactly sure how to interact with them. These *ultras* often manned the front lines at Gezi, with the assistance of experienced activists, but they weren't sure if the "soft and disorganized" protesters behind them appreciated what they were doing. It could be frustrating to engage in real combat, take real risks, and turn around and see a "petty-bourgeois cultural fair."[17]

One day, a huge column of the supporters of Beşiktaş, another club in Istanbul, marched into the square. The procession deeply impressed Eren Senkardes, an artist from an elite neighborhood. They unfurled a large banner reading "BEŞIKTAŞ," except they had drawn the "K" as a communist hammer-and-sickle, and a circle around the "A" in the anarchist style.

Eren watched, absolutely dazzled, as one Beşiktaş *ultra* stood in front of the rest and raised his arm to direct them. "It was truly insane. Their discipline," Eren said. "With every little motion of his hand, the entire squad responded and moved in unison. He had complete control." Referring to a 2002 movie produced in the United States in which the hero controls a complex computer with flourishes of his fingers, he said, "It was like watching Tom Cruise in *Minority Report*."

Another night, another very different procession descended on Taksim. Rihanna was playing a huge show a few blocks away. As she sang, fans in the VIP seats also watched the events in the square, on Twitter. Then they swarmed up the hill, toward Istiklal, and joined the revolt. Eren's girlfriend was in that march. They knew that they didn't exactly hail from the proletariat, but everyone was coming together to fight for their city. Like so many other protesters, Eren was struck in the head with a tear gas canister fired by the police.

This changed his life, and not because the injury was permanent. During the trip to the hospital, he made the kind of deep, unmediated connection with another human being that so many people spoke about in Tahrir in 2011, or Paris in 1968. He wasn't sure if he would survive, terrified by the size of the head injury, which pulsated with terrifying heat. He locked eyes with another man in the waiting room, someone who, he knew, he never would have spoken with before Gezi. But in that moment, they were brothers. The feeling was transcendent, and far more powerful than the pain in the back of his skull.[18]

Zeynep Tufekci, a Turkish sociologist who had been a part of digitally coordinated activist networks since the alter-globalization moment, noticed that the language employed was nearly identical to that which had been produced in New York and Egypt. "If I squinted and ignored that the language was Turkish," she reported, "I felt that it could have been in almost any twenty-first-century protest square: organized through Twitter, filled with tear gas, leaderless, networked, euphoric, and fragile." She also clocked the dual nature of the revolt—it was somewhere between a music festival and the Paris Commune, she wrote. Like Graeber, she rejected the idea that contention is a means to an end. But her interpretation was not based on a prefigurative ideal, but rather on the empirical observation that people were deriving real meaning from these experiences. This was the feeling of "participatory democracy" SDS had dreamed of, except they were running a square instead of the country. Tufekci saw, and felt, that Gezi Park offered an escape from the alienation of everyday life; the ability to exchange products without money inverted the "commodity fetishism" of workaday capitalist society. There was always more blankets or food than anyone needed.[19]

Meanwhile, defenders of the Erdoğan project scrambled to declare that the situation here was very different from the movements it was echoing. In an article for Al Jazeera entitled "Taksim Square Is Not Tahrir Square," two university professors pointed to the presence of radical Kemalists in the square and claimed they were using the revolt to overthrow a government that had "revolutionized center-periphery relations." This was the language of the intellectual left, being deployed to shore up Erdoğan's AKP. "As anthropologists and Marxist academics," they wrote, "we observe that the AK Party still holds the support of the subaltern, the real subjects of a possible revolution. Since 2002, the people on Turkey's periphery have become the centre. Today's chaos threatens to reverse this."[20]

But support continued to pour in from all around the world. Bahar, a wry and impish scientist who worked near the square, very much enjoyed her time amidst the crowd. She joined the Square in defense of secular values (particularly, the scientific method) and against Erdoğan. Gezi was a revelation. She had no idea there were so many people who thought the same way as her in Istanbul. For the first time, she got to know queer and trans people. She met a boyfriend—well, he was more of a "fuck buddy," according to her—in the square.[21]

She was always on Twitter, except for when she was kicked off for mouthing off a little bit too much. In the second half of June, she saw a tweet, coming in from Brazil, reporting that demonstrators in São Paulo were getting tear-gassed. She read that Brazilians had exclaimed, "Love is over! Turkey is here!" as they withstood the onslaught. Bahar saw a flowering of responses, all in solidarity with that other street movement halfway across the globe, appear both online and in the real world. She took a photo of eight people, all in their twenties or thirties, holding green and yellow paper (the colors of the Brazilian soccer team) with a big message spelled out. She posted it online and sent it to the journalist in Brazil who had first posted the viral tweet—that is, to me. Their sign was written in Portuguese—with some mistakes, but totally legible.

"TODO LUGAR É SÃO PAULO—EM TODO LUGAR RESISTÊNCIA—RESISTA BRASIL!—A TURQUIA ESTÁ AO SEU LADO!" Or in English: "THE WHOLE WORLD IS SÃO PAULO—RESISTANCE EVERYWHERE—BRAZIL, RESIST!—TURKEY IS BY YOUR SIDE."

A few days later, thousands of people gathered in assemblies. The older activists with experience—mostly organized leftists who were referred to as "big brothers" in the Park—wanted to use the leverage they had created to reap the benefits (via negotiation and institutional politics) and end the occupation. Young protesters shouted back at them, questioning their authority and yelling that they did not represent them. The faces of the big brothers went pale. They knew they had lost.[22] When it came time for the Turkish government to invite a delegation to negotiate on behalf of the Park, it wasn't clear who was actually supposed to go.

9

The Free Fare Movement

THINGS WERE VERY BUSY FOR the Movimento Passe Livre in the first half of 2013. The city of São Paulo had scheduled a rise in the price of a bus ride (and metro ticket), which would normally go into effect on January 1. But President Dilma asked Mayor Haddad to wait until June to help keep a looming inflation problem under control. Haddad didn't think this made much sense, and they had a small fight over the issue in Brasília. He didn't think transport fees in one city were going to do much to affect prices in the national economy, he told her, and the city badly needed the funds. But she won out. He was going to wait—which meant that the MPL had months to plan their response.

And plan they did. The Free Fare Movement had been studying urban policy and the effectiveness of confrontational street tactics for eight years now. They looked back at what had worked before (Florianópolis in 2004) and what hadn't worked (Salvador in 2003 and São Paulo in 2011). They got together twice a week at the office of the Tortura Nunca Mais (Torture Never Again) human rights group to plan.

Their meetings would last hours, because everything had to be decided by consensus. After school or work, or on the weekends, Mayara sat around with Lucas "Vegetable" Monteiro, Pedro Punk, law student Nina Cappello, rocker Daniel Guimarães, the feisty Elisa "Tinkerbell" Quadros, and twenty or thirty other members. Many of them attended the city's prestigious (and free) University of São Paulo (USP), but they had long ago decided, as a group, to refuse to share biographical details with anyone in the press. They didn't want attention on individuals, as they didn't want anyone elevated above the rest of the group. It was exciting, to plan for the struggle, but it wasn't easy. Meetings could run until two or three in the morning, even when they started before noon.

Their goal was to force mayor Fernando Haddad to reverse the twenty-*centavo* hike on the price of bus rides in the city. Some of them believed they could change Brazilian society in the larger sense; that their movement could lead more people (or the working class) to assert political power through direct action on the streets. But as a collective they had a single, very specific objective, and they came up with a detailed plan to achieve it. As they got closer to June, they began to meet every single day. Members who lived outside the capital, like geography student Oliver Cauã Cauê, descended on São Paulo to prepare for the action.[1]

The Movimento Passe Livre knew that Haddad and the Workers' Party (PT) had developed a robust set of mechanisms for interacting with social movements. Haddad would want a dialogue to incorporate, co-opt, and converse—or, as Vegetable put it, to "put us in meetings, that would lead to a series of meetings, that would create a committee, that would discuss future committees, and then eventually create an agenda based on future negotiations." They chose to deny that possibility and turn their backs on City Hall.

They knew that in order to create the necessary pressure, there would have to be some chaos in the city. Their little group was not big enough to cause the desired conflagration, so they would need to rely on other people joining in. They planned the exact number of demonstrations that they thought would be necessary for Haddad to give in. Of course, they knew that media reproduction of their interventions would be essential. They were deeply distrustful of corporate media (their founding charter urged "caution" when making contact with these "oligarchical" structures), but they had to have a communications strategy.[2] Their organizational model (and the beliefs that underpinned it) would never allow for them to select designated spokespersons. In horizontalism, everyone was equal, and everyone would do everything. So that job would rotate among the members of the Free Fare Movement, and underline that they were truly a leaderless collective. They would only talk about the movement and its objectives, rather than any other political issue. But they would certainly make sure to offer the media the sort of content they loved to run.

They went as far as to plan the exact image they would like to see on the cover of the city's main newspapers after their first intervention. They planned to stop traffic on one of the city's main thoroughfares, 23 de Maio, and mount a barricade, lighting tires on fire (a classic in the Brazilian radical repertoire) and unfurl a giant banner reading:

SE A TARIFA NÃO BAIXAR, A CIDADE VAI PARAR

It rhymes, of course, and scans like a line of poetry. It means "if the fare doesn't come down, the city is coming to a halt." They figured the cops would probably clear them out of there eventually, but not before the press got their shot.

Within City Hall itself, Haddad was having his own problems with the police. Brazilian cops are *military police*, a legacy of the dictatorship, and the most important troops report to the state government. State Governor Geraldo Alckmin, from the center-right PSDB party, was a political rival of Dilma and Haddad, and had very different ideas about public security. Haddad believed that the Polícia Militar (PM) was upset with City Hall over a budgeting issue inherited from the previous mayor. Moreover, the cops were explicitly refusing to collaborate with his "Open Arms" treatment program, which insisted on dealing with homeless crack users as addicts, not criminals.[3] So in May, on the first night of the Virada Cultural, a downtown music festival meant to showcase his vision for the city, they apparently responded with "crossed arms"—that is, they refused to do any policing during the event. I attended. It was absolute pandemonium. My apartment has a balcony overlooking one of the stages, and we watched the band Raça Negra perform live before heading downstairs to check things out. It was as if the military police had asked every small-time criminal in town to put on their best show.

I had nothing other than a half-broken Blackberry and a bottle of *cachaça* on my person, so I wasn't worried about myself. We just looked on, in wonder and in horror, sometimes breaking into horribly manic laughter as teenage boys ripped away every cell phone, backpack, purse, and wallet in sight, and then ran off. The police leaned against a nearby wall and watched.

The MPL marked the first protest for June 6. The Movimento Passe Livre had a group on Facebook that anyone could join. They created an event page for the date, which was a good way to alert people from school, their social circle, and sympathetic activists that something was going down.

Around five thousand people hit the streets that night. Being in the Southern Hemisphere, June is about as cold and dark as São Paulo gets—it's never much chillier than a Los Angeles winter in the city, but it gets cold enough that people like to stay wrapped up at home. So motorists, and the police especially, were surprised to see so many students, punks, and teenagers pour onto 23 de Maio and shut it down. The flames were especially striking, against the black sky, when they lit those tires on fire, and mounted wooden turnstiles on top, to burn along with them. The police called for backup. My friend Piero Locatelli, a reporter at *Carta Capital* magazine, observed what he described as "combat" between the military police and the crowd, just before getting hit with his first dose of tear gas. Piero, no stranger to the punk underground, or rambunctious protests, said he had never seen that many cops in one place in São Paulo before. And he had never seen such a small group of protesters fighting back with such fierce dedication. At one point, the police turned their backs to retreat. The youth cried out—*Amanhã vai ser maior!*—"Tomorrow will be greater!"[4]

I was far away, still reporting on the conflict between indigenous people and ranchers across Brazil's agricultural heartland, but I checked the news every day. I had been working at the offices of *Folha de S.Paulo* for a year now, so I usually looked at that paper first, and then *Estadão*, the more conservative daily in São Paulo. Both papers had the same image on the front page—the Movimento Passe Livre blocking the street and broadcasting their message, with their flames dancing in the dark night. Exactly as they had planned.

The MPL had very few resources, so they had spent a lot of their budget on that banner and the fake wooden turnstiles they burned that night. Starting on June 7, they needed to use everything else at their disposal to help protesters who had landed in prison. At least fifty people were injured. They had to deal with the press, which had printed that photograph but was not exactly sympathetic. One paper reported "vandalism," and the other described "destruction of property," neither of which were technically incorrect.

The MPL had to play a sort of "double game," as Lucas "Vegetable" called it, which was to always blame the government and its repressive apparatuses for the chaos on the streets, to insist that it was the price rise and the police that caused the situation, while they also did what they could to make sure that the chaos remained within the levels they desired. They put a note up on Facebook on June 7, emphasizing the first point. And as expected, the mayor's office reached out. Someone from city hall got the phone number of one of the activists through a mutual friend (this is very much Haddad's style) and called directly, offering to invite her in for a "frank discussion, from citizen to citizen" on transport policy. It was rebuked, on the grounds that this was not the kind of conversation they wished to have.[5] And they were preparing for another protest—that night.

Looking back on the success almost ten years ago in Florianópolis, they had come to the conclusion that unrelenting intensity was crucial for success. So for the second day in a row, they took to the streets.

It wasn't bigger, as those kids had promised the cops—it was about the same size—but they surprised the city by shutting down yet another part of it. On Friday afternoon, around five thousand people gathered in Pinheiros, a richer part of the city and the same neighborhood where a young Haddad had his Marxist pizza parties. When they realized they had the numbers required, they occupied one of the country's largest highways. The military police Tropa de Choque, or "Shock Troops," took aim at the protesters. Some of the counterattackers were "black bloc" participants, fully geared up for the impending clashes. Covering the chaos once again for *Carta Capital*, Piero learned a trick that night from a teenage anarchist. She soaked a T-shirt in vinegar, told him to inhale the fumes, and said that it would help with the effects of the tear gas. It seemed to work.[6]

Over the weekend, the *Estadão* newspaper blamed Haddad, and the alleged permissiveness of the progressive Workers' Party vis-à-vis its beloved social movements, for the "vandals" and the "violence."[7] The mayor himself left the city and traveled to Paris, where he and Governor Alckmin were bidding on the 2020 World Expo for the city of São Paulo. Brazil was already hosting the 2014 World Cup and the 2016 Olympics, and this would be yet another jewel in the nation's crown of expensive international mega-events. When it came to the bus fare, he reasoned he was not exactly pulling a fast one on the people. He had said he was going to raise the price during his campaign, and he won handily. The rise was smaller than overall inflation since the last hike. He believed that raising the bus fare was the right move for the city.

On a personal level, Haddad became increasingly annoyed with the MPL. They did not respect the differences between politicians, he felt; they lumped him in with the conservative repressive apparatus he fought against as a young dissident and was now trying to sabotage his administration. He did not believe he was trying to co-opt anybody; the PT was deeply proud of the mechanisms it had developed over the decades to involve social movements in decision-making and bring the streets into the halls of power.[8] These kids were not only refusing to play by the rules, they were pretending that the rules didn't exist. But the movement couldn't be dismissed entirely. Vice Mayor Nádia Campeão, from the Communist Party of Brazil (PCdoB), skipped Paris and stayed in town to monitor the situation.

On Tuesday, June 11, it rained heavily. Protest number three, which took place that afternoon, was not so much a statement mounted in a single place as a set of battles, appearing and disappearing beneath the downpour, around the center of the mega-city. Water meant no cell phones, and no megaphones, and so, even less organization than usual. Demonstrators tried to enter a bus station to encourage commuters to jump over the turnstiles. The police responded: first with words, and then with tear gas and rubber bullets.

In front of the Tribunal de Justiça, one cop tried to stop a kid from spray painting on a wall. But quickly, the officer found himself surrounded. A group of demonstrators began to hurl rocks at him. One struck him in the head, and he began to bleed. He pulled a gun, and pointed it at the kids, ready to shoot. But he relented, and pointed it back up into the sky, and backed away in fear. If you only caught that scene, it looked very much like a group of punks had almost killed a police officer. This was not something that the MPL as an organization really believed to be productive. It was actually members of the Movimento Passe Livre who pulled the officer out of there and surrounded him to separate him from the crowd immediately afterward.[9] At the same time, it was their public policy to blame all chaos on the state, and to avoid criminalizing resistance. It was a difficult line to walk.

It came as no surprise when this was the image that made the news that day. Sympathy for the officer in the media was overwhelming. Governor Alckmin congratulated him by name in a statement of solidarity. Communist city councilman Orlando Silva used a word from the old Marxist-Leninist canon—"adventurist"—to describe the actions of an irresponsible group that would only destabilize and worsen the country, not actually lead to revolutionary change. Elder statesman Eduardo Suplicy, from the Workers' Party, invoked the legacies of Gandhi and Martin Luther King Jr. to celebrate nonviolent struggle for justice.[10] And Mayor Haddad—returning from Paris—said he placed a call asking the police not to overreact to the youth revolt; but that photo in the papers, of a cop nearly "lynched" by protesters, meant that they wouldn't listen.[11]

On June 13, the morning of the fourth scheduled protest, São Paulo's newspapers delivered a clear message: the police need to crack down on this group. This was not done with innuendo, or with suggestive news coverage, but with frank calls to action. The *Estadão* editorial committee wrote, "The authorities should have determined that the police take more rigorous action, since the very beginning." In an editorial entitled "Retomar a Paulista," or "Retake Paulista Avenue," *Folha de S.Paulo* published this opinion: "The few protesters that seem to have anything on their minds except for hoods justify their violence as a supposed reaction to the supposed brutality of the police." *Folha* continued: "It is time to put a stop to this."[12]

The Free Fare Movement itself was getting stretched thin. They were committed to carrying the plan forward and energized by the struggle, but in addition to shutting down parts of the largest city in South America, fighting with police, and managing their image in the media and on Facebook and Twitter, they needed to provide aid to scores of injured and imprisoned comrades. And on top of it all, they had to hold constant meetings to achieve full consensus for each step they took. There was little time for sleep, but they still managed to come up with the rotation of duties for the protest on June 13. Lucas "Vegetable" Monteiro was going to be working on legal assistance from the mother ship. Mayara was going to be *frento do ato*, serving on the front line, bearing the brunt of any crackdown, and defining the trajectory of the march.

Retomar a Paulista

I got back into São Paulo early in the morning on Thursday, June 13. It was an overnight bus, and I was tired. I knew I was going to the protest that night, so I slept all day, to store up some energy. I didn't expect that this would be news for the *Los Angeles Times*, exactly, but I was very curious. A close friend of mine, Juliana, a freelance photographer who had gone to USP and been heavily involved in the music scene there, knew some of the Movimento Passe Livre, which kept me better informed than the media could.

That afternoon I walked down Avenida Ipiranga, from my apartment on Praça da República, and joined the group congregating in front of the Teatro Municipal. It took me about ten minutes to arrive, and the square felt like a university party. The musical accompaniment to MPL events, the Fanfarra do Movimento Autônomo Libertário, or the "Autonomous Liberation Movement Fanfare Band," a kind of marching drum circle, was warming up. There were kids in ragged clothes—the kind of cheap attire that indicated political affiliation, not poverty. On the edge of the crowd I could see several different flags waving—mostly those of small, left-wing parties, but even the black-and-white standard of a youth movement affiliated with the Workers' Party.[13] I didn't see any cops.

If I had come from the other direction, I might have had a very different experience. Most people did not live as close as me, and they were coming through the Vale do Anhangabaú, one of the strips of São Paulo with an indigenous name. There, military police were stopping people and searching them. Piero Locatelli came up that way, and they pulled him aside and asked to look in his backpack. They found a big plastic bottle of vinegar—cheap stuff from the supermarket that you might mix with olive oil. He had come prepared. The police detained him. Piero couldn't believe it—he was an accredited journalist, and this was no danger to anyone. He switched into the polite, highly grammatical version of Brazilian Portuguese that should indicate he was a respectable professional, and that he respected the officers too. To no avail. He was taken away. Another journalist, a colleague of mine at *Folha de S.Paulo*, did make it into the crowd, though I didn't see her. Giuliana Vallone, twenty-seven years old, worked for the newly founded video section at the newspaper, and took a position far away from the front of the action.

Mayara had a cell phone but not a smartphone. She was working as a waitress at the time, and she had never been able to afford a device with internet access. Mayara would be calling other members of the group constantly to coordinate, as she pulled the mass of people behind her. Along with Pedro Punk, they decided it was time to begin.

We stomped back the way I had come, up past my house, and then we pushed up toward Paulista Avenue. As we moved up Consolação, there was a column of military police staring down at us.

The moment of the attack is seared into my brain. We were looking up at them, up that hill leading to one of the highest points in the city. There were a lot of us, but they had the advantage. The sky hanging right above their heads was black and empty. And then they let loose, with volleys of smoke and fire and noise and canisters and streams of light flickering into the heavens. It was strangely beautiful, in the way that the apocalypse might be. São Paulo is never *pretty*, but it can be terrifyingly beautiful. It can be *awesome*, in the biblical sense. But then the red cloud approached its intended target, which was us, and I stopped looking up.

I don't have good memories of what, exactly, I did next. It was quick bursts of movement, with other small groups of people, here and there. Looking up to see if police were chasing us, and then looking back down to scurry into another little corner, like scared little cockroaches. There was nothing to really "cover," in the journalistic sense, so I just kept looking at my feet, trying to find a way through the maze of the city, back into the open air.

Giuliana Vallone remembers what happened to her. She stumbled onto Rua Augusta, the bohemian stretch of bars and clubs. Dilma was sitting in one of these bars on Augusta in 1970 when the dictatorship picked her up and hauled her off for her interrogation and torture. Giuliana was technically covering the protest, but her phone was dead, and she was exhausted. An older woman got off a bus, lost and clearly in need of help. The commotion had stranded her downtown. Giuliana pointed her in the direction of Avenida Paulista. Seconds later, the woman ran toward her, yelling, "Miss, they are back!" It was the police, climbing down off a big, black Shock Troop vehicle and getting into formation. Giuliana looked toward them and didn't say anything. One of them raised his arm and shot her in the face. The rubber bullet bounced off her skull, and she fell to the ground. Someone snapped a picture.

Like Piero Locatelli, Giuliana Vallone is a Brazilian of Italian extraction, which is one of the most common ethnic profiles among the São Paulo elite. Giuliana was twenty-seven, but she looked younger. She has dark brown hair, and big, round, pink cheeks. By the standards of Brazil or any other country, she is very beautiful. And she worked for *Folha*, the "*New York Times* of

Brazil." In the photo, she is sitting on the pavement, appearing dazed and plaintive, and it looks like she has lost her eye. The image shocked tens of millions of people. Piero was sitting back at work, writing his own story, when he heard shouts go up in the newsroom. They had seen the picture, now flying through social networks. I was still on the street.

Mayara was in a state of panic. She had lost control of the front line, which meant that she had let the movement down. When the first attack came, and blasted the crowd into different crevices, she took shelter in the doorway of a building. In a moment of desperation, a young mother turned to her and asked Mayara to watch her young daughter before rushing into the street to try to rescue her husband. Stunned, she obliged. The little girl turned her face up to Mayara and asked, "Auntie, are we going to die?"

When the mother returned, Mayara tried to get back to the "front" of the march, but there was none. In vain, she attempted to give some structure to the protest, to protect her people, to put the pieces back together, but the waves of attacks kept coming and coming. Finally, she managed to pull out her crappy little phone and call Nina Cappello, who was coordinating things from the base.

"Nina, I have never seen anything more horrible in my life. I feel like I am in a war. I don't know what to do," she cried out, both scared and guilty. "I don't know what to do; please just give me some kind of command."

Nina responded. "Don't do anything at all, Mayara. Grab a beer and relax and watch because we are blowing up on every news channel in the world. You don't need to do anything. We already did it." Mayara couldn't believe it. How could this be success? People were bleeding and wounded all around her.

Television presenter José Luiz Datena is far more conservative than *Folha* or *Estadão*. He runs a sensational and very popular program denouncing crime and celebrating the police. As the events unfolded on the street, he said, "I am against riots, guys," and then opened a poll for viewers to vote on their phones on the question "Are you in favor of this kind of protest?" Over one thousand people immediately voted "yes," and he responded, surprised, "So far…the majority are in favor…I would vote no, I would vote no.… OK, is it possible that we formulated the question incorrectly?" And then he launched a new poll: "Are you in favor of protests with rioting?" Over two thousand of his viewers voted "yes," against less than nine hundred for "no," to which he responded, "Well, the people are so pissed off that they support any protest, as far as I can tell. OK." The monitor behind him continued to transmit images of the streets, and Datena quickly changed his tune. Now the protest was "a show of democracy."[14]

My memory becomes clear again when I arrived near my house. I lived on a big square, so the space was relatively open. Some tear gas hung diffusely in the air, but I could breathe. I regained my composure a bit, chatting with the security guards who worked in my building, and processed what had just happened. I was in one piece, so I decided to go back out. I made it up to the Edifício Copan, the monumental building shaped by legendary architect Oscar Niemeyer. I came upon a loose agglomeration of people, attempting to somehow maintain a presence on the street. Simply being there seemed a kind of stubborn rebuke to the military police, who promptly arrived and put an end to that. As the tear gas canisters landed right below us, the crowd cheered out, "Love is over! Turkey is here!" I scampered back toward my house, defeated again.

I pulled out my Blackberry as I walked and posted this chant to Twitter. I got into my apartment and sat down at my computer. Something weird was happening. This tweet was getting a whole lot of attention, and a lot of likes, and people were retweeting it throughout the world. Something really struck a nerve—the police brutality? The analogy to an uprising in a Muslim country? I didn't understand. Nothing remotely like this had ever happened to me before. Young correspondents in Brazil working for a California newspaper don't exactly have a huge platform. For the first time, I was going viral. I still don't know if I can describe the feeling. It was as if my entire body was being electrocuted with the vaguely pleasant notion that my words were connecting with thousands, millions of people all at once. And then the feeling would vanish until I looked back at the screen, transfixed as I watched the numbers go up and up. It was deeply strange, and I didn't feel comfortable.

I emailed my editor in Los Angeles—this was international news now, I was sure—but as I waited for his response, I concentrated on this feeling. This kind of attention, the fact that I might be bearing witness to a major world event, must be good for my career, I thought, but energy was surging through me that felt even bigger than that. I opened up a document to try to capture the sensation, just for my own memory. I frantically typed out some notes and took screenshots of the numbers. Wryly, in an attempt to check myself against the twisted incentive structures that were appearing clearly before my eyes, I wrote: "Getting tear-gassed is great for engagement."

Hopefully it was good for something. Because for the next several months, I and the rest of the Praça da República would be lulled to sleep, nearly every night, by the faint taste of that familiar chemical compound, 2-Chlorobenzylidenemalononitrile.

10

The Giant Awakens

ON FRIDAY, JUNE 14, THE country woke up to news of police violence. Endless photographs, and eyewitness reports, and journalistic accounts. I had my
little story in the *LA Times*. The *New York Times* ran something (mentioning
protests in Rio, where that correspondent lived), and other international outlets covered it too. Already, catchy monikers were being created based on
the social media reports the previous night. Some called it the "V for Vinegar" movement, referring to Piero's arrest for possession of salad preparation
materials with a play on *V for Vendetta*, whose masks had been present on
the streets on Thursday. But the really dazzling transformation happened
in the mainstream Brazilian media.

I walked to my office, through an absolutely devastated downtown São
Paulo, and got to work. Freelance *Guardian* contributor Claire Rigby had
sent me her report for the *Folha* blog. Of course, like everyone else, we ran
the photo of Giuliana Vallone to accompany the text. Dom Phillips, another
dear friend and contributor to the blog, would put together a video to post
later. After I edited and published Claire's story, and posted it on Twitter,
I began to actually read what the national press had reported. This was a
total about-face. *Folha* condemned the police crackdown that they had asked
for on Thursday. *Estadão* ran interviews with innocent bystanders, commuters, pedestrians, and workers, who all said they suffered from the police

repression. Reporters began to notice that Brazilians do actually spend a large percentage of their income on buses and the metro. (I was also guilty of paying little attention to the issue until June 13.) Outlets opened investigations into the cost of transportation for regular people. Giuliana shared a personal account of her injury on Facebook, where it was immediately shared tens of thousands of times. But newspaper readership in Brazil is low, and reporters aren't famous. It was when television channels began reporting the story in the same way—especially the hugely influential Globo network—that this narrative reached tens of millions of people across the continent. For Monday night, the date that the MPL had planned the next protest, Globo made a big decision. They were going to cancel the transmission of the *telenovela* so they could cover the protest live.[1] For the first time, the papers and the talking heads on TV began to distinguish between "good" and "bad" protesters—affirming that honest citizens were exercising their right to protest, and that a small minority sometimes made trouble. As a result, they granted the movement a legitimacy they had denied a few days earlier.

The MPL rejected this distinction on principle—but they had a lot of other issues to deal with. They spent the entire weekend in a set of endless meetings. Lucas "Vegetable" Monteiro, and many others, were convinced that the demonstrations ran the risk of having their message diluted—that is, given all the new attention, people would bring in their own demands and take the focus off the bus fare. As luck would have it, Saturday, June 15, was the opening match of the FIFA Confederations Cup international soccer tournament in Brasília, a kind of test run for the bigger event set for 2014— and protesters came out, shouting, "We don't want the World Cup, we want health and education." Of course, the MPL activists were deeply opposed to ever telling anyone what to do, but they wanted to keep their message out there. They decided to remain laser-focused on the twenty-*centavo* price increase and engage once more with the country's oligarchical media structures. They planned a press conference and decided that Nina and "Vegetable" would go on a major interview program during the next protest.

On Monday, June 17, the promise that had been made by those kids at the beginning of the protests came true. It was bigger. A lot bigger. Demonstrators were supposed to meet in the Pinheiros neighborhood, at the big "Potato Square." Except you couldn't get anywhere near there. I hopped out of a car that had stopped making progress a full thirty-minute walk from the protest's gathering point, and made my way toward the demonstration.

Except I was already sort of in it. Everyone else on the street was walking to the same place. And I never actually arrived anywhere. The further I walked, the thicker the crowd got, until, imperceptibly, we had become part of a long march making its way across São Paulo. The thing, this thing that we now were, had easily taken the place of all car traffic on the main thoroughfare where the MPL had done battle two weeks ago. Police were nowhere to be found.

I didn't have Instagram in those days, but if I did, I might have seen a post made by Alex Atala on the way to the square a bit earlier. The celebrity chef, who ran a world-famous and very expensive restaurant in São Paulo, appeared on the social network wearing a shirt that read "V for Vinegar." He posted a snippet from the Brazilian national anthem: "You will see that your son does not flee from battle." In response to his photo, the Brazilian fashion designer Alexandre Herchcovitch responded, "I will be there."

The target of the march was the Ponte Estaiada, a big, famous, ugly bridge around seven miles from my apartment downtown. It is really named after the late Octavio Frias de Oliveira, heir to an aristocratic fortune, banker, and owner of the *Folha de S.Paulo* newspaper, but everyone calls it the "cable bridge." I knew, vaguely, that we were headed in that direction, but in practice we were just trudging across freeway, on and on and on.

The people were slightly different. The same punks and left-wing student-union types were there, but there were new people, too. The only way to describe such a varied chunk of São Paulo, I think, is that they were normal Paulistanos, if younger and more privileged than the median. I saw something like the same spectrum of people you might see in a middle-class neighborhood.

As I plodded along, I pulled out my phone. I got a message from Juliana, my photographer friend, on Facebook Messenger. We had taken the cable bridge. The police had lost or given up. She sent me a photograph of that big, gnarly construction, packed with people, all of them now supporting the protests she had been covering sympathetically for weeks. Juliana suffers from depression and is not given to flights of fancy. She is the type of blasé Paulistana who frowns constantly and listens to darkly comic British indie rock. So I will never forget her caption. She wrote: "I don't think I have ever seen anything more beautiful in my life."

Then, in the crowd on my part of the highway, I saw something that I had not seen before. A couple of the protesters, obviously part of the "new" group, were decked out in a novel style. They were wearing all yellow and green, with the Brazilian national football jersey pulled tight over their big muscles. On top of that, they had wrapped the Brazilian flag around their shoulders. They began to belt out a patriotic cheer, the kind you yell in the stadium when the team is playing against Argentina or Germany. "*Eu, sou Brasileiro, com muito orgulho, com muito amor!*"—"I, am a Brazilian, with lots of pride, and lots of love!"

A couple punks, skinny kids with dirty clothes and much darker skin, scampered over to tell them that this was not quite right. They launched into a friendly explanation, the kind that is meant to let the new arrivals know how things worked around here. They had the energy of the nice guys in the mosh pit, who tell the obvious newcomers how to have fun and stay safe (elbows down, don't push smaller people around, pick up anyone that falls). "Empty nationalism at a protest is dangerous," one of the punks said. "We have to focus on concrete political objectives." They explained, very patiently, that some protesters might see the Brazilian flag as a conservative symbol or tantamount to fascism, since in the context of a demonstration (rather than a football game), it was wrong to insist that everyone in the country agrees on everything.

The burly newcomers made it very clear, very quickly, that they didn't give a fuck about any of that left-wing bullshit, and they didn't come here to attend a lecture on political theory from some punks. The kids, sensing trouble, skittered away.

The crowd kept marching. How long had we been walking? Four hours? Six? Was anything going to happen? That was it? Thousands and thousands of us just walking across the city? I peeled off and popped into one of the city's trusty bakery/coffee shop combinations to write up my story for the *Los Angeles Times* and check the rest of the internet for news. The crowds were monstrous in size, according to the people with the expensive cameras and helicopters required to measure these things. Hundreds of thousands of people had participated, in twelve cities, making this the biggest demonstration in Brazil since 1992.[2] Since the 1984 campaign to reinstate direct presidential elections, and the "painted faces" movement to impeach Fernando Collor (the man who beat Lula in 1989), Brazil had not lived through any mass contention. A Globo correspondent in New York, Jorge Pontual, rejected the idea that the internet was responsible for the mass mobilization. He credited his own television station.[3] I was deeply tired, far from home, and you might even say, perplexed. This was all very anticlimactic. I sent in my story from the bakery.

The next morning, I started the now-familiar journalistic ritual of posting articles to the internet, promoting and defending them on Twitter, and discussing the day's events. But there was another battle taking place. Over what had happened the day before. Over what the protests were about. Why people took to the street, and what they wanted.

During the march, Lucas "Vegetable" Monteiro and Nina Cappello had appeared on *Roda Viva*, or "Live Wheel," the interview show where a bunch of journalists literally surround the guests, asking them questions, and they had done incredibly well. It may have helped generate sympathy that one of the interviewers was Giuliana Vallone, sporting a giant black eye from the police violence on Thursday. But they mostly impressed the panel with their deep knowledge of transportation policy in Brazil. They had done their research, and the journalists could tell. "You know, journalists are lazy," Lucas "Vegetable" Monteiro would joke to me later, "so any preparation takes them by surprise." I responded that I might put it differently, that we are bound by the economics of the contemporary industry to immediately produce engaging content with dwindling resources, but I took his point. Crucially, they remained unflappable and disciplined on the show, fully committed to the reduction of the bus fare as the focus of the protests. People may have brought other demands into the streets, they said, but the only thing that united them was support for the initial cause—the real one.

Outside, however, participants and reporters and citizens and officials had seen an incredibly wide range of demands on display. Whether through signs that they brought, things they yelled, or comments they offered to journalists, the message was not exactly clear.

Scrolling Twitter on Tuesday morning, I saw the same divergent set of interpretations, the same dynamic, that participants at Tahrir Square had complained about. I knew a lot of Brazilian journalists personally, and I knew the small community of foreign correspondents very well. I noticed that our explanations of what happened reflected our own biases and ideologies. For example, I tended to emphasize that these were protests about insufficient public services and that concerns about hospitals, schools, and healthcare, as well as the question of public safety, were variations on the initial theme. Another correspondent, a serious and experienced right-of-center commentator at Bloomberg, tended to see the people as rejecting a corrupt state. This had become a favorite conservative talking point since the Workers' Party began running the government. And he was right—some people had brought banners denouncing the PT or calling Lula a thief. You could also find images of citizens denouncing the esoteric PEC 37, a proposed constitutional amendment dealing with the technical legal question of which government agency investigates crimes. It was a favorite bugbear in the right-wing Brazilian publications that, frankly, I rarely read. Dom Phillips, for our little blog at *Folha*, recorded video interviews with a wide range of people, covering the spectrum of the (sometimes contradictory) reasons they came out on Monday.[4] Many protesters now explicitly rejected the message offered by the MPL itself. *"Não é pelos 20 centavos,"* one famous slogan declared—"this is not about twenty cents."

The Globo television station recorded and reproduced patriotic imagery, the "new" yellow-and-green protest style that had surprised me on Monday night. And for all kinds of reasons, Globo was far more likely to blast out photos of photogenic white women with their faces painted green and yellow than skinny punks. Who was telling the truth here? No one, and all of us. We were taking a fundamentally illegible eruption of contention and trying to make it legible. This was a horizontally structured, digitally coordinated, leaderless, mass protest. Concretely speaking, there were as many reasons for participating in the revolt as there were participants. Probably more.

We in the media were, well, mediating the explosion, through our own sets of conceptual apparatuses, and experiences, and unconscious biases, and the sources we had happened to meet. Those sources themselves were defined to some extent by all of the former. As chance would have it, Federico Freitas, the vegan musician who had founded the *Verdurada* or "Veggiefest" punk night (where both the MPL and the Movimento Sem Terra had events over the years) back in 1996, was following me on Twitter, and he put me contact with MPL member Daniel Guimarães, famous in the activist scene for founding the punk band Guerra de Classes ("Class War") and his role in the Free Fare revolts in Florianópolis a decade prior. So I had a source in the original movement throughout most of June. This must have made me more likely to trace things back to the original intentions of that organization. Was this analysis more *true* than all the other possible analyses? I have no idea. This was now a national revolt, and all my experiences were in São Paulo. On June 17, protesters stormed the grounds of Brazil's Congress and danced on the roof. The military police could not, or would not, stop them. Maybe this changed the future of the country more than anything that took place in my neighborhood. And then, as commentators farther and farther away began to weigh in, the picture was painted in broader and broader strokes. That predictable phrase, "Brazilian Spring," was used by ABC News, even though it didn't make much sense to compare a set of winter marches in a democracy with a popular progressive president to the uprisings that toppled North African dictators. The profoundly anti-military MPL certainly was not pushing for anything like the Egyptian solution.

Organizations that explicitly disagreed with the left/anarchist orientation of the Movimento Passe Livre found opportunity in the protests. One of them had international roots. Brazil was home to a small but dedicated group of radical free-market institutions, often linked to the global libertarian movement based in the United States. Estudantes Pela Liberdade was the Brazilian version of Students for Liberty, the free-market think tank funded by the Atlas Network and the Cato Institute, both based in Washington, DC. Founder Fábio Ostermann had learned a thing or two from pro-capitalist comrades in the United States, at free-market seminars in 2008 at the Cato Institute and the Foundation for Economic Education, and as a "Koch Summer Fellow" at a program paid for by the billionaire Koch brothers. Brazilian academic Camila Rocha, who has traced the rise of free-market think tanks in the country, calls the Atlas Network a kind of "neoliberal Comintern," likening the pro-business super-NGO to the Communist International, as it funds and coordinates organizations that promote its own very different ideology across the world.[5] Though Estudantes Pela Liberdade and associated organizations in Brazil (like the Instituto Mises and the Instituto Millenium) promote self-consciously "neoliberal" thinkers, they usually avoid that word (and its negative connotations in South America). They prefer the word *liberal*, which in Portuguese has none of the center-left connotations it does in the United States. It means freedom in a very different sense than the MPL understands it. It means "free markets."

Estudantes Pela Liberdade received funding from Students for Liberty in the United States, which they used to support a small team in Brazil. This also meant that the organization could not participate directly in political demonstrations in Brazil—that would be illegal.[6] But they saw possibility in the unexpected mass demonstrations. They wanted to create a "liberal vanguard" within the protest movement, Ostermann told me. So he contacted a friend, with the idea of repurposing one of their other slogans for the current moment. They created the Movimento Brasil Livre (MBL) and used the new Facebook page to call on people to protest—for the right reasons—on June 18.[7]

In Brazilian Portuguese, "MBL" sounds nearly identical to "MPL." This was intentional. The founding of the MBL was an attempt to enter the fray and redefine the meaning of the protests, Ostermann said. "We wanted MBL to sound similar to MPL as a form of contestation. Because we didn't want free transportation, we wanted a free Brazil, and we had a set of proposals— like the removal of tax breaks and subsidies, the opening of markets, and more competition."[8]

MAYOR HADDAD WAS BACK IN the city and facing intense pressure. The MPL was now amenable to meeting at City Hall. They explained their case and received the support of much of the City Council on June 18. Seven other Brazilian cities lowered transportation prices that day.[9] But Haddad did not want to drop the bus fare. He understood why the country had exploded in response to the violence of the police, which was itself revenge against the injured officer a week before, but that had nothing to do with transportation policy. Giving in was not going to stop it. "If I give in, then all that will be left as a target is you," he remembers telling President Dilma. "It's better I stay out in front and take the hit." Mayara was at the meeting. She was tired, distracted, and nervous. Haddad had always been so arrogant toward them, so dismissive, she felt. But she managed to deliver the standard MPL stump speech to the council. Only afterward did she realize that she had mixed up some of the details. She never liked public speaking. Either way, the city was not going to budge. The Free Fare Movement remained committed to victory on the streets. Later, on Tuesday, June 18, there were more protests across the country. In São Paulo, it started downtown near the grandiose Sé Cathedral, the city's main Catholic church.[10]

It was clear by now that the protesters had not actually defeated the police. The cops had simply stayed away. Except for some small interventions in defense of the governor's palace the night before, they had chosen not to engage. On Tuesday, with the streets to themselves, some of the protesters began to smash up businesses downtown, and another group took aim at City Hall itself. They tried to break into Haddad's place of work and began to demolish as much of the structure as they could. The workers inside called the police for backup. None came. Mayara was on the street nearby, and an older woman ran up to her. She must have recognized her from an appearance in the media. "They are smashing up City Hall! You have to do something. Tell them to stop." Mayara paused to think—it really was not a great idea, actually, to storm and trash those public institutions like that, and to threaten the employees inside. Should she go say something? That was not exactly the role she liked to play (protest authority, never; opponent of direct action, that would be a first). She continued considering her options, until something broke her concentration. Right next to her, a group of protesters surrounded a TV news van belonging to the Record station and set it on fire.

TURKISH PRESIDENT RECEP TAYYIP ERDOĞAN placed a phone call to President Dilma Rousseff. Brazil, especially under the Workers' Party, sought to maintain good relations with all other countries in the "developing" world, and she knew him well after a visit to Istanbul in 2011. She took the call, of course. He wanted to warn her. He believed that something very strange was happening with these digitally coordinated mass protests, and he suspected that both countries—Turkey and Brazil—were the target of some kind of destabilization program. This could be a coup attempt, organized by foreign elements, perhaps in concert with the local deep state or some other shadowy forces. Dilma did not agree. Her theory was that once you deliver citizenship and some of its associated social benefits to a previously oppressed population, they ask for even more. That was only natural. She came up in this country as a dissident, and she was not going to be an anti-protest president. Later, Russian president Vladimir Putin shared a similar message with Dilma. By now, he was convinced that the West had coordinated "color revolutions" in a bid to shake vulnerable nations to the core and expand US hegemony.[11]

On Tuesday June 18, President Dilma went on television. And she praised the spirit of the protests. "Today, Brazil awakened stronger. The grand protests yesterday have proved the energy of our democracy, the strength of the voice of the streets, and the civic spirit of our population," she began. She praised the peaceful protesters—and their patriotic gestures—while distinguishing them from a destructive minority. But overall, she said, it was worth it. "I saw a poster yesterday that I found really interesting, that said, 'Please forgive the inconvenience, we are changing the country.' I want to say that my government is listening to these voices."

The dam broke the next day. Even though around 150 protesters had gathered outside his house the night before, Mayor Haddad started the day believing he was going to stand firm on the price hike. But then, Rio de Janeiro mayor Eduardo Paes called him and said he was giving in on his own. Haddad called in to Brasília, and it became clear there was no way out. He called a press conference and, standing next to Governor Geraldo Alckmin, announced that the fare was coming back down.

Mayara and the MPL, who had barely slept for weeks, absolutely lost their minds. They were delirious with victory. They drank, they cried, and they hugged each other tight. "We never gave up, we never gave up," Mayara said as she embraced a longtime friend. They belted out protest slogans, some now a decade old, that had marked the history of their fight: *"Ei MPL, qual é a sua missão? Abaixar a tarifa e fazer uma revolução!"*—"Hey, MPL, what is your mission? To bring down fares and create a revolution!" Mayara called up Senator Eduardo Suplicy, a little bit tipsy, and sang "The Internationale," the song of the international workers' movement, to him over the phone. At their base at the Tortura Nunca Mais offices, they lit one of their model turnstiles on fire, and danced around it, holding hands, in a circle.

In the meticulous preparations that the Movimento Passe Livre had spent the year designing, they had predicted that they would defeat the bus fare rise on June 19. They had gotten the day exactly right.

There was only one problem, Lucas "Vegetable" Monteiro said. "We had planned every single detail, down to the moment we would succeed. But we had absolutely no plan for what came after that."

THE MPL CALLED A FINAL street action, a celebration more than a protest, for Thursday, June 20. It started before they could even get there. The members of the Free Fare Movement were exhausted, hung over, and unsure how to interact with this particular awakened giant. There had been frenzied discussion among left-wing groups, including the PT, as to whether they should participate on the streets that day. It was well understood by then that they may not be welcome. In the end, they elected to make their presence known, and the MPL decided to form a kind of "security cordon" around them within the protest. This was a novel position for them to take. In years past, of course, they had often whispered to young punks that they should go rip down any flag on the streets. But they weren't an *anti-party* organization. This confusion, between *apartidarismo* and *anti-partidarismo*, worried them, and they put out a note affirming that these groups had been there since the beginning of June.

In over one hundred cities across the country, two million people were on the streets. This was now the largest protest movement in Brazilian history.[12] Only a week had passed since the day of the police attack, but I can remember every single day of the intervening week vividly—every street action, and every twist and turn in the battle to interpret and resignify them online afterward. It felt like time had slowed down. And it felt like the trajectory of history was being hammered out on Facebook, on Twitter, and in the comments section of the Movimento Passe Livre page. I could see the writing on the (digital) wall. I knew that things would be different. There were all kinds of people on the street that day. But all I saw was fighting.

I showed up to Avenida Paulista around sunset. As I got to the avenue, I saw some of the same parties that had been the core participants on June 13, and they had fear in their eyes. They tried to make their way forward, gingerly holding their purple and yellow and red and black flags, but a line of burly men was holding them back and shouting them down. "*Sem partido! Sem partido!*" they screamed in their faces, as more and more of the crowd joined in. "No parties! No parties!" I couldn't see the MPL anywhere, but obviously their defensive plan had not worked. The big men began to push the young leftists, hard, until they were violently expelling them from the avenue onto side streets. The group that spilled out onto my street was from the PSOL socialist party, which had some representation in Congress and committed itself loudly to the defense of LGBT and minority rights. They looked down at the ground, shocked, and dejected, and embarrassed. It was obvious they didn't know what to do. There was a deep sadness in their eyes, and no one could even summon the energy to discuss what had just happened. A few blocks over, a member of the Landless Workers' Movement, the famous MST, made his own retreat. He stopped to speak with Piero Locatelli. "We lost. We lost. It's all over. All we can do is leave."[13]

11

Five Causes, Four Fingers

IN THE MIDDLE OF THE street explosion, the hacking collective "Anonymous" uploaded a video to the internet. These videos always went the same way. There was a man in that *V for Vendetta* mask sitting at a desk. There were some static visual effects, as if the group had infiltrated your computer. Then you hear a male voice, distorted by another cheap video editing tool.

In this video, the man outlined a set of demands. He said that the country must put politics aside and unite behind issues "with no ideological or religious content," which the entire country could agree upon. The "five causes" for which the streets were fighting. First, they would stop PEC 37, that constitutional amendment which would stipulate that only police, not the public prosecutor's office, can investigate crimes. Even for me, someone who had been covering Brazilian politics very closely for years, the consequences of those jurisdictional disputes did not seem especially obvious. Second, Senate President Renan Calheiros must be removed (this one seemed quite political). Third, irregularities in World Cup projects would be investigated and punished. Fourth, congressional corruption would be categorized as a "heinous crime" (this would not change much in practice). And fifth, an end to the "privileged forum," which means that charges against sitting politicians must be tried by the Supreme Court. Notably, none of these demands would lead to concrete, direct benefits for regular people—they were all judicial adjustments or dealt with elite politics—and did not address economic justice at all.

Over the next few days, protest signs in support of "5 *causas*" popped up all over social media. If you wandered the streets of Brazil from June 14 to the end of the month, there were a lot of slogans you might decide represented the movement. There was "V for Vinegar," of course. There was *o gigante acordou*, meaning "the giant has awakened," which dovetailed nicely with a longtime right-leaning slogan, "Wake up, Brazil!" There was *Não é pelos 20 centavos*—which proclaimed that this was about much more than the bus fare price hike. Football came into the mix quickly (and not only because Mayara and other MPL members had coordinated with the *ultras* of Brazil to participate). Riffing on the exacting standards imposed by the World Cup organizers for the (very expensive) stadiums being built, signs read, "We want schools and hospitals up to FIFA standards." This one, to me, seemed to capture the essence of a range of sentiments I had heard over the past several years: we want to actually live like the First World, not just be accepted by them. We want our people to have the comfort and security that a foreigner attending the World Cup will have. And if you liked, if that was the project that spoke to you, it would have been just as possible to claim that the June protests were about the "five causes."

Over the entire week, President Dilma Rousseff developed her own technique for trying to read the streets. She would sit in the presidential palace, watching television feeds of the protests—GloboNews, specifically—with the sound off. If she removed the mediation provided by the channel's commentators, she could stare intently at the people themselves and make note of the signs they were holding. She could try to let them speak to her directly. Of course, this method was limited to the images the Globo conglomerate chose to record and transmit, but it's not like she could wander among the crowd, as I had done—and even if that were possible, demonstrations took place in a hundred cities at the same time. So she sat, and she studied the screen.[1]

After Mayor Haddad gave in to the MPL, President Dilma Rousseff called a set of emergency meetings and considered a number of ways she might respond to the dizzying sets of street manifestations. If you believed—like I did—that the whole thing was fundamentally about better public services, then this was a strange paradox. Given the actual arrangements of Brazilian politics, nobody was pushing harder for an expanded welfare state than the PT (and the closely allied PCdoB). You could view the explosion as an outcry for the government to do more of what it was already doing. This was the basic conclusion that Lula drew in a July *New York Times* editorial.[2] "In the last decade, Brazil doubled its number of university students, many from poor families. We sharply reduced poverty and inequality. These are significant achievements, yet it is completely natural that young people, especially those who are obtaining things their parents never had, should desire more."

At the same time, Lula and President Rousseff definitely saw the antigovernment sentiment on the streets—the denunciations of corruption, and conservative-patriotic outrage directed squarely at their party.

Mayara and other members of the MPL sat down with Dilma Rousseff in Brasília on June 24. It went about as you would expect, Mayara thought, considering that their movement's goals were pretty clear, and the president couldn't change national policy in a single meeting. Arriving in that conference room with the president that day, Mayara realized that despite their political differences, Dilma was "our kind of people." The president realized immediately that the exhausted activists were famished and got someone to feed them some Brazilian cheesy bread. Unlike Haddad, who always came across as academic and aloof, Dilma had the bearing of a fighter, just like them.

But after the meeting, disaster struck. No one and everyone is a spokesperson for the Movimento Passe Livre, and among the many things that the group told the press after the meeting, MPL member Marcelo Hotimsky let fly that Dilma's office was "unprepared" to discuss the issue of public transportation. It was a glib comment, and Mayara was gutted. "Of course the press will choose it as the headline," she thought. By now, some people on both the left and right were claiming, for their own reasons, that the June uprising was a conservative movement aimed at dislodging the Workers' Party and the country's first woman president. Mayara thought those people, as wrong as they were, would use Marcelo's comment to buttress their arguments. They did.[3]

That same day, President Dilma Rousseff announced "Five Pacts with Brazil." She declared her support for the "heinous crime" designation demanded by that Anonymous video, and Congress quickly killed PEC 37, as the man in the mask had wanted. The most important of Dilma's five "pacts" was a proposed referendum to amend the constitution. This would allow for "political reform" of the type that her party had long sought. This would require uniting the rest of Brazil's political class behind the idea—no easy feat, but in the weeks after she put it forward, 68 percent of Brazilians said they supported the project.[4]

Congress was also desperate to do something that would show they were listening to the streets. Senate President Renan Calheiros from the more conservative Brazilian Democratic Movement (PMDB) party (who had definitely been accused of corruption and was definitely not being removed) put forward a big package of legislation that was meant to clean up politics. One of the laws had been in the works for years, the result of international cooperation and pressure from abroad since the early 2000s. It wasn't much noticed in the flurry of changes, but Lei 12.850/2013 would modify the rules for investigating "criminal organizations." Most importantly, it made possible the widespread use of *delações premiadas*, or plea bargain deals, as long as the targets were defined correctly.[5]

Behind the scenes, major players in Brazilian politics—including Vice President Michel Temer, who had not been invited to those weekend emergency meetings—made it very clear to Dilma that they were not going to countenance the kind of political reform she had announced on television. Quietly, the president backed off, and the constitution remained unchanged.[6] But Lei 12.850/2013 soon changed things in the country.

Brazil has a "civil law" system derived from continental European traditions, which is very different from the "common law" system in place in the United States. Notably, judges in Brazil are not as bound by "precedent" as their North American counterparts. Lower courts have a wide range of leeway to rule as they please and are often overturned by higher courts on appeal. The tactic of threatening a suspect with jail time and then offering him a way out if he turns someone else in was not part of the legal architecture. It was largely the influence of the United States that led Brazil to adopt plea bargain techniques. As a result of pressure from Washington, direct contact between Brazilian and US jurists and officials, and the ambient assumption that things in the United States just worked better, authorities had pushed for the ability to investigate the same way as cops in the US for years. And after 2013, they could.[7]

AFTER GEZI PARK FAILED TO unite behind the "big brothers" on the organized Turkish left, Erdoğan's government tried to construct negotiations of their own.[8] On June 12, they invited a group of high-profile supporters, including television actors, to talks. This was widely rejected in the square, so the government came up with a different group, comprising some of the activists and NGOs who had more meaningful connections to the move- ment. This was better; but it was still the state selecting who would represent Gezi Park, not the movement itself. If you care about the ends (not just the means) of your protest movement, then you can't cede the power of represen- tation to some external actor, wrote Turkish political scientist Cihan Tuğal. Certainly not to your antagonist.

To sum up the dynamic at work here—in Egypt, in Turkey, and indeed across the mass protest decade—Tuğal paraphrased one of Marx's most famous lines, in *The Eighteenth Brumaire of Louis Bonaparte*: "Those who cannot represent themselves will be represented."[9]

The Turkish government presented a deal as a fait accompli. The people would keep the Park if the country voted for it in a national plebiscite, but that was it. Nothing else. Take it or leave it. The people in the park were split on that proposal, and there was no mechanism for deciding how to respond collectively.[10] Apparently, many people within the government felt deeply frustrated that they could not find a negotiating partner—the best outcome might have been to give the people (or at least, these influential people in Istanbul) some of what they said they wanted.*

They received no answer from the Square—how could it give one? At an AKP rally in the capital, the prime minister announced the government would clear the park. Authorities did so, by force, on June 15. Assemblies and neighborhood forums sprang up for a while outside the park, but energy began to taper off. Regular people had to go back to their jobs. The groups could not make binding decisions or take concrete action.

ON JUNE 29, 2013, THE Tamarod—"Rebellion"—movement in Egypt announced that it had collected more than twenty-two million signatures demanding that Mohamed Morsi call new elections. From the beginning, the group had represented itself as the heir to the spirit of 2011, the succes- sor movement to Tahrir Square. They were young revolutionaries, using the internet to organize and call for an end to the excesses of the Muslim Broth- erhood government. On June 30, millions of people took to the streets.

---

* At one point, Taksim Solidarity offered five demands: Gezi must remain a park; punish officials responsible for repression; free imprisoned protesters; allow for assemblies to meet in the park; and commit to preserve public spaces and freedom of expression in Turkey.

Gehad, who hated Morsi, went, but she thought this protest was very strange. This was very different from 2011. Back then, she had risen to action after seeing a protester face down police violence. This time, the police were supporting the demonstration, and protesters were taking selfies with cops. The June 30 movement also had the backing of major media, which had been building up to this date for weeks. This didn't feel like an uprising; this was more like a festival. A coordinated nationalist ritual. Military aircraft flew overhead; there were huge Egyptian flags and fireworks everywhere. This felt wrong. On July 3, Defense Minister General Abdel Fattah el-Sisi seized power. For himself. This was a military coup.

As it turned out, Tamarod was never as grassroots as it seemed. Gehad and many others would find out later that Tamarod had been funded by Gulf countries (especially the United Arab Emirates), the military, and wealthy businessmen.[11] Saudi Arabia immediately threw its support behind the new Sisi regime.[12]

"We were played," Gehad said. "Simple as that."

Morsi had millions of supporters in the country who pointed out that he had actually won the only legitimate presidential election in Egyptian history. They occupied the square—not Tahrir, but Rabaa, a few miles to the east—surrounding a mosque. Media spread exaggerated reports that the Muslim Brotherhood was planning violence.[13] The army raided and cleared the square, killing approximately one thousand people.[14] The Rabaa Massacre shocked human rights organizations, but it didn't change the situation for Sisi one bit. The Muslim Brotherhood was banned. Dictatorship was back in Egypt. Simple as that.

In the summer of 2013, Erdoğan would appear in public and make a four-fingered salute in solidarity with Rabaa Square (*rabaa* means "fourth" in Arabic). Even after his government had violently cleared Gezi Park, he still positioned himself as a leader who was in support of popular uprisings, as long as they were the right ones. Rabaa didn't have too many supporters that mattered, however. The rise of Sisi was a huge victory for the Saudi royal family and the version of Gulf-dominated Arab politics that had seemed so threatened since the dawn of a so-called "spring" in 2011.[15] The Turkish Model, and Erdoğan's dream of international influence, were in tatters. In 2013, Erdoğan lost Egypt, he lost much of the secular middle class during the Gezi days, and he was now deeply involved in a bloody quagmire in Syria. It did not look like Turkey was joining the European Union anymore. But his rule itself was not in question; Erdoğan looked forward to easy election victories, as his government gradually became more authoritarian. Not long after the dust settled, the bazaar shopkeeper, Hazar, joined the military and was in for a big surprise when he met the rest of the guys in the barracks. In the square, he felt the entire country was with him—but he found out that most of these guys, watching from rural areas around the country, were against the protests from day one.

THE MOVIMENTO PASSE LIVRE HAD to decide what to do next. After the messy, multimillion-person marches on June 20, the MPL did not call for any more demonstrations. Some of them thought they could have supplied a new demand—perhaps going all the way, for the eponymous Free Fare—to direct the huge amount of energy now on the streets. They found, just walking around town, that people would shout support for them. People would ask what they were doing next. But making such a decision would have required every single member to agree. It is hard to decide on an entirely new campaign quickly if you rely on consensus for your decision-making. Just as importantly, they were dead tired. Some of them were now very ill; others had lost a lot of weight. Mayara had been working the whole time as a waitress while organizing street combat and becoming a minor national celebrity.

They also had to decide how to deal with a flood of recruits who had shown up, though no one had actually asked them to join. How could they integrate everyone into such a tightly knit group? They attended another series of endless meetings, once more at their base at the Tortura Nunca Mais center.

Some members were afraid of inevitable, dreaded bureaucratization if they sought to expand or take advantage of their popularity. One proposal sought to eliminate the necessity that everyone participate in those endless twelve-hour meetings. There would be a general assembly for some things, as well as smaller groups for other things. This was seen as unacceptably Leninist. For his part, Lucas "Vegetable" Monteiro essentially wanted to abolish all of the group's existing structures. After endless discussion, a different proposal won out. The MPL would retreat from the spotlight in the middle of the city, neglect the universities and media, and go down to the people. They would concentrate on outreach in the *periferia*, the poor neighborhoods on the outskirts (or periphery) of the cities. Adjusted for the Brazilian context, this is the exact same thing that the original leaders of Students for a

Democratic Society did back in the 1960s after the media spotlight furnished them with a lot of attention (and, consequently, a lot of new members). "Vegetable" hadn't heard this story before, but when I began to tell him, he was able to finish my sentences for me, and predict exactly what was going to happen. "So people showed up trying to join a movement that didn't actually exist outside the media?" he asked. Right. "*Que loucura.*" What madness.

In Chile, many of the leaders of the 2011 student movement took the opposite approach. They decided to join institutional politics and stood for election in November 2013. Camila Vallejo and Karol Cariola ran for Congress with the Communist Party and pledged to join the "New Majority" coalition with the Socialists. Gabriel Boric and Giorgio Jackson ran as independents, associated with the Autonomous Left movement and the newly founded Democratic Revolution, respectively.

All four leaders were elected. They declared they would have "one foot on the street and another in Congress," but for many people who had joined them on the streets, this was a betrayal. They were joining the system. After Vallejo and Cariola entered the government, their allies back in the student unions quickly lost interest. And for the anarchist currents in the Chilean youth movement, all four of them were now the enemy.[16]

IN 2013, I TRACKED DOWN the man who had uploaded the "Five Causes" video. He wanted to be identified only as "Mario," but he proved to me that he controlled the YouTube channel that hosted the clip. We talked for a while on Facebook Messenger about how he got into politics, and how he heard about Anonymous. He never joined that group, he said—it doesn't work like that. He just liked the stuff he saw, so he got a mask and made a video in the trademark style.

What about the five causes, I asked? How did the group decide on those? "Oh, no one decided," he responded. He had simply made them up. He pieced the "causes" together from stuff he had read on Facebook and came up with a list. Five seemed like a good number.[17]

After the dust settled, the Datafolha polling group (the best in the country) did a new survey on Dilma's popularity. In the first week of June 2013, 57 percent of Brazilians characterized her government as "good" or "great." At the end of the month, the number was 30 percent. That is a twenty-seven-point drop in three weeks.[18] What is astounding is that not one of the issues that caused the June explosion had anything to do with the federal executive branch. Cities control the bus fares—and Dilma had pressured to delay the price rise. State governments control the police—and in São Paulo, the conservative opposition was in command. The Supreme Court is the final arbiter on corruption cases. President Rousseff had lost half of her support in a three-week period in which her administration didn't actually do anything except try to respond to the contradictory messages rising up from the streets. For any analysis that assumes voters act rationally based on access to information about their representatives, this presents a serious conundrum. What could explain the drop? No information became available about Dilma or her governance. Perhaps many people realized that there were a lot of things they didn't like about the country. One common explanation is that citizens believed she had responded poorly to the eruption. But what was the right way? Or, if you bring the media into your understanding of political reality—there is, of course, no national politics without mediation—maybe everyone experienced a few weeks of intense media engagement, weeks in which the government was framed as incompetent, or malevolent, or both. I have never seen a satisfactory answer. Her approval ratings never recovered.

PART TWO

12

Eu Maidan

ARTEM WAS TRYING TO UNIONIZE McFoxy, the burger joint in downtown Kyiv. This was not McDonald's but an obvious imitation, the kind of cheap spot that had sprung up all over since the fall of the Soviet Union. After growing up in a small town in Western Ukraine, Artem had finished his university degree in cybernetic economics in 2012, and he was working fast food to make ends meet. The pay was bad (about $1.50 per hour, even though he was promised $2), he had to work twelve-hour shifts, and the owners were breaking all kinds of laws. He lived in a big, cheap apartment with a bunch of friends, all of whom were interested in activism. Vegetarians, anarchists, socialists, or otherwise, they were trying to somehow make a difference.

So he came home one day and typed into Google: "How to organize fast food." He found a bunch of old American websites with information on a unionization drive at Pizza Hut and followed their lead. This did not work. Artem got fired after two months. So he started working at another restaurant, close to the Maidan, or Майдан Незалежності, "Independence Square," in downtown Kyiv.

On November 21, some people began protesting on the square. As they ate, some of the customers asked Artem, "Why aren't you going?" and he responded, "I have to work, serving people like you!" But really, the answer was more complicated. He thought that these protests were not really for him.

They were not that big, and they were protesting President Viktor Yanukovych for declining to sign an association agreement with the European Union. Artem was certainly no fan of Yanukovych, but as he saw it, a small group of Western-facing students and NGO employees were agitating for the government to take on a more explicitly neoliberal structure. For Artem, that association agreement was something that would help rich people, not regular Ukrainians. It would mean destroying even more of the threadbare welfare state left in the wake of the Soviet collapse.[1] Moreover, it seemed that opposition parties—just as bad as the president with just as many oligarchical ties—were trying to use the small demonstration to push their own agendas.

But then, on November 30, the police cracked down. Images spread through the country of special forces attacking students right in the middle of the capital. Later that day, people began to pour into the square.

This was now about something bigger than that association agreement, Artem decided. It was about rejecting police brutality, and it was about the right to protest. If it was about "Europe," he reasoned, that was an idea that was bigger (and more open to interpretation) than a single economic deal with Brussels. He and his friends needed to plant their own flag in the square and be a part of this. Artem and his friends were going.[2]

To Associate or Not to Associate

Ukraine was a very important part of the Soviet Union. The Communist Party of Ukraine was the largest in the Union (there was no Russian party) of fifteen republics, and Ukraine supplied Moscow with much of its top leadership. Three leaders of the USSR (out of seven total)—Khrushchev, Brezhnev, and Chernenko—had roots in modern-day Ukraine; it would be three and a half, if you count that Gorbachev's mother is from the country. And Ukraine was an agricultural and industrial powerhouse, producing much of the grain, steel, and advanced technology consumed by the rest of the Soviet Union.

Most of Ukraine was part of the Russian Empire before 1917 and joined the Soviet Union in roughly the same manner as the rest of the territories formerly belonging to the Tsar. The Bolsheviks took power after the Russian Revolution. There were certainly people there who wanted things to go differently (forces sometimes allied with the White Army held Kyiv as the capital of an independent Ukraine at different points during the Civil War), as was the case in many parts of the former Russian Empire. Moscow promoted Ukrainian nationalism until Stalin began to view it with suspicion and started to crack down. The Ukrainian Soviet Socialist Republic was devastated by the famine of 1932–1933, which brought mass death to the region as Moscow collectivized agriculture. This part of the nation also fought bravely in the Red Army, beating Hitler's forces back to Berlin after the devastating Nazi occupation of Central and Eastern Europe, and celebrated victory over Germany in 1945.

Another chunk of modern-day Ukraine, in the west, entered the USSR in a very different way. Areas in Galicia and Volhynia (with cities now called Lviv and Lutsk) were part of Poland in the interwar years. During the era of the Molotov-Ribbentrop Pact, the agreement between the USSR and Nazi Germany, Stalin and Hitler agreed to partition Poland. The Red Army went in and took these areas under the justification that it was saving them. Ukraine also incorporated parts of Hungary, and Romania during the war, growing considerably in size by 1945.[3]

It was in the western region that a radical version of Ukrainian nationalism took hold. In the 1930s in Poland, a man named Stepan Bandera, a member of the far-right Organization of Ukrainian Nationalists (OUN), began organizing attacks on local officials. He went to jail, until Hitler's invasion in 1939 allowed him to escape. The OUN welcomed the Nazis as liberators, believing the Germans might allow them to lead an allied Ukrainian state, and helped to massacre Jews in what is now Western Ukraine. But Hitler had other plans, and the Gestapo kept Bandera captive during the war. After the alliance with the Nazis fell apart, Bandera's faction (OUN-B) slaughtered Poles, more Jews, and Ukrainians they considered traitors. Then as the Red Army pushed toward Germany in 1944, the Nazis released him, hoping he would harass the approaching Communists.[4] After the Soviet victory in 1945, the OUN-B and its military wing, the Ukrainian Insurgent Army (UPA), waged a bloody guerrilla war against Communist Ukraine, with some Western support.[5] The KGB finally assassinated Bandera in Munich in 1959.[6]

Finally, there was the third part of the country: Crimea, the strategic peninsula that had been an important Ottoman trading port. It was part of the Russian SSR until 1954 and the celebration of the "Tercentenary of the Reunification of Ukraine with Russia." Both Russia and Ukraine trace their roots to the civilization of Kyivan Rus' (founded in the ninth century, when Vikings established themselves as kings ruling over Slavic lands), and official Soviet propaganda indicated that the 1654 Pereiaslav Council (bringing the Cossacks under the tutelage of the Tsar) brought everyone together again. As a lavish, symbolic gesture of brotherhood, Nikita Khrushchev transferred Crimea to the Ukrainian SSR (which would now also have the task of helping the devastated peninsula recover from the war).

As the Soviet Union collapsed, it appeared for a while that Ukraine and Russia might stay united. In 1990 the Ukrainian parliament declared sovereignty (but not secession), meaning that local laws took precedence over Moscow. Politicians in Kyiv passed a law prohibiting any demonstrations near the parliament building, but dozens of students descended on October Revolution Square and began a hunger strike, demanding the resignation of the prime minister. When the government tried to dislodge the protesters, fifty thousand Ukrainians marched to join them. It worked. Ukraine did not exit negotiations on Gorbachev's new union treaty, as they asked—but the protesters were allowed to present their case on television, and the right to protest was affirmed. This was the first time that "Maidan" could be used as a name for an act of contention, rather than a place, and the moment that taking this square became an established part of the Ukrainian repertoire.[7]

In the March 1991 referendum, 70 percent of Ukrainians voted for a renewed Soviet Union, and 80 percent voted for national sovereignty within that union.[8] In August 1991, US president George H. W. Bush encouraged leaders in Kyiv to stay in a renewed union with Russia. But everything changed after an attempted coup in August 1991.[9] Communist hardliners (some of them visibly inebriated) tried to undo the process that Gorbachev had started in the 1980s and failed spectacularly. In a December 1991 referendum, 90 percent of Ukrainians voted for full independence. This meant the end of the USSR; there could be no Union without Ukraine. That October Revolution Square, the "Maidan," became "Independence Square."

But the second "Maidan" event, in 2004, was far more famous and did much to reshape global ideas of popular contention. After the formation of Ukraine as an independent nation-state, former Communist officials became capitalists and stayed in power. The country experienced the same deep economic decline as most of the post-Soviet world. The collective gains of decades of struggle—the modernization, industrialization, and technological achievements, which came at such high human cost since 1917—were transferred to a small group of well-connected individuals, soon known to much of the world as "oligarchs." But Ukraine did enjoy the right to formal electoral democracy, and a polarization emerged which would be familiar to voters in most rich countries. Corruption was rife across the entire political class, which was intertwined with the oligarchical control of the national economy, but at least there were different teams to choose from.

In 2004, Viktor Yanukovych, a politician from Eastern Ukraine with a checkered past (he had been convicted of robbery and violent assault), faced off against Viktor Yushchenko, a former central banker now championed by the more pro-Western and nationalist camp, and his ally, Yulia Tymoshenko (known as the "gas princess" for the way she made a fortune in the 1990s). Official results indicated that Yanukovych had won, and Putin called to congratulate him. Tymoshenko called on the people to come to the Maidan and protest, and hundreds of thousands of them did, braving the punishing Kyivan winter to camp out for weeks. Yushchenko had deep ties to the US (his wife, Kateryna, was a US citizen who had worked in the State Department), and good reason to be suspicious of Moscow (he had been disfigured by a poison that may have come from Russia).[10] Western politicians and media offered support to the "Orange Revolution"—so named because the protesters wore Yushchenko's campaign color.

It worked. The supreme court invalidated the results and called for a new vote, which Yushchenko won, 52 percent to 44 percent. For many people around the world, this was an inspiring instantiation of "people power" (a designation born out of the 1986 uprising that removed US-backed anticommunist dictator Ferdinand Marcos from power in the Philippines), and it became the most famous of the "color revolutions" that took place in the former Soviet space beginning in Georgia. Like most of those, however, the Orange Revolution did nothing to change the oligarchical structure of the Ukrainian economy. Once in power, Yushchenko and Tymoshenko began to bicker over her business ties, and conditions remained atrocious for regular people.

But culture war is free. Yushchenko was able to throw some red meat to more nationalistic Ukrainians, if he couldn't deliver on bread-and-butter issues. A 2001 census indicated that 78 percent of the country considered themselves ethnically Ukrainian, while 30 percent considered Russian their "language of origin," and even more preferred to use Russian as a primary means of communication.[11] Under the new president, it became harder to do so—only Ukrainian, the official language, could be used in official government business, and Yushchenko pushed for more media in the national language. Many people experienced this new "Ukrainization" as the recovery of the national identity, and others felt it as a repression of minority rights.

In 2006 the government tried to make it illegal to deny that the Holodomor, the "Death by Hunger" in the 1930s, was genocide. While no major politicians denied the fact of the famine, this divided elites. The other side of this argument, as Yanukovych put it: "It was a tragedy, a common tragedy of the states that made up the Soviet Union"—that is, it was something the USSR did to itself, not something Moscow did to Ukrainians. Stalin was Georgian, and many people also starved in Kazakhstan and Russia. That kind of division, the disagreement over whether Ukrainian patriotism necessarily implied drawing Russia as the antagonistic other, was at the heart of two competing visions for the future of the country.[12] Then in January 2010, Yushchenko declared Stepan Bandera a "Hero of Ukraine." That man's organization had slaughtered around one hundred thousand people, and this was a step too far for a lot of people. For Ukrainians who prized the sacrifices their families had made serving in the Red Army, this was an insult. Both the European Parliament and the Simon Wiesenthal Center (the Jewish human rights organization based in Los Angeles, USA) condemned the move.[13] Yushchenko ended his presidency with dismal approval ratings, which dropped to as low as 4 percent in 2009.[14] But on his way out, he said he had stuck to his principles and celebrated the fact Ukrainian support for joining NATO had risen to as high as 33 percent during his presidency.[15]

In the 2010 election, Yanukovych won again. But this time, international observers certified the election as legitimate. Though I have never met anyone who says he was a great president, he was more favorable to economic interests in the east, and he was seen as the best option to the people with a different vision for the country. This "blue" voting bloc, in contrast to the "orange," saw Ukraine as a necessarily pluralistic nation and was suspicious of the version of nationalism based in Western Ukraine and its sometimes far-right traditions. Many wanted to preserve some of the things (especially basic economic security) provided by the USSR. In a 2013 Gallup poll, 56 percent of respondents in Ukraine said the fall of the Soviet Union did more harm than good, while only 23 percent said the end of the USSR benefited their country.[16]

The split between Ukraine's two camps was often portrayed in ethnic and regional terms, but it was more complicated than that, and it often had to do with class and urbanization. Even in very blue regions like Donetsk or Luhansk, it was possible to find people in villages who spoke Ukrainian and identified with ethno-nationalist or right-wing causes. Artem, who is left-leaning and preferred a more pluralistic vision of Ukrainian identity, is from the bright-orange west, but his city was split down the middle during the 2004 Orange Revolution. Identity in Ukraine is not as simple as family lineage, either—the question of who moved into cities, during the Russian Empire or afterward, and underwent proletarianization along Soviet lines, is fundamental to shaping contemporary loyalties. But until 2013, it remained largely true that far-right nationalists tended to be concentrated in the west, especially outside of cities (or in the US or Canada, where the Ukrainian diaspora favored hardline positions).

Putin favored Yanukovych over his rivals, but he did not like him very much.[17] Domestically, his version of government was an incompetent form of crony capitalism. Yanukovych's approval ratings slid downward soon after he took office while the wealth of his family rose. He could not offer his supporters much more than opposition to orange policies on national and linguistic questions. Conditions for ordinary people remained dismal. By 2013, Ukraine was one of only two former Soviet republics (along with Kyrgyzstan) where the GDP had not recovered since the fall of the USSR—the former economic powerhouse was now about as rich as Iraq or El Salvador.[18] After the collapse of the Soviet Union, millions of people left the country, and the total population had shrunk from fifty-two million in 1991 to only forty-five million in 2013. Popular destinations were Poland (which entered the European Union in 2004), where one could earn much higher wages (though immigrating was legally tricky), and Russia.

When it came to geopolitics, Yanukovych (like many leaders in Kyiv) played Brussels and Moscow against each other. The 2012 "Association Agreement" offered by the European Union required liberalization (meaning keeping wages down and cutting pensions), and it was not an invitation to actually join the EU.[19] Vladimir Putin did not want him to take it. The deal would pull Ukraine away from his economy, and could even serve as a prelude to integration into the Western security system. The unexpected, continued expansion of NATO since 1999 had rankled Russian leaders of every stripe.[20] The European Union was asking Kyiv to step over Moscow's red lines, without offering Yanukovych a very good reason to do so. The EU, a young organization that had largely avoided getting involved in geopolitical questions, seemed out of its depth. Russia, on the other hand, offered $15 billion and a great deal on gas (as well as all kinds of threats of sanctions and trade bans). Yanukovych was a crook, but it may have been rational for any Ukrainian leader to take Putin's deal.[21]

Escalation

On November 21, Viktor Yanukovych announced he was not taking the European deal. Mustafa Nayyem, an Afghan-Ukrainian journalist, used Facebook to call for people to gather in the square. A few hundred people, perhaps a thousand, showed up.[22] Maidan 3.0 drew on local traditions of contention—especially the 1989 moment, as well as the Orange Revolution— but it also took inspiration from more recent occupations.

On the first night they had a meeting in a bar, a tacky gastropub across the street from the Maidan. Mustafa said, "Ok—in Egypt they had dedicated people tweeting in English. Who is going to do that for us?"[23]

Maria Tomak was there from the beginning. She worked at the Center for Civil Liberties, a human rights NGO funded by Western donors. But she was inspired more by the legacy of dissidents active within the Soviet Union. Naturally, the Maidan would be a horizontal and "self-organized" movement, with a stage perhaps, but with no leaders, and she and other protesters used Facebook to coordinate.[24]

Social media was important from the beginning, and early demonstrators were largely middle-class and well-connected. But television was important too. Media in the country was controlled by oligarchs, often with television channels identifiably linked with a certain man and his business interests. Yanukovych had angered some (but not all) of this class by placing his own clan at the top of this system. From the beginning, outlets like Hromadske (funded by the Netherlands, the US, and George Soros)—this is where Mustafa Nayem worked—and Channel 5 (owned by chocolate industry magnate Petro Poroshenko) backed the uprising, while stations run by other oligarchs went back and forth as events unfolded, apparently in line with their owners' personal interests. But if you were far from Kyiv and watching Russian television (as many Ukrainians did over the following months), you would have ended up with an entirely different idea of what happened in the square.

In a place like Odessa (a major seaside town in the days of the Russian Empire known as the "Pearl of the Black Sea"), it is easy to find families, or even couples, who disagree among themselves on the very fundamentals of the uprising because they watch different TV channels. But in Kyiv, when the police cracked down on student protesters under the pretext of installing a Christmas tree, both social and traditional media spread the shocking images far and wide. Soon, one hundred thousand people descended on the square.[25]

Artem and his friends brought their own symbols to the Maidan. They took a red flag and sewed the stars of the European Union onto the corner. The idea was that they supported "Europe" in the sense of a social democracy and human progress, a vision of a continental future of prosperity and economic rights. Their priorities were direct democracy and "de-oligarchization": they wanted to put decisions, as well as economic power, into the hands of the Ukrainian people. And, they figured, if you were looking west to Europe, you could not defend any position that was misogynist or anti-LGBT. Their chant was: "Freedom, Equality, and Sisterhood."

This was not the only interpretation on offer. For other people, the third Maidan uprising meant something very different. Euromaidan was more diffuse in its demands than the Orange Revolution, since it was not clearly aimed at changing an election result. And of course, global digital and ideological conditions made structureless uprisings more likely. Just as in Turkey, it was the police crackdown that had set off the explosion, and there was no clear goal that could unite the group except opposition to Yanukovych.[26] Many participants were determined to avoid the perceived errors of the Orange Revolution, which had only effected a transfer of power between existing political elites.

From the beginning, the crowd included liberals who looked west, including those who were professional members of "civil society," such as Maria Tomak. Her group used Facebook to create Euromaidan SOS, a crowd-sourced digital service providing volunteer aid and supplies to protesters in need. The liberal wing in the square included workers in the tech sector—or young professionals who lived like people in Berlin or might have friends who went to graduate school with me in London. They were more likely to believe that the reform package offered by Brussels was good policy, often because those reforms would have benefited their own class. This was the easiest group for foreign journalists to find—in addition to speaking the language of democratic ideals, in English, their organizations have talented, full-time employees trained and paid to interact with people like me.

Veterans of the war in Afghanistan constituted another visible presence in the square. Like soldiers from many other republics, they had invaded that country as part of the Soviet Army. Opposition parties also had a clear interest in getting involved. In 2012 the right-wing Svoboda party had won around 10 percent of seats in parliament, and they controlled a part of the square. It was founded as the Social-National Party of Ukraine, a reference to Hitler's outfit, in Lviv in 1991. But in 2004 they changed their name to Svoboda, or "Freedom," and stopped using the *Wolfsangel* fascist symbol. They were still antisemitic—in 2012 a spokesman said actress Mila Kunis was not really Ukrainian because she was actually a "Jewess"—but they hated Russians most of all. Vitali Klitschko, a former boxer and center-right orange politician, was a constant presence, as was Arseniy Yatsenyuk, the foreign minister under Yushchenko, and Yulia Tymoshenko's Fatherland party. There was Automaidan, a loose group of people who had cars and were willing to use them to help the protest movement. A few Marxist-Leninists even tried to get their message out on the square. And there were also a lot of other people, citizens without clear affiliations or explicit political commitments, who just wanted the government to stop doing such a terrible job—to stop stealing, stop beating protesters, and try to get the size of the economy back to where it was twenty-five years ago. They tended to lean orange, or nationalist, but this was far from uniform.

And then there were the far-right nationalist militants. They are sometimes called "neo-Nazis" as shorthand, but if you get to know them, they will tell you there are different schools of thought within the movement. "Yes, a few of us are National Socialists," they will say, "while others are just fascist, some are arch-conservatives in the monarchist tradition, and others identify as warriors defending the white race."[27] They are mostly united in revering Stepan Bandera. Nationalist militants put up a giant portrait of him on the city council building so that his huge face looked out upon the Maidan

Square.[28] It has always been wrong to claim (as some propaganda narratives do) that in 2013, significant numbers of the Ukrainian population were on the extreme right, or even that the country had more of these violent groups than other countries in the region. But in the special context of the Maidan occupation, the far-night nationalists managed to punch above their weight. They distinguished themselves for several reasons.

First, they had experience fighting, and from the beginning they believed that violence would be necessary. If football *ultras* in Turkey or Brazil might be leftists, the super-fans for a lot of clubs around the world (including in Ukraine) were on the far-right. In addition to actual military training, hooliganism might have been a great way to learn a thing or two about conducting yourself in a riot. Second, they were united in an ideologically coherent project. These were not normal people with disagreements over how to improve economic policy. They were extremists, often ready to die for their cause, who dreamed of a purer Ukraine. And crucially, they were very well organized. These were absolutely not horizontalist organizations. British political scientist Richard Sakwa called these Maidan groups "neo-Leninist bodies of armed men strutting across the square, foreclosing pluralist options and undermining the representative institutions of the state." They were not Leninist in the ideological sense, of course. They hated that man. But they were tightly organized cells, laser-focused on their mission. Means were entirely subservient to their ends.[29]

The most important extremist group was Right Sector. It referred literally to where they stood in the square as well as their ideological orientation—a visual pun—but the group's constituent elements had been training and preparing for something like this since the '90s.

There were also self-defense groups, called *sotnia*, or "hundreds," which were being formed within the Maidan. The name referred to a specific Ukrainian tradition, which came from the days of heroic Cossack rebellions, of forming small cells to fight tyranny.

Artem and his friends, anti-authoritarian leftists, decided that they wanted to form a "hundred" themselves. They were committed to fighting for the cause, and their own self-defense group would reflect their particular vision for the country. They knew that Andriy Parubiy, one of the founders of the far-right Social-National Party (he left in 2004, as it became Svoboda) was overseeing the "registration" of the groups in Ukrainian House, a large building that rebels controlled on the square. One day in January, Artem and his friends got together around sixty leftists, anarchists, feminists, and social democrats, and presented themselves for duty.

Someone went off to deliver the message. As Artem and his friends waited, they took in a bizarre and spectacular scene. Young people with shields and weaponry were sparring and forming scrums and practicing how to push against police lines. They had formed a little revolutionary riot training camp. The anarchists in the group didn't really like the idea of waiting around for some "military-looking guy with a big belly" to give them approval to fight, but they stayed there for an hour. A guy just like that did appear and said, "You don't have enough people. You need one hundred. Come back in exactly forty-eight hours and come unarmed." This seemed weird, since they knew that other "hundreds" were around the same size, but they figured, sure.

Two days later, they returned. C14, the far-right militia, was waiting for them. C14 is the radical youth wing associated with Svoboda and derives its name from the neo-Nazi "fourteen words."[30]* They were definitely not unarmed. They had batons, knives, and chains wrapped around their fists, and they immediately got in their faces. "Get out of here!" they said. They insulted them for being leftists and anti-fascists. "You are not welcome in Euromaidan!" This was not the registration process they had anticipated.

"We decided that they had weapons, and we didn't, so a conflict was probably not a good idea," Artem said. They left. Far-right forces had managed to establish some degree of hegemony over the militant protesters gathered on the square. They did not pull this off because regular Ukrainians supported them—they fought for it, and they won.[31]

The militarization didn't only happen in the square. Starting in January, armed protesters occupied government buildings in Lviv. Militants seized a military arsenal, and hundreds of armed forces poured in from the region to the capital on a daily basis. Insurgents formed "People's Councils" and took power in Western Ukraine.[32]

In a careful analysis of the revolt, Ukrainian sociologist Volodymyr Ishchenko points out why it actually became rational for the radicals to escalate to violence and why the far-right nationalists were well-positioned to take advantage of that situation.[33] Ideally, a resistance movement can employ

---

* The words are "we must secure the existence of our people and a future for white children."

diverse tactics to put pressure on the state—strikes and boycotts are especially effective. These are core tenets of the literature and training, building on the works of US political scientist Gene Sharp, that had informed many activist NGOs and civil society groups since the onset of the "color revolution." But in Ukraine, union structures were weak, much of the industrial heartland didn't actually support Maidan, and boycotts were tepid (this situation is not so unique to Ukraine in the mass protest decade starting in 2010—strikes and boycotts have mostly taken a back seat to highly visible, massive street actions). Generally, the thinking has been that violent uprisings will alienate security forces (who must defect to your side unless you can beat them in a war) and the international community.[34] But after months of deadlock, the extremist minority, who were experienced specialists in the practice of violence, offered another approach. They had top-down decision-making, and they had a coherent strategy. They had been preparing for a war (against the left and Russia) for years. Right Sector was indeed prepared to start a guerrilla war—in which case defeating the Maidan uprising would mean waging a full-on counterinsurgency to retake Western Ukraine, and many people in the government knew it.

Abroad, things were different this time too. Major Western powers condemned the protesters' violence, but not as loudly as they condemned the government's repression.[35] Given this balance of domestic and international forces, more chaos and more conflict were likely to benefit the square in general, and especially the militant minority, more than they would hurt them. It was in their interest to keep the conflict on the streets, which they could control, rather than resolve it at the ballot box. At the height of their popularity in December, only about half of the country supported the Maidan protests, and support began to wane into 2014.[36]

The United States did not hide that it was backing the uprising. Senator John McCain had visited the square and told protesters, "We are here to support your just cause." Victoria Nuland, the assistant secretary of state for European and Eurasian affairs and the wife of influential neoconservative Robert Kagan, strolled the encampments in December and handed out snacks.[37] Actor George Clooney recorded a video in support of the Ukrainians who were "struggling to look forward, and not back."[38] Politicians in the creaking blue coalition were quick to point out that the international reaction might have been very different if armed protesters had set up camp in front of government offices in Berlin or Washington, DC.[39]

Why did the Western powers, and their most prominent media, look at Kyiv in early 2014 and see an uprising of "the people," rather than a specific configuration of political forces in a divided country? A cynical answer is that Ukraine could be used to give a black eye to Russia, which had become an official enemy again after Barack Obama and Hillary Clinton's 2009 "reset" failed and Putin accused the secretary of state of fomenting protests in his country in 2011.[40] But scholar Richard Sakwa points to a deeper set of ideological assumptions that shape the way we interpret events in the West. After 1991, he wrote, we came to believe in "the inexorable advance of liberal democracy and the 'European choice.' Marxist historicism was replaced by liberal historicism, the belief that the telos—or purpose—of history was knowable. This rendered all those who resisted…as not only mistaken but in some way fundamentally evil." On the other hand, the specificities of the forces pushing History toward its inevitable end are rendered invisible. The ugliness of the radical nationalists can be ignored as long as they are shoving the world in the right direction.

ATO

On January 16, the Ukrainian parliament passed a draconian package cracking down on the demonstration by introducing heavy sentences for illegal camps, banning the use of masks in public, and squeezing NGOs with foreign funding (which was most of them, including Maria's). The idea was to end this once and for all. It did the opposite.

The square quickly dubbed these "dictatorship laws." Opposition politicians, including boxer Vitali Klitschko and former foreign minister Yatsenyuk, called for snap presidential elections and constitutional reform. But from the beginning, the Maidan had always rejected the authority of so-called leaders in the political class, and the two men did not actually have any forces behind these proposals, or even any way to pressure for them. The square insisted on going further.[41]

On January 19, Automaidan, the militant car owners' collective, called for a march on parliament. When the procession turned into a violent confrontation, Automaidan backed off and distanced itself from the chaos. Right Sector, however, rose to the occasion and took responsibility for the violence (even if it may not have actually started it).[42] In the three-day riot that ensued, people lost their lives, and the news of the martyrdom of protesters revolutionized the situation indeed. Maria was shocked by the deaths and recalls that for the first time, many of her liberal friends adopted the repertoire—Molotov cocktails, pyrotechnics, and cobblestones—favored by football *ultras* and the radical right. "It was now us or them," she said.

Along with the violent standoff in the capital, the government had now lost control of much of Western Ukraine. This looked like the beginning of many civil wars throughout history.[43]

On February 18, the government tried to crack down on the square, this time by force, and it failed—not because of widespread civil disobedience, but because the armed minority fought back. Twenty-eight people died on that day, including ten members of the Berkut riot police force. On February 19, Yanukovych was ready to negotiate with the opposition on new elections and constitutional reforms. The events to come on February 20 made this impossible.

At 8:00 a.m., bullets began to whip back and forth across the square. Protesters and police both fell to the ground. This was sniper fire. Some shots appeared to come from buildings controlled by pro-Maidan forces. Over fifty people died—mostly protesters. Maidan supporters and international media responded to the massacre with horror. Security forces began to defect, unwilling to kill or die for whatever it was that the Yanukovych government now stood for.[44] Russian media, which had been emphasizing and exaggerating the role of far-right elements on the square, soon claimed that armed militants had carried out a false flag operation to provoke regime change.[45]

February 20 was Artem's birthday. After spending the previous two nights in the square, he was home resting on the day of the massacre. He spent the day receiving horrifying and conflicting reports of the violence, hearing all kinds of theories about the sniper fire, none of which convinced him entirely. By now, he knew that the far-right was a major part of the Maidan movement, but he had decided to remain a part of it, believing that opposition to Yanukovych was the most important cause—even though some of his leftist friends had decided to leave.

On February 21, Yanukovych hammered out a deal with the opposition (including Yatsenyuk and Klitschko) in a process overseen by the EU and a Russian representative in the country. A "national unity" government would run the country until new elections were held in December at the latest; an investigation into the violence would begin; and all sides would agree to an immediate cease-fire.

The Square rejected the deal outright. The Maidan, which now consisted of people willing to shoot or risk getting shot—surely a brave group but not one that could really be said to represent the entire country—wanted Yanukovych out now.[46] The president's life was clearly in danger.* Putin reportedly warned him against fleeing the country. But he did anyway. He hopped down to Crimea and then continued on to Russia, with the help of that country's government.[47] This cemented his legacy as a puppet of Moscow and a traitor, no matter how little Putin actually respected (or controlled) the man a year earlier.

There would be no national unity government. Parliament carried out prompt impeachment proceedings with armed men in the chambers, and without meeting all the legal requirements for removing the executive. Yanukovych continued to insist he was not resigning, and parliament could not assemble the votes needed to impeach. Nevertheless, they proceeded to form an entirely new government on their own, as elites sent representatives to speak with the "people's parliament" formed in the square. This is why critics of the Maidan say that it ended in a "coup," and at this level of analysis, the use of the word largely depends on which connotations one wishes to invoke and the degree of sympathy for the transition.[48] There was a rupture in the constitutional order, but true revolutions often entail some kind of break with preexisting laws. What often matters to participants is what comes next. Maria believes that Ukrainian institutions came close to collapse in those days and is grateful that politicians figured out a way to salvage them. And even if one chooses to use the word "coup," it does not always imply a transition from democracy to dictatorship—a coup can replace a monarchy with a republic, replace one military regime with another, or (as was about to happen in Ukraine) lead a country from flawed democracy back to flawed democracy.

And yes, there would be new elections soon. But for now, Svoboda took key positions in the new government, and eastern Ukraine was practically deprived of representation.[49] Andriy Parubiy, the far-right militant who organized the "hundreds," was now in charge of national security.

---

* In February, Radical Party leader Oleh Lyashko said that Yanukovych would meet the same fate as Gaddafi.

Artem came to the immediate conclusion that this was not a legal government. And it contained radical figures—a "bunch of freaks," he called them—who would not have won in normal elections. But he also questioned whether previous governments in Ukraine were truly legitimate, and he recognized that this group of men was facing a difficult challenge from an aggressive Vladimir Putin.

There was definitely not going to be any "de-oligarchization," as so many people had hoped a few months ago. The new government would remain just as tied to the existing political-economic elite, and its corrupt practices, as the last one. The economy was staying the same. What could they actually give the people as some kind of revolutionary victory? What had been earned through months of struggle and a hundred deaths? The post-Maidan administration could deliver a government that was more proudly nationalist and anti-Russian. Kyiv could turn back to an alliance with the rich First World countries and hope that this would bring some benefits for the country. The strain of Ukrainian identity developed in the western part of the country had moved to the center of national politics. For some people, this was a huge step forward. In the first months of 2014, crowds across the country tore down statues of Lenin, and the entire east and south (the blue half) had only two members in the ad hoc cabinet.

Since 2010, a pattern had emerged in the evolution of mass street protests. They start over something very specific; then they explode to include all kinds of people, accommodating numerous competing or even contradictory visions; finally, the resolution imposes very specific meaning once more. In the middle, infinite possibilities present themselves. At the end, any concrete outcome of the days of quick thinking and unpredictable actions and reactions will disappoint or alienate some people. When "Maidan" stopped meaning a spontaneous, pluralistic expression and came to mean that the elected president had fled for his life, and a more nationalist government took power without elections, this alienated a lot of people.

THE FIRST "ANTI-MAIDAN" PROTESTS had started well before February, mostly in eastern parts of the country, and they were directed by the Yanukovych government. In its final months in power, the Party of Regions did everything it could to get bodies on the streets and in front of cameras. But the formation of a new government led to an entirely new wave of protests with real support. A leaked phone call between Victoria Nuland and US ambassador

Geoffrey Pyatt in which she appeared to be helping to select Yatsenyuk as the new prime minister reinforced the belief that this was Western-backed regime change.[50] The toppling of Soviet statues was deeply divisive.[51] Parliament immediately voted to rescind the right to use any language but Ukrainian in an official capacity. Generally speaking, this anti-Maidan movement was more lower-class than the Maidan protesters, and it certainly did not enjoy sympathetic treatment from major Western media.[52] Some demonstrators wanted to signal opposition to the new government; others wanted defense of minority- (mostly Russian-) language rights, and others wanted a version of federalization for the country (a vote on this possibility was scheduled for May, but later canceled), which would devolve some power to regions outside Kyiv. The counter-mobilization had the support of the Communist Party of Ukraine (KPU)—which had won more votes than Svoboda in the 2012 elections—and even included some radical leftists who had previously tried their hand on the other side in the early Maidan protests.[53]

And then there was the reaction of the Russian government. At the end of February, Vladimir Putin simply took Crimea. It was stunning, both in its blatant violation of international law and how easily he pulled it off. It flew in the face of the international order to send soldiers in disguise into a sovereign country, organize a snap referendum there, and declare it yours. But as self-interested realpolitik, it made perfect sense. The peninsula was home to a hugely important naval base (far more crucial to the Russian military than the US Fifth Fleet in Bahrain was to Barack Obama), and the local population was not going to complain. The annexation was formalized on March 18. The West slapped sanctions on Putin, and he withstood them. The annexation of Crimea was wildly popular in Russia.[54]

THE LOSS OF CRIMEA MADE it even easier for officials in the post-Maidan government to write off the entire anti-Maidan movement as separatist, or a proxy for Russia. This was not true, but now everyone in the country experienced a sudden and unexpected loss. The new central government and its supporters felt they had been robbed of Crimea, while many blue citizens felt their pluralist vision of the country was being ripped away from them. Such universal resentment is very dangerous. Anti-Maidan protests took place in cities like Odessa and Kharkiv throughout March.

In early April, protesters seized local government buildings in three cities. With the added specter of machinations in Moscow, this was the same tactic used weeks earlier in Western Ukraine. New Minister of Internal Affairs Arsen Avakov declared on his Facebook page that the government would crack down on this kind of contention.[55] In the eastern Donbas region, the anti-Maidan movement gave rise to ramshackle volunteer forces, which had a significant degree of public support. Most locals there thought a "coup" had taken place, and many said they feared violent attacks from the right-wing extremists.[56] In April, many residents still hoped for a peaceful resolution within the context of Ukrainian law. Most people in this region, formerly the economic powerhouse of the country, had no separatist pretensions to speak of at the beginning of the year.[57] Most people wanted to stay in Ukraine. But when Russian nationalist Igor "Shooter" Strelkov appeared in the region, leading a commando unit of foreign combat veterans, its fate appeared to be sealed.[58] This was not going to be resolved among Ukrainian brothers and sisters. The government launched the anti-terrorist operation (ATO), with the support of the United States.[59]

We were very far from the digital world that Western leaders had envisaged just a few years prior. Bad things were happening all around, and raising awareness was very far from sufficient to stop them.

In Kharkiv, anti-Maidan protesters were quickly arrested. But in the breezy coastal city of Odessa, protests continued into the end of April. Then, on May 2, pro-Maidan football *ultras* descended on the city (it was match day) and clashed with anti-Maidan protesters. Led by Right Sector (Andriy Parubiy was in the city), the hooligans drove the anti-Maidan demonstrators into the Soviet-era trade union building. Molotov cocktails hurled into the building set it on fire. Some of those who tried to escape were beaten with clubs and knives. The rest burned inside. Nearly fifty people died, and Right Sector leaders declared it "another bright day in our national history." The anti-Maidan movement in Odessa shrank into the shadows in fear as far-right squads continued to threaten those perceived to be leftist or pro-Russian.[60]

The post-Maidan governments conducted trials and investigations into what really happened on February 20, the day of the "sniper's massacre." They have not been completed.[61] In 2014, a survey painted a picture of which types of Ukrainians said they participated in the Maidan uprising. Protesters were older than those in Egypt or Tunisia (most were over forty), and a majority had taken part in the Orange Revolution. Participants were richer than most Ukrainians, but this was less pronounced than in 2004 since the violence pushed some wealthy people away. Citizens who spoke Ukrainian at home were five times more likely to come out to the square; 52 percent of participants supported multi-party democracy; 42 percent believed that Gypsies should be allowed to live in Ukraine; 62 percent agreed with the statement that "strong leaders can do more for our country than laws and discussions."[62]

In the second half of the year, global oil prices collapsed. This was such an obvious blow to the Russian economy that some people asked if the United States and Saudi Arabia had colluded to punish Putin.[63] But as with sanctions, this did not keep him out of Ukraine, while it did affect the rest of the world. The collapse in oil prices pulled the rug out from under Brazil's precariously balanced economy, causing especially serious problems for the Petrobras state-owned oil company. As a result of Putin's actions in Ukraine, the United States pressured Dilma Rousseff to condemn Putin or disinvite him from the BRICS summit scheduled for July. She chose loyalty to that alliance over friendship with Washington, pushing Brazil-US relations to the lowest point in a decade.[64]

The Russian government was now clearly backing the volunteer forces in the Donbas region, though they didn't admit it. A protest had become a kind of a revolution, which became a civil war, which had now become a bloody international quagmire with no end in sight. For some people, especially nationalists who believed that a decisive break with Russia was necessary, the Maidan offered a kind of victory. Even Artem, who was so often disappointed by the direction it took, believed it freed some space for debate and independent media in the country. But things now felt very different than they had just a few months earlier, when almost anyone could pour into the square and articulate what a European future meant for them.

13

The Free Brazil Movement

IN JUNE 2014, BRAZIL HOSTED the opening match of the World Cup. It had been exactly one year since the Movimento Passe Livre started its campaign against the bus fare rise. I had wrangled a press ticket, so I hopped on the metro over to the new Itaquera stadium. I didn't like it as much as the old Pacaembu fields downtown where I used to watch Corinthians matches not far from my house.* The big, expensive stadium, built special for the mega-event, had just been finished. Barely.

This wasn't supposed to happen. Well, at least not according to a meme that had been in the air (and graffitied onto walls) over the past twelve months. *Não Vai Ter Copa*, it declared. "There will be no World Cup." A loose set of demonstrations, carried out with some of the same repertoire the MPL had used, insisted they would stop the tournament from happening, in protest of the lavish spending on stadiums like Itaquera. Over the previous year, the protests had continued, though they grew smaller and more radical in their tactics ("black bloc" participants were more common than yellow-and-green patriots), and lost the support of mainstream opinion over time.

---

* Not coincidentally, Corinthians is Lula's favorite team. The working-class fan base has a long history of opposing dictatorship, most notably when midfielder Sócrates led the Democracia Corinthiana movement in the 1980s. The expensive stadium would become the new Corinthians home pitch.

Brazil had prepared twelve stadiums in total, more than FIFA had asked for, even putting up new arenas in cities without major football teams. The anti–World Cup movement was pulling on one of the strands that emerged in June 2013—insisting money should go to basic social services, instead of soccer. Though circumstances had changed a lot since 2010, this was still one of the main reasons I was in the country—that old, slightly offensive question of "whether Brazil will be ready" for really big sporting events still guided my coverage. So I toured the country and the construction projects. They had certainly spared no expense.

The MPL had not had an easy year. In the first half of 2014, Mayara and many of her friends had felt off or anxious if not downright depressed. They felt that the government was closing in on protest and dissidents. In the run-up to the soccer, the Dilma administration had thrown its weight behind an ominous "antiterrorism law," and was using existing legislation to crack down on many of the people Mayara knew from a decade in the streets.[1] One by one, they began to be arrested for instances of direct action. Her Movimento Passe Livre group had experienced delirious highs in the days when they had unleashed a wave of protest on the streets and had floated on the crest for weeks afterward. They were welcomed and praised all over the city, and were greeted as heroes at small demonstrations in poor neighborhoods. The subsequent crash took them much lower than Mayara had imagined.

When it came time for the soccer to actually start, it felt like the entire nation turned to watch. There was going to be a World Cup, after all. Despite the months of political battles, and despite the feeling of low-level panic my friends in the media had helped to create, I arrived at the stadium with little trouble and took in the scene—nothing fell apart, and there were no angry demonstrators blocking the fans from entering. The crowd was composed of some visiting dignitaries and a lot of rich Brazilians. Tickets for this match were not cheap. Almost everyone was wearing the bright yellow jersey of the national team. As a crowd, they were about as white as me.

During the opening proceedings, they booed President Dilma Rousseff. Or, at least that is what they tell me. I didn't hear this myself; maybe I was distracted at the time, wandering the stands or looking at my phone. But I saw the news spreading through Twitter moments later, as Brazil and Croatia gave us an unimpressive performance. A narrative quickly took shape. The people had rejected Dilma at the opening match of Brazil's own World Cup.

Mayara had to work on opening day, serving beer to gringos in Vila Madalena, the closest thing São Paulo has to a tourist district. She was not looking forward to this; like everyone else, she wanted to watch the game with a glass of her own. But it doesn't matter if you're an anarchist or not, she always said—you have to pay for your beers somehow. On the day of the match, she woke up to terrible news—a few of her friends from the activist scene had been arrested and hauled off to jail early in the morning. She tried to keep this out of her mind as she worked.

As the game began, five police cars zoomed up the street and suddenly came to a stop in front of her bar. Her boss saw the look on her face and took her tray from her hands. Mayara ran into the bathroom, and her coworkers locked her inside. Moments later they knocked and told her that the cops had gone; they had just ordered something and left. But Mayara was still in panic. She couldn't move. She couldn't leave the bathroom. Finally, she stepped out and took a huge glug of *cachaça*. Her boss put her in a taxi and told her to get out of there.

The MPL members were watching the games too. But they decided to organize a protest a few days after the opening to try to put the focus back on the Free Fare cause. This was a disaster, Lucas "Vegetable" Monteiro said. They asked the government not to police the event; the idea was that they could avoid any unnecessary clashes during the tournament. They were going to put on a football match in the middle of the street. What ended up happening was a crowd they attracted split off and completely destroyed a high-end car dealership. Totally demolished it. It only served to reinforce the idea, now too common, that their type of resistance was uncontrollable and criminal, he said. Later in the tournament, on the way to a game in Rio, I saw another car dealership smashed up by anti–World Cup protesters.

I watched the semifinal match, Brazil against Germany, on July 8 in downtown São Paulo. I stood outside among a giant crowd, in front of a giant screen, in the same concrete Anhagabaú valley where Piero Locatelli was arrested for possession of vinegar a year earlier. Neymar, the scraggly young star from São Paulo state, was out with an injury, but the fans were undaunted. The nation was fully committed to victory. Brazil had won five World Cups in its history, more than anyone else, and this was home turf.

Germany went up 1–0. No big deal. Then they scored again, only twenty-three minutes into the game. The crowd went silent. Being down 2–0 is a serious problem in a semifinal. And then Germany scored again, and again, and again. It seemed Brazil had given up—or forgotten how to play. I am not sure if I can adequately explain the emotional shift in the crowd during those fifteen minutes, from the second to the fifth goal. This was a journey into the depths of the human heart. Initial dejection quickly transformed into horrified shock, which became stunned disbelief, which quickly transformed into a kind of manic eruption of laughter, with fans cackling in mad delight as they now openly cheered for Germany. "*Gol da Alemanha!*" the announcer cried out. "*Gol da Alemanha! Gol da Alemanha! Gol da Alemanha! Gol da Alemanha! Gol da Alemanha!*" The final score was 7 to 1. Then Germany won the World Cup.

IN OCTOBER, PRESIDENT DILMA ROUSSEFF faced reelection. Her main challenger came from the same party that had placed second in 2002, 2006, and 2010. Their candidate, Aécio Neves, came off as a bit of a playboy, but he was the scion of a family with democratic credentials. His grandfather served in the government of João "Jango" Goulart (the president ejected by a US-backed coup in 1964) and had played a major role in the redemocratization of the country. Most foreign journalists, myself included, labeled Dilma a "center-left" president and Aécio a "center-right" challenger. Brazil had apparently settled into the same two-party polarization that would be familiar to voters in many rich countries.

From a global perspective, there were not huge differences between the two candidates. Dilma's camp accused her opponent of wanting to roll back all social gains made by the Workers' Party and give the country back to rich elites. It helped her case that in 2014 the United Nations finally removed Brazil from its Hunger Map, which illustrates the countries that suffer from significant undernourishment, and praised the country for huge improvements over the previous ten years.[2] But Aécio said Dilma had mismanaged the economy, and he would do better. His program called for more "market-based" solutions, a script that is uncontroversially considered right-of-center around the world. But Aécio's camp and many supporters firmly rejected that they were to the "right" of anything at all. In Brazil, this was seen as something more like a slur than cold description. To be "right" here still meant to be antidemocratic and reactionary.

Then there was a third candidate. Marina Silva, an environmentalist from the Amazon and a former member of the Workers' Party. It is hard to spend time with her without coming to the conclusion that she has a pure heart. She carries herself like a gentle priestess. But there were two problems, at least as her critics saw things. People with pure hearts may not be great for politics in general, and they may be especially ill-suited for a Brazilian polity facing real economic problems. Aécio was not wrong that progress had stalled, or that many economists had criticized Dilma's governance—growth had nearly come to a halt in 2014. Keen observers could see that a storm was brewing.

Marina didn't have a strong party behind her, and she didn't have a network of support in Congress. Given Brazil's system, it might be incredibly difficult to hold a government together if she won on her own. The last person who tried something like that was Fernando Collor, impeached in 1992 for corruption. And on top of that, she was an evangelical Christian. Dilma supporters attacked her on this front, with success.

This dynamic led to a typically absurd North American intervention, perfectly crafted by the digital era. US actor Mark Ruffalo (who played Hulk in *The Avengers* franchise) made a video declaring his support for Marina Silva and uploaded it to the internet. He clearly thought the save-the-rainforest candidate was the progressive choice, and with the click of a button he told hundreds of millions of people to vote for her. But then, he was inundated with tweets from Brazilians telling him that Marina did not support LGBT rights, and that Dilma was the real progressive candidate. Ruffalo immediately apologized and withdrew his endorsement.[3]

Locally, the campaign became very heated, very quickly. During 2013, some left-wing protesters had taken aim at Brazilian media. I distinctly remember a group outside the *Folha* offices, shouting that the newspaper was owned by *latifundários* (the elite landowning class) and assisted the dictatorship in repression, because I witnessed one prominent reporter in the newsroom discover to their shock that both accusations were true.[4] But the 2014 campaign was the first time I saw and felt attacks coming from the right. On social networks, increasingly vocal Brazilians questioned the legitimacy of both the government and the journalistic apparatus.

As the election loomed, it looked like Dilma might actually lose, ending the PT's twelve-year tenure in the presidential palace. Her team pushed things to the limit, on both the discursive and administrative fronts, to reach for victory. The campaign slogan, *Muda Mais*, or "Change More," promised that social improvements would only deepen. It was the same response that Lula had prescribed the year before in his *New York Times* op-ed. The government also did everything it could to lessen the pain for the moment, putting off any difficult adjustments to budgets and salaries until after the election.[5]

Many members of the Movimento Passe Livre were anarchists, or otherwise rejected participation in elections as a matter of principle. As a group, the MPL never takes any position on political campaigns of any kind. But for many of them, the upcoming election was terrifying. It appeared that, for the first time since 1998, the right could actually win. The possibility that Aécio could take power seemed like the end of the world to many people on the left, and a totally unacceptable outcome to the Free Fare activists. So they voted for her. Mayara didn't feel the slightest twinge of doubt. She cast her ballot for Dilma Rousseff. Aécio lost by 3 percent in the runoff.

VERY QUICKLY AFTER DILMA WON, it became clear that we were not going to live through a socialist revolution. She appointed a finance minister whom most of the left considered to be a neoliberal. Cuts were coming.

The score of that traumatic soccer game, 7 to 1, had become a cultural meme. As bad news began to pile up—well after the end of the World Cup— Brazilians would say that "every day brings another 7 x 1." "My bus is late, again—another 7 x 1 for me." "Dilma is going to cut social spending—that's another 7 x 1 for the country."

Even though she had won, Dilma needed to shore up support with the other power centers that matter in Brazilian politics. These moves were seen as a signal to the "business community," both in the country and internationally, that she would keep things under control. Don't pull your investments. But the Workers' Party had always been walking this very thin line.

Far more shocking was the response of Aécio Neves to his election defeat. He gave credence to suspicions bubbling around on right-wing corners of the internet that the election had been stolen. His formerly boring, respectable party called for an official investigation into the results.

I had watched the final count come in at the offices of *Folha de S.Paulo*, where the journalists seemed to be split as to whom they preferred. It was high drama, of course, but no one was going to cry about either outcome. Things were different for the right wing, especially for the well-organized and well-funded institutions that had been trying to push *liberal* ideas for years. They experienced the defeat as a profound and shocking loss. The Workers'

Party had been in power for three terms now. Would they ever leave? At one election party in the southern state of Rio Grande do Sul, the news came as a lightning bolt. The organizer ran to the bathroom, locked himself inside, and began to weep. On corners of Facebook I barely knew about, they began to plan.

Just six days after Dilma's victory, they called for a protest to demand her impeachment. The event got the support of Olavo de Carvalho, an esoteric reactionary philosopher living in the United States with a committed online base, and they managed to put over two thousand people on the streets. On Twitter, I watched top Brazilian journalists chuckle at the folly of all this. This was just some kooks letting off steam. The only politician at the first protest was Eduardo Bolsonaro, the son of a shouty, extreme-right provocateur and long-term congressman named Jair Bolsonaro. This all seemed ridiculous. You can't try to impeach someone who hasn't even started her second term yet.

The Movimento Brasil Livre (MBL), the right-wing free-market protest vehicle born in June 2013, sprang back to life. Fábio Ostermann called up his comrades in the *liberal* movement and suggested they use the MBL structure to establish a presence in the anti-Dilma movement. It worked. Immediately, they were recognizable leaders of a new wave of protests. Alongside them there was Vem Pra Rua, or "Come to the streets," a group founded by businessmen and right-wing professionals in 2014.[6] Just like the name "MBL" itself, this was language taken from the Movimento Passe Livre.* The MBL excelled at presenting itself as a young, grassroots, tech-savvy street movement. Most of the public-facing leadership was under twenty-five, and one, Kim Kataguiri, who especially excelled at getting people riled up online, was only eighteen. Unlike most of the people in Aécio's party, they dressed like they knew what music was. A colleague of mine, a correspondent at Spain's *El País*, ran a piece on the group with this headline: "It's not an indie rock band, it's the anti-Dilma vanguard."[7]

The MBL and Vem Pra Rua were clearly appropriating the language, posture, and repertoire of contention that entered the national consciousness in 2013. But these were not anti-authoritarian, self-funded punks and committed horizontalists who would rather cease to exist than tell anyone what

---

* Piero Locatelli's 2013 book on the protests is entitled #VemPraRua.

to do. They got money from some of Brazil's richest people (and right-wing institutions based in the United States) to pursue clear political goals. That didn't matter. Their messaging strategy was effective. After one huge protest, the Atlas Network—that "neoliberal Comintern" in Washington, DC—publicly congratulated the MBL for organizing protests and "working to tear down Brazil's barriers to liberty."[8]

The MPL was under a lot of stress. Unable to direct energy on the streets, the group had begun to turn on itself. If the movement was supposed to prefigure a better society, some thought, then surely it could not be acceptable that the group appeared to reproduce some of the *machista*, or racist dynamics that are present in wider Brazilian society. As they fought internally, the appearance of this new protest movement was a knife deep in the stomach. It was obvious the MBL was stealing from them to trick people, and that it was working.

"This is a typical maneuver employed by fascists, going back to the 1920s. They take elements from the left and invert their meaning," Lucas "Vegetable" Monteiro said. The new MBL even performed a commitment to leaderlessness. "They take this anti-systemic pose, they adopt the aesthetics of the anti-globalization movement, they say they have no party affiliation. But they take money from politicians, and have the goal of destroying a single political party"—that is, Dilma's Workers' Party, he said.

Mayara ran into her aunt at a family event. This was one of her more conservative relatives, a woman who had chastised her for her political militancy when Mayara was younger. To her surprise, the aunt turned to her smiling and said—you will never believe it! I actually went out protesting, to one of your events. Mayara was perplexed—oh really, which event? Last year? Back in June? No, no. Her aunt was talking about one of the recent protests, the ones calling for impeachment.

14

Under My Umbrella

BENNY TAI, A LAW PROFESSOR at the University of Hong Kong, published a column with a proposal for a mass protest.[1] If the electoral reforms Beijing planned to announce soon did not deliver meaningful democracy, they should take action. Inspired by Occupy Wall Street in the United States, they should "Occupy Central," the downtown business district of the city, which had been a Special Administrative Region of the People's Republic of China since 1997. He and two colleagues, a professor and a Baptist minister—who collectively came to be known as "the Occupy Trio"—created an organization to prepare. This ad hoc civil society group, Occupy Central with Love and Peace, had pushed ahead of the official legal opposition, the "pan-democrats" in the local government.[2]

On August 31, 2014, the National People's Congress in Beijing revealed the anticipated reforms. The "chief executive," the top position in Hong Kong's very strange postcolonial governance structure, would now be elected through universal suffrage, but the candidates themselves would be selected by a nominating committee. This is certainly not what the "Trio" had in mind. Occupy Central with Love and Peace called for an occupation to start on October 1, the anniversary of the day that Communist China was born.

Two student groups—Scholarism and the Hong Kong Federation of Students—beat them to it. After a demonstration on Friday, September 26, Joshua Wong and other young Hong Kongers climbed a fence into Civic Square, outside government headquarters, and stayed there. On Sunday, September 28, Benny Tai recognized what had happened. Occupy Central was already underway, though it started earlier than planned, and in a slightly different location. The kids had pushed ahead of the Occupy Trio.[3]

More and more protesters began to flood Admiralty, the famous stretch of coast that got its name when the British Navy still ruled these waters, and they spilled over into a huge eight-lane highway. Overwhelmed, police tried to disperse the crowd with tear gas. Hong Kong is a very rich and well-ordered little corner of Asia, and most people had not seen any kind of repression like this since the 1960s. Live television, social media, and international outlets produced and reproduced shocking images of police cracking down on students. More protesters came out. And a single image stood out as especially poignant. A lone man emerged from clouds of tear gas, holding up two defiant little umbrellas.

The crowds got bigger and bigger. Chief Executive C. Y. Leung ordered cops to disperse, and the police ceded the streets to the uprising. In the center of Admiralty, protesters fashioned a makeshift podium, dubbed the "main stage," from ladders and planks. Central Hong Kong was now indeed occupied, and what the global press quickly dubbed the "Umbrella Movement" had begun.[4]

THE BRITISH EMPIRE TOOK POSSESSION of this small piece of land in 1842. After the First Opium War, in which Queen Victoria's invading forces successfully asserted Britain's right to sell addictive drugs on Chinese territory, the Qing Dynasty was forced to hand over Hong Kong in negotiations. The Queen herself complained that they should have gotten even more. After the Second Opium War, in which combined French and British forces crushed renewed Chinese attempts to impose limits on free trade, they did. Britain would now also control the large Kowloon Peninsula, and then in 1898, they got even more. These "New Territories" were not granted in perpetuity, just for ninety-nine years—and the lease would run out in 1997.

The British never ran Hong Kong democratically, and until the end of World War II, it wasn't even their preferred place to do business in the region. Shanghai, the Western-facing jewel in their Asian collection, was where they placed the main branch of the Hongkong and Shanghai Banking Corporation (HSBC) in 1923. But after the Japanese left, defeated in World War II, and Mao Zedong's Communist Party began to make progress against the US-allied *Guomindang* (Nationalist) forces, free-wheeling free-market energy began to move south. It was not just money but emigrants from the mainland that arrived in Hong Kong. People ranging from "fashion designers and filmmakers to merchants and mobsters," and of course lots of regular people seeking work, moved to the city. The People's Republic of China took control of the mainland in 1949, but stopped short of making a bid for Taiwan (now controlled by the Nationalists) or Hong Kong, and this mix of new people began to congeal into a stable society of its own.[5]

It was in Hong Kong that key elements of the global repressive repertoire were born; in the 1950s, British police began to fire wooden bullets at the ground with the aim of wounding protesters' legs, rather than killing them.[6] Experimenting more in Northern Ireland, this approach evolved into rubber bullets. (Tear gas was developed by the French who used it in World War I, and then to control uprisings in North Africa.)

During the Cultural Revolution, launched in 1966 by Mao Zedong to shake up the bureaucratic authority structures his own revolution had created, Hong Kong was rocked by a burst of contention. The Hong Kong Federation of Trade Unions (HKFTU), a pro-Beijing trade union federation, led a series of strikes after the Hong Kong Artificial Flower Company tried to cut wages and benefits for its workers. Beijing's representatives and sympathizers on the island turned their focus on the colonial system itself, while revolutionary protesters waved copies of Mao's *Little Red Book*. Clashes turned into mysterious bomb attacks, and then into mass arrests. But British imperialism had learned some tricks over the centuries, and officials mixed in some co-opting with their crackdown. Authorities liberalized the colonial system a little after the revolts, reducing working hours and introducing health and safety regulations for the territory. The colonial officials also tried to encourage a new sense of Hong Kong identity, distinct from a Chinese one—something that was quite novel at the time.[7]

But it was only after Margaret Thatcher and Deng Xiaoping hammered out the terms of the final 1997 handover that British authorities began to introduce democratization measures. The last governor introduced a flurry of reforms just before heading for the exit, leading many in Beijing to believe he was more concerned about undermining the transition than ensuring fundamental rights for his colonial subjects.[8]

Prime Minister Thatcher was perhaps one of the most assured liberal teleologists in history, and she believed as a matter of course that the flowering of capitalism would mean the arrival of a liberal democratic system. She was also very eager to avoid any disagreements that might result in mass migration from Hong Kong to Britain.[9] Paramount leader Deng, the man who introduced a series of market reforms after Mao Zedong's death, believed in maintaining the primacy of the Party, and he knew that the PRC was not even close to catching up with the West. At the time of the handover, Hong Kong (only 0.5 percent of the total PRC population) accounted for nearly 20 percent of the nation's GDP. The two leaders hammered out the wobbly concept of "One Country, Two Systems," and the "Basic Law," which maintained some of Britain's strange colonial system and promised (in ambiguous terms) the eventual provision of universal suffrage, for the election of the executive and the legislative council (LegCo).

In the late 1980s, the PRC itself saw an uprising of contention after the government started to experiment with some neoliberal "shock therapy" reforms similar to those enacted in Russia a few years later. When students and protesters filled Tiananmen Square in 1989, Hong Kongers became intimately involved in the uprising. Whatever sense of unique identity had been developed, many citizens—liberals and leftists and capitalists alike—felt that their future was intertwined with that of mainland China, and they acted in solidarity with counterparts in Beijing. The protests in central Beijing began as a celebration of deceased former Party chief Hu Yaobang, and for a time had the backing of many journalists in the country's state-run media outlets. The movement contained elements that pushed for further liberalization, as well as some that defended aspects of the old socialist system—though media abroad often read them as (or found voices that allowed them to appear to be) simple demands for a Western-style system.[10] Hong Kongers held a benefit concert for the protesters and funneled resources to the Square. The central government moved to crush the movement, violently clearing the demonstrations from the square—triggering a huge march in Hong Kong—and the Party remained firmly in control.

The PRC never fully embraced shock therapy, settling on a flexible, more tentative approach to participating in the market economy. Chinese economists called it "crossing the river by feeling the stones." That process—slow, careful, and constantly readjusting—worked a lot better than the package imposed on the former Soviet Union. In the twenty-first century, China caught up to the West (in economic terms) more quickly than anyone predicted in the 1980s.

From 1990 to 2017, Russia's share of world GDP was cut in half, while China's share increased sixfold.[11] It was this growth that played such a large role in powering Latin America's (much more modest) achievements in the Lula years. Countries in South America exported raw materials to the PRC, which used them for a boom in infrastructure construction.[12]

The Communist Party of China (CPC) had developed a deep relationship with the people of the mainland over the past sixty years, forging ties through Maoist people's war, the ups and downs of the Cultural Revolution, and the economic growth that brought hundreds of millions out of deep poverty. To carry out its national project, it relies on repression, of which 1989 is only one example, but the Party does not rule with the stick alone. The CPC is a massive organization of more than ninety million members, who are often accessible to citizens. They have learned to be responsive to (some kinds of) demands. A study conducted by Harvard's Ash Center from 2003 to 2020 found that a large majority of Chinese people expressed satisfaction with the central government, far surpassing comparable numbers in the US (though Chinese citizens gave lower marks to local officials).[13]

The Hong Kong Special Administrative Region had a relationship to the People's Republic of China that was not dissimilar to Western Ukraine's relationship to the Soviet Union: it joined the country late, after occupying pivotal space in the Cold War, and its residents shared little of the history, the vocabulary, and the triumphs and tragedies of the long socialist struggle understood by people in the larger country.[14]

As the 2010s started in Hong Kong, and digitally coordinated explosions spread around so much of the world, its governance mechanisms had not evolved very much. Half of the seats on the LegCo were handed out directly to special interest groups: "real estate and construction" and the accounting group got one each, for example, while financial interest groups got two. This system of "functional constituencies" was set up in 1984 under British rule, and it is the kind of blatant crony capitalist system that most rich democracies have to at least hide behind the scenes. The other half of the LegCo was elected on a district basis, and the "pan-democrats" managed to maintain a decent presence there, winning around a third of total seats in the 2012 vote.[15]

The people of Hong Kong had neither the network of communist officials that mainlanders have, nor did they have anything resembling Western democracy. Objectively speaking, the Special Administrative Region is materially privileged; it is much richer than the mainland and the other countries in the region. But from the standpoint of meaningful representation, "One Country, Two Systems" was the worst of both worlds. Even though the mega-rich "tycoons" (elsewhere they might be called "oligarchs") continued to do very well, Hong Kong became less and less important for the Chinese economy overall. By 2014, Hong Kong now represented less than 3 percent of the total Chinese GDP, and the city itself had become more and more unaffordable for locals.[16] Confidence in One Country, Two Systems had crashed, from 78 percent in 2008 to 37 percent in September 2014. The march of progress had stalled for Hong Kongers, both politically and economically.[17]

IF IN THE 1950S THE umbrella symbolized the futility of human resistance to nuclear devastation for a small group of British protesters, in Hong Kong the umbrella came to stand for plucky opposition to state violence. But after that first night, the Umbrella Movement was not marked by vigorous contention with security forces. Indeed, many Hong Kongers said they'd never had any poor interactions or negative feelings about the police at all. That attitude may have been limited to the Cantonese-speaking majority, locals with full citizenship, but it would be incomprehensible in places like Egypt, Brazil, or the United States. Hong Kong had famously lionized its police force in its martial arts movies over the years, and throughout 2014, the international press would report with shock and delight on the dynamic between Hong Kong protesters and local authorities. One New York Times headline declared that "Hong Kong Protests Are Leaderless but Orderly," reporting that the youth was "diligently clean" and "exceedingly polite," even picking up their own trash.[18]

The Western press especially loved Joshua Wong, who provided them with the narrative of a "teenager taking on a global superpower."[19] He made the cover of Time magazine as "The Face of Protest." Unlike the instant celebrity of Camila Vallejo in Chile, however, the devout Lutheran did not have a well-defined ideology, or the structure of a disciplined party, nor had he been elected to lead a well-established student association. He had gained national attention in 2011 when, at just fourteen, he and a small group of students converged as Scholarism to oppose new elements of "moral and national education" introduced by the chief executive that would, among other things, sidestep the events of Tiananmen Square. They led a large, peaceful protest in 2012 and occupied government headquarters for a week, until the Hong Kong chief withdrew the reform proposal. It seemed that whatever Hong Kong's special little political system actually was, protesting worked.

But the 2014 Umbrella Movement could not be truly "leaderless" because there was a stage. Joshua Wong, along with the Occupy Trio and a few other student leaders, controlled this platform, and thus, informally, the movement. They gave speeches or decided who else would. Indeed, for some of the participants, the idea of "the stage" came to represent the concept of leadership itself. Just as Brazil's Movimento Passe Livre might reject any "vertical" structures within a political struggle, some Hong Kongers would come to insist on "no stage" to signify something like horizontalism. Stages are, after all, quite literally above the crowd. The Umbrella Movement also cemented one of those national two-color schemes that our form of contemporary society loves to generate—from now on, the "yellow" camp would be pro-democracy, and more Western-facing, while the "blue" camp would be more pro-Beijing and supportive of the police.

Unlike most people on the streets, retired teacher and longtime activist Au Loong-Yu had been in a contentious demonstration before 2014. He was old enough to participate in solidarity efforts for Tiananmen in 1989, a year that was comparatively safe in the Special Administrative Region.[20] In 2005, he and other left-leaning Hong Kongers had participated in a wave of protests against the World Trade Organization in the Hong Kong manifestation of the alter-globalization movement. The young (and pro-democracy) Hong Kong Confederation of Trade Unions took part, as did visiting demonstrators from countries like South Korea. Police used tear gas, but the crackdown on dedicated, ideologically driven, and raucous protesters (many of them working-class foreigners) did not inspire widespread revulsion. Things were very different when the chemical was used on unarmed local students in 2014—this "instantly turned many people who had been passive observers of the movement into strong sympathizers," wrote US historian Jeff Wasserstrom.[21] Au Loong-Yu took to the streets with the kids and was arrested at the beginning of June.

Au Loong-Yu had spearheaded a group called Left21 and run a quarterly journal. As a longtime student of global politics, he was painfully aware that the official opposition, civil society groups, and the trade union movement possessed very little organizational strength. The largest "yellow" party won votes every few years, but they had less than a thousand actual members. The Umbrella Movement had no capacity to impose any costs on the government. An attempt to organize a mass strike fizzled. PRC authorities also represented 1.36 billion people on the mainland, and there was no widespread pressure to change the rules of governance in the Special Administrative Region.

The Umbrella Movement initially sought to copy Occupy Wall Street (which was a copy of Tahrir Square, which was inspired by success in Tunisia), but they also drew on other repertoires of contention from around the world. They erected a "Lennon Wall," which was a reproduction of a site in Prague (named after British pop singer John Lennon) that hosted graffiti starting in the 1980s. Hong Kongers covered the wall with colorful Post-it notes describing why they were protesting. A projector nearby displayed messages of solidarity coming in from around the world. They also employed tactics that obviously came from contemporary global media. After police murdered Michael Brown in Ferguson, Missouri, and supporters of the nascent Black Lives Matter movement in the US held up both arms, chanting, "Hands up, don't shoot," Hong Kong protesters also made the gesture, though some didn't know where it came from.[22] Then there was the influence of Hollywood. Some protesters began to hold up three fingers. This gesture didn't come from another city, at least not one in our world—it was from *The Hunger Games*, a film series produced in the United States in which lead character Katniss Everdeen (played by Jennifer Lawrence) holds up three fingers to signal opposition to a tyrannical regime.

Hong Kong only had seven million people in it, but it was home to the offices of a lot of Western corporations, and it became clear to some protesters that the selection of symbols, and tactics, took place in a constant feedback loop with media representation. Kids might choose something because they thought it would go viral, and then the sign or the tactic that actually did go viral would come to represent many more kids than had actually used it, and then some other kids would gravitate toward the approach that they believed had been an established media success.

In concrete terms, it became clear to many participants that the movement amounted to the broadcast of messages to authorities in Beijing. A significant portion of the Hong Kong population wanted to choose the chief executive in the same way that Western countries picked their presidents, and Western media would naturally amplify this with sympathetic coverage. But Beijing already knew all of that. This had been the fundamental impetus behind "pan-democrat" politics since its inception decades earlier.

Au Loong-Yu took the stage to give a speech, and he also acted as an educator in ad hoc "street forums" in downtown Hong Kong. As the occupation dragged on, he took note of some obvious divisions emerging in the movement. "Some 'localists' began to mount attacks on the so-called 'left pricks,'" he said. "Eventually the localists would emerge as the major beneficiaries of the Umbrella Movement."[23] Neither of these terms translate perfectly to English, and thus require a little bit of explanation. The "localist" movement had started as a defense of traditional Hong Kong structures—beginning with a beloved old pier—from cross-border development. But some of this group came to reject Chinese investment or even China itself. On one end of the localist spectrum, some (though not everyone) articulated outright xenophobic politics, attacking working-class immigrants from the mainland in racist terms. As a rule, this group was opposed to what they called the 左膠, something like "plastic leftists" or "left pricks," the translation that Au Loong prefers. "This was always more of an attack, or a straw man, than a coherent statement. Hong Kong barely had any left. This started as a city of refugees, a capitalist colonial outpost, and it very much became an 'everyone for himself' kind of town." The right-localists, especially, did not like the HKFS student federation, or any prominent activists, and warned that they were going to betray the movement.

The localists were the ones who attacked the "stage" and the idea of leadership and representation in general most forcefully. They opposed the use of any flags on the streets, or any kind of assembly structure. This was all summed up in the slogan, which was both literal and metaphorical: "tear down the main stage."

The Hong Kong government responded to the pressure on the streets, though in a different way than in 2012. It called upon representatives of the Umbrella Movement to participate in a debate broadcast on live television on October 21, 2014. On one side sat five members of the Hong Kong Federation of Students, and on the other, Chief Secretary Carrie Lam would lead a team of five government officials. Most of these politicians had not been elected, and neither had the students. In any case, people were watching outside at Admiralty, cheering along for the students on a big screen. And then, not much else happened. The government listened but did not address the key demand for open elections. That decision had been hammered out in Beijing, anyway.

In November, numerous taxi and minibus companies filed injunctions requiring protesters to unblock the city's streets. On December 11, the government cleared the roads.

15

No Gods, No Representation

IN THE BEGINNING OF 2015, my editor asked me to meet as many Syrians as I could in Brazil. The war in that country was dragging on—four years had passed since the initial uprising and crackdown during the so-called Arab Spring, and millions of people had fled the violence. They left seeking to make homes elsewhere, all around the world. Including in Brazil. The idea, at my newspaper, was to drive home the message that this was truly a global story, and that the waves of refugees were transforming the entire world.

There were quite a lot of Syrians in São Paulo, and I began to attend *iftar*, the evening meal during Ramadan fasting season, in a working-class neighborhood east of downtown. I got especially close to Firas, a wickedly funny man from the north of the country whose story flew right in the face of both the xenophobic and liberal stereotypes about Arab immigration. He has a master's degree in chemical engineering, and he is not particularly religious. Brazilians were nice, he said, but he didn't want to stay here, thank you very much. The public schools were terrible, and there was far too much crime. He was trying to get to the United States. This was a *Los Angeles Times* investigation, predisposed to be sympathetic to refugees, but he certainly wasn't going to reproduce any of the sentiments that *bien-pensant* Californians learn to associate with stories of immigration. Was he looking for the land of the free? A better life? Grateful for the opportunity? No, not really. He would have preferred to stay in Syria, but conflict and criminal foreign intervention had destroyed it. Northern Europe had the best healthcare and education and packages for refugees, but unfortunately the United States was the best option available to him, he said. If he had to rip his children away from Syria, then the best he can do for them is to get to a really rich country. Brazil wouldn't really work for him. I laughed out loud all the time as he spoke, but I knew this kind of talk probably wasn't going in the story.

Some other Syrians decided they would stay in São Paulo, and they didn't have much trouble doing so. By global standards, Brazil has virtually no immigration. There are around a million people who were born elsewhere, but that adds up to less than 1 percent of the country. In many ways, the United States and Brazil have similar structures. They are both Western European settler colonies with a very clear racial hierarchy—whites on top, then groups of immigrants that came more recently, with the descendants of enslaved peoples excluded from official white society for centuries and surviving indigenous populations living on the margins. But racialization works slightly differently in Brazil. Arabs have a long history in São Paulo. One of the most popular fast-food joints is Habib's. The mayor, Fernando Haddad, was of Lebanese descent. In Brazil's mainstream politics, there was not much anti-immigration sentiment.

The story was very different in the world's richest countries, which were shaken by the question of what to do with so many new arrivals. On continental Europe, confident stateswoman Angela Merkel decided to welcome one million immigrants to Germany, while other countries set up a deadly invisible border in the Mediterranean Sea. In the United States, an unimaginative but media-savvy and endlessly entertaining television personality turned his attention on an already-deadly invisible border nearer to home. Real estate heir Donald Trump launched a bid for the presidency by saying that many Mexican immigrants were "rapists" and then refusing to back down when mainstream media criticized him. His campaign was largely powered by shocking and newsworthy proclamations on Twitter, and by the fact that producers knew he was good for ratings. A veteran of the world of

New York gossip, Trump knew how to manipulate the media; or, at least, he knew how to appear on TV. At the event that launched his campaign, he hired actors to pretend to be his supporters (and then didn't actually pay them).[1] In the United Kingdom, a loose coalition of conservative politicians took the provocative side of a somewhat unexpected contest to decide if the country would remain in the European Union. Prime Minister David Cameron called the referendum so his side could easily win it, and he could get on with business. Famously, his opponents on the pro-"Brexit" side ran a menacing ad, with hordes of Muslims marching on the nation, like some kind of reverse Crusade.

In the broader sense, the anti-immigration reaction in the First World was not only caused by reverberations from the so-called Arab Spring, or cultural differences, or even by racist attitudes built deeply into North Atlantic societies. It was objectively true that, seventy years after the beginning of formal decolonization and Third World movement, the planet was wildly unequal. With the exception of Communist China, which experienced decades of rapid growth, every large country in the Global South remained in the same relationship to the First World it had inherited just after World War II.[2] Far more than skill, luck, or hard work, the material contours of the life of any human being are dictated by where they are born.[3] A country like the United States is not just a little bit richer than Guatemala, the country where a US-backed dictatorship killed hundreds of thousands of people a generation ago. GDP per capita in the United States is fifteen times higher than it is in the Central American nation. In Egypt, the minimum wage is under $100 per month. Although a form of liberalism born from Enlightenment ideals appeared to enjoy some kind of global hegemony at the beginning of the twenty-first century, the idea of equality of opportunity at the planetary scale was so distant from reality that it was never even discussed. As Yugoslav-born economist Branko Milanovic points out, given this configuration of the global system, it is entirely predictable that many people would be desperate to cross borders and change their lot in life, and it is no surprise that citizens in rich countries try to jealously guard their privileges.[4]

To the great shock of the liberal press, and the political establishment, Brexit carried the vote, with 52 percent of the country voting to leave the European Union.

Anti-politics

In addition to its xenophobic turn, something else about the Brexit campaign surprised political analysts. The attitude might have been summed up by the answer that Lord Chancellor Michael Gove gave to a journalist who pointed out that many experts believed leaving the EU would actually harm Britain's economy. Gove told him that "the people of this country have had enough of experts with organizations with acronyms saying that they know what is best." More than just a question of policy, Brexit was an opportunity to stick it to the establishment.

When given this chance over the past few decades, citizens around the world have almost always taken it—from 2003, when Arnold Schwarzenegger was elected governor of California, to Brazilian clown Tiririca's overwhelming victory. In Britain, it didn't matter that this sentiment was delivered by a middle-aged government official with the title of "Lord Chancellor"—it got people excited.

By the middle of the decade, scholars were paying attention to this posture, to an attitude that was not just apathetic toward politics but actively opposed to all of its formal and institutional manifestations. The term "anti-politics" named a phenomenon that came to profoundly shape the world in the 2010s. This was more than just a vibe, a feeling detected by pundits; empirical studies confirmed this was a real and growing international tendency. A 2014 survey of sixty countries around the world found a majority no longer had much confidence in government or political parties.[5]

There is some overlap between anti-politics and the ideological articulation of neoliberalism that emerged in the anglophone world. US president Ronald Reagan famously said that "the nine most terrifying words in the English language are 'I'm from the government, and I'm here to help.'" But that was more properly a posture in opposition to state involvement in daily life. In that worldview, politics still had its place: selecting leaders, enforcing and reproducing free-market conditions, buying weapons, and using them to intimidate geopolitical rivals. Since the 1980s, US (and British) politicians had loved to pose as "outsiders" while running for elections, and then constantly declare that they didn't want to "play politics" after winning them. Barack Obama's election was driven to some extent by this kind of discourse; the man that offered "Hope" and "Change" was encouraged to run because he had spent little time in Washington, DC, and was not perceived as an "insider."[6] But over the years, anti-political sentiment had grown into something more complete, and it had become more widespread and virulent. At its extreme end, it could mean a rejection of democracy itself.

In a careful study of politics published after Brexit, academics Nick Clarke, Will Jennings, Jonathan Moss, and Gerry Stoker found that anti-political attitudes had increased both in scope and intensity since the middle of the twentieth century. While people theoretically support "informal politics"—participating in civil society campaigns, volunteering, etc.—as an alternative to formal politics, they don't actually do much of it. What is left is a distaste for politics in general and especially for the highly visible figure of the politician. In recent years, it has been trivially easy to find people saying that "all politicians are the same," and then quickly follow up with the contradictory statement that "they need to stop fighting and get things done." Though the four researchers focused primarily on British politics, this was the same attitude you might hear in a São Paulo taxicab. Another incredibly common opinion, they found, is that politicians are a joke. They're all clowns, and clowns would make better politicians.

None of this would be possible without the specific ways in which mass media in tandem with social media depicted politicians, found Clarke and his cowriters. Large publications, now owned by profit-maximizing private firms, cultivated very specific (and very demanding) expectations of politicians as individuals. These men and women (in the past, mostly men) used to only appear in the public eye when discussing policy and addressing the public. Now there was the possibility of a twenty-four-hour performance of humanity and professionalism. Making a gaffe by demonstrating the lack of any of the above could easily be caught by the media. Meanwhile, less visible, but deeply important, structural issues moved into the background.[7]

In 2013, many members of the Movimento Passe Livre knew that their "a-party" stance had been confused with an "anti-party" attitude that ultimately became violent. By 2015, many of them realized that the "anti-party" wave had been transformed, or widened, into a much larger "anti-politics" movement sweeping the country. The most visible manifestations of this tendency were the impeachment protests organized by the likes of the MBL and Vem Pra Rua, the groups that had appropriated their own legacy. In one 2015 survey, 96 percent of participants at one of these events said they were unsatisfied with the political system; a majority said that someone "outside of politics" would be needed to solve the country's problems. And from the beginning, some protest organizers called for military intervention—that is, a coup—to end the Dilma government, unsettling some of the more principled liberals. A military dictatorship would be one way to solve the problem of actually existing politics by simply demolishing it. And as a rule, any politician that showed up for those rallies in 2015 would be greeted with boos—except for one.[8]

Jair Bolsonaro was a disgraced army captain who left the service after being accused of planning a false flag bombing in Rio de Janeiro as a scheme to get a pay raise from the military.[9] He did very little in Congress except try to direct more money to police officers and promote the legacy of the defunct military regime. But as a media figure, he had developed a reputation as the far-right answer to everything and anything about the political system that developed after the fall of the dictatorship. And his outbursts were certainly attention-grabbing. In a 1998 television interview, he proclaimed that the military regime had not killed enough people. He said: "Voting won't change anything in this country. Absolutely nothing! Things will only change, unfortunately, after starting a civil war here, and doing the work the dictatorship didn't do. Killing some 30,000 people, and starting with FHC. If some innocents die, that's just fine." When he was referring to "FHC," he was calling for the execution of then president Fernando Henrique Cardoso. You can't get any more anti-political than that.

Baby, You Can Wash My Car

In 2015, two new figures burst onto the political scene in Brazil, but neither of them were politicians. Working the courts was a hard-charging judge, and out on the streets, a cool cop. On a quest to clean up this country, this duo was taking names and breaking the rules, the story went, and the media absolutely loved them.

Corruption had been endemic to the Brazilian political system since the reintroduction of democracy. Indeed, corruption was rife during the dictatorship too—it just worked differently, and people rarely found out about it. For good reason. In 1979, one prominent diplomat let slip that he was working on memoirs in his retirement, in which he would recount malfeasance carried out by the military regime. One week later he disappeared—kidnapped, tortured, and murdered by the secret police.[10] But since the introduction of the 1988 constitution, every effective government had existed in tandem with a particular type of corruption. In order to maintain an unwieldy coalition in Congress, the ruling party distributes political and economic resources to the dozens of others. Cabinet positions, publicly funded projects, and money are handed out not just to allies, but to putative rivals as well. This system financed expensive political campaigns, both legally and illegally, with money often shaved off of big government contracts. This happened under Fernando Henrique Cardoso, it happened under Lula, and it happened under Dilma. No evidence has ever emerged that has sustained convictions of those presidents, as individuals, for corruption—but they certainly sat at the top of a system in which it was customary.

Before June 2013, around 5 percent of Brazilians believed that corruption was the biggest problem facing the country. That number steadily began to rise, starting with the explosion of protesters (and protest causes) that month. Two years later, the number was up to 21 percent.[11] But by 2015, it was clear that it was no longer the dynamic of the representation of that eruption that was powering the ongoing surge in concern. Everyone knew that it was Operação Lava Jato, or "Operation Car Wash," and Judge Sergio Moro appearing on the television almost every single day.

Just as there had always been corruption in Brazil's new democracy, there had always been judges, would-be vigilantes who attempt to mount an attack on the system. But those attempts were usually blocked by higher courts, which would rule that they had stepped out of legal bounds to do so. In another era, Sergio Moro might have been one of these failed chancers.[12]

Lava Jato, meaning "Car Wash" or "Jet Wash," was named after a small gas station scam that gave rise to the operation.[13] Launched in 2014, it quickly grew into an ambitious and powerful investigative force. Lava Jato was different from those previous attempts for two major reasons. First, the task force made ample use of the practices made possible by Lei 12.850/2013, the law passed in the flurry of reactions to the June 2013 protests. They arrested people for the purposes of interviewing them (condução coercitiva), they threatened to throw the book at them, and then they offered a plea deal (delação premiada) in exchange for someone giving up a bigger fish. And second, they made ample use of the media.

Back in 2004, Judge Sergio Moro had written an article on *Mani Pulite* (Clean Hands), the anti-corruption charge that took place in Italy in the 1990s. Leaving aside the fact that the *Mani Pulite* didn't actually reduce corruption in that country, Moro celebrated that the Italians had made strategic use of the mass media to create the pressure necessary for success. Publicity "guaranteed public support for the judicial measures, stopping public figures from obstructing the work of the judges," he wrote, and "arrests, confessions, and publicity created a virtuous cycle, adding up to the only explanation for the magnitude of the results" in Italy.[14] Since studying there in 1998, Sergio Moro had forged relationships in the United States, and he was up to date on all the latest international techniques available in these types of operations—namely the introduction of plea deals, which had been the result of long-term North American pressure on the Brazilian system.

Lava Jato certainly had willing media partners in Brazil.[15] Morning after morning, TV viewers and newspaper readers were treated to the shocking scene of some politician or major businessman being hauled away to prison. We got news of larger and larger numbers of dollars allegedly diverted from contracts with major Brazilian companies, most shockingly from the state-run Petrobras oil company, until figures reached the billions.

The scenes of the arrests generated a little cultural meme—an anti-corruption action figure. One federal police officer, a gray-haired Japanese-Brazilian man, was often present in the operations. He always wore big Ray-Ban sunglasses, and he always remained calm as he dragged away powerful establishment figures. Thus, the *Japonês da Federal*, the "Japanese Fed," became an internet sensation. And then there was the figure of Sergio Moro himself.

When speaking, Judge Moro is not impressive. He has the accent, cadence, and diction of a confident provincial lawyer, always searching for big, impressive words and unaware that he found the wrong ones. In photographs, though, he has the strong jaw and thick hair you might draw on a cartoon superhero. And the media treated him like one. He was all over the covers of magazines, and his popularity shot up around the country.

It was well-known that Lava Jato was pushing the limits of the law to pursue their investigations and ensure convictions. This was why they often called it a "crusade," and this was celebrated as courageous. But if you took a step back, it was obvious that Moro was only looking at abuses committed by one type of actor—corruption in the military or the judiciary went unmentioned, as his team zeroed in on the nexus between politicians and strategic national corporations. And if you looked closely, it was already clear they were pushing past those legal limits. They hid information to maintain jurisdiction over the cases; they arrested people without reason; and they aimed their probe very squarely at one political party.[16]

I did not know about any of this. I had no special insights into the Lava Jato operation, nor did I do investigative work into its inner workings. Like most other foreign journalists, I was reacting to the constant, unending, bombastic parade of media spectacles. Most of us didn't have the expertise to understand the legal intricacies of the investigation, even if we had been granted access behind the scenes. But I had a slightly different ideological apparatus for interpreting an "anti-corruption crusade." For our little *Folha* blog in late 2013, I wrote a piece saying that media depictions often got it wrong. Corruption—surely a serious problem in the country—manifested itself concretely through corporate influence over the state and public life; not—as was too often depicted—some *político* filling a giant bag with cash and running. Regular people were far more affected by the special rights granted to big construction companies and banks and the concerns ravaging the Amazon rainforest than they were by the amounts of money actually kept by politicians themselves. But those companies generated profits and provided the funds that kept the government operating. Moreover, I didn't quite see how a flash of judicial-punitive force would lead to any fundamental reconfigurations. At best, these kinds of operations had succeeded in forcing a game of musical chairs at the level of elite politics.[17]

So I never personally praised Lava Jato or wrote effusively about how it might clean up Brazil. This set me apart from most major outlets in Brazil and in the English language. That said, I didn't criticize Lava Jato at the beginning, either; I covered it with a matter-of-fact tone, watching and waiting to see what happened.

By the beginning of 2016, it seemed things were getting out of hand. For the *Folha* blog, I commissioned Alex Cuadros to write a piece, called "The fog of war—corruption and media in Brazil," that worried the press was dropping journalistic rigor during the anti-corruption frenzy, and mentioned specific outlets by name. My editors told me that we had broken a rule within the newspaper; we were not supposed to cite other publications directly without notifying them first. They had gotten pushback from the other Brazilian media. I had never heard of this rule, but I agreed that we could show them texts of this kind in advance in the future. Admittedly, we had not been maintaining the blog like we used to. One week later, *Folha* told me the project was being discontinued after four years.[18]

Jubilant coverage continued within Brazil and without. At the beginning of 2016, the pan-American anglophone publication *Americas Quarterly* ran a big special on anti-corruption operations in Latin America. *Americas Quarterly* is funded by the Council of the Americas, a group of businesses promoting free trade in Latin America. On the cover, they had posed Sergio Moro as a Ghostbuster, armed with a proton pack for blasting the undead. The headline read, "Corruption Busters."[19]

The Crisis of Representation

As the twentieth century came to an end, with Old Left structures in decay and links with representation clearly fraying, some thinkers found a way to turn the crisis into an opportunity. Most famously, thinkers shaped in the tradition of the original Italian *autonomismo* asserted that masses had been replaced by a "multitude" of individuals that did not need organic links with one another, or any relationship to a representative body, in order to transform society. At one extreme of that logic was the insistence that all representation is either a distortion or an authoritarian imposition. It is always, to some extent, a lie and has no place in true democracy. Commentators were left to decide whether this was an optimistic reading of the progress of History, but it seemed clear that we had become more disconnected than ever.[20]

This insistence on rejecting representation entirely, rather than trying to reconstruct it, has appeared to some extent in most of the mass protest explosions in the era that began with Tahrir Square. Some version of it was expressed in Egypt, Spain (*no me representan*), Greece, Chile, Turkey, Occupy Wall Street, and Brazil, even if the amount of people who actually felt this way varied widely.*

Chilean political scientist Juan Pablo Luna wrote in 2016 that political representation was in crisis. The links between the people and the state, supposedly the foundation of liberal democratic politics, had become

---

* In North Africa especially, the movements were more concretely horizontal than they were self-consciously horizontal*ist*.

increasingly weak, and often rendered invisible. The real links, stronger and stronger, were between the government and business interests. People had lost faith in old parties, he found, and new parties tended to fall apart immediately—hundreds of them appeared and disappeared in recent years in Latin America. In Chile, the number of people choosing not to identify with any political party was 53 percent in 2008; in 2016, it was 83 percent. But Luna was quick to point out that this was not just a national crisis. It was "the local manifestation of something very serious," he wrote: "the exhaustion of the global model in place since World War II."[21]

No media distortion, no focus on empty spectacle, no twisted corporate agenda is required to generate the feeling that politicians do not fully represent their constituents. By all accounts, they do not. There is widespread agreement that the political systems in advanced societies have become distant from the sovereign people that putatively grant them their power. In the United States, so often a default reference point for liberal politicians in Latin America and the rest of the Global South, one famous study indicated that "economic elites and organized interest groups play a substantial part in affecting public policy, but the general public has little or no independent influence." Researchers at Princeton and Northwestern Universities found that the preferences of average citizens have almost no influence on the form of government, unless wealthy actors and powerful interest groups want the same thing.[22]

By the middle of the 2010s, in the English language, if someone asked about "representation," it was more likely they were asking whether members of a certain racial or identity category were appearing in entertainment products designed for mass consumption, rather than whether designated representatives can actually carry out our will. The idea of willfully empowering someone to act on your behalf because you trust and (to some extent) control them seemed impossibly quaint.

Among the world's well-functioning polities, no approach is more different from that of the United States than the governance of China carried out by the Communist Party. But Wang Hui, a participant in the Tiananmen Square protests and now one of the most eloquent voices on the "New Left" published in the People's Republic of China, says that the CPC itself has suffered a "breakdown in representation." Originally forged in the doctrine (and practice) of people's war, the party has become more of a bureaucratic administrative apparatus, and it has lost a strong connection to the people. This happened after the end of the Cultural Revolution, when the

Party became depoliticized and charged with overseeing market reforms. So while Wang believes the Party is very different from the political forms in the West, he concludes in 2016 that China is part of the global "crisis in representation [which] is a product of neoliberalism in the political sphere, in that it is a consequence of depoliticization."[23] It seems that not even the Maoists and the Dengists escaped this particular malaise.

Without mass party politics or union participation, it falls to nongovernmental organizations to put pressure on the state. But someone has to pay for them. In Ukraine, even Maria Tomak, a proud veteran of the Center for Civil Liberties and Euromaidan SOS, admitted that unfortunately, most "civil society" in her country consists of NGOs funded by Western donors. Even if there were more civic participation in national politics, as she hopes there will be in the future, regular Ukrainians can never punch with the might of the truly rich. In the 2014 election that followed the transitional Euromaidan government, voters (with Crimeans and citizens in the Donbas region now excluded) chose chocolate industry oligarch Petro Poroshenko from among the options on offer. His Channel 5 had been one of the earliest and most consistent media supporters of the uprising that began in 2013. Poroshenko had good relations with Russia while amassing his billions, but he now presented himself as a nationalist and would take the reins as heir to the Euromaidan legacy.[24] Corruption would not decrease, nor would the economic power of regular people increase.

In her famous short essay on "The NGOization of Resistance," Indian author Arundhati Roy claims that while there are organizations doing valuable work, the broader role of the NGO has been to fill the vacuum created by a state retreating in the neoliberal era—except they don't fully plug the gaps, and they are only accountable to funders, not citizens. They "dole out as aid or benevolence what people ought to have by right," she claims. "It's almost as though the greater the devastation caused by neoliberalism, the greater the outbreak of NGOs. Nothing illustrates this more poignantly than the phenomenon of the U.S. preparing to invade a country and simultaneously readying NGOs to go in and clean up the devastation."[25]* In Egypt, one of the reasons that the Muslim Brotherhood—in contrast to the rest of civil

---

* The 2014 study cited above focused primarily on attitudes in rich countries, but as early as 1990 anthropologist James Ferguson called the global development system, led by entities such as USAID, an "anti-politics machine" in the former Third World.

society—was so organized in 2011 is that the Islamist group played the role NGOs play in so many other Global South countries.[26]

In Chile, Luna noted that the student movement had been caught in a loop, attempting and failing to re-create 2011 every single year. But people had stopped paying attention. In any case, a big part of what made them so exciting was not their concrete (left-wing) politics, back in 2011, but that they were *anti-establishment*.[27]

In 2015, both Gabriel Boric and Camila Vallejo served in Congress. Boric had turned heads upon taking office when he showed up with messy emo-rock hair, a trench coat, and no tie. This caused some degree of outrage, and the twenty-eight-year-old said he didn't care—indicating clearly he was from a new generation and a new culture. But he quickly threw himself into doing the actual day-to-day work of a congressman, taking pride in always showing up for legislative sessions, and he grew in popularity among Chileans. Vallejo, firmly ensconced in an organized Communist Party, was a part of Michelle Bachelet's ruling coalition. As has been common for Marxist-Leninist parties in Latin America, she remained committed to socialist ideals in the long term and concrete governance in the short term. Boric was independent and officially "Autonomist."

The Movimento Passe Livre is one of the groups that made its rejection of representation most explicit. To some extent, horizontalism is synonymous with anti-representation politics. That is why they switched their spokespersons constantly, even as some of them demonstrated skill and gained the trust of the public, and others made serious mistakes.

In 2015 as Lava Jato blasted holes in Brazil's democratic system, Lucas "Vegetable" Monteiro published an open letter with a devastating message. "Is the Movimento Passe Livre Over?" the headline asked, and his text immediately rendered his verdict. The Movimento Passe Livre had "reached its end." This was not a decision the group had made itself. He was speaking out of turn and representing the group in the media without the others' consent. One could not imagine a less horizontalist move.[28]

He wrote that in their quest to reject the "old left," and Leninist practices, they had turned their principles into a rigid dogma of their own. In language that is remarkably reminiscent of Jo Freeman's influential essay "The Tyranny of Structurelessness," he said that the group's focus on formal consensus meant the employment of intense social pressure, with some militants exercising profoundly undemocratic influence. Then in language that is remarkably reminiscent of SDS founding member Todd Gitlin, he said that they could not integrate new members into an organization that was based on the ties of close personal friendship. In the comments section and in the media, other members furiously denied that the MPL was over. But this was a punishing blow. Splits over the past, and the future, of the MPL led Mayara to fall into depression.

In Tunisia, the people were now represented by a parliament, and a prime minister, and a president. There were twelve parties in that parliament, and the government was not very stable. In 2016, the nation was on its seventh administration since the revolution.[29] In Egypt, everyone had a very clear representative, at least on the global stage. Field Marshal Sisi had been firmly entrenched in power since 2013. That didn't change in 2015, when a visiting Italian researcher was arrested, tortured, and killed. Who was representing Syrians? That depended on where you lived—your territory might be controlled by Assad himself, or by leftist Kurdish militias, or by ISIS, or forces backed by Turkey and the United States, or Sunni militants backed by Saudi Arabia. In Yemen, the fragile order imposed four years earlier fell apart violently. The National Dialogue Conference, meant to resolve the problem of a Saudi-imposed leader with no popular mandate, stalled for years until the Houthis, an armed group in the north of the country that had been in conflict with the central government since before 2011, took over parts of the capital. Saudi Arabia itself then attacked the country with US support, maintaining that the Houthis were backed by Iran. Thus began a long and deadly civil war. And Libyans didn't have much representation to speak of at all.

16

A Tale of Two Impeachments

THE PRESIDENT OF SOUTH KOREA had a secret adviser. She was writing her speeches, shaping key policy, and reading secret documents. The two women had met back in the 1970s, when the adviser's father said he could communicate with the president's mother even though she had been murdered by North Korean assassins. Because he could speak with her in the afterlife.

The dead woman in question was the wife of President Park Chung Hee, whose dictatorship began after a coup in 1961 and ended when he himself was killed after a night of heavy drinking in 1979. His daughter assumed the presidency in 2013. She had remained close friends with the medium's daughter, Choi Soon-sil, the entire time. In office, Park Geun-hye helped raise millions of dollars for foundations benefiting Choi Soon-sil. Some of the money went toward family horses in Germany.

Soon after all of this was revealed by the press, Choi Soon-sil told prosecutors, "Please forgive me, I have committed a sin that deserves death."

Due to the supernatural elements of the story, and the power that Choi apparently had over Park, the press said that a "Rasputin-like figure" may have infiltrated the heights of South Korean politics. Tens of thousands, and then hundreds of thousands, and then more than a million people came out

204 If We Burn

into the streets, in what became known as the Candlelight Demonstrations. Approval ratings for President Park Geun-hye dropped to 5 percent, and then lower than that. Political elites in Seoul came together behind the idea of impeachment. They moved to remove President Park Geun-hye.

And yet, that may not have been the strangest—or most consequential—impeachment to take place in 2016. There was the removal of Dilma Rousseff in South America's largest country. As I write, years later, the consequences of that impeachment have still not been fully resolved.

Leaks

In the pantheon of Brazilian *políticos*, across the spectrum of corruption in Latin America, Eduardo Cunha is an especially devious character. On one end, we might place the individuals who interact with a dirty system in order to make life better for regular people. They don't take money for themselves, they try to stay clean, but they know they will inevitably become a little bit muddied if they care about results. At the other end, you have people who make things worse for their citizens, who abuse the representative system for selfish reasons, and who are taking far more than they put in. By all accounts, Eduardo Cunha, serving as speaker of the lower house of Congress in 2016, was the latter.

Cunha, an evangelical Christian, was a leading figure in the unruly coalition of lawmakers that provided Dilma with congressional support. These men and women (but mostly men) never liked Dilma as much as they liked Lula. They perceived her as combative and assertive, insisting too forcefully that she was the president and could set the agenda (including an early anti-corruption drive), while Lula was a master at making every kind of important man in Brazil feel special. Early in 2015, Cunha had received members of the free-market Movimento Brasil Livre, who presented a request for the impeachment of Dilma Rousseff (despite continuing to insist they were an "a-party" movement). But by the end of 2015, it was clear that the maelstrom blown into life by Lava Jato was about to consume Eduardo Cunha himself. The man wasn't just moving money here and there to keep the wheels greased, investigators were discovering. Eduardo Cunha had a secret Swiss bank account, and he had allegedly stolen tens of millions of dollars by laundering it through one of his churches. A congressional ethics committee began a process to strip him of his mandate.

Privately and then publicly, Cunha tried to make a deal.[1] If the Workers' Party killed the ethics committee investigation, saving his hide, they could keep him as an ally. If they did not, he was going to start impeachment proceedings. Dilma scoffed at this request. This was a wild threat made by a desperate man; nobody took impeachment seriously. Remove her for what? She had not been implicated in any Lava Jato investigation.

At the same time, her second term was not going well at all. The economy had gotten much worse, as everyone had expected (but Dilma had not admitted) at the end of 2014. And Lava Jato was decimating confidence in the political class. A year into her second administration, Dilma's approval ratings had plummeted—only 12 percent thought she was doing a good job, versus 65 percent who gave her negative reviews.[2]

The Workers' Party chose to go forward with the investigation into Eduardo Cunha. The same day, he made good on his threat. He held an impromptu, frenetic press conference in the halls of Congress and announced he was beginning impeachment proceedings.[3]

To be impeached, the Brazilian constitution stipulates the president must have committed a *crime de responsabilidade*, something that might translate as "high crimes" in the United States. A trial of sorts takes place, and both the lower house and the Senate vote on the removal of the executive. As this impeachment request had been formulated, the accusation was that President Rousseff had violated budgetary rules. Under Dilma, the government had delayed payments to public banks as a form of creative accounting that made state finances appear more solid than they were. This practice is called *pedaladas fiscais*, or "fiscal pedaling," and it has been quite common since the 1990s. It is certainly a kind of manipulation, but it is not theft. It is probably not even illegal.[4] Making the case that this was a *crime de responsabilidade* would be a real stretch.

At the same time, the impeachment movement that had emerged on the fringes before her second term even began now had something to hold on to. The MBL, Vem Pra Rua, and other right-wing groups that had been active since late 2014 now had a chance. All they had to do was pressure the political class into casting a vote for an existing measure. How would they do this? Of course, they drew on the same repertoire that had been adopted in the country since June 2013. This would be mass protest, and they would take to the streets; more specifically, they would take Avenida Paulista. The date for the big show of force was set for March 13, 2016.

But first, on March 4, Lava Jato brought Lula in for questioning. They showed up at his home early in the morning and took him to the airport in a federal vehicle. This was very strange because the task force employed a judicial mechanism used on material witnesses that refuse to be interviewed. But they had not even called Lula in for questioning, and he had never refused to offer evidence. It all seemed like it was meant as a spectacular gift to enemies of the PT, a demonstration that Lava Jato had the power to arrest him. Of course, all sympathetic media was secretly informed in advance. Lula called this faux arrest a "pyrotechnics show."[5]

Then, as planned, the impeachment movement took to the streets of Brazil. For the first time since 2013, the numbers exceeded the June protests unleashed by the Movimento Passe Livre. This was now the biggest protest in the history of the country.[6]

Of course, the pulsating crowds were yellow, with splashes of green. By now this uniform, the shirt of the national football team, was the clear choice for any right-leaning street demonstration. Millions and millions of people now dressed like those two people I had seen back in June 2013, locked in futile conversation with those punk teenagers.[7]

But for people who had been on the streets back then, this protest was strange. This was very different than 2013. Back then, people had risen to action after seeing protesters face down police violence. This time, police were *supporting* the demonstration. The impeachment protests also had the backing of major media, which had built up to this date for weeks. This didn't feel like an uprising; this was more like a festival. A coordinated nationalist ritual.

Seasoned protesters felt the same way that Gehad did in Cairo, in June 2013. They watched befuddled as the event played out on social networks. These people were not facing off against the state. These people were taking selfies with cops. This felt wrong.

The Avenida Paulista protest was the largest of dozens in the country. Crowds gathered under one of the favorite symbols of this movement: a giant inflatable doll portraying President Lula in a black-and-white prisoner's uniform. They cheered out, "Viva Sergio Moro!" "Viva Lava Jato."

A few days later, Judge Sergio Moro gave these people another gift.

President Rousseff wanted to bring Lula back into government as her chief of staff. Yes, this would be admitting that she was in trouble, that she needed the help of her mentor. But there was little question about that anymore. It seemed that Lava Jato had nothing on her, but it was pulling the tide up around the administration quickly. Best to get all hands on deck.

On March 16, 2016, Moro sent a recording to the Globo media group. Lava Jato had been bugging calls between Lula and Dilma. Moro took a conversation about Lula's entrance into the government, and he made it public.

This phone tap was not authorized, and even if it had been, any evidence obtained in this way must remain under protection during an investigation—not turned into a political tool in the public arena. Moro not only violated the right of the president of the republic to have private conversations, he told the press how to interpret them. They proved that Lula knew he might go to prison, the story went, and that Dilma had offered him the government post so he could stay out of jail (a cabinet position would take jurisdiction away from Moro and transfer it to the Supreme Court).

Did those conversations actually prove that? Well, no—none of this is on the recordings. But this was an explosion at the heart of government, and it gave the country the impression that the Dilma administration was falling apart. How can you govern a country if a rival faction within the state is recording and leaking your calls in order to weaken you?

I can remember exactly where I was sitting when this happened. For those of us who followed Brazilian jurisprudence, this was a rupture in the space-time continuum. I was in downtown Los Angeles, thinking my time in Brazil (five years at that point) might be over. After hearing the news, I went right back to São Paulo.

When I arrived, I met up with some friends who were drinking heavily, and they turned to me, thinking I might know more than them. "What is happening? Is it true?" they asked. "Is there going to be a coup?"

The answers were coming fast. The supreme court moved to block Lula's appointment to Dilma's administration, saying it could hinder a federal investigation. Then on April 8, the center-right PSDB announced it was getting behind impeachment. That included Aécio, it included former president Fernando Henrique, and it included São Paulo governor Geraldo Alckmin.[8] Congress was actually going to vote on this thing.

That month, a polling firm asked Brazilians what they wanted to happen and offered three different options for the resolution of the political crisis. In response, 25 percent said they wanted Dilma to stay. Sixty-two percent said they wanted to hold new elections. Legally speaking, this option was viable if the electoral court (the Tribunal Superior Eleitoral, or TSE) found there had been irregularities in the 2014 election.[9] They would then annul the outcome and call for a new vote. But that was not the option the political class began to coalesce around in April—they were looking to impeach Dilma and simply hand the presidency over to Michel Temer, her vice president and establishment insider (from the centrist PMDB party, the same as Eduardo Cunha). In the poll, 8 percent of Brazilians said they preferred that option.[10]

The debate over the use of the word *golpe*, or "coup," became intensely politicized. This is a term imbued with deep meaning in Latin America. At the nitty-gritty, juridical level, the question revolved around whether the constitution gave Congress the right to simply declare anything they wanted to be a *crime de responsabilidade*, or if that word implied some objective legal standard. In the larger historical and connotative sense, the argument was whether this process should be in the same category as the CIA-backed overthrow of Salvador Allende, or the military coup that installed the dictatorship that tortured Dilma herself. Due to recent history, that question had serious implications. In general, the mainstream (center-right) Brazilian media portrayed anyone using the word in reference to the impeachment campaign as a diehard supporter of the government. International media largely did the same. No prominent foreign publication called this a "coup," and at least one journalist was called in by management for social media posts that allegedly indicated sympathy for the president.[11]

My approach to the impeachment was different from my approach to covering Lava Jato. I was not carefully neutral; I wrote about the process critically from the very start. I didn't assert this was a coup outright in my own voice, but I presented this interpretation as prominent and credible, and I made two points that I thought were even more important than the fight over terminology. First, this was a politically motivated charge to remove the president on a technicality. On March 28, I published an investigation for the *Los Angeles Times* with the headline "The Politicians Voting to Impeach Brazil's President Are Accused of More Corruption Than She Is," showing that a majority of the lawmakers were being charged or investigated for serious crimes, and Rousseff was not. And second, impeachment would create a government without clear democratic legitimacy. This was a very dangerous prospect just a quarter century after the end of a dictatorship. The whole country was going to see very clearly that Congress was switching out the elected leader for someone they preferred.

Furthermore, the motivation may have been to save their own hides. In March, Senator Romero Jucá had a phone call with an important former Petrobras official, Sergio Machado. They discussed a plan to "stop the bleeding" in the political class. "The easiest solution is to put Michel [Temer] in there.... A deal, a grand national pact," said Machado. "With the Supreme Court, with everyone," said Jucá. This was more damning than anything in Lula's conversation with Dilma, but this phone call didn't leak until after the impeachment vote.[12] Senator Jucá's gambit indicated that parts of the political class saw impeachment as a desperate attempt to stop Lava Jato from consuming them. They could offer Dilma as a *bode expiatório*, or sacrificial lamb, and see if it worked. What did they have to lose?

Smile for the Camera

The Congresso Nacional was designed by legendary Brazilian architect Oscar Niemeyer. A lifelong communist, Niemeyer never gave up on the high modernist idea that humanity could transform the world as we wish, that we can turn this life into something else entirely. Like much of Brasília, the congressional buildings look like they might actually sit on the surface of another planet—concrete and steel representations of man's vision of a utopian future. At the same time, Niemeyer said that many of his designs emulate the curves of a woman's body. Congress looks like a more elegant, more corporeal version of something from *The Jetsons*. The Senate is a giant white dome. The lower house is its inverse, an upraised cylinder resembling a huge teacup. The sky above is always a brilliant shade of blue. All the action happens underground.

On April 17, 2016, we all poured into the building. It was time for Congress to vote on whether or not they would go forward with impeachment proceedings. Then it would go to the Senate for approval; but that part was just a formality. This was going to be decided today.

But how? We in the press had no idea. We had heard rumors of last-minute deals, frenzied lobbying, desperate begging, threats, and secret promises. It was only very recently it had dawned on the country that this might actually happen. This thing that seemed an absolute joke, the dream of cranks and extremists, just months ago.

We journalists wandered the halls, speaking to whomever we could. Brasília was intentionally built far from Brazil's economic center, São Paulo, and the former imperial capital, Rio de Janeiro. It can feel like an island in the middle of the vast nation. It is perhaps for this reason that the June 2013 uprising never forced the government to actually stop functioning; there aren't too many people here. Once you get inside Congress, it is quite easy to mingle with the political class. I spoke to representative Jair Bolsonaro in the hallway and asked about the international repercussions of the vote. He came back with a fanatically anticommunist, Cold War–era provocation that I figured wouldn't really work for my article. He wasn't the story here; this was a fringe figure, and anyway, everyone already knew how Bolsonaro was going to vote. I moved on to another group of congressmen.

We were going to be in the hallways as the voting took place, but this didn't make much of a difference. You could see right into the main chambers or watch it on monitors, and you could speak to people right after they voted. Yet somehow, the Movimento Brasil Livre had acquired passes to actually stand on the floor of Congress. They weren't dressed as little indie rockers anymore; they were in the suits and ties that were required of them to enter the building.

I stepped outside, into the heat of the *planalto*, the Brazilian highlands. Police had set up barricades with clear demarcations for two different "protests" that would take place that day. On the left, people would show to up to indicate that they didn't support impeachment. On the right, people would show up to indicate that they did. Of course, the people on the right would be wearing yellow and green. The people on the left would be in red. These rules were obvious by now. In three years, Brazil had gone from a country with overlapping, contradictory protest repertoires to one with very clear rules governing the use of street actions. Certainly some camera up in the sky, owned by some media outlet and attached to a drone or a helicopter, would soon transmit images of the comparative agglomerations, showing everyone which group had won. Idly I walked up to the crowds and stared at the sea of people. What were these, really? How could they both be protests if one side is going to get what they want? Here, perhaps the Portuguese word *manifes-tações*, or the Spanish *demonstraciones*, works better. This is not civil disobe-dience or direct action. No one is imposing any costs on anyone in power. They are showing up to be counted. But, every adult is already counted— in theory, at least—in elections. Or, less officially, in polls. By now, almost everyone in the country had an opinion on the proceedings that day. So then, both teams were showing how many of their local supporters they could get out of the house, or how many could afford to book a trip to the capital?

I went back inside. The real show had begun.

Anyone who thought Congress would spend that day proffering opinions on the serious nature of Dilma's offenses or engaging in thoughtful analysis of the nature of a *crime de responsiblidade* was sorely mistaken. This was a circus. Representative after representative walked up to the microphone and delivered whatever little speech they wanted to give. One congressman said he was voting "yes" because "bandits want to destroy Brazil by making chil-dren change their sex." Another wished his granddaughter happy birthday. A few praised Sergio Moro or Lava Jato. Those of us in the press, huddled on the ground outside, were stunned. Surely they know this doesn't look good. And it didn't, collectively. But individually, the members of Congress were smarter than we were; they had perceived the true nature of the proceedings. They were all being handed an invaluable resource—free media time. For a few seconds, the whole country would pay attention to whatever they said, no matter how small their state or their party. They were taking advantage of their moment in the spotlight.

The long, strange show became so repetitive that some people stopped paying attention. Then—an explosion of murmurs in the hallway, and then, shouting. Tiririca had voted for impeachment! After winning in 2010, he donned a tie and took the business of Congress seriously, boasting that he was one of the only legislators to attend every session.[13] Over the years, he became a relatively important political asset due to his continued electoral popularity. And until this morning, he had been considered a solid *Não* vote. Something or someone must have flipped him. There was a lot of this hap-pening. A physical scoreboard, with little numbers in red and neon green, indicated that people were changing sides and abandoning the nation's first woman president. In the chamber, men waved little yellow signs embla-zoned with the words *Tchau, querida*, in English something like "Bye-bye, sweetie." This message accomplished two things at once: it made reference to the phone call Sergio Moro had leaked in March by repeating Lula's parting words, and it made the sexist nature of the proceedings explicit.

And, as it turns out, I was wrong. We didn't actually know how Jair Bolsonaro was going to vote. He took the microphone and delivered remarks that were obviously prepared in advance. "For the memory of Colonel Carlos Alberto Brilhante Ustra, the terror of Dilma Rousseff, for the army, for Brazil above everything, and God above everyone, my vote is yes." He had dedicated his vote, the man who tortured Dilma Rousseff during the dictatorship.

This was a stab to the heart of Brazilian democracy, a surprise attack on everything established as the national values since the fall of the dictatorship, and as they listened, some people in the country felt physically disoriented. Jean Wyllys, the first openly gay member of Congress, lost control. He lunged at Bolsonaro, screaming, and tried to spit on his face. The room erupted, as men began to physically restrain each other. Bolsonaro had surely made use of his time. With one incisive media performance, the seven-term congressman had become an outsider. With one violent provocation, he had declared holy war on the Brazilian political system.

The votes were in. They had won. The most famous members of the Movimento Brasil Livre huddled in a group just outside a circle of journalists, camera crews, and talking heads. Their faces were sober, if not a bit stressed and puzzled. They were clearly planning something. Why were they pulling their group to this specific spot? Then it became clear. They pulled their faces into big, exaggerated smiles, and then pushed in front of all the cameras. They hugged, beamed, and pumped their fists into the air. They performed a victory ritual, acting as if this was the moment they found out they had won, and they huddled close. Just as expected, the cameras turned to them and recorded the images of the upstart group of kids that had done it, that had toppled this government, after years of fighting.

I knew I was supposed to be cold and objective about these things. I had spent the day observing carefully, trying to gather as much information as possible, and I had sent in my professional report to my newspaper. But when I saw this, all of that changed. I felt rage bubbling up inside of me from the pit of my stomach to my heart, lungs, and then my head until my mind was awash with waves of hot, red fury. I didn't care if these guys, just a little bit younger than me, were right-wing. They were *lying*. They had tricked people, including members of the Movimento Passe Livre's own family, into believing that they stood for something similar. They lied when they said that they were apolitical, and nonpartisan. They hid the nature of their group and who funded it. And now they were lying about their feelings, putting on another show of what they thought people wanted to see.

IN MAY, MICHEL TEMER ANNOUNCED he was forming an entirely new government. He ejected the entire cabinet formed by Dilma Rousseff after her election. In Brazil, it is very common to select a vice presidential running mate from a different party to garner more institutional support, and Temer, a member of the PMDB party, had remained mostly invisible during both the 2010 and 2014 campaigns. Temer (another Lebanese-Brazilian, like Haddad) had his own career before running alongside the Workers' Party; but he had certainly never sketched out an alternative vision for the country to its voters. But now, with Dilma removed by Congress, he took the nation in an entirely new direction with a much more conservative administration. They were far more "pro-market" than any PT administration, and Temer made no attempt to hide the radical nature of this shift. You just had to look at a photo. In his new cabinet of twenty-two people, all twenty-two of them were white men.[14]

There are other words that can be used to describe this, but those people who called all of this a parliamentary "coup" were not wrong.* No one voted for this new executive branch, and nobody would. That seemed to be the point. The country veered to the right, just as economic elites wanted, and there was nothing that regular people could do about it. Sure, there were protests. Big ones. But these were already coded as partisan, pro-PT demonstrations. The media did not give them the right to stand in for "the people," as we had to demonstrators in the second half of June 2013. These red rallies did not count as History; they were seen as predictable manifestations of support for a particular party. There was no surprise, and they were not treated as major news.

On August 5, 2016, the day of the Opening Ceremony of the Rio de Janeiro Olympics, I was on a bus, scrolling Twitter, on the way to the famous Maracanã Stadium with other foreign journalists. In 2009, when Brazil won

---

* The word "coup" is misleading here if it connotes a military takeover or the long-term abolition of democracy, and it carries a lot of this historical baggage in Latin America. But as a term that denotes a break in the institutional order (in this case, to subvert popular will and help elites), I think its use is justified. *Golpe* is often used to mean "blow" or "scam" in Portuguese, and I think those translations work too.

the right to host this Games, it symbolized Lula's success and the arrival of a great democracy on the world stage. Now the contest would be overseen by a man who had stabbed his predecessor in the back and installed an all-white, all-male administration after shoving her aside. As we approached the stadium, I tweeted that the country was now ruled by "interim" president Temer, putting it in quotes to allude to the widely held understanding that he would hold on to power once the proceedings were formalized, and that he did not enjoy universal democratic legitimacy. A columnist from *Estadão* newspaper responded, furious. This reflected unprofessional partisanship. She sent messages to my editor, trying to get me fired.

We got to the stadium. The Opening Ceremony was beautiful. Michel Temer nearly escaped the boos that had greeted Dilma Rousseff two years earlier. That's because he didn't show his face, and the announcers were smart enough to never even say his name. They knew what would happen if they did. They knew how the people felt about "interim" president Temer.[15]

That June, Newton Ishii, the *Japonês da Federal*, was arrested for corruption.

Cows and Candles

The Republic of Korea was born in 1948, after the United States occupied the southern half of the peninsula in World War II. South Korea came into being on the front lines of the Cold War, and from the beginning, its program of pro-Western development was far more concerned with perceived communist threats than it was with democracy. President Syngman Rhee (a Christian who had been living in the United States) crushed left-wing uprisings against his government, killing over one hundred thousand people. After the Korean War (1950–1953), he continued to practice a form of party "democracy" that did not require him to ever actually cultivate mass support or compete with his socialist rivals.[16] He was overthrown in the 1960 April Revolution, mass protests that began after police killed a student demonstrating against rigged elections. But a year later, General Park Chung Hee carried out a coup, putting an end to a short period of apparently unacceptable political instability, and established his own dictatorship, which he claimed was a continuation of the 1960 uprising from below.

After democratization in the 1980s—itself the consequence of a cycle of uprising, repression, and protests—the most important mass protest came in 2008 as part of the alter-globalization era. During that wave of contention, hundreds of thousands of Koreans poured into the streets to stop the flow of US beef into their country. Some reformers had tried to actually involve the masses in party politics in the way that the Workers' Party had in Brazil, but South Korean rules allowed political elites to pick candidates, severely limiting their contact with the population during campaigns.

As it turns out, South Korea's intelligence director had ordered staff to support Park, the daughter of the dictator, as early as her 2012 election. Before the scandal broke, many people at the top of national politics must have known about her deep, illegal collusion with "adviser" Choi Soon-sil. But it was in October 2016 that news of the crimes became mainstream, and the obvious response was mass protest. They used social media to organize weekly protests, holding up candles and singing songs in downtown Seoul— the same repertoire that was put into practice eight years earlier during the alter-globalization era. This took place outside of the official channels of establishment politics, and small parties like the Greens and the center-left Justice Party were prominent in the Citizens' Movement for Park Geun-hye's Resignation. But it was not actually the streets that toppled President Park. That happened in Congress, where the opposition Democratic Party joined the impeachment movement. Unlike the case mounted against Dilma Rousseff, it was very easy to demonstrate that Park had broken the law. Crucially, her own party split—enough of her former allies wanted to distance themselves from Park.

Moon Jae-in, a former human rights lawyer and chief of staff under one of the main pro-democratic reform figures, was elected in May 2017. He immediately reached out to North Korea, with the hope of eventually reuniting the two countries. Technically, the Korean War never ended; many people want to re-create one Korea—as difficult as that may be—while many others simply want peace and friendship in place of war and fear.

I got to attend the next Olympics, the 2018 Winter Games in Pyeong-Chang, as well. As a result of Moon's overtures, the South and North competed as one team, as fans in the South Korean mountain region waved the United Korea flag, and cheerleaders from the Democratic People's Republic of Korea sang songs in support of the women's hockey team.[17]

17

I Was in the 212

IN NOVEMBER 2016, REAL ESTATE heir and reality television star Donald Trump defeated Hillary Clinton and was elected president of the United States of America. This was a deep shock to liberals in the United States. He wasn't supposed to win. He wasn't even supposed to be in the contest after he made racist comments on day one of the campaign. All of the predictive models had been wrong; all of the assumptions about what America stood for in the twenty-first century had to be reexamined.

The most prominent representatives of this faction began to look at the internet itself, specifically actions carried out on the California-based social media platforms that had taken center stage a decade ago, as potential culprits for this radical disruption. Awkwardly, many companies in Silicon Valley now employed prominent former members of the Obama administration who had entered these hugely profitable firms immediately after leaving politics.[1] Within firms like YouTube and Facebook, workers denounced their own machines for promoting whatever drove the most engagement because, they realized, "bullshit is highly engaging."[2] Researchers were discovering that nothing got people's attention like moral outrage. But US liberals looked outward, specifically at Russia. They looked at websites whose articles were widely shared across these social media platforms, and they started to realize that on the internet, you could write anything. It was becoming clear that people might just believe whatever they saw, or whatever they wanted.

We were now very far from the days of 2010 and 2011 when the Democratic Party—and indeed, Hillary Clinton herself—had believed that the internet would make the world more like the United States. Now, the internet was something that could be used by malevolent foreign powers to undermine the American project. As late as 2016, former Politico CEO Jim Vande-Hei said that Facebook founder and CEO Mark Zuckerberg should run for president. Now, the most powerful state in history began to look at how these companies actually operated.[3]

This was the discursive context in which I arrived in Jakarta, the capital city of the world's fourth-largest country by population. I would be based in Indonesia, but I was going to cover all of Southeast Asia for the *Washington Post*. Certainly, this would not have happened if Jeff Bezos, the CEO of Amazon, the online retailer based in the United States, had not purchased the newspaper in 2013. When I started at the *LA Times* in 2011, that newspaper had a larger global presence than the *Post*. But since Bezos bought the newspaper (for $250 million, or 1 percent of his net worth), *WaPo* had been expanding its coverage.

As I arrived in Jakarta, the city was rocked by yet another Facebook-inspired mass protest in a Muslim-majority country. But we were very far from the world of Tahrir Square and the We Are All Khaled Said page that set off the largest country in the so-called Arab Spring. This was a flavor of digitally coordinated uprising that would have been very difficult for progressives and leftists like "Sandmonkey" or "3arabawy" to imagine just six years prior.

AFTER THE US-BACKED MASS MURDER of approximately one million people in 1965–1966, Indonesia became one of the most important allies of the West during the Cold War. A general in the armed forces, Suharto, was rewarded with foreign aid and investment after overseeing the slaughter, and he ruled comfortably (and with record levels of corruption) into the 1990s. But as the 1997–1998 Asian financial crisis hit the country, the dictatorship began to wobble, and his support began to dry up.[4]

During the final moments of his thirty-two-year tenure, riots erupted throughout the country, and in May 1998, some people took aim at the country's ethnic Chinese population in North Jakarta. The Chinese-Indonesian

2 219

minority had been an easy scapegoat, and target of intermittent violence, even before US-backed pogroms in the early 1960s sent part of the population into exile, and the wildly anticommunist Suharto government banned all Chinese-language materials in the country. As his dictatorship fell apart, numerous ethnic and religious groups began to jockey for power, and once more, the Chinese were labeled as traitors, or part of a global cabal of financiers. Approximately one thousand people lost their lives in 1998, and many more decided to leave the country. After Suharto's fall, Indonesia began a bumpy transition to democracy and established a functioning but imperfect system across the country's six thousand inhabited islands (in total, there are about eighteen thousand). As in Brazil, the economic order remained broadly the same as that established during the dictatorship, but in Indonesia, the military remained more influential.

In 2012, former furniture maker Joko "Jokowi" Widodo was elected governor of Jakarta, one of the most prominent political offices in the country. Jokowi might be called Indonesia's Lula, as he was the first postdictatorship politician to emerge from outside the country's military ranks or traditional political elite. But a better comparison is Obama, not only because the two men look very much alike, but because of the way he actually governed. Jokowi was a member of the fiery-red Democratic "Struggle" Party, the same as Megawati Sukarnoputri, the daughter of deposed president Sukarno, considered the founding father of Indonesia, whose national motto was "Unity in Diversity."

During that election, Jokowi's vice gubernatorial candidate was Basuki Tjahaja Purnama, but everyone called him by his Hakka Chinese nickname, "Ahok." The fact that his name was Basuki Tjahaja Purnama in the first place is evidence of the deep anti-Chinese sentiment officialized during the US-backed dictatorship. Many ethnic Chinese citizens were forced to change their names, adopting something that sounded Javanese or Muslim.

Jokowi excelled in the world of Indonesian politics, and he ran for president of the republic and won in 2014. Ahok took over, and the Daerah Khusus Ibukota ("Special Capital Region") of Jakarta, and its over ten million residents, now had a "double minority" as a governor. In addition to his ethnic Chinese heritage, Ahok is also a Christian. Around 87 percent of Indonesians are Muslim; constitutionally, Indonesia is a multiethnic, multifaith country. Balinese Hindus, Dayak Catholics, and Sunda Muslims are all citizens with equal rights. But politically, it is tricky to be Chinese and

Christian and run Jakarta. I would often tell people in the United States to imagine a Muslim running for governor of New York. It might be hard to get elected. Or, if they got in there and did well, they might be very well-liked. This is what happened with Ahok. He had approval ratings of over 70 percent in 2016. His success, to a Western observer, looked a lot like proof of Indonesia's tolerance and pluralistic democratic credentials.

Until he ran for reelection. On the campaign trail, he mentioned the Qur'an. His words were: "It is possible that in your hearts, some of you won't vote for me because of lies about Surah Al-Maidah 51," a verse that some Muslims (but certainly not all) believe prohibits voting for a Christian. "That is your right."[5] Ahok was saying that he believed Islam allows its faithful to vote for him (if he didn't, it wouldn't make much sense to run in Jakarta). His campaign uploaded the mostly unremarkable speech, made to a small community on the Thousand Islands, an archipelago north of the large island of Java, to his YouTube channel. But then on Facebook, someone uploaded an edited version. It now appeared that he had said the Qur'an itself contains lies. The video went viral. Conservatives began to demand his imprisonment for "blasphemy," a notoriously ill-defined criminal offense in the country.[6] He got death threats. And tens of thousands of people used Change.org petitions to attack, and then defend him. The Indonesian Ulema Council (MUI) issued an official judgment, or *fatwa*, declaring that Ahok had committed blasphemy (later, one key cleric admitted he signed the *fatwa* without actually watching the video).[7]

For the backlash, the combined Islamist, conservative, and anti-Ahok forces would draw upon the global repertoire of made-for-media contention. They would hold a mass protest designed to reverberate on social media. They would all wear the same color—pious white was the obvious choice, in this case—and they would gather in Independence Square. They would give their movement a hashtag-friendly title and post about it online. It was obvious what this could accomplish. Even though the whole city was about to vote on whether the governor would stay, they could make a bid to represent the nation themselves. Certainly, they could get everyone's attention.

THEY HAD THEIR FIRST PROTEST in October. But then, when pro-Ahok forces planned a "counterprotest" (always an ambiguous term, to say the least), they marked the date for a mega-event: December 2, or in local date format, 2/12. Everyone was going to call it "212."

It wouldn't be right to call this a "leaderless" movement, partially because it wasn't really a movement at all. It was a small set of discrete actions with a well-defined purpose. The events were structured in a way that anyone could come, and then you went home. That was it. But there were organizers and prominent figures whose profiles were boosted by the event. The National Union of Fatwa Guards organized the first protest. The group Hizbut Tahrir, or "Party of Liberation," from the same Arabic word that gave the name to the square in Cairo, claimed to be the brains behind part of the operations. Tommy Suharto, the son of the late, mass-murdering dictator, supported the 212 and may have donated some money to event organization because fostering Islamist currents in the country would be good for his political dynasty.[8] And the Islamic Defenders Front (FPI—or Front Pembela Islam) gained a significant amount of notoriety during the demonstrations. Its leader, Rizieq Shihab, made news soon after by claiming that the Indonesian currency had subliminal communist imagery in the form of hidden hammers and sickles on the notes. (I wrote one of the articles reporting this story.) Was the 212 "spontaneous"? It certainly came together very quickly, and it made its presence known. But by this point in the decade, smart people were asking if that word meant much of anything.[9]

AHOK LOST HIS REELECTION BID. The governorship would go to Anies Baswedan, an altogether more conventional Indonesian politician. For the type of people who were most likely to interact with foreign journalists in Jakarta—the English-speaking elite, well-paid NGO workers, cosmopolitan liberals, broadly the same type of people who were at the very early Maidan protests—this was a real blow to their vision of Indonesia. But things would soon get worse. In May, Ahok was sentenced to prison. He was convicted of blasphemy.

The year 2017 would remain one of surprise reaction in Indonesia. In September, a small group of academics and activists tried to hold a conference on the 1965 mass killings. Mobs besieged Jakarta's Legal Aid Institute, where they had gathered, and left them fearing for their lives. In Indonesia there was now an almost complete overlap between the radical anticommunist movement and the radical Islamist movement. Rumor has it that radical anticommunists spread the word—that is, the rumor—on the WhatsApp messaging service (owned by Facebook since 2014, and widely used outside the United States) that the conference was actually part of an effort to reestablish the Partai Komunis Indonesia, which would be both illegal and wildly implausible fifty-two years after the anticommunist atrocities began. That was a lie—but it may have been effective at getting people out to attack the terrified historians and survivors. A group called the Muslim Cyber Army was particularly proficient at this kind of digital warfare, and I found myself in their sights soon enough. Throughout the region, fake news and online attacks became the way that politics was done.

In the nearby Philippines, President Rodrigo Duterte had swarms of particularly ardent defenders on social media (I found myself in their sights soon enough, as well), and it emerged that they were paid to do this kind of thing, just like some people in Russia, Saudi Arabia, Israel, Turkey, and many other places. This was a political tactic that would generate high returns on the low cost of digital labor. In countries like Myanmar, journalists and human rights activists had already learned the costs of a national conversation taking place on computers controlled in California. Fueled by racist fake news on Facebook, murderous riots continued unabated as desperate locals sought to locate whomever was supposed to be controlling the website.[10]

It also became clear, later in 2017, that conservative forces in Indonesia were willing to use the red-baiting strategy against the president himself by intimating that Jokowi was somehow a communist when it served his purposes. He was evidently chilled by the successful campaign against Ahok. It was clear that he would not initiate any kind of "truth and reconciliation" committee, or investigation into the 1965–1966 mass killings, as many human rights groups had hoped when he first won the election. It soon became clear that he would not really stand up to military power, or to conservative religious forces. His former running mate languished behind bars.

But former governor Ahok found a way to cope. In jail, he read the Bible intensely and began to date a young police officer. They married soon afterward. Increasingly, I personally turned away from contemporary news and began to investigate the legacy of 1965 anticommunist mass killings.

18

O Mito

THERE WAS A PROBLEM WITH the theory offered back in 2016 that Lula was going to join the Dilma government to avoid his imminent arrest. When he did not enter the government at all, no one arrested him, despite ample evidence that Sergio Moro and the Lava Jato team would have liked to do so. Evidently, they didn't have grounds. It came out later that they knew Lula only agreed to join that administration after allies repeatedly asked for his help.[1] If Lava Jato was really paying such close attention to his conversations, they should have known that too.

At the beginning of 2018, with a presidential election on the horizon, Sergio Moro and the Lava Jato team began to close in on the former president. They still had the full investigative power they had accumulated over the years, and they were still in frequent contact with international authorities, but they settled on a relatively weak accusation. Defenders of this strategy said that this was how the North Americans brought down Al Capone; they had to get Lula however they could. When pressed, they admitted they had to meet a deadline—the judge had to nail him before the Brazilian people could reelect him president.[2]

In the humble beach community of Guarujá, one of the country's major construction companies owned a building overlooking the ocean. According to Lava Jato, the firm renovated a three-level apartment, a "triplex," as a gift to Lula, who allegedly planned to buy the place as a beach house. (Plenty of Paulistanos have a second home on the coast, but few rich people these days are buying them in chaotic, crowded, crumbling Guarujá.) The case hinged on an interview given by an executive in exchange for a plea deal. Even if that executive had been telling investigators the truth about his company's plans, Lula never bought or used the place, so he never actually received any benefit from anyone.[3]

Sergio Moro issued an arrest warrant. His ability to do so hinged on a recent Supreme Court decision allowing the imprisonment of defendants before final rights to appeal had been exercised—a move that analysts chalk up to the successful media campaign and popular pressure on the justices themselves during Sergio Moro's crusade.

As they awaited Moro's move, Lula spent his final days holed up at the headquarters of the outfit where he got his start in public life. Surrounded by sympathetic demonstrators at the ABC Metalworkers' Union on the outskirts of São Paulo, wearing a jacket with indigenous stitching given to him by Bolivian president Evo Morales, he consulted with his lawyers.[4] Some of his supporters thought he should seek exile in a nearby country (which wouldn't be hard) or mount some kind of physical resistance to the arrest. But Lula decided to give himself up. The former president was taken away to prison in Curitiba, the home base of the "Car Wash" operation from the beginning. Courts there decreed that while in prison, the most popular president in Brazilian history would not be allowed to give interviews to the press.[5]

MAYARA WAS HAVING A HARD time in São Paulo. She remained deeply entrenched in the activist scene, but it was harder and harder for her to put up with the situation in Brazil. She was tired of hearing, in left-wing media and from people who had not been there in 2013, that she and her friends in the MPL were responsible for the coup. This was now a common narrative, especially favored by militants in the PT, and it drove her crazy. She agreed that the energy unleashed on the streets had been redirected or appropriated or conquered by the right, but that was not their fault. That was the fault of the PT itself, she said. It should have taken advantage of the uprising, rather than insisting on the impossible task of trying to quell it. A huge wave had been unleashed in June of that year, and yes—they failed to stay on top of it for very long themselves. But the Workers' Party should have caught it, instead of trying to hold back a tsunami.

She had experienced real depression, especially since the MPL began to split into pieces. As a result, she began to have trouble thinking about what had happened in the past in a rational way. Her memories could become scattered or even disappear. And she was sick of people blaming her for the state of the country.

That little cultural meme, "7 x 1," had not gone away. Indeed, Brazilians had found far too many opportunities to invoke the legacy of the 2014 World Cup game against Germany. The onset of serious economic hardship? Another 7 x 1. The Temer government? Another 7 x 1. That administration became less popular than any directly elected president ever had. His approval rating in 2018 hit 4 percent.

Support collapsed for the establishment center-right parties that had backed impeachment and put him in power as the far right loomed larger and larger. In March 2018, gunmen murdered Marielle Franco—a Black, queer city council member who had spoken out against police violence—right in the middle of Rio de Janeiro. To call that a "7 x 1" would have been a cruel joke. Also during the Temer government, I lost someone—Olavo, the Amazon defender who used to guide me around the country, was onboard a plane that crashed in the jungle.[6] His family suspects that someone made good on one of the many death threats he received. Things in the country were sinking to lows that made even black humor difficult to marshal. Mayara didn't know of any way to fix things, and all of this was dragging on her.

So she moved to Chile. She had some contacts there, and she was eager to do two things: get better at Spanish and trek through the Andes as often as possible. Santiago has amazing hiking trails just outside the center of town and absolutely majestic ones a little bit further out. She worked odd jobs, essentially as an illegal immigrant, but life was great.

In her new environment, a couple things jumped out at her. First, Chile was a very neoliberal country. She had known that, but she was shocked at the way this seeped into daily life. Her peers went deeply into debt to pay for a college education. They also had to wrangle with a complicated, expensive private medical system. Brazil's 1988 constitution meant that no one had to worry about either thing—both public universities and healthcare were free, no questions asked. She also noticed that the people of Santiago even *acted* neoliberal. At a party where everyone was drinking, she saw someone offer to *buy* a cigarette, and then they *actually paid for it*, handing over a little bit of change right by the dance floor. This was unthinkable in Brazil. But these Chileans would monetize even the smallest little transactions. Or you would go to dinner at someone's house, and they might ask for everyone to donate some money because they were trying to raise funds for an aunt who needed surgery. She couldn't believe it—that was terrible! She had only seen that kind of thing in media from the United States.

But Chile had an exciting tradition of contention based on opposition to neoliberalism. No one had come close to reproducing the huge explosion of 2011, but in early 2018, Chilean women launched a set of protests against sexual abuse and violence, which flowered into the Mayo Feminista, or "Feminist May." Sebastián Piñera, the same right-leaning billionaire in charge in 2011, had come back into office. He offered a modest package of legislation in response to the wide set of demands, but the former student leaders who were now serving in the government denounced them as insufficient. The ongoing No más AFP, an explicitly anti-neoliberal protest campaign that had begun back in 2016, continued to take aim at Chile's privatized social security system. But it wasn't like Mayara could forget about Brazilian politics. As the horrors of the presidential election back home became more clear, she got involved with the local community of Brazilian expats. They wanted to do everything they could to affect the outcome back home—like protesting in front of the embassy, and urging everyone to vote in October. They were desperately trying to elect Fernando Haddad.

THROUGHOUT 2018, POLLS INDICATED THAT Lula would win reelection if he were allowed to run. An August poll gave him 39 percent of first-round intended votes. Geraldo Alckmin, the former governor of São Paulo (during the June 2013 protests) from the center-right PSDB could get a predicted 6 percent in that scenario. His party had been badly bruised since its support for impeachment in 2016. The real challenger, the candidate with serious momentum, was extreme-right provocateur Jair Bolsonaro. That phrase he had delivered at Dilma's impeachment hearing, "Brazil above everything, God above everyone," was now a campaign slogan. In that same poll, 19 percent of Brazilians said they would vote for him, putting him in second place behind Lula.[7]

But Lula was in jail, and if he stayed there, he wasn't running. While the Workers' Party insisted he was officially the candidate, they also had to find somebody to run if Lava Jato kept him locked up. Lula invited Haddad to visit him at Curitiba. "The candidate is going to be you," he told him. The former mayor responded, "Well, if it is my mission to carry out, I accept."

This obviously was not going to be easy. Haddad would have to stand in for an imprisoned (and more popular) candidate. He was a last-minute replacement and would have very little time to mount a real campaign of his own. After Michel Temer's treachery, they wouldn't take the risk of selecting a vice-presidential candidate from the other side of the aisle. He would run with Manuela d'Ávila from the loyal Partido Comunista do Brasil (PCdoB). All year Bolsonaro had been on the offensive, turning the presidential race into a parade of aggressive provocations. He and his supporters, often inspired by right-wing politics in the United States, got in the habit of making machine gun shapes with his two hands, which would represent the increased number of firearms he wanted to see in the country. More to the point, candidate Bolsonaro said he would *fuzilar*, or "gun down," the Workers' Party. Without Lula in the race, polls indicated he would win the most votes in the first round of the contest.

It was unthinkable to Mayara that a man like this could run Brazil. Her old rivalry with Haddad, from the "V for Vinegar" days, could not matter any less. And she had certainly never—not for a moment—abandoned political struggle. After the trauma of what happened to the June 2013 movement, it seemed that a generation of Brazilians had given up on the idea of protests itself. That was not Mayara. She got to know much of the Brazilian community in Santiago and organized a show of support for the PT candidate in the election coming in October. It was a novel and interesting kind of activism for her. These were people far outside her usual circles. Some were intense supporters of the Workers' Party. Others were the kind of "progressive middle class" and moderates that didn't have fully formed political ideologies but knew they didn't like Bolsonaro. They named their movement after the politician who had been killed months before in Rio and was now an LGBT and left-wing martyr: it was the Comitê de Luta Marielle Franco, or the "Marielle Franco Struggle Committee."

In September, Bolsonaro met with a crowd of supporters in the state of Minas Gerais. Camera phones captured the moment from every angle. Videos show him carried through the streets on the shoulders of his fans. Then, in all the clips, a lone man comes up to him and stabs him in the torso. Watching any one of the many videos you can see Jair Bolsonaro, wearing a bright yellow shirt reading "my party is Brazil," slump forward in pain and grab for his stomach. Supporters immediately apprehended the attacker, a man named Adélio Bispo de Oliveira. Adélio said he was on a "mission from God" and gave authorities the impression that he was mentally unstable. But he used to be a member of a socialist party, and it didn't take long for the budding Bolsonarista movement to unite behind the narrative that he had survived an assassination attempt carried out by the left. That narrative wasn't entirely fabricated—this was definitely an attempted murder—but everything indicated Adélio suffered from paranoid delusions and acted alone. By this point, though, the Brazilian right wing excelled at using social media to spread the message that worked best for them. Soon, Bolsonaro's family (his three adult sons were politicians) posted a photo of the candidate in his hospital bed, making machine gun hands.

Bolsonaro did not have a political party of his own. Or rather, he had spent the last thirty years jumping from one to another without much concern for their official ideological content. He was now on number nine. As the slogan on that T-shirt indicated, the entire Bolsonarista movement was framed as a kind of "anti-party" revolution. Rise above division and "politics," it proclaimed, and unite behind patriotic common sense. But he still had to belong to one in order to run for president, and he was in the small Partido Social Liberal. He would not get very much time on television, as political advertising in Brazil is divided in accordance with the size of the party. All the received wisdom indicated that TV commercials shaped the outcome of presidential elections.

It turned out that by 2018, this was no longer the case. The Bolsonaro campaign made use of social media firms such as Twitter and Facebook. It became trivially easy to post something online and receive a large number of responses from pro-Bolsonaro bots. But the real action was happening on WhatsApp. Huge groups of supporters formed in each state to transmit messages to all their friends and family. I secretly monitored two of these to get a sense of the emerging ideology. There were also operations to blast out Bolsonarista messaging automatically—definitely illegal, and definitely funded with a lot of cash. A lot of these messages were fabrications, or "fake news," a term from the United States that had now entered Brazilian Portuguese. For example, one video claimed Fernando Haddad was distributing "dick bottles" to toddlers so that they would drink milk from plastic shaped like a penis. The Workers' Party, according to this narrative, was preparing the country's youth to perform oral sex. These kinds of things sound outlandish and unbelievable, until you meet people who believe them. Bolsonaro's hardcore supporters, though they always formed a minority of the country's population, were prepared to place their faith in his mission. They liked to call him "*o mito*," which translates to something like "the myth" or "the legend."

Jair Bolsonaro was set to debate Haddad, along with the other candidates. He said that he couldn't come due to his poor health after the attack. This didn't seem very convincing because he was doing media again. He was first in the polls. Fernando Haddad, unlike Lula, was not well known around the entire country. He had only just entered the race, and Haddad longed for the chance to face down Bolsonaro on the national stage. Instead, while the debate between the rest of the candidates aired, Bolsonaro gave a one-on-one interview on TV Record, a channel owned by evangelical Christians.

As expected, Bolsonaro and Haddad made it to the runoff round, with Bolsonaro in first place. Haddad pleaded, challenged, and dared him to debate. He said he would do it in the hospital. Once again, Bolsonaro refused.

I came back to Brazil for the election. I interviewed a lot of voters across polling sites in major population centers, from upper-middle-class São Paulo to the very poor outskirts of Rio de Janeiro. It is important to make a distinction between Bolsonaristas and people who voted for Bolsonaro. Bolsonarismo is on the extreme right, with its base in the white middle class, and comprises a violently antidemocratic current that existed in Brazil well before the man came onto the scene. There are a lot more men than women. But there were also a lot of other people who voted for Bolsonaro. Regular Brazilians who wanted to try something else after four PT governments. They voted for him because he said he would reduce crime, or because the economy was bad and he promised something better. This group, quite large, was not particularly committed to the man or his ideology and often believed the media was exaggerating about him. They had often gotten some snippet of positive news on WhatsApp from a family member, or a church, or some other seemingly reliable source. The attitude "let's see how he does" was particularly common among working-class people. So was the answer: "I'd vote for Lula if he were running."[8]

Members of the Movimento Brasil Livre were now supporting Bolsonaro. They were also running for office themselves. That whole "nonpartisan" thing was out the window. Two prominent members had joined the right-leaning Democrats party, one of the country's most established, and were taking aim at Congress. Another had already taken a seat in the government in São Paulo.

Until the last second, Mayara held on to hope that Haddad could win. She refused to give in to defeatism, despite what all the polls were indicating. Then she got the news in Santiago. Bolsonaro had won, 55 percent to 45 percent. Mayara began to weep, and hugged her friend tight. The Chileans, including her new boyfriend, Pancho, are not quite as expressive as Brazilians, which is why Mayara thinks her lamentations and those of the rest of her community shocked the locals in the bar that night. Their Chilean comrades huddled around them, trying to comfort the expats. I was sitting in an apartment near the water in Rio de Janeiro, typing away, looking out on the diverse neighborhood below. The mood changed immediately. All day long, women had walked the streets or watched the news in dirty little bars with purple stickers reading "Haddad/Manuela" planted on their torsos. As soon as the victory was announced, groups of men, clearly rich and clearly dedicated to strength training at the gym, began to scream at them, hounding them off the street. "Communists! Communists!" Lula was still in jail.

JAIR BOLSONARO ANNOUNCED THAT SERGIO Moro would be joining the new administration. He would leave his role as judge in the small state of Paraná and become justice minister. Effectively he would take on two roles, performing the duties previously carried out by the minister of justice and a separate minister of public security. Everyone would call him the "super justice minister." The anti-corruption crusader, the Lava Jato mastermind, was being rewarded with high political office.

This was obviously corruption in itself. Even before 2018, it was clear that Moro had broken the law in the pursuit of his version of justice. Lava Jato had obviously helped Bolsonaro win—Moro had put his main adversary, the frontrunner, in jail earlier in the campaign year. And now he was very publicly profiting.[9]

His acceptance of a position in a far-right administration also confirmed suspicions that his "crusade" was political all along (he had always promised he would never run for office) and disappointed his cheerleaders in the liberal press.[10] But things quickly got worse than all of that. A series of explosive revelations, published by the *Intercept Brasil* in 2019, demonstrated that he had been far more unscrupulous than previously understood. He wasn't bending the rules; he was smashing them. Moro was actively and secretly collaborating with the prosecutor to secure convictions. Leaks confirmed that Lava Jato had remained in close contact with the United States government, especially the Justice Department and the FBI, throughout the prosecutions.[11]

Bolsonaro announced that he would be abolishing the Environmental Ministry. But this was the first moment that his brand of provocative anti-politics clashed with reality. Just because you believe your country can get rich if it stops listening to the politically correct, gay, rainforest-loving, communist environmentalist scientists does not mean it's actually true. Brazilian agribusiness already quite liked the current setup in the country, and they told him it would be against their interests to abolish the ministry. So he didn't. But by starving the indigenous defense and environmental defense agencies of resources, and clearly aligning with extractive interests in the Amazon, he gave illegal miners and loggers space to increase their violent dominion over parts of the vast rainforest.

Official Bolsonarismo quickly established its own repertoire of "protest." These were essentially rallies in support of the executive branch, but they always managed to take aim at someone else, whether it was the Supreme Court or Congress (both of which the Bolsonaro family openly discussed shutting down). It became very easy to identify a Bolsonarista event if you happened to see one on Avenida Paulista. Yellow or green shirts, of course, and lots of flags. But not just the Brazilian flag. They loved to fly the US flag—which made sense, as the United States government had always appeared to support the forces of anticommunist reaction in Latin American history, and the Bolsonaro family was fiercely dedicated to supporting US president Donald Trump.* You would see the Israeli flag—the Bolsonaro family also loved that country, admired its militarism, and brought Israeli specialists to Brazil to help deal with the fires burning across the Amazon, which exploded in the first year after he took office.

And you may have seen flags from Ukraine. Perhaps the national flag, but they also flew—or wore as a kind of a cape—the flag for Pravyi Sektor, or

---

* When he regained his right to speak with the press, Lula would claim that Lava Jato had been guided by the FBI and State Department, who sought to weaken Brazilian construction firms and industrial development. In this reading, the goals would be economic, rather than just Washington's traditional opposition to the left. "Car Wash" left many of Brazil's would-be "national champions" in tatters.

Right Sector, the group formed in the middle of the Maidan uprising in 2013, which became formalized as a paramilitary battalion and political party afterward. As Bolsonaro began to clash with other branches of government, his supporters began to call to "Ukrainize Brazil."

Of course, these radical Bolsonaristas were not inspired by the early days of the Maidan and the diverse demonstrations in support of "Europe" and against police violence. They were celebrating the radicalization of the street movement and calling for the creation of armed paramilitary groups in Brazil, which could "wipe clean" the political establishment in a manner similar to the way that (they believed) Ukrainians carried out a clean break with the previous order in their country. Key figures in this movement were in contact with a Brazilian living in Kyiv, and Sarah Winter, a prominent "ex-feminist" Brazilian activist, said she had gone to Ukraine for training. To put it simply, these people wanted to carry out a violent right-wing coup.[12]

Eduardo Bolsonaro, the third son of the president, took inspiration from Ukraine when he proposed a new law in Congress, where he had served since 2015. After his father became president, he pushed to make "apology for communism" illegal. This would mean the criminalization of a significant portion of the political opposition. His main reference point for the proposed law, he said, was the "de-communization" process carried out after the Maidan uprisings. In addition to banning the previously influential Communist Party (KPU), which had its base of support among older voters, the government in Ukraine under Petro Poroshenko had outlawed leftist symbols like the hammer and sickle, as well as old Red Army memorabilia.[13] But in interviews, Eduardo Bolsonaro also pointed to the example of Indonesia, which officially made communism illegal during the mass murder of approximately one million people in 1965–1966.

IN UKRAINE ITSELF, THE PEOPLE got a chance to elect a new leader in early 2019. Volodymyr Zelensky, a well-known Russian-speaking Jewish comedian, threw his hat into the ring. His political party—Servant of the People—had the same name as the television show in which he starred as a regular guy who became president of Ukraine. During the campaign he avoided traditional media and appealed directly to voters, using his fame, YouTube, and stand-up comedy (along with ample funding from oligarch Ihor Kolomoyskyi) to drive home the message that he was a new kind of politician who would take on the corrupt establishment. During the campaign,

Zelensky said that he was most inspired by the examples of French president Emmanuel Macron and Jair Bolsonaro.[14]

Zelensky promised to end the ongoing conflict in the Donbas region. His TV show had mocked the country's radical ethno-nationalists. Sitting president Petro Poroshenko, much of the post-Maidan political class, and *Foreign Policy* magazine claimed that he was dangerously pro-Moscow.[15] He won in a landslide and took office in May. A representative of Zelensky's government had to react and quickly explain to the Brazilian press what the government in Kyiv actually stood for when far-right Brazilians started hoisting Ukrainian flags to represent their own radical ideas.[16]

Zelensky's victory can be considered part of the global "anti-politics" wave that crashed across the world in the 2010s and rewarded all kinds of apparent outsiders with high office.* Normally, these figures floundered, became unpopular, and were replaced with experienced insiders in the next election. But floundering was not really an option in Ukraine after his election, and Zelensky would soon be presented with a number of serious challenges.

---

* Like Bolsonaro himself, Emmanuel Macron may be considered part of this internet-driven anti-politics wave. The investment banker created an entirely new political party in 2016, and then declared he wanted to France to be a "start-up nation."

19

A Tale of Two Explosions

IN 2019, THE WORLD PRODUCED another burst of contention rivaling 2011 in the sheer number of people who took to the streets, if not in the changes they unleashed (as of yet). Mass protests took place in Sudan, Iraq, Algeria, Australia, Indonesia, and all over Latin America, not to mention India, Lebanon, and Haiti. More than thirty-seven countries experienced massive protests that year, rounding out a decade that surpassed any other in the history of human civilization in its number of mass street demonstrations.

But two explosions stand out across the globe in 2019, and not only because they both built directly on earlier, unfinished movements born in the decade's first wave of protests. They also pushed their respective countries to a breaking point and forced a reconstruction of the existing order. In the crucial, defining moments of the raucous rebellions, the tactical and organizational questions we have been tracing since the twentieth century—verticalism versus horizontalism; hierarchy versus "spontaneous" self-organization; the questions of representation, meaning, and technological mediation—became hotly contested and shaped all subsequent history in both places.

And the two movements experienced two very different outcomes.

If We Burn, You Burn

In 2019 Carrie Lam was serving as chief executive in Hong Kong—chosen in the way proposed by Beijing in 2014, contrary to how the "yellow" camp in the Umbrella Movement hoped to select leaders for the Special Administrative Region. She was the same woman who had faced off with student representatives on television at the height of their movement, representing the "pro-Beijing" camp.

In February, her government introduced new extradition legislation. Apparently, they did not expect that this would be very controversial.[1] In 2018, a Hong Konger had murdered his girlfriend in Taiwan, but he couldn't be sent back there to face trial due to legal loopholes. The new legislation would fix this—but it would also mean that Hong Kongers could be shipped off to the mainland for trial. The actual text of the law was fairly unremarkable, by international standards. But many people didn't trust the government.

There was a fundamental disconnect between many people and the Hong Kong administration on this issue, not only because five employees of a local bookstore had disappeared in 2015, showing up later in custody in the PRC. My little community of foreign correspondents had been shocked in late 2018 when *Financial Times* journalist Victor Mallet was expelled from the city, apparently for hosting an event with a speaker from a pro-independence party.* More importantly, ever since the British conquest of the island, no government had established effective representation that the local people accepted as legitimate. The yellow camp suspected that the extradition bill was another infringement on local autonomy.

Then there was the case of Xiao Jianhua in 2017. The billionaire businessman and Canadian citizen had been accused of corruption on the mainland. But he was living in an elegant suite in the Hong Kong Four Seasons, apparently untouchable. Until he got touched. A group of unidentified men entered the hotel, overpowered his eight female bodyguards, drugged him, put him in a wheelchair, and took him away. Normally, Hong Kong's (very rich) economic elites had tried to stay out of mainland politics. But the extradition

* My friend Joe Leahy, who had been covering Brazil for years, left São Paulo to take his place.

bill worried them. It was no secret that many of the Hong Kong "tycoons" got rich while breaking a lot of laws. "When we started to open up factories in China," admitted Felix Chung Kwok-pan, a pro-business legislator representing the textiles sector, "a lot of things had to be done by special ways, through corruption, bribery, or whatever." Xi Jinping had been running an anti-corruption campaign in the PRC since 2012 (this was a big decade for anti-corruption crusades), and many tycoons thought they might be vulnerable to more of the same.[2]

But it was the Civil Human Rights Front (CHRF) that began to plan protests starting on March 31. Members of this group were considered plastic leftists or "left pricks," by the more radical and nativist factions in Hong Kong. Formed in 2002–2003 during a successful movement against a proposed national security law, they were a large, organized, and legal outfit that brought together fifty civil society groups and unions, and they planned events well in advance. They picked the tactic that Hong Kongers knew best, which was a big march across the little city, and they invited everyone.[3] After weeks of preparation and hard work, about ten thousand people turned out at their first event. They planned another one for April 28. Even more people came out to the streets, and once again, the political parade was characteristically civilized. Their efforts had paid off, and the "yellow" camp was waking up. Carrie Lam said that the people didn't understand the bill, and her government hemmed and hawed before finally setting June 12 as the day the law would be introduced at the legislature. The CHRF set another protest date—the ninth of June.

But before that, the Law Society of Hong Kong came out against the bill. Lawyers—both local and foreign—staged a silent march on June 6 with the goal of rallying support for the event three days later. It was in their interest to do so: they could feel their role in an international business hub slipping away.[4] Just as in Tunisia nearly a full decade prior, the appearance of this class lent professional respectability to the growing movement.

And it really had grown. The event on June 9 was to rely on the most conventional script in the Hong Kong repertoire. They would have a big, peaceful march from Victoria Park to government headquarters. The surprise was that quite a lot of people showed up. They packed into the streets until perhaps one million people were visible to the cameras in the sky. In size, this now rivaled the city's movement to support the demonstrations in

Beijing back in 1989. As was usual in Hong Kong, things ended in an orderly manner, and most people went home.

But a group of people stayed gathered around the LegCo government building, wondering what to do next. Should they take the protest up a notch? Leave? A young philosophy student named Derek Tai, remembering that protests were against the law past midnight, realized that their activities had technically become illegal. Sure enough, the cops were telling him that it was time to go home. But some friends nearby called for help, and he joined in with the group pushing on a metal railing to clear space for the protesters. A cop snatched him from behind. He was shocked. There had not been any clashes with cops that day or, actually, ever in his life.

At the station, Derek got to speaking with one of the officers, who said they hadn't expected any kind of conflicts that day. They got scared and over-reacted, the officer admitted, and Derek didn't really hold it against them. He could see that they hadn't even brought helmets. He never had a problem with cops. He believed the police officer's version of the story, and they got along just fine. Derek figured his case would be resolved quite soon.[5]

On June 12, another group of young Hong Kongers decided on a more direct strategy. They planned to invade the LegCo and stop the bill from being tabled. The speaker of the city legislature had in fact postponed the reading planned for that day, but thousands of people arrived, intent on occupying the building. Many thought this could go down like nearby Taiwan's (successful) 2014 "Sunflower Revolution." Also known as "Occupy Taiwan Legislature," the movement took over government spaces in the center of Taipei in protest of a trade bill. But this was a very new strategy in Hong Kong.

Something else had changed in Hong Kong, especially when compared to the days of the "Umbrella Revolution" five years prior, and even since the mass marches that had started in March. There was now "no stage," and no leaders governing the planned occupation. Young residents (and those who were not so young, like Au Loong-Yu, the progressive veteran of activist causes going back to 1989) had been coordinating their plans online before-hand using the Telegram messaging app. Police used rubber bullets and tear gas in an attempt to hold them back. It didn't work. They succeeded in enter-ing the building and disrupting proceedings.

Police commissioner Stephen Lo called this a "riot," which immediately sparked outrage.[6] This was civil disobedience, activists responded, carried out by a group that (as June 9 had shown) had a whole lot of people behind them. On June 15, Carrie Lam gave in—sort of. She didn't kill the extradition bill, but she announced that it was temporarily suspended.

On June 16 there was another mass march, and this one was even bigger. By some counts, two million people marched on the street that day. Even the lowest estimates (police put it at around 350,000) would still probably indicate the largest protest in Hong Kong history, measured on a like-for-like basis.[7] This was a staggering number of people. There were only 7.5 million residents in Hong Kong as a whole, including children and the elderly. Any journalist or historian who chose to say that "the people" had spoken on that day would be well within their rights, to the extent that a mass of discrete individuals can ever actually do so. The message was quite legible, as these things go, and it was twofold: a whole lot of Hong Kongers really did not want this extradition bill passed, and a whole lot of Hong Kongers did not like the way the authorities treated the June 12 demonstrators at the LegCo. Carrie Lam apologized to the people of Hong Kong. But the young citizens were still energized; the movement still had momentum. They were not going to stop with the temporary suspension of an extradition bill.

Finn Lau, a student in the United Kingdom, was active on LIHKG, the online forum where a lot of strategies and tactics were being hashed out for the protest movement. LIHKG is often compared to Reddit, a forum in the United States that leans right and male, but this was a "lo-fi" Cantonese-language site used by a lot of Hong Kongers (that also happened to lean right and male).[8] After participating in protests in London in early June, Lau began trying to organize international efforts to put pressure on the Hong Kong lawmakers.

He never used his real name on LIHKG. He signed off his posts with 攬炒, or *laam chau*, a Cantonese phrase that denoted an aggressive poker strategy—"embrace fry," or mutually assured destruction. On one post, he decided to insert an image along with its English translation. It read, "if we burn, you burn with us," which he had taken from *The Hunger Games* film series. One of his posts unexpectedly went viral, and he gained a certain notoriety on the forum. He began to form an international action group on Telegram.

I asked Finn Lau, later, if he realized the wave of global protests that began at the beginning of the decade actually started with a man who set himself on fire in Tunisia. He was only eighteen back then, he said, and he wasn't paying attention to the Arab world.[9]

IN HONG KONG ITSELF, YOU could join Telegram protest groups by walking up to now-resurrected "Lennon Walls" and scanning the links posted there. Or, if you had an Apple device (which many people at the Hong Kong protests did), you could turn on the AirDrop feature on the subway and receive messages about the demonstrations.[10] This was one of many ways that the Hong Kong protests became incredibly decentralized, even more so than in 2014. In addition to an increasingly right-wing orientation, they were something like the polar opposite of a Leninist movement. The Telegram groups had a "poll" function, which allowed for ad hoc voting on tactics—then people did what they liked. And while the Russian revolutionary leader was obsessed with discipline and secrecy, anyone in Hong Kong, including cops, could just walk up to the Lennon Walls and join these groups too.

Before the next protest, planned for June 21 (not by the Civil Human Rights Front, but by the "leaderless" online communities, and with the support of newspaper *Apple Daily*), a tactical approach emerged from the Hong Kong cultural repertoire.[11] "Be water!" was a quote from actor and martial arts superstar Bruce Lee, who in turn had taken the lesson from the teachings of Taoist master Lao Tse: "Empty your mind. Be formless, shapeless: like water.... Water can flow or crash. Be water, my friend."[12] For the especially dedicated yellow protesters still on the streets (now sometimes known as the "dark yellow" movement), this meant that they would not take a fixed position; they would not go on a predictable march or "occupy" anything, but rather swarm and then disperse. They would splash throughout the city until they managed to shut down key buildings for the day. Then they took off. This last tactic was called "leave together"—just as cops showed up, ready to charge, the protest would disappear. Effective at disrupting business as usual, and very frustrating for the police.[13]

At the end of June, the protesters made very clear just how much money they could command for their cause. They raised millions of Hong Kong dollars, then took out full-page advertisements in the *New York Times*, *The Guardian*, and a number of other major global newspapers. The position of the United States government had changed since 2014, and China was now an outright rival, with Donald Trump waging a trade war on the PRC. The US government was supporting the protesters, but they could raise a lot of money from local supporters without much trouble too.[14] Wong Yik Mo, one of the original protest organizers at the Hong Kong Human Rights Front, would come to worry that it was actually too much money. There was now a huge amount of energy, a huge amount of resources, and a huge amount of bravery, but not a clear strategy for turning all of that into concrete results. The mass, broad-based movement was now in the past, and a more radical minority was eager to act but unable and unwilling to negotiate with the people in power.

July 1 is always a protest day, as it marks the day that Hong Kong became a part of the People's Republic of China. Carrie Lam was supposed to attend a flag-raising ceremony at dawn. That wasn't going to happen—her security deemed it unsafe.

By the middle of the morning, someone had unfurled a very different flag in downtown Hong Kong. There was a huge, blood-red banner on display on Harcourt Road, now blocked by protesters. It read, "If We Burn, You Burn With Us."[15]

Five Demands, Three Fingers

Later that day, on July 1, upwards of hundreds of thousands of people turned out for a march. This was smaller than June 12, but it was a lot of people. Then, as night came, protesters once more made their way toward LegCo. This time the building was left unprotected except for a few pan-democrats, the official legal opposition, who tried to ask the frontline demonstrators to stop. They pushed right past them.[16]

By now, this group of protesters, wearing black and intent on entering the building, had expanded their cause. Or rather, they now had "five demands." These were:

1. Formal withdrawal of the extradition bill
2. An end to the characterization of June 12 demonstrators as "rioters"
3. Amnesty for arrested protesters
4. An independent inquiry into police behavior
5. Universal suffrage for the chief executive and the LegCo

Who came up with them? It seems they emerged out of online discussions. That is, they were crowdsourced in Telegram groups and LIHGK, which meant that the vanguard making decisions for the streets would be the well-connected youth, or those with a lot of popularity among them. They probably took inspiration from five claims, emblazoned on a banner held by thirty-five-year-old Marco Leung Ling-kit before he fell to his death on June 15. The nature of the demands shifted slightly in the weeks that followed, as did support for the constituent elements.[17]

Was this the old strategy of "demand the impossible," made famous in Paris 1968 and meant to push the confrontation toward further radicalization and a revolutionary break, or was there a credible plan to demobilize if the government gave in? Or could Carrie Lam call in some representatives to work out a compromise? There may have been answers to these questions, but her administration didn't know them. It was clear, however, what the frontline protesters, who would now come to be known as "the braves," would do to apply pressure—they would impose costs on the city and the government.

After some chaotic discussions and some attempts to take a vote, a number of protesters broke into the LegCo building. Once inside, some of them began to smash things, and others sprayed graffiti on the walls. And then, a few of them unfurled the colonial-era flag, the banner that used to wave over the city when it belonged to the United Kingdom. Unsurprisingly, this got a whole lot of media attention.

Eventually, Carrie Lam confirmed that the bill was dead, not just suspended. But that was no longer what this was about, and the stakes were raised even higher on July 21. This protest was organized by the Civil Human Rights Front, and the police gave them legal right to march, up to a point. When they got to that point, the cops simply stepped aside, and many of the protesters kept going, and going—until thousands arrived at the Central Government Liaison Office, the seat of Beijing's power in Hong Kong. They threw eggs at the building, and then spray-painted the wall. "Respond to the Five Demands," someone wrote. Then someone else: "Down with the Communist Party." And then, "Fuck Chee-na," an anti-Chinese slur.

Au Loong-Yu, the leftist who had participated in the Tiananmen Square solidarity movement in 1989, who had organized with protesters from around the world against the World Trade Organization, and who had been in the Umbrella Movement from the beginning, felt a deep sense of sadness when he saw this. He knew that Hong Kong would lose as soon as it was in a battle *against* China, instead of a struggle *alongside* the people of the mainland. No matter how just your cause, he felt, you simply weren't going to beat the People's Republic of China in open conflict. The idea of "revolution in one city" was not something that had much of a place in political history, nor could anyone envision how it would work here.[18] "This was too far, too far," he said. Chee-na is not something that is lightly offensive. This is the term that imperial Japan used when they were conquering the country and murdering its people.

Au Loong-Yu also knew that with this kind of a protest movement—diffuse, formless ("be water"), and "leaderless," an uprising with "no stage" (Brazilians might say horizontalist)—outside forces would end up imposing meaning on the revolt. They would be able to pick and choose the images that represented the uprising. It would be trivially easy for Chinese media to show that graffiti to hundreds of millions of people in the PRC and portray the Hong Kong revolt as a bunch of rich kids who were simply anti-Chinese racists.

Indeed, there was an actual overlap between the most xenophobic people (racism certainly did exist) and those who pushed for "no stage" the loudest. Notably, one prominent localist, Edward Leung, had called out, "Reclaim Hong Kong, revolution in our time." This slogan would echo through the streets in the second half of 2019. But it was not clear how this revolution would work, or who would carry it out. Au Loong-Yu worried that it simply got people fired up, it got their blood going, but that in practice it was identical to "If we burn, you burn"—cause maximum disruption and hope that this will force a positive outcome. Under the paving stones, the beach.[19] And Mung Siu Tat, the head of the pro-democracy Hong Kong Confederation of Trade Unions (HKCTU), which had been organizing strikes since the 1990s, began to be alarmed by the tyranny of structurelessness. "Some people were indeed making decisions, but they had not been authorized to do so. There was a real gap between the idea of spontaneity and reality of authority," he said. Directives like "no stage" or "you cannot bring a flag" or "you cannot shout a slogan" are actual rules, he said. "That is discipline, and perhaps even more 'authoritarian' than any formal structure would have ever been."[20] Au Loong-Yu put it this way: "Certain braves, in the name of being anti-stage became actual leaders, yet they were not accountable to anyone."[21]

Something else raised the stakes that same day. As some protesters emerged from public transportation elsewhere in the city, men in white shirts attacked them with bamboo canes. They were apparently linked with triads, organized crime groups active in the region. They specifically targeted young people and those wearing black. Forty-five people were injured. Everyone already knew there was a sizable "blue" population in the city, and that many people were pro-Beijing and pro-police, but now someone was organizing a violent anti-yellow backlash. Rumors swirled that a local politician with a bad reputation was responsible for the attacks, and that more could be coming. This was feeling more and more like a war.

On July 26, protesters took the airport. If the goal was to impose costs on the city, and to garner media attention, this was a highly effective strategy. People around the world watched cops face off with kids throughout the brightly lit halls, as cameras were poised and ready to catch them in any act of brutality. An international hub like Hong Kong could not do without an airport, but authorities could not crack down in such a visible area, either. Then on July 28, the dark-yellow camp escalated things again. At the "battle of Sheung Wan," many protesters showed up in "full gear"—that is, yellow hard hats, eye goggles, and gas masks on top of their "black bloc" style clothing. It became routine for wealthier braves to engage in combat with police, ripping up the street and throwing stones or building barricades, and then simply ditch the "full gear" on the street at the end of the night in order to return home undetected. In addition to the "three finger" salute from *The Hunger Games*, members of the movement drew on other aspects from global popular culture—like *The Avengers*, *Star Wars*, or *Neon Genesis Evangelion*—to shape representation of the movement. Antony Dapiran, who was deeply sympathetic to the movement, wrote, "The barricade sociality had given the protesters an identity, and forged them into a cohesive unit that could match the police play for play. And if the protesters' full-gear outfits were a uniform, they were also in this sense a costume. Some became increasingly elaborate in their theatricality, reveling in a dystopian post-apocalyptic sci-fi chic: this was a protest of cosplay."[22]

These kinds of performances got ample attention from international journalists, whom the braves normally regarded as allies.[23] The battle of Sheung Wan forged a new, Hong Kong–specific repertoire that would become familiar to audiences in the city and around the world over the weeks that followed.

On July 29, however, a representative of the government in Beijing made a surprising statement. He acknowledged the efficacy of the initial peaceful protests and issued a thinly veiled criticism of Carrie Lam. If the young Hong

Kongers spoke the language of the CPC, if they were amenable to negotiating, this might have been an opening. But these were two entirely different political cultures, which had been part of the problem ever since 1997.[24]

Apple Daily, the tabloid newspaper founded by local tycoon Jimmy Lai, had become the most vocal media supporter of the ongoing protest movement. In the years leading up to 2019, it had bothered a lot of activists with sexist or xenophobic coverage. It was a populist rag, not high-minded political commentary, and (it was later revealed) Jimmy Lai's business aide Mark Simon, who previously worked for US naval intelligence, used company money to fund right-wing conspiracy theories in the United States.[25] But at the beginning of August, the newspaper became the main mouthpiece for a general strike.

The HKCTU (which had received some funding from the NED) was taking the lead on the August 5 strike.[26] According to that union group, hundreds of thousands of people participated in sectors across the city, most crucially in the aviation industry. Airlines had to cancel hundreds of flights. Chinese authorities responded by declaring they would ban staff who participated in the strikes from flying into the mainland, which is tantamount to losing your job for a Hong Kong airline worker. Supporting a workers' insurrection was a strange position for a newspaper owned by a tycoon with links to the US Republican Party, but that is where *Apple Daily* lined up in 2019.

There was another group that had an interest in imposing meaning on the diverse, diffuse uprising. Republican congressmen in Washington, DC, and the media outlets that supported the Donald Trump administration could find evidence that this was actually an anti-China uprising, if they chose—and they did. They framed it as an affirmation of the moral leadership of the United States on the world stage. Only a small minority of Hong Kongers supported independence from the PRC—a much larger number wanted more democracy within China—and only a tiny minority of protesters did things like wave American flags or hold up pictures of the president of the United States.[27] But those images went far and wide. Finn Lau's little group, formed on Telegram, was working with lawmakers in the United States and the United Kingdom to impose costs on the government of Hong Kong. Within the US government, the Hong Kong protests had their most visible supporter in Marco Rubio, the Republican senator from Florida. As an outspoken anticommunist who had tried to incite a coup in Venezuela earlier that year, his association with the movement gave a lot of Hong Kongers—especially the "left plastics" who had been at the forefront of early organization efforts since 2014—reason to worry. Did US politicians actually want to help Hong Kong, or just to make China look bad? But what was everyone supposed to do, vote on this? Finn Lau was operating on private Telegram groups, and longtime Western media darling Joshua Wong, who went to Washington to offer testimony to Rubio and other US lawmakers, did not actually *represent* anyone—except in the media.

At another airport protest, on August 13, the crowd identified two mainland Chinese men among them speaking Mandarin. They beat one and dragged him through the departure hall. Another apparent mainlander said he was a member of the media and announced to the press and everyone present: "I support the Hong Kong police. You can beat me now." They did. It turned out he was an employee of the PRC's *Global Times* newspaper. This was a propaganda victory for Beijing, whether they had been looking for it or not. This could offer more proof that Hong Kong was now dominated by anti-Chinese riots.[28]

Lam formally withdrew the extradition bill on September 4. Protests continued. This was now about the "five demands," of course, but many members of the local government in Hong Kong, including some who had previously supported universal suffrage, now feared there was an internationally coordinated effort to destabilize the city and all of China.[29]

A large crowd of people marched to the US consulate on September 8, asking Washington to pass the bill that would punish the local government. By now, the protesters were more likely to be localists than the crowds on the streets in June and July.[30] We do not know what the officials in Beijing decided to do. If they chose to simply do nothing, and let the movement spend its energy and bleed support as the year wore on—as many yellow Hong Kongers now believe they did—then that could have been an effective strategy. Many people who had participated in the mass marches in June felt things had gone too far.[31]

When Finn Lau came up with "If we burn, you burn," he thought that Beijing could not tolerate chaos in as important a city as Hong Kong. He began to realize that he was wrong. They definitely could, and they did. In 2019, Hong Kongers were still much, much richer on average than people in the mainland—but its economy was small enough that the central government could tolerate a few months of fires.

It's Thirty Years

On October 7, 2019, students at the Instituto Nacional de Santiago took aim at the city's subway stations. Brazilians would call this a round of *catracaços*, but Chileans simply call it *saltando torniquetes*. They blocked and jumped turnstiles, forcing mass fare evasions, and soon came into conflict with police. They were protesting a small rise in the price of transportation.

Evadir, no pagar, otra forma de luchar! they yelled. "Evade, don't pay, another way to fight!"—except, of course, the original rhymes.

The Instituto Nacional is an elite high school, and its politically active student body has often played an important role in Chilean history—before, during, and after the US-backed Pinochet dictatorship. With these kids on the front line, this raucous bout of contention was naturally going to be a rejection of that legacy; it was an anti-neoliberal revolt. But Chilean youth had been trying to organize another big one ever since 2011. The most famous leaders of that first student movement—Camila Vallejo, Gabriel Boric, Giorgio Jackson, Karol Cariola—were still in Congress, playing institutional politics since they chose to run in the 2013 elections.

Sebastián Piñera, who was back in office, was certainly not Dilma Rousseff. He was not a man whose political career was forged in struggle. His administration was not made up of people who understood what it meant to work for a living and pay for public transportation. His economic minister shocked a lot of people when he said that if commuters wanted to avoid the rush hour price hike—thirty pesos or around four cents in US dollars—they could catch the train before 7:00 a.m. and pay a reduced fee.

The president's response to the protesters was to declare a "state of siege," impose a curfew, and bring the military into the streets for the first time since the people kicked Pinochet out of power. He said that Chile was "at war with a powerful and relentless enemy."[32]

If we can use a bit of journalistic imprecision, we can safely say that the Chilean people rejected this intervention.

Citizens poured into the streets en masse, explicitly defying the president. Chileans were shocked that he would declare "war" on high school students from Santiago. They were terrified that Piñera was bringing back harsh measures that should have been buried with the dictatorship. "From nearly one day to the next," the government's crackdown turned this small student movement into a "national urban awakening."[33] This was now an explosion, or an *estallido social* as the media quickly dubbed it, signifying a kind of social "popping" in the way that an overstuffed balloon might loudly break open, spilling its contents into the atmosphere.

Right away, feminist groups sprang into action to coordinate support for the protesters who were in orbit around the Plaza Baquedano, a huge square in the center of the city that marked the divide between rich suburbs in the foothills and the working-class flatlands downtown. Members of Abogados Feministas, or "Feminist Lawyers," a group formed during the 2018 protest wave, quickly built a group on WhatsApp to meet and plan a response. Danitza Pérez Cáceres, a founding member who lived nearby, could not believe how fast things had exploded and felt excited and afraid at the same time. The Abogadas Feministas began to provide support for protesters at the plaza (soon renamed the Plaza de la Dignidad by the movement), as well as legal aid, meeting the same demand as Euromaidan SOS in Ukraine and the @TahrirSupplies Twitter account (assisted once in a big way by Andy Carvin) in Egypt in 2011.[34]

On October 25, over one million people took to the streets in the largest protest in Chilean history. All kinds of citizens came out to protest, including many that seasoned activists had never seen before. This was 2019, so the kids were no longer on Facebook. Over the years, that company had fiddled with the algorithm on its service to maximize profitability, radically changing the type of post that would appear to users, and the kinds of groups and discussions that had driven uprisings from 2011 to 2013 were not happening there anymore, if they were even still possible. Just as importantly, the site had become associated with older people. Instead, the meaning of the demonstrations was often hammered out on Instagram (another service that was now owned by Facebook), especially on its image-based Stories function, where public back-and-forth was impossible.[35]

A few slogans quickly emerged out of the morass of contradictory opinions and conflicting reasons for being in the streets, both of which were remarkably similar to the ones that took over the streets in Brazil in 2013. "The country has awakened," everyone began to declare. And then: "It is not about thirty cents, it is about thirty years." Except unlike the "it is not about twenty cents" cry in Brazil, the meaning was not left indeterminate. Thirty years meant something a bit more specific—this was the amount of time since the dictatorship ended, and the era in which insufficient democracy had been delivered to the Chilean people. The period in which the country had not gotten far enough away from Augusto Pinochet.

Mayara couldn't believe her eyes. It was all happening. She had been in the capital for a little more than a year and was suddenly living through a mass protest explosion that was very similar to the one her group had set off in 2013. Except it was better, she thought. First, there was no need for an MPL here, no small group that had to decide when to call protests, or what to say to the media, or how to withstand the pressure of exponential growth in a short period. And here, the president was right-wing. So there was no reason for any elements of the institutional left to worry about weakening the government, try to hold things back, or attack the young activists for adventurism.

Once more, after all the years she had spent depressed, or battling accusations that she had made Brazil worse, she threw herself into the movement. She could stop being an individual with a job, and money problems, and her own personal issues once more. She hurled herself into the *estallido* and became part of the crowd. Part of this giant, euphoric ball of people growing and pulsating and reshaping reality. Part of History.

President Sebastián Piñera made a bid to define the meaning of the uprising. He called the huge demonstration on October 25 a "happy, calm, and peaceful march" and said it was "without political colors." It was true that not everyone on the streets that day was a leftist. But a whole lot of people were calling for his removal. The rejection of neoliberalism and the rejection of the Pinochet dictatorship, as well as the rejection of Piñera himself (or at least, the rejection of his response to the initial protests), remained at the center of attention and shaped the possible paths that the "pop" could take.

The musical group One Thousand Guitars for Victor assembled near the square to sing a song from the days of the Allende government. They began to play the classic "El Derecho de Vivir en Paz." Its composer, Víctor Jara, was a beloved folk musician who was tortured and murdered in the first days of the military junta in 1973. Thousands and thousands joined in until the ecstatic people in the crowd were shouting, affirming, and demanding "the right to live in peace."

For what it's worth, this was the viral clip that made it to me that day as I sat in my apartment in Jakarta. Another iconic image, the kind of photographic reproduction of reality that is copied and posted and reposted around the world, showed a mass of people climbing up the statue at the center of the Plaza de la Dignidad, waving Chilean flags. But at the very top, someone was waving a flag of the indigenous Mapuche people, who had brought their decades-long struggle into the square as well. And if you looked into that Víctor Jara song, it was not just about the police leaving you alone. It praises Ho Chi Minh and his heroic struggle against murderous US imperialism in Vietnam. It is a ghostly denunciation of the same violence that would take his life and a deeply left-wing anthem. It would be hard for this to work out well for Piñera.

Neighborhood assemblies, or *cabildos*, sprang up all over the country. Residents came together to discuss their grievances with the government, what the uprising meant for them, and what they should do next. These were "spontaneous" and organic in that no institutional political actors came up with the plan to form them. They were horizontally structured and self-governed, and anyone could come. But they drew on local traditions of popular power, and they were shaped by the earliest and most active participants. As such, they tended to be left-leaning, feminist, and young like the rest of the *estallido*. Regular people spoke about their day-to-day problems in contemporary Chile, while more committed activists might talk about legislative proposals that could reduce violence against women, or about forming a whole new legislative system entirely.

Then there was the *primera línea*, the front line, the people engaging in active combat with the police. The people who lost an eye when struck with a tear gas canister, or were blasted back with water cannons, or got hauled off to jail. This group drew on local traditions of contention, namely the figure of the *encapuchado*—or "hood"—who wears a black sweatshirt and covers her head. A friend of Mayara, a Chilean anarcho-feminist named Alicia, designed her own knit balaclava—black and purple with flowers and holes and protection for her neck—and gained a little notoriety in the press as an "icon of the feminist struggle." Young, punk, and anti-authoritarian types were important for the front line, as were minors who actually lived on the street. These might have been orphans or the urban poor that had been abandoned or abused by the system, and maybe used cheap drugs. And then there were the football *ultras*. As in so many other mass protests since 2011, committed soccer fans had the bulk, bravery, and background to provide real assistance in street combat. But very much unlike the situation in Kyiv, and despite Piñera's best attempts, this was an explosion where left-wing themes remained dominant.

Romina A. Green Rioja described what it felt like for a feminist historian like her on the streets. There was: "the feeling of joy, the acceleration of history, and the sense that politics was happening everywhere."[36] Danitza Pérez Cáceres and her colleagues just kept working and helping people. Days were long, and they would all blend into each other until her memories of events felt somehow nebulous, something more than real. There was no time to stop and think, or to be afraid.

The uprising had come quickly, and it was intense. In one month, more than a dozen people had lost their lives. Central Santiago stopped functioning as anything other than a site of contention and a furnace of history. It couldn't burn like this for long. "This was a climate of real instability, and that forced authorities to act," Danitza said. "When the city center is being destroyed, this creates a very real sense of urgency." Even some residents who supported the uprising and participated daily left their downtown apartments empty to stay with friends or relatives a little bit outside the impact zone.[37] Back in the days of the Old Left, most people would know that classic Marxist analysis asserts the primary task of the bourgeois state is to reproduce the conditions for the accumulation of capital—to make sure the business class stays in business. These conditions were disrupted. Things got even worse, from the standpoint of those who were carefully monitoring the Chilean economy, when dock workers began to strike in port cities like Antofagasta and San Antonio, bleeding millions of dollars out of Chile's trade flows.[38]

The country's elected representatives needed to find a way out of this. In the middle of November, congressional leaders got together and began negotiations that lasted deep into the night. Not all parties were there—the Communist Party was absent, for example—but enough assembled to get something done. What could they give the streets that would respond to their demands without pulling the rug out from under their own feet? Since 2011, and even before that, a wide range of civil society groups had been calling for a new constitution to replace the 1980 document inaugurated under Augusto Pinochet. For obvious reasons, this cause was especially close to the hearts of the left, and the generation of student leaders that took to the streets eight years ago often found they bumped up against the "invisible glass ceiling" of the old constitution as they made their demands. And while there were many other demands being made outside, right now, the call for a new constitution was on the streets. It was often at the center of conversations taking place in the neighborhood *cabildos*.

So these political representatives came up with a peace deal—an *acuerdo por la paz*. Soon, they proposed, Chileans would vote in a referendum to decide if the country would write a new constitution. If that referendum passed, voters would elect representatives to sit in a constitutional convention and write it. This was not a deal, *un acuerdo*, made between the political class and the streets. This was a deal made *within* the political class.

The only leftist from the 2011 generation to cross the aisle, the only "autonomist" radical to sign the accord with the rest of the establishment, was former student leader Gabriel Boric.

Canceled

"The Square" rejected the deal. Or at least, many of the individuals who were on the front lines, in the streets, at the center of the uprising, and vocal about its meaning thought that this was a betrayal. According to any kind of horizontalist reading of the situation, it was an authoritarian act; this was an outside actor imposing its own will on the revolt. The meeting had taken place at night, behind closed doors. No one asked the people who had actually begun the protest, and no one had asked the people who were still out there, risking their lives. Clearly, the relationship between Congress and the plaza was *vertical*—and the political class was trying to *represent* them. Since the cry of *no me representan* back at the Plaza del Sol in Madrid in 2011, this kind of thing had been off limits, at least for a very vocal current within the mass protests taking place over the decade.

The major split was over how to re-found the country. Many people wanted an assembly to decide the future of the country, rather than a convention. In the first scenario, it would be the people that would dissolve sovereign power in Chile and constitute a new government. A convention—the road favored by the actually existing government—would recognize the legitimacy of the actually existing government and rely on its rules to define the steps forward. Calling an assembly was the solution favored by Alicia, Mayara's anarcho-feminist friend, and much of the anti-authoritarian left. In some ways, *asambleísmo* is close to the Chilean word for "horizontal-ism," and it has a long tradition in the country—long enough for the Communist Party to have an official document outlining why it is a trap.[39]

Not everyone was paying attention to the philosophical distinctions between an assembly and a convention. There were many protesters who had focused their ire on Piñera and refused to accept a situation in which he was allowed to stay in office. As was the case going back to Egypt, some of the most radical people insisted that a riot itself was the revolution and could be expanded and transformed into a new society. And a lot of these people knew who had betrayed them—Gabriel Boric. He inspired special indignation. He had led the uprising in 2011, only to enter politics, and then—in an act of profound treachery—he lent his name to the establishment solution. He helped make this *acuerdo* possible and, even worse, he gave the political class a way to pretend that the youth and the streets were part of the deal.

Danitza used a new term, which had recently emerged from US digital culture, to describe what happened to Boric. *Él fue cancelado*—he was canceled. It happened first online and in the media, but then the thirty-three-year-old politician felt the physical manifestation of the phenomenon—which was quickly reproduced digitally. One day, as he was sitting on a park bench downtown, a group of Chileans came up to him and poured beer all over him, throwing trash on the congressman and shouting him down. "The people believed in you!" one man yelled. "We all believed in you!"

The next meetings of the neighborhood assemblies went ahead as scheduled. And the *primera línea* came out again to defend the square and battle with the police. The punks and hoods had not made a deal.

However, the (informal) leaders of the *cabildos* began to notice that attendance was down. At some assemblies, a lot of people were in favor of the accord, others less so. Even when this wasn't any source of conflict in the meeting, the numbers were dropping. The *cabildos* had never really known what to do with the decisions made by their collectives, and now they didn't know what to do with dwindling interest.[40] They were confronting one of the tough questions that often arise from horizontalist practices, identified by thinkers like Paolo Gerbaudo in the middle of the decade: How do you decide who is in, and who is not? If a lot of working-class people stop show-ing up, are they still a part of it?[41] Is the *cabildo* just as legitimate?

And more importantly (for the people trying to run a capitalist econ-omy), the disruptions were less intense, and there was less violence on the street. Downtown Santiago was still a bit of a mess, and people were defi-nitely coming out to protest at the Plaza de la Dignidad (the last time I vis-ited, in 2022, this was still true), but you could just about start to conduct business as usual again. At least, things seemed to be heading in that direc-tion. The political class planned to give the people its referendum on a new constitution in 2020. Sebastián Piñera was set to end the year with an 11 per-cent approval rating, but was still the president. The next elections would not take place for two more years.

IN HONG KONG, AUTHORITIES INSTITUTED an emergency "mask ban" in October, meant to stop the radical "braves" from hiding their faces. Carrie Lam's government was not offering a peace accord or a referendum any time soon.

The movement was now led by the individual braves themselves, rather than any mass protests or broad-based organizations. As Chile entered its summer in the southern hemisphere and Hong Kongers felt the approach of winter, international media could barely keep up with the other protest explosions rocking the globe. An uprising in Algeria, that forced the resig-nation of President Abdelaziz Bouteflika, raged on. It was the largest revolt since the end of the country's civil war. In Baghdad, hundreds of thou-sands of Iraqis called for an end to the sectarian political system created by the 2003 US invasion and occupation. The government (now friendly with Iran, something that George W. Bush had certainly not hoped for back then) cracked down with the aid of Shia militias.[42] Then, in Bolivia, mass protests erupted after election results came in, and the military stopped recognizing the leftist Evo Morales as the legitimate president. In the wake of the coup, a right-wing president with no popular support took over the country.[43]

In November, the Hong Kong braves ended up abandoning the "be water" strategy. They occupied two universities in the city and bunkered down inside. Antony Dapiran reported what this looked like from the inside of Polytechnic U: "Through the smoke a protester emerged wearing an old, World War II–style gas mask and wielding a bow and arrow. This was no longer a protest, or even a riot. It was medieval siege warfare." But China was better at war than the young people of Hong Kong. One police officer on the scene said, "It's common sense that you have to face the penalty if you break the law, just like you have to pay the bill after having a meal in a restaurant. No worries, if you are stubborn, we can stay here and wait for you until Christmas."[44]

In Washington, DC, Congress passed the "Hong Kong Human Rights and Democracy Act of 2019" put forward by Marco Rubio. In addition to punishments for Beijing, the law stipulated that Washington would periodically evaluate if Hong Kong was imposing sanctions on countries already sanctioned by the United States. Seasoned activist Au Loong-Yu felt that the "tying of Hong Kong human rights to US foreign policy is a mockery of human rights."[45] For other Hong Kongers, like Finn Lau, this felt like some kind of a win. Beijing promised to retaliate immediately. But by the end of 2019, the smart minds in the United States government had something else to worry about in China.

Happy New Decade

In December 2019, scientists identified a novel strain of the coronavirus in Wuhan, central China. Not long after, authorities in the People's Republic of China began to press citizens to stay indoors to reduce the spread of the disease. These kinds of responses, which became widely known as "lockdowns" in English, did not immediately spread across the world. But soon, they would force existing street movements to retreat and transform into something else. On most of the planet, the threat of immediate death would supersede the widespread desire to engage in mass protest. New bouts of contention would emerge and take forms that were surely shaped to some extent by the presence of the virus. At the time of writing this, that pandemic has not entirely ended, and it is (quite intentionally) outside the scope of this study to ask how things will have been remade when it ends.

But as the decade came to a close, before COVID-19 (named for 2019, the year it was first identified) froze a global wave of contention in place, the explosion of mass protests since 2010 had already effected profound historical shifts in the countries where they took place. This was true in Africa and the Middle East, and in the former Communist world, and in Brazil, and it was true in Hong Kong and Chile.

In Santiago, many of the young people (or those who were no longer so young) who had been active on the streets since 2011 could ring in the new year looking forward to a constitutional referendum, whether or not it was coming in the exact way they wanted. Danitza and other feminists fought behind the scenes for rules that would make a likely constitutional convention more aligned with the values of the uprising.

Finn Lau spent New Year's Eve in Hong Kong. He was still studying in London, but he had come home in December to participate in the movement he had assisted from abroad. The university occupations had been a major blow to the ranks of frontline braves. He was still known as 攬炒, or "If we burn," his signoff on the LIHKG forum, as his public identity had never been revealed. The demonstration planned for the next morning, January 1, was deemed illegal. But they weren't going to call it off. On the first day of the new decade, along with hundreds of other people, Finn Lau was arrested.

20

Reconstructing the Past

TIRIRICA, DESPITE HIS MANY TALENTS as a clown, was wrong about history. His campaign back in 2010 struck a powerful chord when he declared *pior que tá não fica*, and millions of internet users made his clip "go viral." But anyone who thought that was tragically mistaken. It can get worse. Things got worse in Egypt, where an even more brutal dictatorship has taken the place of the Mubarak regime. Things surely got worse in Libya, which became a failed state. In 2010, the country had the highest Human Development Index in Africa, according to the United Nations. By 2017, human beings were bought and sold for hundreds of dollars in a shocking revival of the African slave trade.[1] Only a small minority, a group of the most fanatical Bolsonaristas, would claim that Brazil was better off at the end of the decade. It is unquestionable that, from the point of the organizers of the June 2013 protests, the country had gotten much worse. We can go on and on, citing other countries as examples, but there is no need to belabor such a depressing point. It can always get worse.

As I spent years traveling around the world, talking to the people that helped create the mass protests described in this book, and interviewing the experts and government officials who tried to grapple with their meaning, I would always ask what they thought had happened. But I never did so to cast blame or to establish that mistakes were made. Most people who spoke with me know very well that things can go terribly wrong regardless of intentions, and the conversations often became difficult. Many of these individuals have suffered for years trying to understand the events of the past decade.

I always put my question something like this: "If you could speak to a teenager somewhere around the world right now, someone who might be fighting to change history in some kind of political struggle in their lifetime, what would you tell them? What lessons did you learn?"

The first very obvious lesson, perhaps now too clear to require much explaining, is that history continues to unfold after the explosion. A revolution is a difficult process and does not start and end with a single bolt of lightning. Too often, it seemed that the approach employed in the 2010s could be summed up, fittingly, in a tweet:

1. Protests and crackdowns lead to favorable media (social and traditional) coverage
2. Media coverage leads more people to protest
3. Repeat, until almost everyone is protesting
4. ????
5. A better society

It is with some bitter irony, and a big helping of his self-deprecating wit, that Mahmoud Salem, the blogger who crossed the Nile to fight for Tahrir Square in 2011, recalls that final battle scene from the movie trilogy *The Lord of the Rings* when Sauron is defeated. Why did they think that if Mubarak fell, all evil would simply disappear from the land? When Lucas "Vegetable" Monteiro told me that the Movimento Passe Livre had made no preparations for what happened after they successfully killed the fare hike, he smiled and then burst into humbled laughter. They had forgotten quite a big detail!* Theo, a young Hong Konger who fought alongside the braves in 2019, looks back wistfully on the approach they took in the second half of the year.[2] They certainly weren't going to beat Beijing in an open confrontation, so what was the endgame? History does not possess a supernatural, metaphysical quality that pushes it forward relentlessly. Many people in my

---

* Similarly, Barack Obama has said that the biggest mistake of his presidency was "failing to plan for the day after" in Libya. At the level of the world's only superpower government, however, this may strain credulity. One might conclude that ultimately, the US was willing to accept a failed state.

generation (and I think I, too, was guilty of this teleological mode of thought at the beginning of the decade) thought that if you simply gave the thing a kick, it would come unstuck and move in the right direction. Paradoxically, liberals, socialists, conservatives, and anarchists alike have all thought that way, even as they define "the right direction" rather differently.[3] But if you burn down your building, divine providence does not supply you with a better one. If you chop down a tree, you do not immediately get a bigger tree. Sometimes you are just left with a stump. As industrial society becomes ever more complex, the range of possible unintended consequences grows larger. If your car isn't running well, it is not recommended to light it on fire and hope that a better one comes along.

You have to have a way to get from where you are to where you want to be, many people told me, or at least a road map to somewhere better, and you need, if not a plan already prepared in advance, then a strategy elaborated quickly and effectively as events unfold. Simply being right is not enough. Some of the Hong Kong protesters cited Mao in 2019—"a revolution is not a dinner party" appeared on posters around the city, so I don't feel it's inappropriate to cite the way that Wang Hui, both a leftist and a protester in 1989, characterized the Chinese revolutionary: "Mao upheld the righteousness of the revolution but was not blinded by this righteousness," he wrote. "Rather, he combined this sense of righteousness with strategic analysis."[4]

In this book, we looked closely at ten mass protest explosions: in Tunisia, Egypt, Bahrain, Yemen, Turkey, Brazil, Ukraine, Hong Kong, South Korea, and Chile. While Occupy Wall Street, Spain, and Greece were important for shaping the rest of the decade, the protests themselves did not dislodge the respective political structures from their foundations, or generate an institutional rupture; likewise, the Indonesian case changed politics in the world's largest Muslim-majority country, but the system itself was not disrupted by the street movement. While mega-protests elsewhere helped cause the events in Libya and Syria, armed intervention began to shape outcomes at least as much as any broad-based demonstrations.

If we view the outcomes from the perspective of what the mass protests asked for (and this is complicated, though I think it is crucial), then seven of these countries experienced something even worse than failure. Things went backward. The South Korean Candlelight Revolution can be marked as a success; not coincidentally, its goal was very clear and achievable. I believe that Euromaidan can be called a kind of draw. It generated a mix of successes and failures, depending on your perspective. For those who thought that the most important thing was to reintroduce Ukrainian nationalism into the heart of the polity, and to force a separation from Russia, the years after 2014 could be experienced as a kind of victory. And many people told me they felt exactly this way. But "de-oligarchization" absolutely did not happen—quite the contrary—and opportunities did not increase for normal people.[5] In the years after the Maidan, Ukrainians continued to look elsewhere for a better life—from 2014 to 2020, millions more people left the country.[6] In a December 2019 survey, 38 percent of respondents said they would support Euromaidan, if they had a chance to redo history—and pollsters could no longer ask people in Crimea, Donetsk, or Luhansk.[7] It is not as if the world's leading powers showered the country with riches, or even provided it with basic security from invasion, after so many Ukrainians died to turn the country toward "Europe."

At the level of elite political and economic power, Maidan forced a kind of game of musical chairs with the players now required to don Ukrainian nationalist garb. Volodymyr Ishchenko and Oleg Zhuravlev call this type of uprising "deficient revolutions," and the victorious pose requires a forgetting of many of the revolt's original goals.[8] These kinds of things always do. In Ukraine there were certainly losers—not only the "blue" Ukrainians who felt that they had been disenfranchised by the end of the Yanukovych government, or people in places like Odessa that had protest movements annihilated. For some people, the rise of right-wing nationalist ideology in Kyiv politics, and the affirmation of Ukrainian identity as necessarily anti-Russian and anticommunist, was something like an assault on the nation they believed they were a part of. Many people told me they felt exactly this way. And this is leaving aside the people of the Donbas, whose neighborhoods were decimated by civil war.

Obviously the decisions to violate Ukrainian sovereignty—to snatch up Crimea and ultimately to invade the country—fall on Vladimir Putin. Those are his crimes and he is responsible for the consequences. But if there were no men like him, no political struggle would ever be necessary. A more audacious analysis might ask if a different type of revolution was possible. Some early participants told me they hoped that the Kyiv uprising would create dissenting groups that would push for economic justice from below, but they were surprised at the degree to which conservative elites were organized and succeeded at delivering a top-down cultural revolution instead.

As a rule, the people who sat down with me did not want to stop their analysis at the recognition that repressive forces were repressive; they did not want to simply blame their enemies for behaving badly. If all of that were not the case, there would be no reason for contention in the first place. Those kinds of answers were too easy. They wanted to hold themselves to a higher standard. The last two uprisings that we followed, those in Chile and Hong Kong, probably had the most wildly divergent outcomes—a delicate victory and a devastating defeat. In June 2020, Beijing introduced a National Security Law for Hong Kong, and what has happened in the Special Administrative Region in the following years amounts to about the exact opposite of what the "yellow movement" had asked for: mass arrests and many young people going into exile, a crackdown on media, and the end of the "pan-democrats" in the LegCo. After Beijing disqualified some of its colleagues for violating their duties or endangering national security, the rest of the opposition resigned. Afterward, pro-Beijing lawmaker Regina Ip told me that "as our democratic experiment has not worked well, I don't think we are likely to elect our chief executive and legislature by universal suffrage for a long time." She said that "with the pan-dems gone, we are now able to function much more efficiently and productively."[9]

Things went very differently in Chile. In October 2020, voters overwhelmingly approved their referendum to call a convention and write a constitution to replace the document put in place under Pinochet. Then it was time to replace Sebastián Piñera. In 2021, the thirty-five-year-old Gabriel Boric, the leader of the 2011 student protests who entered congressional politics in 2013 and signed the "peace accord" in 2019, was elected president. He declared, "If Chile was the cradle of neoliberalism, it will also be its grave." Boric fell behind the Pinochet-defending José Antonio Kast in the first round, but rode a wave of support in the runoff to defeat him, 56 percent to 44 percent. He made Camila Vallejo the secretary general in his cabinet and brought in Allende's granddaughter to run the Ministry of Defense.

In 2022, I met a lot of people who initially opposed Gabriel Boric's decision to sign the acuerdo por la paz, but then became full-throated supporters of the constitutional project. They decided they were glad he did what he did. I believe this reveals something crucial about the dynamics that emerge from the particular repertoire of contention put into play in the mass protest decade—we will come back to this soon—but this was also the hard work of feminists, militants, and other Chileans working behind the scenes after the high point of the "social popping" had passed. So far, the Boric government has struggled to make real the dreams of the *estallido social*—mirroring the historical experience of most social democratic governments in the Global South—but they got into office, and so they got their shot. It is entirely possible that the Boric government will fail, or provoke an effective right-wing backlash. But setting aside the possibility of a fully fledged revolution that defends itself against the inevitable counterattack, you cannot do much better than win power, and get to work. Not as a result of this kind of mass protest.

Mahmoud Salem now lives abroad, as do Hossam el-Hamalawy, Gehad, and almost everyone from Egypt who could speak to me for this book.* When I was in Cairo, I felt a climate of repression unlike anything else I had experienced in my career. I wasn't even trying to uncover any secrets or break any news, and yet, everyone told me to be extremely careful; any conversation about politics in public could get me—or worse, my Egyptian contacts—arrested. I met friends of friends, before other friends of friends said that those friends might be spies, and that actually, anyone could be. Don't judge them, they said, as they may have been forced into it against their will. And US president Trump was characteristically brash but revealingly honest when he called Sisi "my favorite dictator." In the capital cops might stop you on the street and search your phone for anything political, and then take you to jail. The repression in recent years is worse than at any other moment in Egyptian history, said Hossam Bahgat, a human rights activist in Cairo. What explains this? It seems Sisi is terrified of another 2011, another Tahrir Square. It's not clear if or how the Egyptian leader understands the process that led to his regime.

In Bahrain, I was able to have lunch with Ebrahim Sharif at his home, now that he is out of jail. But those photos of the Sunni monarchy, the kind he was forced to kiss under threat of torture, are still everywhere in his country. In Turkey, Istiklal Avenue is now mostly alcohol-free, and the dream of a Turkish Model and EU membership seems like an absurd joke. Ukraine has been invaded. Yemen is under attack and suffering from mass famine caused by the Saudi-led blockade and invasion. During the COVID-19 pandemic, the neighborhood in front of my downtown São Paulo apartment came to look like a film about the end of the world: roving gangs of teenagers trying

* Among a litany of other self-criticisms, both "Sandmonkey" and "3arabawy" now regret their calls to boycott the 2012 election.

to steal enough to survive; families living on the streets, huddling around fires arising from big trash cans and warming their hands or heating up discarded noodles. In 2012, when I moved to Praça da República, that scene would have been unimaginable. In 2022, my dear friend Dom Phillips, one of the main contributors to our little blog for *Folha*, was murdered in the Amazon doing his job. Bolsonaro said he was asking for it and then suggested that piranhas might have eaten his body. In Tunisia, I went back to the market where Mohamed Bouazizi worked before setting himself on fire, and then to his grave outside Sidi Bouzid, where he had been buried as a martyr in the more optimistic days of the revolution. "I knew him. He was a nice guy. But this revolution did not benefit the Tunisian people. Tunisia did not take one step forwards. It moved backwards," said Ismael Awled Nasser.[10] I heard a lot of the same from the nice women who were doing their best to sell their fruit, to make ends meet, while dealing with yet another foreign journalist. Near his grave, some local teenagers were less diplomatic. "Mohamed Bouazizi, may he rest in peace. But most people hate him."

But as I said, the point was not just to notice that the mass protest decade hasn't really worked out. The idea was to understand why.

I PUT THE QUESTION TO Mayara Vivian and Fernando Haddad. At the beginning of the twenty-first century they formulated two very different responses to the onset of neoliberal globalization, and back in 2013 they had faced off in an epic battle on the streets of São Paulo. When speaking about the MPL, Haddad still becomes visibly upset, sitting upright in his chair and crossing his arms. Nine years after the events of June 2013, I asked them the main lesson they learned. They both said the exact same thing.

Não existe vácuo político—"There is no such thing as a political vacuum."

The idea is that if you blow a hole in the center of the political system, taking power away from those who have it, then someone else is going to enter the empty space and take it. Unclaimed political power exerts an irresistible gravitational pull on anyone who might want it, and at every moment in recorded history, someone has wanted it. Personally, in the years since 2013, I would often use the language of a theatrical performance to say something similar. If you want to knock the main players off the stage, you should be paying attention to who is going to take their place. These might be local or foreign actors. If is not going to be you, then you had better like the people who are waiting in the wings.

The particular repertoire of contention that became very common, almost appearing to be natural, from 2010 to 2020—apparently spontaneous, digitally coordinated, horizontally organized, leaderless mass protests—did a very good job of blowing holes in social structures and creating political vacuums. There's a reason we so often call them "explosions." As a very simple rubric for understanding the outcome in each country, we just have to look at who was ready and waiting to rush in. In Egypt, it was the military. In Bahrain, it was Saudi Arabia and the Gulf Cooperation Council, who literally marched in to fill in the gaps. In Kyiv, it was a different set of oligarchs, and well-organized militant nationalists found a little bit of space that they could occupy too. In Turkey it was ultimately Erdoğan himself, though he took up more space than a leader should in a democratic country that hopes to enjoy global prestige and the support of cultural elites in Istanbul. In Hong Kong it was Beijing. In Brazil, Dilma Rousseff was not removed, not immediately; but to the extent that she lost influence in June 2013, that power did not fall to the anti-authoritarian left, as the Movimento Passe Livre would have liked. Traditional power structures, and the economic oligarchy, regained some of the influence they lost when the Workers' Party was firmly in control. The Brazilian center-right blew open another hole by supporting impeachment, and the far right walked into that space. And so on.

In the mass protest decade, street explosions created revolutionary situations, often on accident. But a protest is very poorly equipped to take advantage of a revolutionary situation, and that particular kind of protest is especially bad at it. If you believe that you can forge a better society, if you are willing to run the risk of trying, then you should enter the vacuum yourself. But a diffuse group of individuals who come out to the streets for very different reasons cannot simply take power themselves, at least not *as* an entire diffuse group of individuals. Once someone goes in there and takes power in the name of the masses, you are talking about a type of vanguard—a particular ideological project, and a minority of people who dare to try to *represent* the rest of the population. In some of the more utopian strains of anti-authoritarian thought, the riot is supposed to become the new society, but this has not worked out so far.[11] Perhaps it might, someday, but it would probably not work very well in the actually existing Global South, which is surrounded by so many foreign actors that might be sucked very quickly into an apparent power vacuum by the possibility of easy profit and plunder.

If some new group boldly steps into the vacuum, manages to stay there, and transforms society, then that's a revolution. But if you find your political system broadly acceptable, or you don't think you can replace it with something better, then the thing to do is to negotiate. That is called reform. You can use your power on the streets to extract concessions, if you play it right. But once more, this necessarily entails representation.

It was not just Mayara and Haddad who overlapped in their answers to my question. I heard it very often—it came in different forms, but I heard it more than any other response. I think Hossam Bahgat put it best, or at least, the most directly.

"Organize. Create an organized movement. And don't be afraid of representation," he said without hesitation, in his office in Giza, as his world fell apart around him. "We thought representation was elitism, but actually it is the essence of democracy." I heard answers like this over and over, confirming research compiled by scholars. As early as 1975, William Gamson found that movements succeed more often when they deploy hierarchical forms of organization. In a wide-ranging 2022 study, Mark Beissinger found that loose uprisings of the Maidan type tend to increase inequality and ethnic tensions, while they do not consolidate democracy or end corruption.[12]

"After Maidan, I decided I do not believe in self-organization," said Artem Tidva, the young leftist who brought a red European Union flag to the square, as we grabbed a bite to eat in central Kyiv in the summer of 2021. "I used to be more anarchist. Back then everyone wanted to do an assembly; whenever there was a protest, always an assembly. But I think any revolution with no organized labor party will just give more power to economic elites, who are already very well-organized." Unlike some of his former comrades, Artem never gave up on the Ukrainian uprising and stayed active in the post-Maidan political scene, working to push for center-left, anti-racist alternatives in the context of the new political order. But in Ukraine, it seemed clear that the uprising had benefited the groups that had already formed coherent, disciplined organizations before the uprising began, and we had seen more evidence of that earlier in the day.

I had coffee with Solomiia Bobrovska, a member of the Euromaidan SOS Group (and a coworker of Maria Tomak) who entered Congress with the liberal "Voice" Party in 2019. I was mostly asking about Maidan—its tactics and goals, and the lessons she had learned—and not trying to talk about extremists. But she began to complain that she received criticism for working with

C14, the far-right youth group, when in reality people should realize they are allies united with people like her against Russia. After the interview finished, I texted Artem to ask where we were meeting. He would need a minute, he said. He and his friends had just been attacked by C14.

"I definitely don't have the same views on these things as I did before 2013," said Lucas "Vegetable" Monteiro. He still believes that a better society must be born out of this one, not just created after some revolution seizes state power. But he now thinks that the Movimento Passe Livre turned the principles of horizontalism, autonomy, and prefiguration "into a dogma, into a kind of religion, and we could not turn them into real political practice. Instead, they became a kind of identity. And we ended up quickly crashing into barriers that we ourselves had created." The MPL still exists, but no one who was in the group in 2013 is still a member. Looking back on 2019 in Hong Kong, Theo told me, "[It] was very fun to see the China building defaced, I had a lot of fun on the streets, but the decentralized nature of the movement meant that there was no room for discussion about how it should work, or how a coherent strategy could be developed."

Not everyone I met came out of the decade adopting positions in favor of formal structures, in support of "verticalism" and hierarchy, insisting that representation matters. Mayara, for example, remains mostly true to the ideals she adopted as a young punk.[13] But everyone moved in the same direction. I spent years doing interviews, and not one person told me that they had become more horizontalist, or more anarchist, or more in favor of spontaneity and structurelessness. Some people stayed in the same place. But everyone that changed their views on the question of organization moved closer to classically "Leninist" ones.

But we should not make the same old mistake of assuming that all those elements—apparent spontaneity, leaderlessness, horizontalism, digital coordination, and public mass protest—automatically go together. Even within the anarchist tradition, there was no expectation that they should. We should take them one by one. First, I often put the word "spontaneous" in quotes in this book because it may not survive close scrutiny. Rodrigo Nunes, the young Brazilian who set up the clown-performance school in the alter-globalization days, has spent years trying to rethink political organization. He points out that no one does anything spontaneously; or rather, they do everything spontaneously. You may have protests that have been planned very far in advance, or that come together very quickly; you may have formal structures, or you may have a mass of individuals; either way, each person has made a decision to participate based on what they have seen and heard and what they understand to be the right way to react. It is important to understand that injustice in society does not "spontaneously" lead an "unorganized" mass of people to take the correct action required to move them closer to a perfect society—that is magical thinking. Usually these days, spontaneous protest just means big and fast, planned in a hurry, or one that grew more quickly than expected.

Digital coordination is something that emerges with the internet, and (specific types of for-profit, advertising-driven, engagement-maximizing) social media, and as Tufekci points out, they allow for the existence of big protests that come together very quickly—so quickly, perhaps, that no one knows each other, people are trying to realize contradictory goals, and after the initial energy fades, nothing remains.[14]

However, "leaderlessness," "horizontalism," and "prefiguration" are ideological elements; they are ways you might think political movements should be structured, or ways in which it is morally correct to do so. Again, these are tricky to pin down in practice. Since Jo Freeman's essay in 1972, it has seemed clear that any putatively "leaderless" movement will have unofficial leaders, as long as the group gets big enough, whether they admit it or not. The question is how they arise—did they self-select based on their social power in the group, were they chosen democratically by its members, or were they appointed by foreign media and engagement on social media? Even the most ardent horizontalists admitted that it is never fully possible. "Horizontalism is a horizon," Daniel Guimarães in the MPL used to say, reproducing a famous quote that also appears in Marina Sitrin's 2006 book. Prefiguration may be understood symbolically, as a way to communicate the movement's values; it may be a way to get people fired up and excited to participate; it may be mystical and even religious; it may be understood as the point of the movement itself, which is seen to be generating new political forms during the uprising; or it may be a concrete way to show the masses what you want to do, and prove to them that you can do it, convincing them during a revolutionary situation to allow you to represent the people.[15] But regardless of the way it is conceived, the prefigurative approach tends to constrain the range of outcomes. Self-consciously horizontalist movements have a hard time drawing the line between who is in and who is out, and they struggle to pivot quickly when circumstances change (as the MPL learned in 2013), or to expand rapidly when their popularity increases. More broadly, prefiguration often means that you insist on being (internally) better than the structures you are confronting, and it always means devoting some attention to means, rather than a bloody-minded focus on ends.

Then there was the decision to take to the streets and pour huge numbers of people into highly visible public spaces, which can be seen primarily as a media action. Citizens also staged confrontational interventions to impose costs on the state—during the mass protest decade, this mostly took the form of destruction of property and fighting with police, rather than strikes and boycotts, which are often more effective. How did this particular repertoire become hegemonic? Why did global "protest" so often look like this from 2010–2020? In one sense, the mystery is not only why this package of contention didn't work, but why we thought that it would.

I believe that a preexisting set of ideological currents, developed in moments of anti-Soviet and neo-anarchist thinking, gained particular momentum in the era of the "end of history" (the 1990s) and then found elective affinity with technological and corporate developments made in the 2000s. Social media firms made it much easier to scale up the size of horizontal mass gatherings, and their services also made it very likely that citizens would see disturbing imagery of states abusing their power. Given that representative government and perhaps even representation itself is in crisis, and that many human beings appear to be more individualistic than we have ever been, all of this proved to be a dynamite combination.

David Graeber insisted, as the alter-globalization movement gave birth to a new protest repertoire, that the means were the ends. He recognized that anarchist-inspired approaches do not work very well in a war. But the problem, at least in the mass protest decade, is that if you are actually successful, someone is going to declare war on you. This might be political warfare, or it might be literal, violent war. If you score any kind of political victory, there is likely going to be someone who feels they will lose, and these people usually go on the attack—and have no philosophical objections to using hierarchy, formal organization, and "authoritarian" internal command structures—in a phrase, effective collective action, the kind of stuff that works really well, especially in a conflict. In the 2010s, the dominant repertoire of contention ended up working too well if the idea was to avoid war. The mass protest decade made unexpected trouble for powerful forces, and they fought back.

IT SHOULD BE OBVIOUS THAT humans do not spontaneously adopt the correct response to a given set of injustices. If they did, we would not have seen so many movements copying things they had seen elsewhere—either in the past decade, or throughout human history. Even the French Revolution grabbed at language and practices that had existed long before, as both Karl Marx and Charles Tilly famously documented. But the process of adoption and assimilation sped up rapidly in the twenty-first century, so much that it seemed to happen unconsciously. Over the past ten years, movements not only employed repertoires that were developed in radically different national-political and cultural-historical contexts, but they adopted repertoires that didn't even work where they were originally developed. They may have provided a few moments of inspiring media spectacle, but more careful attention given to developments in the years afterward would have been sobering. Emulation of the Tahrir-style mass occupation, for example, continued after Egypt fell to the Sisi dictatorship. I spoke to many people who said they wished they had studied revolutionary history more deeply or paid more attention to recent events around the world and the ways mass movements worked out—or failed—in the era of digital coordination.

If we spontaneously, intuitively adopted the correct response to injustice, presumably there would have been a lot less examples of people imitating Hollywood. After our last conversation, Hong Kong protester Theo began to walk away, then he stopped himself and turned back. "One more thing," he said. "I think it is also a little sad, and definitely very unfortunate, that we got so many of our ideas from pop culture."

But we are the global generation raised after the end of the Cold War, after the process that Odd Arne Westad called "Americanization"—what so many others called "globalization." Like much of the internet, the major social media firms are all based in the United States (the decade ended just as TikTok began to really take off outside China), and my hometown of Los Angeles produces the biggest, most recognizable movies in the world. *V for Vendetta* (the film, not the graphic novel) may have had famously incomplete ideas about how a revolution would work (neglecting the question of what happens after the regime falls), but everyone still knew about it. Even more importantly, intellectual production happens in a way that reflects the hierarchical nature of the global economy.

For obvious reasons, North Americans played an outsize role in the online communities born in the alter-globalization era. New York and

London have (relatively) well-funded, globally respected, left-leaning publishing houses, not to speak of the ideological state mega-apparatuses promoting the more mainstream ideas of democracy and liberalism. A Brazilian or Cameroonian intellectual may very well want to get their work published in the United States; the opposite is rarely true. And personally, it is unlikely I would have gained access to the resources required to write this book if I had not been born in the US and spent my career in high-prestige English-language media.

Looking back, my friend Piero Locatelli, the journalist who brought vinegar to the protest that fateful day in June, chuckled as he described the way US consumer culture had influenced the Brazilian anti-authoritarian left. "A lot of my generation was inspired by the Zapatistas in Mexico," he said in 2022. "But how did we find out about the Zapatistas in the first place? From Rage Against the Machine."

Repertoires and philosophical approaches usually flowed from north to south, not the other way around. Several people told me they believed their movements had unconsciously taken on positions developed in the First World that may not be so applicable in the Global South. One Egyptian revolutionary put it to me this way: "In New York or Paris, if you do a horizontal, leaderless, and post-ideological uprising, and it doesn't work out, you just get a media or academic career afterward. Out here in the real world, if a revolution fails, all your friends go to jail or end up dead." He was pointing to something that nagged at him, and me, and many others who have taken time to look back at political struggles since the 1960s. Is it perhaps that a lot of these approaches were developed by a New Left, back in the US and Western Europe, that didn't fundamentally care if they won? Some of the figures in those movements expressed sentiments that suggested as much. Wini Breines wrote that it was correct that they were often willing to sacrifice victories to remain loyal to their organizational or prefigurative principles.

Somewhere like Egypt, it really matters if you win. But Hossam "the Bedouin" el-Hamalawy, another revolutionary from the same country, disagrees slightly on the importance of struggle in the First World. "It is foolish to dismiss the working class in the West, because my liberation as someone in the Global South will never be achieved unless power falls away from the Global North."

Iranian American sociologist Asef Bayat, who lived through both the Iranian Revolution in 1979 in Tehran and the 2011 uprising in Cairo, makes sure to distinguish between subjective and objective conditions for the uprisings starting in 2010. On the one hand, the so-called Arab Spring took place in opposition to neoliberal policies, but it also took place in a society shaped by neoliberal subjectivity. It was carried out by individuals with a certain way of looking at the world. "The Arab revolutions lacked the kind of radicalism—in political and economic outlook—that marked most other twentieth-century revolutions," he wrote in his book *Revolution Without Revolutionaries*. "Unlike the revolutions of the 1970s that espoused a powerful socialist, anti-imperialist, anti-capitalist and social justice impulse, Arab revolutionaries were preoccupied more with the broad issues of human rights, political accountability, and legal reform. The prevailing voices, secular and Islamist alike, took free market, property relations, and neoliberal rationality for granted."[16] A generation of individuals raised to view everything as if it were a business enterprise was de-radicalized, came to view this global order as "natural," and became unable to imagine what it takes to carry out a true revolution.

Looking back on 2013, Fernando Haddad tied the form of the uprising to the outcome. "After 1999 [the year of the Seattle protests] we saw the rise of a certain anti-state left, with a kind of neo-anarchist charm, that kept its distance from governments and any instantiation of political representation in general," he said. When brought to Brazil, "the innovation short-circuited. The form of the protests, much more than their demands, allowed other causes to enter the streets and contest their meaning." Italian sociologist Paolo Gerbaudo, who was present at so many of the decade's explosions, said something even more forceful: "At the end of the day, horizontalism is a reflection of individualism." This might, indeed, make sense for a movement that had so much overlap with a musical subculture born out of generational warfare and absolute rebellion.[17]

In our age, we tend to think that you are not really involved if you are not deciding everything for yourself—if every individual is not a leader in a "leaderful" or leaderless movement. The format of the mass assembly, all the talking, was perfectly suited to the "hyper-articulate and educated middle class that tended to dominate protests in the 2010s," wrote Turkish theorist Cihan Tuğal.[18] But throughout history, people have contributed to causes greater than themselves in a wide manner of ways, no less heroic for relying on different skills. We all understand that the coach is not the most important figure on a soccer team, and that the famous striker cannot exist without the defenders. In a political movement, the "leaders," the people who make strategic decisions or stand in front of cameras, must not be seen as superior to the people delivering food, or risking their lives in battle, or caring for the sick and wounded.

THERE ARE MANY REASONS WHY things are fundamentally different outside the North Atlantic, which I have tried to sketch throughout the book. But another obvious one I have mostly left aside is the fact that the First World confronts no group of countries that are much more powerful. If a power vacuum were created in the United States, it might be filled by any number of groups. But it cannot be filled by a more powerful country—there are none. When one of the main tasks of the neoliberal project was to make all the world's states porous to international capital and open up all the planet's resources for extraction and commodification, it's easy to see how simply weakening a small state can provide opportunities to governments or companies abroad. That is, if no group with real legitimacy takes over what has been lost. I think the mass protest explosions in the past decade primarily emerged from local dynamics. But taking this very wide view of the global system helps us to understand why this particular type of revolt can reinforce preexisting power dynamics. There is no such thing as a political vacuum.

During my last meeting with Artem, I mentioned that Lenin had said "spontaneous" uprisings would simply adopt the ideology that is dominant in the air around them. "Of course," he said, "that is exactly what happened." If you want to reshape or oppose the larger global system, you probably want to dig in your heels and make it very clear what you stand for. If, on the other hand, ideologically diffuse mass uprisings tend to create opportunities for, or reinforce, larger power structures, then it would make sense why the world's richest countries might tend to welcome them. But all of this would be based, necessarily, on an incomplete reading of events.

For this book, I focused on first-person testimony and built the story based on the things that we already know. But if the past seventy years are any guide, then it is safe to wager that over the next few decades we will begin to learn about secret foreign interventions and provocations that will be shocking, if not in their effectiveness, then in their deviousness.

Back in 2013, when Turkish president Recep Tayyip Erdoğan called Dilma Rousseff and warned her that an attempt to destabilize her country, with foreign support, may have been underway in Brazil, she didn't agree with that analysis. In an interview in 2021, she said she has changed her mind.[19]

Wong Yik Mo, one of the original organizers of the 2019 Hong Kong protests, is far from certain that foreign involvement was helpful to his cause at all. He worries, looking back, "that we were used, that the Trump administration wanted to sacrifice us as part of their propaganda war against China." The goal in that case would not have been for them to win, but to fail, and be repressed—very publicly.

Historically, successful revolutions have had to defend themselves against ousted elites and their foreign allies. Against counterrevolution and invasion. What would have happened, I would often ask, if there were a full revolution in Egypt? What if some kind of Arab nationalism, or Arab Socialism, returned, or even just mild social democracy in the world's largest Arab country? The United States has relied upon Israeli and Saudi Arabian power in the Middle East since the Cold War, and real democracy in Egypt would almost certainly mean a pro-Palestine position. Offering people basic freedoms and a half-decent life would undermine Saudi Arabia. When Tunisians explained why things went relatively well for them (for a while), they would often point (in addition to strong preexisting political organizations) to the fact that their country was too small to matter for geopolitics.

But those are more elegant explanations than usually emerge when looking back on the mass protest decade. In North Africa, Brazil, Hong Kong, and throughout the world, there is fundamental and often acrimonious disagreement on what the movements were all about. In 2022, as he launched his book on Bolsonarismo at a Palestinian bar in São Paulo, Rodrigo Nunes put it this way: "If someone starts a sentence saying, 'June 2013 was...' then they are already wrong." I am not sure we have even gotten so far as to interpret what the uprisings meant. Is it even possible to do so?

Representation Matters

In seven of the ten places we analyzed in this book, the explosion was facilitated by viral images of state repression. We can see that protests took off after evidence emerged of police brutality, or a crackdown. And in Tunisia, Egypt, Turkey, Brazil, Ukraine, Hong Kong, and Chile, the crucial spark consisted of visible repression against a particular type of citizen, against someone who was not supposed to be hurt, or be murdered. In Brazil, the press did not mind much when the cops were beating and arresting punk anarchists—indeed, they asked them to please do more of that—but when middle-class journalists Giuliana Vallone and Piero Locatelli suffered state repression, the nation was shocked. In Egypt it was not the plight of striking workers that powered the mass Facebook group—it was the death of Khaled Said. I spoke with countless people in Ukraine who told me that it was when Yanukovych cracked down "on the students" that they decided to take to the streets. This was also the dynamic in Chile and Hong Kong; in Turkey it was the woman in an elegant red dress, not a militant, who went viral.

After a mass protest event, social scientists and journalists begin to look for structural explanations. That country has a lot of inequality, they may say. Unemployment was high; the price of food has risen; democratic reforms are needed. All of that is hugely helpful and part of the story. But I think that after taking an extremely wide view of the decade, looking at these events in comparison to one another makes it clear that this isn't quite enough. Employing just those methods, you can't really explain why Chile's uprising happened in 2019 instead of 2015, or why Brazil had one at all.

At a very human, emotional, and even cognitive or phenomenological level, a person is always reacting to what they see or hear or feel. An individual does not really stand up, open their front door, and walk to the square in the center of the capital because of inflation. Not for that reason alone.[20] One is often stirred to action by some passion—either anger, or shock, or the taste of righteous euphoria. And I believe one usually has to believe that what is happening outside is a good thing; you have to believe that it will be fun, or exciting, or inspiring, or you have to believe that you will be doing something noble, that this action will put you on the "right side of history." No matter how angry you are, or how much you despise your government, few individuals are going to join an event they believe to be a reactionary mob (though some will!), a self-destructive riot, or (worse) troublemaking organized by foreign meddlers.

That means media are fundamental, both social and traditional. Every single modern nation-state relies upon the use of violence and repression. Cops will physically restrain and haul away anyone who violates property rights or defies their authority. "Repression is literally what the police are supposed to do. That is necessary for maintaining this type of society," reflected Lucas "Vegetable" Monteiro, looking back on 2013. "The cops were doing their job." Police might be prone to frequent violence, as in Egypt, or they may be relatively respected, as they were in Hong Kong a decade ago. You may believe that police should disappear in a future, more perfect society, or you may think that they should always be around. But in basically every country that exists, you can get a cop to beat you up.

Until very recently, however, it was unlikely for a regular person to ever see this violent repression in action. Indeed, it is a recent technological invention that allows human beings to see any things that aren't actually happening in front of their eyes—the age of photography occupies a tiny percentage of our history. Our bodies will still react physically to anything they experience, as if it were happening to us. And it is far from clear that the most visible and affecting power dynamics are the most important ones in a complex society. They may be the tip of the iceberg, or just the intermittent interventions needed to reproduce more generalized injustice. Perhaps sometimes, at a really granular level, we were really protesting our phones. Media gave us reason to be shocked; and media (whether that be supplied by big corporations or our friends and family) framed some reaction as positive, productive, or inspirational.

But why did the media play such a large role in defining what these protests were about? I think this has to do with the structure of contemporary mass contention. Back in the days of the Old Left, or even the civil rights movement, you could simply ask the movement what it stood for. The Communist Party might tell you its position on a given issue and why it was mobilizing; a union might tell you that it was striking in order to achieve a very specific salary objective; the highly disciplined SCLC and SNCC would tell you they were marching to Montgomery so that Black people in the United States would be able to exercise their right to vote. That is because the members of these groups signed up for the type of collective action that would allow someone else to represent and speak for them.

Protests, after all, are communicative events aimed at existing elites. That is right there in the name, and it becomes even more clear in Latin America—in Spanish or Portuguese they are "manifestations" or "demonstrations." This is a fundamental reason why they do so poorly in revolutionary situations. By taking Tahrir Square, the Egyptians were sending a message to somebody else rather than forming a new government. At its most basic level, a protest says, "I don't like this—you fix it." As history shows, the mass protest only came together, piece by piece, in the era of mass communications.

Ten years after June 2013, Juliana, the photojournalist friend who sent me that euphoric text message from the Estaiada Bridge, has found her own memories trampled on by contradictory narratives and media power. "I watched the whole thing from close up, and I know all the nuances," she said. "But now, does the real, original meaning of the protest matter to anyone? These days I find myself thinking that knowing the whole story just makes us more traumatized, rather than more enlightened." I told her that to this day, Lucas "Vegetable" Monteiro is fond of citing a poll conducted on June 20, 2013, indicating that transportation was the most important motivation for the turnout that day.[21] "Poor guy," Juliana responded. "Does he actually think data has anything to do with the historical meaning of that protest?"

After looking at events like this across the world, I have come to the conclusion that the horizontally structured, digitally coordinated, leaderless mass protest is fundamentally illegible. You cannot gaze upon it or ask it questions and come up with a coherent interpretation based on evidence. You can assemble facts, absolutely—millions of them. You are just not going to be able to use them to construct an authoritative reading. This means that the significance of these events will be imposed upon them from the outside. In order to understand what might happen after any given protest explosion, you must not only pay attention to who is waiting in the wings to fill a power vacuum. You have to pay attention to who has the power to define the uprising itself.

When analyzing the June 2013 coup in Egypt, Cihan Tuğal helpfully summarized Marx, saying, "Those who cannot represent themselves will be represented." I think we must take this one level further when explaining the mass protest decade, and say movements that cannot speak for themselves will be spoken for.

With this in mind, it is interesting to consider the case of the most successful explosion in the 2010s. In Santiago in 2019, many people in the plaza said Boric was imposing a deal on them that they didn't ask for—that he was interpreting the movement from a position of power, handing down meaning in an authoritarian way. And I think that, fundamentally, they were right. But it was always going to go that way; given the form of the explosion, it must go that way. The *estallido* was never going to ask for, or agree to, anything. Chile was lucky enough that it ultimately had its meaning imposed by a generation that understood the streets, had entered power at an earlier moment in the decade of interconnected struggles, and actually had the political legitimacy to pull something off. Boric and the rest of Congress were elected representatives, after all. This is the key to their victory. The streets had (relatively good) representation, even if they didn't ask for it.

This is not the only way this thing goes, of course. In the center of Tahrir Square, the Sisi government maintains a monument to the 2011 uprising and still officially traces its rise to the revolution. But if you get anywhere near the thing to try to read its inscription, cops will physically stop you.

During illegible revolts, the dominant media take on an even larger role than they might otherwise. They not only portray the things in a positive or negative light, influencing the number of people who might choose to go. The journalists (and I was one of these) try to provide some kind of explanation, which can end up reshaping the very object of our reporting. The weaknesses of mainstream corporate media are well known; recent opinion polling indicates that few people need to be convinced of their limitations.[22] From ownership structure to the (often seemingly desperate) need to chase eyeballs and clicks, to the narrow band of class and the ideological perspectives offered by major outlets, we do a very imperfect job. But I think another one of our blind spots needs considering when it comes to these uprisings.

It's safe to say that many journalists at the top of our global media hierarchy in the past decade did not really understand the aspirations of the Global South, or the profound revolutionary transformations that would actually be required for the world's less rich peoples to live the way that the rich nations do. A talking head on CNN or a columnist at the New York Times has almost certainly lived a life of wealth and privilege that is unimaginable for most of the world's population, mostly if not entirely in the United States, and the best that they could usually do in the mass protest decade was to interpret the people to be yearning for freedom and promise in vague terms that good things would come if Westernization and democratization won the day. Then they would move on. Too often, "democracy" has been conflated with a desire to join the West, or some idealized version of it—that is, to join the small club of rich and developed countries. Too often the only question asked about a protest movement was if the government in a given country was a bad one. Even those of us a little bit closer to the ground (and I include myself here) failed by getting too excited about the explosions and failing to ask where the pieces would fall. By representing and re-representing the upswing with messianic imagery, paying too little attention to the underlying structures and the way they fell apart.

I hope that in the future, my cohort will look carefully at the constituent elements of any new protest movement, and where it could lead. That we will ask: Who comprises this movement, what specifically are they asking for, and what is likely to happen if they win?

Given the existing configuration of global media, it may have been precisely the least effective elements that got the most attention. One only needs to think of how a big television station in the United States might cover "spontaneous, leaderless mass protests" apparently espousing broadly liberal, pro-Western goals compared to a revolt led by a disciplined group with a clear ideological project. If something does not appear to be ushering History along its path, it may be painted with different colors. That is inevitable; media will always employ some kind of framing. But in the case of "horizontal" uprisings, those decisions change meaning, they elevate (unofficial) leaders, and they become part of the event. I don't personally think this works in a conspiratorial way (and Fernando Haddad told me the same thing), but journalists simply interpret events using the beliefs and experiences they already have.

Which leads me to myself and gives me an opportunity to recognize the way my own perspective has twisted the shape of this book. I hope it was clear that my little tweet in 2013, the one that that made it to Gezi Park, had absolutely no influence on the course of events in Turkey; even in Brazil, I had very little importance. I was one of a few dozen people representing the explosion beginning on June 13. Collectively, we probably had a role in shaping the way the protests were understood—and I don't think this is a good thing—but no responsible historian would put me in any part of this story. I included my own experiences to be honest, but even more so to show the subjective conditions of journalistic practice and the incentive structures that appear before our eyes. I think it is a real problem that we are drawn so powerfully to the production of whatever will go viral on social media.

I also wanted to make clear, throughout the story, that things could have gone differently. To assume or imply that June 2013 always must have led to Bolsonaro (or Tahrir to Sisi, Maidan to war, and so on)—or to only select the facts that establish a link from the former to the latter—would be to tell the story backward, and to fall victim to the same type of teleological thinking that I believe has proved a barrier to meaningful change in our century.

Along with representation itself, traditional media is in crisis. This may appear self-serving, as this is my industry, so I will not begrudge anyone who chooses to ignore me. But I think we can draw a broad analogy between media and the world's actually existing states. Like any representative government, the media is deeply imperfect and needs to be criticized constantly, both from within and from without, in order to keep it honest. We should seek to create media that are better and more democratic. But we should not fall victim to cheap wishful thinking and believe that if we simply blow up the media, something better will appear out of thin air. You have to pay attention to who will rush into the vacuum.

But leaving the media aside, the problems of illegibility and virality scrambled reality for the major actors across the decade as well. If you are the government of Brazil, you should not find yourself responding to demands articulated by a single guy in a mask on YouTube, just because his video got a lot of views. And if you are a protest movement taking on the most powerful government in the history of Asia, you should not pick your strategy based on which post gets the most upvotes on a forum like Reddit. We can be certain that any worthy opponent is not making its decisions that way.

21
Building the Future

THERE IS ONE MORE THING I heard over and over, across five continents. In the face of obvious setbacks, serious tragedies, and widespread depression, people would tell me: this is just the beginning. We have planted the seed for something bigger. In the long term, these struggles can be part of something greater, and we can come back stronger than ever and win. Not everyone said it. But this possibility hangs over the entire project. Without it, there would be no reason for these people to give me their time in the first place.

I think that this possibility teeters on the edge between obvious truth and teleological self-deception. A major lesson that emerged from the experiences they shared with me, a historical fact that emerges in the 2010s, is that failure is an option. In order to win, you have to accept that possibility. As we have seen, there is a huge amount of desire to see change in the structures that comprise our global system. And as we have shown, that desire was not enough, and neither was being right. At least, not yet. It is of course possible that, in the future, these struggles will be seen as crucial steps toward a better world that has come into being. But for that to happen, movements like these and the people inspired by them will have to actually succeed. If failure is also possible, what does that mean? It means that we have to learn from this decade and make it happen. Step by step, piece by piece. That is why so many busy, demoralized people, including those who took serious risks, chose to speak with me.

GEHAD AND AHMED BUILT THEIR relationship looking back on the Egyptian revolution and its failures. From the beginning, they connected over their shared understanding of what happened in 2011, and they spent years talking about what it meant, and how it felt. I met a lot of people who spent the past decade this way. Egyptians, like Brazilians and people from so many other countries, will often stare into the distance when asked about the uprising that rocked their lives before launching into an endless, sometimes contradictory set of explanations. But Ahmed and Gehad have also built a family. Their young daughter is entering a world facing political crisis and environmental collapse, and she will soon be old enough to take part in political struggles of her own. They don't have to stop looking back, but they must also look forward.

That was the other half of the question I asked everyone. "If you could speak to a teenager somewhere around the world right now, in Peru or Korea or Tanzania, someone that might be fighting to change history in some kind of political struggle in their lifetime, what would you tell them? What advice would you give them, as they attempt to build the future?"

The answer was never that we should give up. It is not like you can avoid the arrival of historical struggle, even if you wanted to. That is why we have been so careful throughout the book to delineate between political resistance in general and specific forms of contention. Though eminently understandable, it is a grave mistake to fall victim to "Do Somethingism," to think that every action is equally valuable. Mayara, and Hossam "3arabawy" Bedouin, and Artem, and many others told me that they have obsessively gone back over every little detail of certain days, wondering what could have gone differently. Mahmoud Salem, the "Sandmonkey" blogger, told me that he never wants anyone to feel the guilt that he does, the knowledge that he asked teenage boys to risk their lives and watched them die, only for the entire movement to experience defeat. When trying to do something as difficult as changing society, there are no guarantees that anything will go as it should.

Of course—I am just a journalist. I have never built a political party or carried out a revolution. I am keenly aware that a lot of my conclusions are much easier said than done.* But I think we came up with a fairly coherent set of first responses.

Organizations are effective, and representation is important. Collective action has a proven record of success and works best when it is truly collective. There is a reason that the powerful have sought to "divide and conquer" since before the birth of Jesus. All else being equal, individualization tends to re-enforce existing power structures. That is why unionization—something that undoubtedly worked for achieving certain goals—consists primarily of a kind of de-horizontalization. Leaders, vertical structures, and hierarchies tend to emerge in large groups of people. One must either be prepared for this, or—the classic solution—construct a self-consciously democratic organization that ensures this happens in the most legitimate and transparent ways possible.

One must be very aware of what a "protest" is doing, and how it will lead to a positive outcome. One must not confuse tactics and strategy; a particular type of contention may get you through one phase of a struggle, but not the next. If the goal is to put pressure on existing elites, then strikes and boycotts often work much better than people walking back and forth across a city. If enough leverage is created to make demands—that is, to enact reform—then someone must represent the group causing problems and negotiate the victories. If the existing elites can actually be removed—a revolutionary situation—then some group must be prepared to take their place and do a better job. In both of those cases, this has always been a relatively small group, compared to the rest of the population. The question is whether the people give this minority permission to speak for them.

But none of that means you have to dismiss unplanned mass action or decline the participation of all kinds of regular people who may not have the time or inclination to join a political party, union, or formal organization. Indeed, even the most disciplined and radical revolutions have relied upon them, and they are likely to come along again in the future, unless the configuration of many things (society, the internet, and dominant political ideologies) changes drastically. It is entirely conceivable that the 2020s will surpass the 2010s as the decade with the most protests in human history.

---

* The turn to formal organizations brings a whole set of its own problems. The US government responded to the formation of the (Marxist-Leninist) Black Panther Party with infiltration and assassination.

Rodrigo Nunes was one of the evangelists of the Brazilian alter-globalization movement in its fully horizontalist phase. Looking back on the 2010s and looking forward to a new era of organization, he reached for a metaphor that is more appropriate to the challenges of our planet—in *Neither Vertical nor Horizontal*, he writes about an "ecology" of organizations and affirms that different types of organizational schema can, and should, interact with one another. To put it in the terms that emerged in this book, a mass explosion can make a ruckus and create a political vacuum, and it would be rational to do so if the people back the group that will fill it. The crucial distinction is to not use the explosion in order to *form* the organization. In the second decade of the twenty-first century, it was the groups that were already there, prepared, that did the best when the explosion came—whether they were Hoxhaist Communists in Tunisia or the nationalist extremists in Ukraine, these groups punched above their weight.

Sitting with me in Rio, just days before Bolsonaro stood for reelection, Nunes said that trauma had a lot to do with what had happened to Brazil. Progressives traumatized by the direction taken in 2013 felt that they had lost control of the streets. They were paralyzed in the face of extreme-right insurgence. Any new mass protest action might, once more, serve the interests of their enemies. But the direction taken in 2013 had to do with an earlier trauma experienced by the left: the sins of the Soviet Union, Iran, or any other revolutions that led to messy, imperfect realities after victory. As Nunes wrote, Brazil has been stalked by "the fear that the organization necessary to change the world will be the same that stops us from doing so—from there flow feelings of impotence and melancholy."[1]

Of course, the actual Leninists never went away, and the whole time they were there insisting on discipline and coordinated action. As we saw, they played a role in getting things started in places like Tunisia and Egypt. But it is striking to see someone like Rodrigo Nunes rethink so many of the assumptions that powered the mass protest decade. Drawing on Jacques Derrida (who draws on Plato, who draws on Socrates), he speaks about organizations as a *pharmakon*, something that can be medicine or poison. In simpler terms, organization works, and you can use it for good or for evil. It was an overreaction to reject them simply because they led to trauma in the twentieth century, and it is a mistake when "the establishment of structures of any kind is sensed as the start of a slippery slope towards the gulag." Yes, we have to confront that they have the potential for misuse. But if you refuse to use the tools that work, you are not really building; you are refusing to take responsibility, and you are ceding your power to other people.

Nunes comes from the tradition that is deeply critical of the legacy of the Soviet Union. But in recent years, even he has begun to speak, half-jokingly, of "networked Leninism."[2]

All of this—a post-teleological orientation, an insistence on the serious analysis of causes and effects, and an awareness that political action is dangerous, even to your moral purity—points to the importance of timing. If you cannot carry out a revolution and are not in a position to negotiate reforms, then perhaps it is acceptable to do nothing at all. Better yet, to organize, analyze, and strategize—to put yourself in the best position for the next opportunity. Sometimes, the right action may be to wait. At the least, recent history suggests you should not try to effect maximum disruption at any moment that this appears possible.

Even within the very radical Marxist-Leninist tradition, the concept of revolutionary "retreat" is important. Winning all at once—that is Hollywood. There is a right way to lose, there is a right way to wait, and there is an effective way to regroup. "Victory is impossible unless one learns how to attack and retreat properly," Lenin wrote in 1920.[3] Given the complexity of the world's problems at the moment, there is no reason to believe that victory is right around the corner, no matter one's idea of triumph.

As two very different men put it (though they are both French)—the future lasts a long time.*

If you want to help people, if your goal is to confront the problems facing humanity, that means a focus on ends, and it means constructing a movement that can stand the test of time, in addition to remaining democratic and accountable. In Brazil, the Movimento Passe Livre is gone—at least, all of its members in 2013 have left the organization. But Oliver Cauã Cauê still wore one of the old black shirts, illustrated with a foot kicking over a turnstile, when we met nine years later. We got to talking about the problematic relationship between means and ends in the MPL. I asked—what if it were possible to achieve the twenty-cent fare reduction through quiet negotiation or back-channel activism, rather than via the glorious struggle in the streets? Without the heroic battle with the cops? Would the MPL have taken that

---

* The second man, who used it for the title of a memoir, *L'avenir dure longtemps*, was Marxist theorist Louis Althusser. The first was Charles de Gaulle.

route? "Absolutely not," he said with a smile. For many people in the movement, the point was the fight.[4]

BUT WHAT ABOUT THAT FEELING? What about that intense, life-changing collective euphoria? This was an issue on which my interlocutors were split. What about those magical, radiant days, the moments when you felt that your very soul became fused with the forces of history, that you were bigger and more powerful. That all your differences melted away, and that you and your fellow revolutionaries were literally remaking the world, with each and every thing that you did. This supernatural experience was something that took place all around the world, and everyone agreed it was important. Some people said they would relive those days for the rest of their lives. The disagreement was about what came next.

For some of them, the horrible comedown, the plunge into depression that came after things did not work out, was something like a hangover. You can get yourself all fucked up on revolutionary élan, just like you can drink alcohol or take drugs. But it warps your senses and causes you to make poor decisions. It isn't real, and you're going to pay for it later. If you want the feeling of mass ecstasy you should go to a music festival instead of encouraging vulnerable young people to go out and get killed. Indeed, it seems you can probably draw a line from the ethos of the New Left and the arrival of Woodstock, and then, ultimately, to Coachella.

Then there was another interpretation, just as common. It is the most real thing that one can ever feel. It is not an illusion at all; it is a stunning, momentary glimpse of the way that life is really supposed to be. It is how we can feel every single day in a world when artificial distinctions and narrowly self-interested activities melt away. When our society truly is participatory, when we are truly forging history in every movement and acting in love and harmony with our fellow human beings, we will be able to feel this way all the time. Over four years of interviews, across ten countries, people went back and forth.

As I said, they couldn't decide which one it is.

Acknowledgments

I DON'T KNOW IF IT was possible to write this book at all—to cover the strange events of this decade in a volume of this size—at least, I am not sure if it was possible to do it well. That is up to the reader to decide. But I do know that I could have never written it on my own.

It is a bit ridiculous that only my name is on the cover. A number of people contributed crucial reporting, research, or revisions, and they should be considered coauthors. In a newspaper story, there is a slot for "additional reporting by"—in a movie, there are the credits. But in a book, all I have is this space to recognize the people who actually made this thing come together. So, I want to start by thanking everyone who worked with me, whether they spent a few hours helping me with sources in Arabic, or a few days introducing me to people in Istanbul, a few weeks chasing down materials in Russian and Ukrainian, or dedicated months to fact-checking the manuscript and saving me from myself. I am extremely grateful to Arwa Gaballa in Egypt, to Hiba Tlili in Tunisia, to Vanesse Chan and Jessie Lau from Hong Kong, to Peter Korotaev in Kyiv, to Adham Youssef and Farah Abouzeid at the American University in Cairo, to Ömer Yavuz in Turkey, to Jack McGinn and Taif Alkhudary at the London School of Economics, and finally, to Cos Tollerson in New York. Moreover, out of the kindness of their hearts Laurel Chor, Alice Gutneva, and Murad Alhayki provided me with meaningful guidance and important connections.

Then, I want to thank my friends and family for putting up with me since 2019. I am not sure if everyone understood why I was constantly working on my second book, why I had chosen to do something that was so stressful, but it meant a lot that you went along with it. My heroic mother and lovely sister and two beautiful nieces are already at the front of the book; here I want to express my appreciation for my brothers Rory and Hugh, and for my deeply selfless father, Ron. My loving family has made everything possible. I also want to apologize to the friends I annoyed while trying to write this thing, especially Tarsila Riso, Dragan Sasic, Sung Tieu, Alex Press, and Sundeep Grewal.

But of course, this book is really about the interviewees, and the stories of the people who were generous enough to sit down with me and share their experiences. I will never be able to pay back this act of trust and kindness, so let me just say that I will never forget this. I truly hope that I have honored your contributions, and your memories. I want to thank Mayara Vivian, Fernando Haddad, Lucas Monteiro, Piero Locatelli, Jawaher Channa, Ezequiel Adamovsky, Hossam el-Hamalawy, Gehad, Mahmoud Salem, Ebrahim Sharif, Evan Henshaw-Plath, Hamdeen Sabahi, Furkan, Frederico Freitas, Hazar, Eren Senkardes, Bahar, Fábio Ostermann, Artem Tidva, Maria Tomak, Wong Yik Mo, Derek Tai, Mung Siu Tat, Au Loong-Yu, Finn Lau, Danitza Pérez Cáceres, Theo, Hossam Bahgat, Juliana Knobel, Rodrigo Nunes, Ahmed, and Oliver Cauã Cauê for appearing in the book. Last names were dropped when requested and not relevant to the story.

I am also indebted to each person whose name does not appear in the main text. Every single conversation deeply shaped the way that the narrative is told, and I am eternally grateful for all of them. The order is chronological, and the names with an asterisk are pseudonyms, but they know who they are. I want to thank Juliana Cunha, Kamal Gaballa, Omar Robert Hamilton, Sharif Abdel Kouddous, Mohamed Zaree, Magd Zahran, Osama Badie, Kareem Megahed, Tarek Shalaby, Hichem Amri, Ahmed Gaâloul, Naoufel Eljammali, Hamza Ben Aoun, Wael Naouar, Kais Bouazizi, Anouar Jadawi, Ayouni Moncef, Ayman Gharbi, Ismael Awled Nasser, Radia Nsiri, Zohra Saadouni, Ibrahim Mastouri, Ivan Verstyuk, Taras Bilous, Vitalina Kutsyba, Victoria Voytitska, *Natalya Podil, Polina Godz, *André Korchuvate, Oleg Shelenko, Uladzimir Shcherbau, Daryna Akselerat, Solomiia Bobrovska, *C 14 Boyeviki, Svitlana Chorna, *Paula X. Odesa, Maksym Voitenko, Vyacheslav Azarov, Moris Ibrahim, Lera, Dennis, Shaimaa Fayed, Hassan Saber, Sener Sahin, Celil Kapar, Aydin Celik, Berfu Demir, Ayse Ertung, Ramazan Demir, Serkan Özabacı, Berker Ersoy, Efe Oğur, Abdulnabi Al-Ekri, Radhi Almosawi, Farida Ghulam, Nabeel Rajab, José Chrispiniano,

Neuri Rossetto, Jampa Filho, Isabella Souza, Cris Gouvea, Luciana Santos, Pedro de Oliveira, André da Silva Takahashi, Sâmia Bomfim, Lieta Vivaldi, Alicia Maldonado Mirando, Alvin Lum, Octavio Del Favero Bannen, Rodrigo Karmy, Hernán Herrera, Camila Musante, Felipe Espinosa, Giovanna Roa, Daniela Serrano, Chan Ho-Him, Joey Siu, *Abigail Chan, Regina Ip, Nury Vittachi, Carlos Martinez, Jun Pang, Ronny Tong Ka-wah, Derek Tai, JN Chien, Promise Li, Daniel Cheung, Jessie Lau, Raymond Lee, Tsang Yok Sing, Julia Damphouse, Thomas Traumann, and Selvi May. I also want to thank those who live under such duress and political uncertainty that they chose not even to supply a pseudonym and so do not appear here at all—but they know who they are.

Profound, sincere gratitude is owed to the scholars who reviewed the manuscript and offered much-needed comments and corrections. Fabio de Sa e Silva, John Chalcraft, Cihan Tuğal, Jeffrey Wasserstrom, and Volodymyr Ishchenko provided an invaluable service to the project; any errors that made it into the final book are entirely my fault.

I also want to recognize the real experts, fellow journalists, and accomplished scholars who spoke to me about the mass protest decade. Their input was often just as important as the interviews with witnesses and participants. I apologize for the journalistic method, irritating as it may be, of asking intentionally stupid questions. Thank you to Erica Chenoweth, Patrick Iber, Nils Gilman, Loren Balhorn, Fadil Aliriza, Branko Milanovic, Samuel Moyn, Luke Yates, Vijay Prashad, Daniel O'Connell, Michael Walker, Jack Shenker, Najib Abidi, Amr Magdi, Said Sadek, Anne Alexander, Mohamed-Dhia Hammami, Max Ajl, Andrew Roth, Max Seddon, Christopher Miller, Matias Spektor, Amro Ali, Tatiana Roque, Eduardo Mello, Flávia Biroli, Kenneth Bunker, Paolo Gerbaudo, Christopher Szabla, John Bartlett, Tobita Chow, Joe Leahy, Stephan Ortmann, Sean Scalmer, Evgeny Morozov, Alex Hochuli, Andrew Fishmann, Andreas Harsono, Jann Boeddeling, Daniel Vukovich, Merlyna Lima, and Simone Chun.

Every single person who has taken an interest in my work—who has read *The Jakarta Method*, or picked up this volume, or never read anything I have written but still has given me a vote of confidence in person or online—I offer my real and heartfelt gratitude. I have been overwhelmed by the support and generosity over the past few years, which put pressure on me to make absolutely sure that this was a serious and diligent study. I hope I have not let anybody down.

But far before I started writing, as well as after I finished the manuscript, a whole team of people helped turn it into a real book. My agent Rob McQuilkin and my editor Clive Priddle deserve credit for giving this project life, and I am so grateful that Athena Bryant agreed to do the first edits with me again. I also want to recognize everyone at PublicAffairs, especially Miguel Cervantes, Anupama Roy-Chaudhury, Kiyo Saso, Johanna Dickson, Pete Garceau, Amber Hoover, Laura Piasio, Caitlyn Budnick, Duncan McHenry, and Shena Redmond, as well as Max Moorhead and Ellie Roppolo at Massie & McQuilkin. Big thanks are in order to Siddhartha Mahanta, who commissioned and edited the piece that turned into my first book, and who commissioned and edited the piece that foreshadowed this book.

I would not have been able to do this work without the British Library, the Biblioteca Mario de Andrade in downtown São Paulo, the New York Public Library, the Staatsbibliothek zu Berlin, and all of their staff. I thank them all, and every library that manages to continue to exist.

I would be extremely unsurprised to find out, somewhere down the road, that one or more people on the long list above are not who they claim to be. So, I want to thank the world's myriad intelligence and security agencies for all their hard work. The man who followed me around Moscow in particular made me feel very special.

Allow me to offer my deepest acknowledgments to everyone I mentioned, and my apologies—and very deep thanks—to anyone I have forgotten.

Notes

Introduction

1. In addition to historical declarations made by the Bolsonaro family, Rio de Janeiro governor Wilson Witzel threatened criminals with summary execution and very publicly celebrated the death of a suspect in 2019. Italo Nogueira, "Governador que só pensa em morte reclama de política sobre caixão," *Folha de S.Paulo*, September 23, 2019.

2. Santiago Wills, "The Brazilian Spring: An Explainer," *ABC News*, June 24, 2013.

3. Samuel J. Brannen, Christian S. Haig, and Katherine Schmidt, "The Age of Mass Protests: Understanding an Escalating Global Trend," CSIS Risk and Foresight Group, March 2020.

4. I came to this conclusion before starting this project and discovering Charles Tilly's foundational insights into the ways "protesters" draw on preexisting repertoires of contention, but his work shapes the approach to come and is cited accordingly. The fact that a journalist ignorant of this scholarly work would stumble onto the same broad understanding based on experiences over the last fifteen years is, I believe, further proof of its ongoing relevance.

5. This is the number of interviews, not interviewees; some subjects sat for multiple interviews. Research was carried out in Bahrain, Brazil, Chile, Egypt, Germany, Hong Kong, Indonesia, South Korea, Tunisia, Turkey, the United Kingdom, and the United States.

6. Georgi Derluguian, *Bourdieu's Secret Admirer in the Caucasus: A World-System Biography* (Chicago: University of Chicago Press, 2005), 158–159 and 264; for a discussion of Braudel's "longue durée" in the context of the so-called Arab Spring, see Sara Salem, "Critical Interventions in Debates on the Arab Revolutions: Centring Class," *Review of African Political Economy* 45, no. 155, 2018.

7. This is widely attributed to him, especially since 2001, but it is not in any published works and may be apocryphal.

8. Mark Beissinger, *The Revolutionary City: Urbanization and the Global Transformation of Rebellion* (Princeton: Princeton University Press, 2022), 41.

9. For a discussion of the ways that history is shaped by rapid responses to errors and unexpected difficulties, see Charles Tilly, "Invisible Elbow," *Sociological Forum* 11, no. 4 (1996): 589–601.

10. Beissinger, *The Revolutionary City*, 200–218.

Chapter 1: Learning to Protest

1. In the *Phaedrus*, Socrates famously complains that writing rips speech away from its speaker and from the context that gives language its meaning, allowing for misinterpretation. No one is there to explain what the words are supposed to mean. He was probably right, this changed language forever; but we spent over two thousand years developing techniques for using and interpreting written text.

2. Benedict Anderson, *Imagined Communities: Reflections on the Origin and Spread of Nationalism* (London: Verso, 2016).

3. Charles Tilly, "Speaking Your Mind Without Elections, Surveys, or Social Movements," *Public Opinion Quarterly* 47 (1983): 461–478.

4. Charles Tilly, *The Contentious French: Four Centuries of Popular Struggle* (Cambridge, Mass.: The Belknap Press of Harvard University Press, 1986), 4–30.

5. Ultimately, they sought the disbandment of the British armed forces entirely. Sean Scalmer, *Gandhi in the West: The Mahatma and the Rise of Radical Protest* (Cambridge: Cambridge University Press, 2011), 138–155.

6. Mike Davis and Jon Weiner, *Set the Night on Fire: L.A. in the Sixties* (New York: Verso, 2020), 50–63.

7. Scalmer, *Gandhi in the West*, 71.

8. Ibid., 150 and 215.

9. Wini Breines, *Community and Organization in the New Left, 1962–1968: The Great Refusal* (New York: Praeger Publishers, 1982), 11.

10. Students for a Democratic Society, *The Port Huron Statement*, 1962.

11. Jeremy Suri, *Power and Protest: Global Revolution and the Rise of Détente* (Cambridge: Harvard University Press, 2003), 89–92.

12. Todd Gitlin, *The Whole World Is Watching: Mass Media in the Making and Unmaking of the New Left* (Berkeley: University of California Press, 2003), 27.

13. Ibid. For "judo," see page 29; for the decisions on protests and media response, page 79; for the statement in response, page 91.

14. Gitlin claims the "Prairie Power" new arrivals, called such because they came from middle America, were more likely to call themselves anarchists. *The Whole World is Watching*, 131.

15. Breines, *Community and Organization in the New Left*, 36.

16. Gitlin, *The Whole World Is Watching*, 45.

17. Breines, *Community and Organization in the New Left*, 15 and 112.

18. Vladimir Lenin, "What Is to Be Done?," in *The Essential Works of Lenin*, ed. Henry M. Christman (New York: Bantam, 1966).

19. Daniel Guérin, *Anarchism: From Theory to Practice* (New York: Monthly Review Press, 1970), x–xi.

20. *The Essential Works of Lenin*, 83 and 128–130, on spontaneity and the need for special revolutionary training, respectively; for a response, see "Organizational Questions of Russian Social Democracy" by Rosa Luxemburg. Unlike the way that twenty-first-century activists have often understood "spontaneity," Luxemburg also insists on an organized Marxist party, though one that is less centralized than Lenin's version.

21. For a recent overview of the term and its uses, see Luke Yates, "Prefigurative Politics and Social Movement Strategy: The Roles of Prefiguration in the Reproduction, Mobilisation and Coordination of Movements," *Political Studies* 69, no. 4 (2020): 1–20; for pathbreaking employment of "prefigurative politics" to explain the New Left, see Breines, *Community and Organization in the New Left*, chap. 4. The quote is from the Preface to the Second Edition, published 1989.

22. Uri Gordon, "Prefigurative Politics between Ethical Practice and Absent Promise," *Political Studies* 66, no. 2 (2017): 1–17.

23. Jura Federation Circular, 1871. Cited in Gordon, "Prefigurative Politics Between Ethical Practice and Absent Promise."

24. Breines, *Community Organization and the New Left*, 14.

25. Bertrand Russell, *Autobiography* (London: Unwin Paperbacks, 1978), 612–613. Cited in Scalmer, *Gandhi in the West*, 226.

26. Vladislav M. Zubok, *A Failed Empire: The Soviet Union in the Cold War from Stalin to Gorbachev* (Chapel Hill: University of North Carolina Press, 2007), 182–200; Ali Kadri, *The Unmaking of Arab Socialism* (New York: Anthem Press, 2016), chap. 1, especially page 68.

27. Adam Hanieh, *Lineages of Revolt: Issues of Contemporary Capitalism in the Middle East* (Chicago: Haymarket Books, 2013), 24–25; Hazem Kandil, *Soldiers, Spies, and Statesmen: Egypt's Road to Revolt* (London: Verso, 2012), 56–60.

28. Alessandro Brogi, *Confronting America: The Cold War Between the United States and the Communists in France and Italy* (Chapel Hill: University of North Carolina Press, 2011), 95–102.

29. Leon Trotsky said that "the first task of every insurrection is to bring the troops over to its side." Cited approvingly by Mark Beissinger in *The Revolutionary City*, 29.

30. Beissinger, *The Revolutionary City*, 57.

31. For footage of demonstrations and interviews with participants, see Chris Marker, *A Grin Without a Cat*, Dovidis, 1977.

32. Gerd Koenen, *Das Rote Jahrzehnt: Unsere kleine Deutsche Kulturrevolution 1967–1977* (Cologne: Kiepenheuer & Witsch, 2001), 46–47, 49. Cited in Julia Lovell, *Maoism: A Global History* (New York: Alfred A. Knopf, 2019), 278.

33. Suri, *Power and Protest*, 90 and 188.

34. Kristin Ross, *May '68 and Its Afterlives* (Chicago: University of Chicago Press, 1988), 42–45.

35. "Hard core" is translated from *noyau dur*. Ibid., 38.

36. Gavin Grindon, "Revolutionary Romanticism: Henri Lefebvre's Revolution-as-Festival," *Third Text* 27, no. 2, 2013; Charles de Gaulle himself made a reference to the concept of the *chienlit* during the events of May 1968.

37. Giovanni Arrighi, Terence K. Hopkins, and Immanuel Wallerstein, "1989, the Continuation of 1968," *Review* (Fernand Braudel Center) 15, no. 2 (Spring 1992), 221–242.

38. I follow Suri and Arrighi et al. in broadly considering the Cultural Revolution as part of a "global 1968." For a dissenting view, see Jeffrey Wasserstrom, "Did China Have

a 1968?," *American Historical Review* 123, no. 3, 2018. For my purposes it does not matter that the anti-bureaucratic frenzy was directed from above, but rather that the movement took aim at an "Old Left" party structure. For a brief overview of the Cultural Revolution itself, see Rebecca E. Karl, *Mao Zedong and China in the Twentieth-Century World* (Durham, NC: Duke University Press, 2010), chaps. 8 and 9.

39. Kandil, *Soldiers, Spies, and Statesmen*, 96.

40. Lara Marlowe, "Paris provoked CIA and KGB alarm," *Irish Times*, May 9, 1998.

41. Arrighi et al., "1989, the Continuation of 1968," 223.

42. André Gorz, "The Way Forward," *New Left Review*, November and December 1968.

43. Ross, *May '68 and Its Afterlives*, 63.

44. Martine Storti, *Un chagrin politique: de mai 1968 aux années 80* (Paris: L'Harmattan, 1996), 53. Cited in Ross, *May '68 and Its Afterlives*, 188.

45. Nina Antonia, *Too Much Too Soon: The New York Dolls* (London: Omnibus, 2003), 166.

46. Greil Marcus, *Lipstick Traces: A Secret History of the Twentieth Century* (London: Faber and Faber, 1989), 3, 53, 62.

47. Francis Fukuyama, *The End of History and the Last Man* (New York: Free Press, 2006), 8; Zubok, *A Failed Empire*, 265.

48. Odd Arne Westad, *The Cold War: A World History* (New York: Basic Books, 2017), 619.

49. Derluguian, *Bourdieu's Secret Admirer in the Caucasus*, 307.

50. Zubok, *A Failed Empire*, 310.

51. Stephen Kotkin, *Armageddon Averted: The Soviet Collapse, 1970–2000* (Oxford: Oxford University Press, 2008). For the analysis that the USSR could have easily "continued muddling on for quite some time" and that support for the army and Soviet patriotism were strong, see pp. 2–27. For the assertion that a strong allegiance to socialism was a part of ordinary people's worldview, see p. 44. For the latter analysis, Kotkin cites Donna Bahry, "Society Transformed? Rethinking the Social Roots of Perestroika," *Slavic Review* 52/3 (1993).

52. Beissinger, *The Revolutionary City*, 208.

53. Branko Milanovic, "For Whom the Wall Fell?," *The Globalist*, November 7, 2014; for a moving picture of life at the end of Communist Albania (a country outside the Warsaw Pact), and the ways in which "freedom" failed to arrive after its death, see Lea Ypi, *Free: Coming of Age at the End of History* (London: Penguin, 2022).

54. Zubok, *A Failed Empire*, 303.

55. Evgeny Morozov, *The Net Delusion: How Not to Liberate the World* (London: Penguin, 2011), 55.

56. Hans Modrow, "I Was the Last Communist Premier of East Germany," *Jacobin*, November 9, 2019.

57. "How much did reunification cost," *Deutsche Welle*, September 29, 2015.

58. Branko Milanovic, *Income, Inequality, and Poverty During the Transition from Planned to Market Economy* (Washington, DC: World Bank Regional and Sectoral Studies, 1998), 4.

59. Isabella M. Weber, *How China Escaped Shock Therapy: The Market Reform Debate* (London: Routledge, 2021), 3–6.

60. Milanovic, *Income, Inequality, and Poverty*, 67 and 102–103.

61. Weber, *How China Escaped Shock Therapy*, 1.

62. Milanovic, *Income, Inequality and Poverty*, 71.

63. Odd Arne Westad, *The Global Cold War: Third World Interventions and the Making of Our Times* (Cambridge: Cambridge University Press, 2005), 387.

64. Derluguian, *Bourdieu's Secret Admirer in the Caucasus*, 14 and 79.

65. Vincent Bevins, *The Jakarta Method: Washington's Anticommunist Crusade and the Mass Murder Program That Shaped Our World* (New York: PublicAffairs, 2020).

66. Nils Gilman, "The New International Economic Order: A Reintroduction," *Humanity* 6, no. 1, Spring 2015, 1–16.

67. Bret Benjamin, "Bookend to Bandung: The New International Economic Order and the Antinomies of the Bandung Era," *Humanity* 6, no. 1, Spring 2015, 33–46; Guiliano Garavini, "From Boumedienomics to Reaganomics: Algeria, OPEC, and the International Struggle for Economic Equality," *Humanity* 6, no. 1, Spring 2015, 79–92.

68. Patrick Iber, "Worlds Apart," *New Republic*, April 23, 2018.

69. Quinn Slobodian, *Globalists: The End of Empire and the Birth of Neoliberalism* (Cambridge: Harvard University Press, 2018), 5–12.

70. Weber, *How China Escaped Shock Therapy*, 3; Michel Foucault, *The Birth of Biopolitics: Lectures at the Collège de France, 1978–1979* (New York: Palgrave Macmillan, 2010), 19–35, 278.

71. Mitchell Dean and Daniel Zamora, *Foucault and the End of Revolution* (London: Verso, 2021), 213–215.

72. Ross, *May '68 and Its Afterlives*, 80–92.

Chapter 2: Mayara and Fernando

1. This section is based on author interviews with Mayara Vivian in São Paulo, 2021 and 2022.

2. Paolo Gerbaudo, *The Mask and the Flag: Populism, Citizenism, and Global Protest* (London: Hurst & Company, 2017), 20–21.

3. The Radiohead website is how I discovered *No Logo*, which I read, in the early 2000s. This promotion is noted in *Q Magazine*, October 2000.

4. The history of Indymedia Brasil is based on interviews with André Takahashi in São Paulo, 2021 and 2022.

5. This section is based on interviews with Frederico Freitas, by phone, 2021 and 2022.

6. Rodrigo Lopes de Barros, *Distortion and Subversion: Punk Rock Music and Free Public Transportation in Brazil, 1996–2011*, 10–12; Pablo Ortellado, "Sobre a passagem de um grupo de pessoas por um breve período da história," in *Estamos Vencendo! Resistência Global no Brasil*, Pablo Ortellado and André Riyoki (São Paulo: Conrad, 2004), 9.

7. David Graeber, "The New Anarchists," *New Left Review* 13, January/February 2002, 69–71. Emphasis reproduced from the original.

8. Author interview with Rodrigo Nunes in Rio de Janeiro, 2022.

9. All passages on Fernando Haddad are partially informed by author interviews with Haddad in São Paulo, 2021 and 2022. Where I draw on published material, these sources are cited below.

10. Diogo Bercito, *Brimos: Imigração sírio-libanesa no Brasil e seu caminho até a política* (São Paulo: Fósforo, 2019), 164.

11. Clara Becker, "O Candidato da Esquerda," *Revista Piauí*, Edição 61, Outubro 2011.

12. Fernando Haddad, *Em defesa do socialismo* (São Paulo: Editora Vozes, 1998), 59–60.

13. Lincoln Secco, *História do PT* (São Paulo: Ateliê Editorial, 2011), 26–27 and 81–82; for Lula's early life, relationship to the PCB, and his participation in the founding of the party, see Fernando Morais, *Lula, Volume 1* (São Paulo: Companhia das Letras, 2022), chaps. 9–15.

14. John Paul Rathbone, "Debt Crisis Lessons from Latin America," *Financial Times*, December 4, 2011; Greg Grandin, "Why Stop at Two?," *London Review of Books* 31, no. 20, October 2009; Secco, *História do PT*, 179–180.

15. Haddad, *Em defesa do socialismo*, 49–51. The emphasis is his.

16. Fernando Henrique Cardoso and Enzo Faletto, *Dependency and Development in Latin America* (Berkeley: University of California Press, 1979).

17. Camila Rocha, *Menos Marx, Mais Mises* (São Paulo: Todavia, 2019), 74.

18. William Nelkirk, "Even in Brazil, President Can't Escape Probe Queries," *Chicago Tribune*, October 15, 1997.

19. Piero Locatelli, *#VemPraRua: As revoltas de junho pelo jovem repórter que recebeu passe livre para contar a história do movimento* (São Paulo: Grupo Companhia das Letras, 2013), 2–3; author interview with Juliana Cunha in São Paulo, 2021; Elena Judensnaider, Luciana Lima, Marcelo Pomar, and Pablo Ortellado, *Vinte Centavos: a luta contra o aumento* (São Paulo: Veneta, 2013), 9.

20. All discussions of "Vegetable" are based on author interviews with Lucas "Vegetable" Monteiro in São Paulo, 2021 and 2022.

21. Ezequiel Adamovsky, *Más allá de la vieja izquierda: Seis ensayos para un nuevo anticapitalismo* (Buenos Aires: Prometeo Libros, 2007), 107–108; for more of Adamovsky's reflections on his time in this movement, see Ezequiel Adamovsky, "Pots, Pans, and Popular Power: the neighborhood assemblies of Buenos Aires," in *We Are Everywhere: The Irresistible Rise of Global Anti-Capitalism* (New York: Verso, 2003); author interviews with Adamovsky, 2022.

22. Marina Sitrin, *Horizontalism: Voices of Popular Power in Argentina* (Edinburgh: AK Press, 2006).

23. Fukuyama, *The End of History and the Last Man*, xiii.

24. To the credit of Francis Fukuyama's often-criticized volume, the North American liberal theorist did not claim this process was automatic, and the book attempts to articulate the concrete dynamic that might create a universal Historical path. The "End of History" did not mean that things would stop happening, but that History in the sense of the conflict over the world's organizational form would come to an end. In the end of the twentieth century, it seemed that even some Soviet leaders agreed; for a serious treatment of Fukuyama's thesis and its implications for the mass protest decade, see Alex Hochuli, George Hoare, and Philip Cunliffe, *The End of the End of History: Politics in the Twenty-First Century* (London: Zero, 2021).

25. Karl Löwith, *Meaning in History: The Theological Implications of the Philosophy of History* (Chicago: University of Chicago Press, 1949). On cyclical and linear time, see pages 2–5; on the emergence of contemporary teleological thinking, see chaps. 2–9; on the tensions buried within the idea of historical development in a world "as Christian

as it is un-Christian," and a society which is both "progressive and profane," see pages 200–201.

26. Hanieh, *Lineages of Revolt*, 4–5; Maha Abdelrahman, *Egypt's Long Revolution: Protest Movements and Uprisings* (London: Routledge, 2014), Introduction.

27. Beissinger, *The Revolutionary City*, 96.

28. Alex von Tunzelmann, "The toppling of Saddam's statue: how the US military made a myth," *The Guardian*, July 8, 2021.

Chapter 3: Pior que tá não fica

1. Jonathan Wheatley, "Olympic accolade sets seal on progress," *Financial Times*, November 4, 2009.

2. "Lula 'é o cara', diz Obama durante reunião do G20, em Londres," *G1/GloboNews*, March 2, 2009.

3. Helder Marinho, "Brazil's Lula Leaves Office with 83% Approval Rating, Folha Says," Bloomberg, December 19, 2010.

4. Vincent Bevins, "Brazil president holds her own as Lula successor," *Los Angeles Times*, October 16, 2011. "Sweep" here is a free translation of *faxina*. I have previously also used "cleaning house."

5. Locatelli, *#VemPraRua*, 3.

6. Movimento Passe Livre São Paulo, "Luta contra o aumento de 2011."

7. "Teenage Riot," *Vice News*, 2013.

Chapter 4: More Than an Uprising

1. Based on interview with Kais Bouazizi, Anouar Jawadi, Ayouni Moncef, and Ayman Gharbi in Sidi Bouzid, 2021.

2. David Siddhartha Patel, "Comparing Explanations of the Arab Uprisings," *Project on Middle East Political Science*, October 2–3, 2014. Prepared for "The Arab Uprisings Explained" workshop.

3. Joel Beinin, *Workers and Thieves: Labor Movements and Popular Uprisings in Tunisia and Egypt* (Stanford: Stanford University Press, 2016), 30–35.

4. Cihan Tuğal, *The Fall of the Turkish Model: How the Arab Uprisings Brought Down Islamic Liberalism* (London: Verso, 2016), 154; Beinin, *Workers and Thieves*, 2 and 83–92.

5. All passages about Jawaher draw upon author interviews in Tunis, 2021.

6. Thessa Lageman, "Remembering Mohamed Bouazizi: The man who sparked the Arab Spring," *Al Jazeera*, December 17, 2020; Ali's party affiliation was mentioned to me as a matter of course in Sidi Bouzid, but some accounts prefer to leave out this detail, since PDP did not drive the revolutionary upsurge. I believe, however, that—along with myriad factors—his background as a savvy and experienced activist is also relevant to the story.

7. Author interviews with anonymous former PCOT members in Tunis and Sidi Bouzid, 2021.

8. Merlyna Lim, "Framing Bouazizi: 'White lies', hybrid network, and collective/connective action in the 2010–11 Tunisian uprising," *Journalism* 14, no. 7, 2013; he was certainly not a college graduate, and the officer has always denied striking Bouazizi.

9. Tuğal, *The Fall of the Turkish Model*, 157; for a discussion of this particular story and its relationship to the broken promises of development, see John Chalcraft, "Egypt's uprising, Mohamed Bouazizi and the failure of Neoliberalism," *The Maghreb Review* 37, no. 3–4, 2012. Small business owners, liberated from the shackles of socialist governance, were supposed to be the vanguard of the new liberal revolution.

10. My account focuses on media and party participation in the early days of the uprising, because of the ways they will resonate with other stories in the decade. For analysis which challenges this kind of framing, see Jann Boeddeling, "From Resistance to Revolutionary Praxis: Subaltern Politics in the Tunisian Revolution," The London School of Economics and Political Science, 2020.

11. For an account of trade unionists demonstrating on December 25, see *Swiss Info*, "في تونس.. الإعصار الاجتماعي المنبعث من سيدي بوزيد يهدّد "قوانين اللعبة"," December 27, 2010; for a discussion of the overall timeline, indicating that large-scale demonstrations in the capital began on December 27, see Ryan Rifai, "Timeline: Tunisia's Uprising," *Al Jazeera*, January 23, 2011.

12. Photograph posted to Twitter by Mohamed Dhia Hammami; Ben Youseff, "REVOLUTION, dix ans après: sous les pavés, la rage," *Le Temps* Tunisia, January 1, 2021.

13. Deutsche Welle, "أحداث سيدي بوزيد تتحول إلى معركة إعلامية رأس حربتها فيسبوك," December 29, 2010.

14. International Crisis Group, "Between Popular Uprising and Regime Collapse: Popular Protests in North Africa and the Middle East (IV): Tunisia's Way," *Crisis Group Middle East/North Africa Report*, no. 106, April 28, 2011.

15. João Roberto Martins Filho, "A Influência Doutrinária Francesa sobre os Militares Brasileiros nos Anos de 1960," *Revista Brasileira de Ciências Sociais* 23, no. 67, 39–50, 2008.

16. "US Summons Tunisia ambassador over handling of protests," *BBC News*, January 7, 2011; "Tunisia closes schools and universities following riots," *BBC News*, January 10, 2011."

17. "Tunisian authorities urged to protect protesters following deadly weekend," Amnesty International, January 10, 2011.

18. Aasef Bayat, *Revolution without Revolutionaries: Making Sense of the Arab Spring* (Stanford: Stanford University Press, 2017), 8–9.

19. All sections on Hossam el-Hamalawy draw upon author interviews in Berlin, 2021 and 2022.

20. After months of pro-Palestinian protests throughout Cairo, Egyptians filled the square in September 2001. Adel Abdel Ghafar, *Egyptians in Revolt: The Political Economy of Labor and Student Mobilizations 1919–2011* (Oxfordshire: Routledge, 2017), 157; author interviews with anonymous activists and protesters in Cairo, in 2021.

21. All information on Gehad based on author interviews, 2021 and 2022.

22. Kandil, *Soldiers, Spies, and Statesmen*, 107–130.

23. US journalist Barbara Walters was famously shocked by how few Egyptians showed up to the funeral. Kandil, *Soldiers, Spies, and Statesmen*, 171; see also Mohamed Heikal, *Autumn of Fury: Assassination of Sadat* (London: Andre Deutsch, 1983), Introduction.

24. Adam Hanieh, *Lineages of Revolt*, 31.

25. NED cofounder Allen Weinstein said, "A lot of what we do today was done covertly 25 years ago by the CIA." David Ignatius, "Innocence abroad: the new world of

spyless coups," *Washington Post*, September 22, 1991; for an overview of this relationship in historical perspective, see Greg Grandin, *Empire's Workshop: Latin America, the United States, and the Making of an Imperial Republic* (New York, NY: Picador, 2021), 278–279.

26. On remittances, see Kadri, *The Unmaking of Arab Socialism*, 20–25, and Hanieh, *Lineages of Revolt*, 85–128; on the importance of shopping malls, see Jack Shenker, *The Egyptians: A Radical Story* (London: Allen Lane, 2016), 85–95; on increasing social problems, and deterioration in investment and growth rates in comparison to the previous era of state-led economic policy, see Karen Pfeifer, "How Tunisia, Morocco, Jordan and even Egypt became IMF 'Success Stories' in the 1990s," *Middle East Report*, no. 210, 1999.

27. Kandil, *Soldiers, Spies, and Statesmen*, 198.

28. Shenker, *The Egyptians*, 198.

29. Beinin, *Workers and Thieves*, 79.

30. The short 2011 Al Jazeera documentary "Seeds of Change" annoyed some Egyptian revolutionaries, by giving the April 6 Youth Movement more credit than they may have deserved, but shows the group's conversations with Otpor; for the support from Freedom House and subsequent controversy, see Ron Nixon, "U.S. Groups Helped Nurture Arab Uprisings," *New York Times*, April 14, 2011. Unsurprisingly, many Egyptian activists were deeply suspicious of the United States, which backed both Mubarak and Israel; Hossam el-Hamalawy says that the April 6 Movement appealed to global media precisely "because they claimed to be post-ideological, which is very sexy to the West."

31. Amro Ali, "Saeeds of Revolution: De-Mythologizing Khaled Said," Al-Jadaliyya, June 5, 2012.

32. The World Bank, "Individuals using the Internet (% of population)," International Telecommunication Union (ITU) World Telecommunication/ICT Indicators Database data, cited in Beissinger, *The Revolutionary City*, 310.

33. For "distortion," see Shenker, *The Egyptians*, 11; the word "magic" emerged from author interviews with anonymous revolutionaries.

34. Kandil, *Soldiers, Spies, and Statesmen*, 224; Bayat, *Revolution without Revolutionaries*, 116–126.

35. Author interviews with Egyptian revolutionaries, including anonymous sources, 2021.

36. Bayat, *Revolution without Revolutionaries*, 94–113.

37. Author interview with Wisner Jr., 2018; see also Sheryl Gay Stolberg, "Frank Wisner, the Diplomat Sent to Prod Mubarak," *New York Times*, February 2, 2011.

38. Robert Tait, "Whose Side Is History on After Egypt's 'Berlin Moment'?," *Radio Free Europe*, February 12, 2011.

39. CNN: Anderson Cooper, "In Egypt, fear has been defeated," CNN YouTube Channel, February 12, 2011.

40. Mark Landler, "Obama Cites Poland as Model for Arab Shift," *New York Times*, May 28, 2011.

41. John Chalcraft, "Horizontalism in the Egyptian Revolutionary Process," *Middle East Research and Information Project* 262, Spring 2012. See also *The Square*, Noujaim Films, 2013.

42. Shenker, *The Egyptians*, 224 and 251–252.

43. Originally in Gerbaudo, *The Mask and the Flag*, 65; restated to the author by Salem in different form in 2021.

44. Author interviews with Mahmoud Salem, 2021 and 2022.

45. Beinin, *Workers and Thieves*, 105; France 24, "مجلس انتخاب يعلن المؤقت الرئيس"
تأسيسي في 24 يوليو/تموز," March 4, 2011.

46. Kandil, *Soldiers, Spies, and Statesmen*, 233.

47. Beissinger, *The Revolutionary City*, 295–312; while high unemployment likely played a role in instigating revolutionary participation, Beissinger notes, the highly educated unemployed did not participate at a higher rate than the highly educated and employed.

48. *United Nations Development Programme*, "Human Development Report 2010: The Real Wealth of Nations," 144; Libya is ranked fifty-third, just behind Croatia and Uruguay.

49. Alan J. Kuperman, "A Model Humanitarian Intervention? Reassessing NATO's Libya Campaign," *International Security*, 2013, 105–136, 116; Peter Beaumont, "'War weary' Libya reflects 10 years on from Gaddafi and Arab spring," *The Guardian*, April 26, 2021.

50. Claudia Gazzini, "Was the Libya Intervention Necessary?," *Middle East Research and Information Project* 261, Winter 2011; Matthew Green, "To What Extent Was the NATO Intervention in Libya a Humanitarian Intervention?," *E-International Relations*, February 6, 2019; Patrick C. R. Terry, "The Libya intervention (2011): neither lawful, nor successful," *The Comparative and International Law Journal of Southern Africa*, 2015, 162–182.

51. Green, "To What Extent Was the NATO Intervention in Libya a Humanitarian Intervention?," 3; Human Rights Watch, "Unacknowledged Deaths, Civilian Casualties in NATO's Air Campaign in Libya," May 13, 2012.

52. Mira Rapp-Hooper and Kenneth N. Waltz, "What Kim Jong-Il Learned from Qaddafi's Fall: Never Disarm," *The Atlantic*, October 24, 2011.

53. Corbett Daly, "Clinton on Qaddafi: 'We came, we saw, he died,'" *CBS News*, October 20, 2011.

54. Ministry of Foreign Affairs of the People's Republic of China, "President Hu Jintao Meets with French Counterpart Sarkozy," March 30, 2011.

55. Richard Sakwa, *Frontline Ukraine: Crisis in the Borderlands* (London: I.B. Tauris, 2015), 6; Kim Ghattas, "What a Decade-Old Conflict Tells Us About Putin," *The Atlantic*, March 6, 2022.

56. Theodore Karasik and Heinrich Matthee, "Russia's Emerging Defense and Security Doctrine: Impact on Europe and the Near East," *Institute for Near East and Gulf Military Analysis*, June 8, 2014; Sakwa, *Frontline Ukaine*, 30.

57. Biblioteca da Presidência da República, "Discurso da Presidenta da República, Dilma Rousseff, na abertura do Debate Geral da 66ª Assembleia Geral das Nações Unidas."

58. Nikolaos Van Dam, *Destroying a Nation: The Civil War in Syria* (London: I.B. Tauris, 2017), 62–79.

59. Linda Matar and Ali Kadri, *Syria: From National Independence to Proxy War* (Cham: Palgrave Macmillan, 2019), 66.

60. Justin Gengler, *Group Conflict and Political Mobilization in Bahrain and the Arab Gulf* (Bloomington: Indiana University Press, 2015), 13–41; on the dissolution of the National Assembly, see page 237.

61. All material on Ebrahim Sharif informed by author interviews, in Bahrain and by phone, 2021 and 2022.

62. Gengler, *Group Conflict and Political Mobilization in Bahrain and the Arab Gulf*, 202.

63. The site is now called "Al Farooq Junction," a reference to Umar ibn al-Khattab.

64. Bayat, *Revolution without Revolutionaries*, 76; Barack Obama, *A Promised Land* (New York: Crown, 2020), 652.

65. Ala'A Shehabi and Marc Owen Jones, *Bahrain's Uprising: Resistance and Repression in the Gulf* (London: Zed Books, 2015), 9; Pepe Escobar, "Exposed: The US-Saudi Libya deal," *Asia Times*, April 2, 2011.

Chapter 5: Around the World

1. Gerbaudo, *The Mask and the Flag*, 36.

2. For insistence a year later that the movement was always "horizontal, without representatives," see *ABC España*, "Y ahora . . . ¿cuál es la Democracia Real Ya?" March 24, 2012.

3. Gerbaudo, *The Mask and the Flag*, 54

4. Cristina Flesher Fominaya, *Democracy Reloaded: Inside Spain's Political Laboratory from 15-M to Podemos* (Oxford: Oxford University Press, 2020), Ch. 10.

5. Gerbaudo, *The Mask and the Flag*, 18 and 38.

6. Zeynep Tufekci, *Twitter and Tear Gas: The Power and Fragility of Networked Protest* (New Haven: Yale University Press, 2017), 97.

7. Colin Moynihan, "Occupy Wall Street Activists File Suit Over Control of Twitter Account," *New York Times*, September 14, 2014; Gerbaudo, *The Mask and the Flag*, 154.

8. Adam Tooze, *Crashed: How a Decade of Financial Crises Changed the World*, (New York: Penguin, 2019), 394–395.

9. See David Folkenflik, "Tracking The Media's Eye On Occupy Wall Street," NPR, October 13, 2011. He writes that "early sympathetic columns in the *New York Times* and the *Boston Globe* were largely dismissive." In language that recalls Todd Gitlin's lessons from the 1960s, he says that this is because Occupy Wall Street "proved difficult for the media to categorize and therefore to cover."

10. André da Silva Takahashi, a founder of both Indymedia and the MPL, put it this way: "This is the Third World, and downtown São Paulo is already occupied: by drug users, poor people living on the streets, and by small-time criminals. In the end, the lumpenproletariat expelled the activists."

11. "Ocupa Sampa completa um mês no centro de São Paulo," *Rede Brasil Atual*, November 14, 2011.

12. Author interviews with Chilean student activists in Santiago, 2022.

13. Marisa von Bulow and Sofia Donoso, "Introduction: Social Movements in Contemporary Chile," in *Social Movements in Chile: Organization, Trajectories and Political Consequences*, ed. Sofia Donoso and Marisa von Bulow (New York: Palgrave Macmillan, 2017), 16 and 33.

14. Sofia Donoso, "'Outsider' and 'Insider' Strategies in Chile's Student Movement, 1990-2014," in *Social Movements in Chile*, ed. Donoso and von Bulow, 108–123.

15. Nicolás Somma and Rodrigo Medel, "Shifting Relationships Between Social Movements and Institutional Politics," in *Social Movements in Chile*, ed. Donoso and von Bulow, 59–88.

16. Francisco Goldman, "Camila Vallejo, the World's Most Glamorous Revolutionary," *New York Times*, April 5, 2012.

17. Author interviews with Giovanna Roa in Santiago, 2022; Donoso, "'Outsider' and 'Insider' Strategies," 133.

Chapter 6: A Social Network

1. I was not paid to run the *From Brazil* blog, though *Folha* paid contributors like Claire Rigby and Dom Phillips for each post. I only received the desk space and use of the newsroom infrastructure; the Ford Foundation helped train the so-called Chicago Boys, the economists who shaped policy in Chile's military dictatorship. In Brazil, Ford initially supported the US-backed 1964 coup and the consequent regime, but eventually shifted to funding civil society groups and pro-democracy dissidents. For the former see Sebastian Edwards, *The Chile Project* (Princeton: Princeton University Press, 2023), chap. 2. For the latter see Richal Wimpee and Abamby Steve Estrada Raymundo, "'Distasteful Regimes': Authoritarianism, the Ford Foundation, and Social Sciences in Brazil," *Rockefeller Center*, October 20, 2021.

2. Yasha Levine, *Surveillance Valley: The Secret Military History of the Internet* (New York: PublicAffairs, 2018), 70–127.

3. Vincent Bevins, "Surfin' USA," *The Baffler*, January 4, 2021.

4. Marcos Nobre, *Limites da Democracia: De junho de 2013 ao governo Bolsonaro* (São Paulo: Todavia, 2022). It is significant that the early adoption of the internet by upper-middle-class residents in a given nation (in this case, Brazil) shapes the digital culture that forms.

5. Levine, *Surveillance Valley*, 107–133.

6. The man who created the "like" button came to regret it, and limited his own use of what he called intentionally addictive and time-wasting social media services. Paul Lewis, "'Our minds can be hijacked': the tech insiders who fear a smartphone dystopia," *The Guardian*, October 6, 2017.

7. Author interview with Evan Henshaw-Plath, 2022; Harry Halpin and Evan Henshaw-Plath, "From Indymedia to Tahrir Square: The Revolutionary Origins of Status Updates on Twitter," *WWW '22: Proceedings of the ACM Web Conference 2022*, Virtual Event, Lyon, France, April 2022.

8. Morozov, *The Net Delusion*, 180–184 and 217–231; Levine, *Surveillance Valley*, 248–254; "Special Briefing to Announce the Alliance of Youth Movement," US Department of State, November 24, 2008.

9. Nicholas Kristof, "Tear down this cyberwall!," *New York Times*, June 17, 2009.

10. Urmee Khan, "Twitter should win Nobel Peace Prize, says former US security adviser," *The Telegraph*, July 07, 2009. This case is cited in Morozov, *The Net Delusion*, 1–4.

11. Katharine Viner, "Internet has changed foreign policy for ever, says Gordon Brown," *The Guardian*, June 19, 2009.

12. Author interview with Evgeny Morozov, 2022; articles in the *International Herald Tribune* and the *New Republic* are cited in Morozov, *The Net Delusion*, 41.

13. "Internet foi ferramenta de luta contra regimes autoritários em países árabes," *Globo/G1*, November 12, 2011.

14. Jack Shenker, "Egyptian Vote on Constitution Reveals Deep Divisions," *The Guardian*, March 18, 2011.

15. After Nasser, he has cited Lula as his main political inspiration. Author interview with Hamdeen Sabahi, 2023; for better-publicized references to Lula after the 2012 election, see "«صباحي»: هدفي القضاء على الفقر.. وتحقيق التنمية المستدامة", *Al-Masry Al-Youm*, March 17, 2014.

16. "Gay Girl in Damascus: Tom MacMaster defends blog hoax," *BBC News*, June 13, 2011.

17. Rafeef Ziadah, "Saudi-UAE interventions: Arms, aid and counter-revolution," Transnational Institute, October 27, 2021.

18. "Popular Protests in North Africa and the Middle East (IV): Tunisia's Way," International Crisis Group, April 28, 2011.

Chapter 7: Cowboys and Indians

1. Gautam Nair, "Most Americans vastly underestimate how rich they are compared with the rest of the world. Does it matter?," *Washington Post*, August 23, 2018.

2. Joe Leahy, "Rousseff to tackle sharp rise in the real," *Financial Times*, January 5, 2011; Brazil became the world's sixth-largest economy (but not for long) starting at the end of 2011.

3. "The loneliness of the right-wing legislator," *The Economist*, April 3, 2014.

4. For a description and photos of this routine, see Vincent Bevins, "Brazil's special forces wage uphill fight against Amazon destroyers," *Los Angeles Times*, July 10, 2015.

5. For a retrospective analysis of results in this area, see Roberto Goulart Menezes and Natália Fingermann, "Cooperação Sul-Sul no governo de Dilma Rousseff (2011–2016): Retração ou transformação?," *Sociedade e Cultura* 23 (2020).

6. Jonathan Wheatley, "Brazil Basks in Petrobras Spotlight," *Financial Times*, September 24, 2010; "Filling Up the Future," *The Economist*, May 11, 2011.

7. "Quero humanizar São Paulo," *Carta Capital*, March 24, 2012; "Um Tempo Novo para São Paulo," *Plano de Governo Haddad Prefeito*, 2012.

8. Rosana Pinheiro-Machado and Lucia Scalco have called this "inclusion through consumption." See "From Hope to Hate: The Rise of Conservative Subjectivity in Brazil," *HAU: Journal of Ethnographic Theory* 10, no. 1, 2020, 21–22.

9. Vincent Bevins, "Huge shopping malls change landscape of Brazil," *Los Angeles Times*, October 1, 2014.

10. Alex Cuadros, *Brazillionaires: Wealth, Power, Decadence, and Hope in an American Country* (New York: Spiegel & Grau, 2016), 124–127.

11. Reinaldo Azevedo, "Haddad é o Taliban de bicicleta; é o Estado Islâmico sobre duas rodas," *Veja*, November 20, 2015.

12. Vincent Bevins, "Brazil's Dilma Rousseff is popular, but not among news media," *Los Angeles Times*, March 3, 2013.

Chapter 8: Minority Report

1. Jacob Poushter, "Prime Minister Erdogan popular in Turkey broadly, but less so in Istanbul," Pew Research Center, June 5, 2013.

2. Gürkan Özturan, "Before Gezi there was Emek: The demolished heart of Turkish cinema," *Kaitoikos World*, December 14, 2016.

3. Author interviews with Furkan and other activists, Istanbul 2021.

4. A timeline and in-depth report is available at Amnesty International, "Turkey: Gezi Park protests: Brutal denial of the right to peaceful assembly in Turkey," October 2, 2013.

5. Author interview with Hazar, Istanbul, 2021.

6. Dexter Filkins,"The Deep State," *New Yorker*, March 12, 2012.

7. Tuğal, *The Fall of the Turkish Model*, 271; of course, the term "Third World" was not used in this way during Atatürk's lifetime.

8. Westad, *The Global Cold War*, 59. This volume incorrectly refers to potential bases at the "Straits of Hormuz," an error which I regrettably reproduced in early editions of *The Jakarta Method*.

9. Tuğal, *The Fall of the Turkish Model*, 69–92.

10. Ahmet Insel, "The AKP and Normalizing Democracy in Turkey," *South Atlantic Quarterly* 102, April 2003.

11. Tuğal, *The Fall of the Turkish Model*, 7 and 93.

12. Author interviews with middle-class Turks living in London at the time. They reported being glued to Facebook, until they simply splurged for a flight back home to Turkey.

13. Tuğal, *The Fall of the Turkish Model*, 263.

14. Like Peronism in Argentina, Kemalism comes in different flavors.

15. Alexander Christie Miller, "Occupy Gezi: from the fringes to the center, and back again," *White Review*, July 2013; Ahmet Samin, "The Tragedy of the Turkish Left," *New Left Review*, March/April 1981.

16. Tuğal, *The Fall of the Turkish Model*, 259.

17. Author interviews with Vamos Bien members in Istanbul, 2021.

18. Author interviews with Eren Senkardes in Istanbul, 2021.

19. Tufekci, *Twitter and Tear Gas*, xv and 89–93.

20. Ali Murat Yel and Alparslan Nas, "Taksim Square Is Not Tahrir Square," *Al Jazeera*, June 12, 2013.

21. Author interview with Bahar in Istanbul, 2022.

22. Tuğal, *The Fall of the Turkish Model*, 256.

Chapter 9: The Free Fare Movement

1. This entire chapter draws on author interviews with MPL members, especially Lucas "Vegetable" Monteiro, Oliver Cauã Cauê, and Mayara Vivian, in São Paulo, 2021 and 2022.

2. Movimento Passe Livre, "Carta de Princípios."

3. Fernando Haddad, "Vivi na pele o que aprendi nos livros," *Revista Piauí*, June 2017.

4. Locatelli, *#VemPraRua*, 4–6; *Amanhã vai ser maior* or "tomorrow will be bigger / greater" was the name of a documentary about the Free Fare protests in Florianópolis, eight years earlier; see Lopes de Barros, *Distortion and Subversion*, 43.

5. Judensnaider et al., *Vinte Centavos*, 36.

6. Locatelli, *#VemPraRua*, 12.

7. "Puro vandalism," *O Estado de São Paulo*, June 8, 2013.

8. Author interview with Fernando Haddad in São Paulo, 2021.

9. Locatelli, *#VemPraRua*, 14.

10. Judensnaider et al., *Vinte Centavos*, 73–75.

11. "Lynched" is the language used by *Estadão*, "Chegou a hora do basta," June 13, 2013; for an account of this call, see Haddad, "Vivi na pele o que aprendi nos livros," *Revista Piauí*.

12. "Editorial: Retomar a Paulista," *Folha de S.Paulo*, June 13, 2013.

13. This would be the *Levante Popular da Juventude*; that day it was also easy to see members of PSOL, PCO, and PTSU on the street.

14. Judensnaider et al., *Vinte Centavos*, 99; it is still easy to find this clip online: see for example "Datena surpreendido em pesquisa! Passe Livre 13/06/13," published by Fabio Hemeg on YouTube.

Chapter 10: The Giant Awakens

1. Locatelli, *#VemPraRua*, 50.

2. Simon Romero, "Thousands Gather for Protests in Brazil's Largest Cities," *New York Times*, June 17, 2013: Romero cites 100,000 for Rio alone; "Protesto em São Paulo é o maior desde manifestação contra Collor," *Folha de S. Paulo*, June 17, 2013.

3. Locatelli, *#VemPraRua*, 7.

4. Dom Phillips has tragically passed away, so I cannot ask him for permission. But I don't think he would mind sharing the footage he sent me that day. Still online (in 2023) at: https://vimeo.com/68591988, Password saopaulo.

5. Rocha, *Menos Marx, Mais Mises*, page 121 on the Koch program, page 31 on the "Comintern," and page 23 on the word *liberal*. For the "neoliberal Comintern" characterization, Rocha is quoting British historian Richard Cockett; author interview with Fábio Ostermann in 2022.

6. Marina Amaral, "A Nova Roupa da Direita," *Agência Pública*, June 23, 2015. This explanation is given by Juliano Torres, executive diretor of Estudantes Pela Liberdade.

7. Accessed in 2023, the June 18 Facebook post reads, "Protestar, sim! Mas pela(s) causa(s) certa(s), por favor . . ." with a link to the Instituto Ordem Livre; Ostermann confirmed this must have been one of the first MBL posts, if not the first.

8. Author interview with Fábio Ostermann in 2022.

9. Judensnaider et al., *Vinte Centavos*, 187.

10. Author interviews with Fernando Haddad and Mayara Vivian in 2021 and 2022.

11. See the 2021 Dilma Rousseff interview with Diário do Centro do Mundo (DCM), "Dilma fala sobre o telefonema de Putin alertando sobre o golpe," *DCM TV*.

12. Two million is an optimistic estimate for any given moment on January 20 but a safer bet to describe the movement as a whole that week. Jonathan Watts, "Brazil erupts in protest: more than a million on the streets," *The Guardian*, June 21, 2013; in 1992 the *New York Times* estimated the street movement against President Collor at 750,000 and called it the largest in Brazilian history. See James Brooke, "Huge Rally Demands Brazil Chief's Impeachment," September 20, 1992.

13. Locatelli, *#VemPraRua*, 34.

Chapter 11: Five Causes, Four Fingers

1. Author interview with Thomas Traumann, 2022.
2. Luiz Inácio Lula da Silva, "The Message of Brazil's Youth," *New York Times*, July 16, 2013.
3. André de Souza, Paulo Celso Pereira, and Luiza Damé, "Após reunião, MPL diz que Presidência é despreparada," *O Globo*, June 24, 2013.
4. Datafolha Instituto de Pesquisas, "Maioria defende constituinte para reformar política," July 1, 2013. Published online by *Folha de S.Paulo*.
5. Fabiana Alves Rodrigues, *Lava Jato: Aprendizado institucional e ação estratégica na Justiça* (São Paulo: Editora WMF Martins Fontes, 2020), 44.
6. Thomas Traumann, *O Pior Emprego do Mundo: 14 ministros da Fazenda contam como tomaram as decisões que mudaram o Brasil e mexeram no seu bolso* (São Paulo: Planeta, 2018), 254.
7. Alves Rodrigues, *Lava Jato*, page 26 for the number of overturned cases, pages 9–14 and 60 on international pressure for the reforms.
8. Tufekci, *Twitter and Tear Gas*, 70–72.
9. Tuğal, *The Fall of the Turkish Model*, 214.
10. Tufekci, *Twitter and Tear Gas*, 72–80.
11. Arwa Ibrahim, "Leaks from Sisi's office allege far-reaching UAE 'interference' in Egypt," *Middle East Eye*, March 2, 2015; Neil Ketchley, "How Egypt's generals used street protests to stage a coup," *Washington Post*, July 3, 2017.
12. Marc Lynch, *The New Arab Wars: Uprising and Anarchy in the Middle East* (New York: PublicAffairs, 2016), 157–163.
13. Afterward, they built this narrative into a polished television drama. Abdullah Al-Arian, "The Lasting Significance of Egypt's Rabaa Massacre," Middle East Research and Information Project, August 23, 2022.
14. Human Rights Watch, "Egypt: Rab'a Killings Likely Crimes against Humanity," August 12, 2014.
15. Sisi's debt to his Gulf Arab backers, Chatham House, April 20, 2020.
16. Melissa Sepulveda, the new president of the Universidad de Chile's student federation, said: "I wouldn't vote for Giorgio Jackson . . . for Camila Vallejo neither. . . . The possibility for change isn't in congress." Pablo Navarrete, "Chile's 'Penguins' Student Revolution Grows up," *International Business Times*, November 18, 2013.
17. Vincent Bevins, "From YouTube to law: How the '5 causas' of Brazil went viral," *Los Angeles Times*, July 17, 2013.
18. Datafolha Instituto de Pesquisas, "Aprovação a governo Dilma Rousseff cai 27 pontos em três semanas," June 29, 2013. Published by *Folha de S.Paulo*.

Chapter 12: Eu Maidan

1. For a November 2013 explication of this view on the Association Agreement, see "Гладун Андрій, До Європи без змін," *Commons*, November 26, 2013. Commons.com.ua is a left-leaning Ukrainian publication.
2. All sections on Artem based on author interviews with Artem Tidva in Kyiv, 2021, and by phone, 2022 and 2023.

3. Serhii Plokhy, *The Gates of Europe: A History of Ukraine, Revised Edition* (New York: Basic Books, 2021), 222–225; 247–254.

4. Grzegorz Rossoliński-Liebe, *Stepan Bandera: The Life and Afterlife of a Ukrainian Nationalist: Fascism, Genocide, and Cult* (Stuttgart: Ibidem, 2014), chaps. 2–5.

5. Serhiy Kudelia, "Choosing Violence in Irregular Wars: The Case of Anti-Soviet Insurgency in Western Ukraine," *East European Politics and Societies and Cultures* 27, no. 1, 2013; Kevin C. Ruffner, "Cold War Allies: The Origins of CIA's Relationship with Ukrainian Nationalists," Central Intelligence Agency, 1998.

6. Rossolinksy-Liebe, *Stepan Bandera*, 531.

7. Plokhy, *The Gates of Europe*, 292–308.

8. Sakwa, *Frontline Ukraine*, 9.

9. Plokhy, *The Gates of Europe*, 308–310.

10. Sakwa, *Frontline Ukraine*, 19; Roman Olearchyk, "Russia to help analyse Yushchenko poison," *Financial Times*, September 12, 2007.

11. State Statistics Committee of Ukraine, "All-Ukrainian Population Census 2001." "Language of origin" is probably a better translation than "mother tongue," as it is an identity claim, rather than the language spoken at home during childhood.

12. This division comes complete with two coherent and mutually exclusive versions of Ukrainian history. Dominique Arel and Jesse Driscoll, *Ukraine's Unnamed War: Before the Russian Invasion of 2022* (Cambridge: Cambridge University Press, 2023), 47–50.

13. Simon Wiesenthal Center, "Wiesenthal Center Blasts Ukrainian Honor For Nazi Collaborator," January 28, 2010.

14. Oleg Shchedrov, "Russia wades into Ukraine polls," Reuters, August 11, 2009.

15. "Yushchenko attributes his low popularity ratings to adherence to his principles," *Kyiv Post*, November 28, 2009; in the entire pre-2014 period it is possible that support never even got this high. See Volodymyr Ishchenko, "NATO Through Ukrainian Eyes," forthcoming in G. Anderson (ed.), *Natopolitanism: The Atlantic Alliance since the Cold War* (London: Verso, 2023).

16. Neli Esipova and Julie Ray, "Former Soviet Countries See More Harm from Breakup," Gallup, December 19, 2013.

17. Sakwa, *Frontline Ukraine*, 78–79; the Party of Regions is better seen as a vehicle for serving Russian-speaking elites within Ukraine, rather than effectively serving Russia itself. Arel and Driscoll, *Ukraine's Unnamed War*, 17 and 62–63.

18. "GDP (current US$)—Ukraine, 1987–2021," The World Bank; Sakwa, *Frontline Ukraine*, 72.

19. Elizabeth Piper, "Special Report: Why Ukraine Spurned the EU and Embraced Russia," Reuters, November 19, 2013.

20. In 1997, George Kennan wrote that NATO expansion "may be expected to inflame the nationalistic, anti-Western and militaristic tendencies in Russian opinion; to have an adverse effect on the development of Russian democracy; to restore the atmosphere of the cold war to East-West relations, and to impel Russian foreign policy in directions decidedly not to our liking." George F. Kennan, "A Fateful Error," *New York Times*, February 7, 1997.

21. Tooze, *Crashed*, 20 and 495–497. In addition to saying that the Association Agreement would have spelled "political disaster" if Yanukovych took it, Tooze notes

that only 39 percent of Ukrainians polled in November 2013 wanted the EU deal; 37 percent favored economic ties with Russia.

22. Maria Tomak told the author there were "hundreds" at most; sympathetic outlet Pravda Ukrainska (where Mustafa Nayyem previously worked) estimated 1,500 at most; На Майдан пришло уже около 1500 возмущенных остановкой евроинтеграции, Украинская правда, November 22, 2013.

23. Author interview with Max Seddon, who was present, 2022. Free translation.

24. This enthusiasm for "self-organization" was shared by participants from across the political spectrum. See for example "Евромайдан. Кто? Что? И как?" НІГІЛІСТ," December 13, 2013, for a leftist affirmation of this concept; for a liberal celebration, see Antonina Kolodii, "Про націєтворчу роль та історичні корені Майдану," Wildon Center, January 10, 2014; for a right-wing encounter with the practice, see "Позивний 'Воланд': Спогади футбольного ультрас про Майдан," *Digital Maidan*.

25. Alan Taylor, "Days of Protest in Ukraine," *The Atlantic*, December 2, 2013.

26. While only 39 percent of Ukrainians had supported the Association Agreement with the EU, 74 percent of the population opposed the police violence in late 2013. Arel and Driscoll, *Ukraine's Unnamed War*, 99.

27. Author interviews with C14 militant group in Kyiv, 2021.

28. The banner may have been brought by C14, but Maidan forces controlling City Hall did not object. See "На будівлі КМДА вивісили портрет Бандери," ipress.ua, January 14, 2014.

29. Sakwa, *Frontline Ukraine*, 85.

30. "Radical Group C14 Files Lawsuit Against Hromadske," *Hromadske*, July 5, 2018; "Yes, It's (Still) OK to Call Ukraine's C14 'Neo-Nazi,'" *Bellingcat*, August 9, 2019.

31. Artem was busy working during the very early days of Maidan. But another member of his organization reported being attacked by right-wing forces even before the crackdown on November 30: "Ukraine 'Left Opposition' Activist Reports on Maidan Movement," Marxist-Humanist Initiative, March 16, 2014; For another left-wing defense of remaining on the square, despite its right-wing elements, see "Левые на Майдане: конфликт," openleft.ru.

32. Sakwa, *Frontline Ukraine*, 83.

33. Volodymyr Ishchenko, "Insufficiently Diverse: The Problem of Nonviolent Leverage and Radicalization of Ukraine's Maidan Uprising, 2013–2014," *Journal of Eurasian Studies* 11, no. 2, 2020.

34. Erica Chenoweth and Maria J. Stephan, *Why Civil Resistance Works: The Strategic Logic of Nonviolence* (New York: Columbia University Press, 2011), 41–51; Gene Sharp, *From Dictatorship to Democracy: A Conceptual Framework for Liberation* (New York: The New Press, 2012), 7–11.

35. Volodymyr Ishchenko, "Insufficiently Diverse," 9.

36. "Евромайдан поддержали 50% украинцев, антимайдан—28%," zn.ua, December 27, 2013; "Майдан поддерживает половина украинцев,–опрос R&B," lb.ua, December 10, 2013; for an outline of the ways support wavered throughout the uprising, and the relationship to violence, see William Jay Risch, "Heart of Europe, Heart of Darkness: Ukraine's Euromaidan and Its Enemies," in *The Unwanted Europeanness?*, ed. Branislav Radeljic (Berlin: Walter de Gruyter, 2021), 134–135. In February, 28 percent of the country said they would vote for Yanukoyvch

in the first round of a hypothetical election, unchanged from three months earlier in December 2013. In 2010 he received 36 percent in the first round of the election he ultimately won.

37. Sylvie Kauffmann, "How Europe Can Help Kiev," *New York Times*, December 23, 2013.

38. "George Clooney supports Ukrainain demonstrators," on Vitali and Wladimir Klitschko's YouTube channel KlitschkoOfficial, December 9, 2013; "George Clooney explains his support for Ukraine's EuroMaidan, Yulia Tymoshenko," *Kyiv Post*, February 9, 2014.

39. Laura Smith-Spark, Diana Magnay, and Victoria Butenko, "EU Official Meets Ukraine's Yanukovych amid Protest Stalemate," CNN, January 24, 2014.

40. Peter Baker, "U.S.-Russian Ties Still Fall Short of 'Reset' Goal," *New York Times*, September 2, 2013.

41. Maidan's would-be leaders had also eschewed violence since 2013. But they were not actually leaders. Arel and Driscoll, *Ukraine's Unnamed War*, 74.

42. Ischchenko, "Insufficiently Diverse," 6.

43. For a careful analysis of the dynamics that make "civil war" a relevant term here, see Arel and Driscoll, *Ukraine's Unnamed War*, especially chap. 1.

44. Serhiy Kudelia, "When Numbers Are Not Enough: The Strategic Use of Violence in Ukraine's 2014 Revolution," *Comparative Politics* 50, no. 4, July 2018.

45. To bolster their case, *Russia Today* published a leaked conversation between EU foreign affairs chief Catherine Ashton and Estonian foreign minister Urmas Paet in which they discussed the possibility. Ewan MacAskill, "Ukraine crisis: bugged call reveals conspiracy theory about Kiev snipers," *The Guardian*, March 5, 2014.

46. While middle-class people from Kyiv used to dominate the square, the Maidan now consisted of a large number of villagers from Western and Central Ukraine, who came to the capital to fight. Risch, "Heart of Europe, Heart of Darkness: Ukraine's Euromaidan and its Enemies," 143.

47. Sakwa, *Frontline Ukraine*, 89; for the threat that Yanukovych would end up like Gaddafi, see David Blair and Roland Oliphanht, "Ukraine Protests: 21 Killed Amid 'Sniper Attacks' as Fresh Fighting Breaks Kiev Truce," *The Telegraph*, February 20, 2014.

48. Adam Tooze wrote that the final Euromaidan victory, "even if it had the support of a considerable faction of the Ukrainian people, was of dubious legality and was undeniably Western inspired." See *Crashed*, 497.

49. "Ukraine's revolution and the far right," *BBC News*, March 7, 2014; Arel and Driscoll, *Ukraine's Unnamed War*, 97.

50. Bob Dreyfuss, "The Not-So-Secret Ukraine Phone Call," *The Nation*, February 10, 2014.

51. In one 2016 poll, 48 percent of respondents opposed the destruction of all Lenin monuments, while 41 percent supported it. Fidel Castro was more popular than Bandera. See "Отношение к отдельным историческим личностям и процессу декоммунизации в Украине," Рейтинг, November 17, 2016. The survey did not include Crimea.

52. Keith Gessen, "Western Journalists in Ukraine," *N+1*, no. 24, 2016.

53. Ута Вейнманн, "Денис Левин: 'У нас ещё есть третий путь для Украины,'" *Sensus Novus*, January 23, 2014.

54. "Russians Want Crimea; Prefer Luhansk and Donetsk Independent," Chicago Council on Global Affairs, April 3, 2019; many residents of Crimea celebrated the annexation, and support for remaining within Russia stayed above 80 percent from 2014 to the end of the decade. Gerard Toal, John O'Loughlin, and Kristin M. Bakke, "Six years and $20 billion in Russian investment later, Crimeans are happy with Russian annexation," *Washington Post*, March 18, 2020.

55. "Ukraine: Pro-Russians storm offices in Donetsk, Luhansk, Kharkiv," BBC News, April 7, 2014.

56. Oleg Grytsaienko, "The Crisis in Ukraine: An Insider's View," *Russie.NEI.Visions*, no. 78, June 2014. Cited in Sakwa, *Frontline Ukraine*, 149.

57. Keith Gessen, "Why not kill them all?" *London Review of Books* 36, no. 17, September 2014.

58. For a discussion of Strelkov's relationship to Moscow, see Arel and Driscoll, *Ukraine's Unnamed War*, chap. 1.

59. "Ukraine says Donetsk 'anti-terror operation' under way," *BBC News*, April 16, 2014.

60. Stephen F. Cohen, "The Silence of American Hawks About Kiev's Atrocities," *The Nation*, June 30, 2014.

61. Bohdan Nahaylo, "Unsolved Maidan massacre casts shadow over Ukraine," Atlantic Council, February 18, 2020; Ivan Katchanovksi at the University of Ottawa analyzed testimony and evidence from years of trials and claims they point to sniper fire from buildings that were not controlled by the government. Ivan Katchanovski, "The Maidan Massacre Trial and Investigation Revelations: Implications for the Ukraine-Russia War and Relations," *Russian Politics* 8, no. 2, July 2023. The Zelensky government has blamed Ukrainian special forces under Yanukovych for the massacre. A verdict is expected in 2023.

62. Beissinger, *The Revolutionary City*, 306.

63. Tooze, *Crashed*, 503.

64. "BRICS neutrality on Ukraine a diplomatic win for Putin," Reuters, July 14, 2014.

Chapter 13: The Free Brazil Movement

1. "Right to protest under threat as Brazil pushes 'terrorism' law ahead of World Cup," Amnesty International, May 12, 2014; Pedo Marcondes de Moura, "A controversa prisão de manifestantes gera revolta entre os movimentos sociais," *El País*, June 27, 2014.

2. "The state of food insecurity in the world 2014," Food and Agriculture Organization of the United Nations.

3. Filipe Matoso, "Após gravar vídeo, ator de Hollywood retira apoio a Marina Silva," *Globo/GI*, September 30, 2014.

4. "CNV chancela versão de que a Folha emprestou carros para a ditadura," *Carta Capital*, October 12, 2014; "Empresário foi obstinado por independência e novidades," *Folha de S.Paulo*, April 30, 2007.

5. Traumann, *O Pior Emprego do Mundo*, chap. 6.

6. Rocha, *Menos Marx, Mais Mises,* 150–153; author interview with Fábio Ostermann, 2022.

7. María Martín, "Não é uma banda de indie-rock, é a vanguarda anti-Dilma," *El País*, December 12, 2014.

8. "Students for Liberty Plays Strong Role in Free Brazil Movement," Atlas Network, April 1, 2015.

Chapter 14: Under My Umbrella

1. 公民抗命的最大殺傷力武器, *Hong Kong Economic Journal*, January 2013.

2. Anthony Dapiran, *City on Fire: The Fight for Hong Kong* (Melbourne: Scribe, 2020), 38.

3. Jeffrey Wasserstrom, *Vigil: Hong Kong on the Brink* (New York: Columbia Global Reports, 2020), 48.

4. Dapiran, *City on Fire*, 45.

5. Wasserstrom, *Vigil*, 24–28.

6. Beissinger, *The Revolutionary City*, 352.

7. Dapiran, *City on Fire*, 149–150.

8. Wasserstrom, *Vigil*, 35.

9. Chi-Kwan Mark, "To 'Educate' Deng Xiaoping in Capitalism: Thatcher's Visit to China and the Future of Hong Kong in 1982," *Cold War History* 17, 2017, 10–12.

10. Jeremy Brown, *June Fourth: The Tiananmen Protests and Beijing Massacre of 1989* (Cambridge: Cambridge University Press, 2021). On Cold War media representation, see the preface. On journalist support and diverse goals, see 55–75; Wang Hui, "The Year 1989 and the Historical Roots of Neoliberalism in China," *Positions: East Asia Cultures Critique* 12, no. 1, 2004, especially 7–25.

11. Weber, *How China Escaped Shock Therapy*, 2, 145, and 249–260, on the Russia-China comparison, the "crossing the river" philosophy, and the 1988–1989 crises, respectively.

12. John Paul Rathbone, "Doubts Come to Surface About 'the decade of Latin America,'" *Financial Times*, May 12, 2013.

13. Edward Cunningham, Tony Saich, and Jessie Turiel, "Understanding CCP Resilience: Surveying Chinese Public Opinion Through Time," Harvard Kennedy School Ash Center for Democratic Governance and Innovation, July 2020.

14. For Western Ukraine, the "pivotal space in the Cold War" was formative CIA experimentation just after the end of World War II. Vincent Bevins, *The Jakarta Method*, 28–29; Jeff Rogg, "The CIA Has Backed Ukrainian Insurgents Before. Let's Learn from Those Mistakes," *Los Angeles Times*, February 25, 2023.

15. Wasserstrom, *Vigil*, 45.

16. Josh Noble, "Economic Inequality Underpins Hong Kong's Great Political Divide," *Financial Times*, October 21, 2014.

17. Francis L. F. Lee, Gary K. Y. Tang, Samson Yuen, and Edmund W. Cheng, "Five Demands and (Not Quite) Beyond: Claim Making and Ideology in Hong Kong's Anti-Extradition Bill Movement," *Communist and Post-Communist Studies* 53, no. 4, December 2020, 25.

18. Chris Buckley and Austin Ramzy, "Hong Kong Protests Are Leaderless but Orderly," *New York Times*, September 30, 2014.

19. Dapiran, *City on Fire*, 46.

20. All mentions of Au Loong-Yu informed by author interviews, 2022 and 2023; references to published materials are cited below.

21. Wasserstrom, *Vigil*, 50.

22. Author interviews with anonymous Hong Kong protesters.

23. Au Loong-Yu, *Hong Kong in Revolt: The Protest Movement and the Future of China* (London: Pluto Press, 2020), 11–14.

Chapter 15: No Gods, No Representation

1. Philip Bump, "Even the firm that hired actors to cheer Trump's campaign launch had to wait to be paid," *Washington Post*, January 20, 2017.

2. See Vincent Bevins, *The Jakarta Method*, Appendices One and Two, which look at the world's largest twenty-five countries by population. South Korea, number twenty-eight, is the largest country to buck the trend, moving to high-income status, and is included as a notable exception. For this reason, I consider South Korea to be outside of the traditional First World.

3. Branko Milanovic, *Global Inequality: A New Approach for the Age of Globalization* (Cambridge, Mass.: The Belknap Press of Harvard University Press, 2016), 130–140.

4. Branko Milanovic, "Migration's Economic Positives And Negatives," *Social Europe*, January 29, 2016.

5. Nick Clarke, Will Jennings, Jonathan Moss, and Gerry Stoker, *The Good Politician: Folk Theories, Political Interaction, and the Rise of Anti-Politics* (Cambridge: Cambridge University Press, 2018), Introduction.

6. Carl Hulse, "Obama Cleared Way for Today's Outsider Candidates," *New York Times*, February 1, 2016.

7. Clarke et al., *The Good Politician*, 126–156 and 220–222.

8. Rocha, *Menos Marx, Mais Mises*, 150–165.

9. Rubens Valente, "Bolsonaro admitiu atos de indisciplina e deslealdade no Exército," *Folha de S.Paulo*.

10. Hellen Guimarães, "Diplomata foi morto pela ditadura antes de denunciar corrupção no regime, confirma nova certidão," *O Globo*, September 21, 2018.

11. Rocha, *Menos Marx, Mais Mises*, 143 and 154.

12. See for example Operação Castelo de Areia, or "Operation Sand Castle," blocked in 2011, and the case of Luiz Francisco Fernandes de Souza.

13. Very technically, "Jet Wash" is the right translation.

14. Sergio Fernando Moro, "Consideração Sobre a Operação Mani Pulite," *Revista CEJ*, no. 26, 2004.

15. This was obvious to all of us in the country, but see Alves Rodrigues, *Lava Jato*, 77, on the importance of media support.

16. Alves Rodrigues, *Lava Jato*, 148; for a more recent, retrospective study, see Mariana Mota Prado and Marta Rodriguez Machado, "Turning Corruption Trials into Political Tools in the Name of Transparency" in ed. Sandra Botero, Daniel M. Brinks, and Ezequiel A. Gonzalez-Ocantos, *The Limits of Judicialization: From Progress to Backlash in Latin America* (Cambridge: Cambridge University Press, 2022).

17. Vincent Bevins, "Corruption: it's the private sector," *Folha de S.Paulo*, December 13, 2013.

18. The official reason given for the end of the blog was cost-cutting, but I responded that I had never been paid. I have written notes about this interaction because I emailed blog contributors, such as Claire Rigby and Dom Phillips, to ask how we should react. The consensus was that we should celebrate what we had done and move on, rather than make a fuss.

19. AS/COA Annual Report, 2019. The language the organization uses is "open markets." COA was founded at the behest of John F. Kennedy to combat the influence of Fidel Castro in Latin America; because of its ample and stable funding, *Americas Quarterly* can pay journalists to cover all of Latin America. I have contributed one article, in 2018. See Vincent Bevins, "Brazil's 'Other' Election—and Why It's So Important," *Americas Quarterly,* August 16, 2018.

20. Paul Rekret, "Generalized Antagonism and Political Ontology in the Debate between Laclau and Negri," in *Radical Democracy and Collective Movements Today* (Oxfordshire: Routledge, 2016).

21. Juan Pablo Luna, *En Vez Del Optimismo: Crisis de representación política em el Chile actual* (Santiago, Catalonia, 2018), chaps. 4 and 14.

22. Martin Gilens and Benjamin I. Page, "Testing Theories of American Politics: Elites, Interest Groups, and Average Citizens," *Perspectives on Politics* 12, no. 3, September 2014.

23. Wang Hui, *China's Twentieth Century: Revolution, Retreat and the Road to Equality* (London: Verso, 2016), 39, 153–155, 296; it should be noted that Wang Hui himself has said he prefers the term "critical intellectual" to "new left."

24. Alexander Nekrassov, "Ukraine and the battle of the oligarchs," *Al Jazeera,* July 1, 2014.

25. Arundhati Roy, *The End of Imagination* (Chicago: Haymarket Books, 2016), 335.

26. Nadim Mirshak, "The Muslim Brotherhood in Egypt: A Gramscian re-examination," *Current Sociology* 71, no. 3, May 2023, 489–508; Kadri, *The Unmaking of Arab Socialism,* 62.

27. Luna, *En Vez del Optimismo,* chap. 2.

28. "O Movimento Passe Livre Acabou?" *Passa Palavra,* August 4, 2015.

29. Sharan Grewal and Shadi Hamid, "The Dark Side of Consensus in Tunisia: Lessons from 2015–2019," Brookings Institution, January 2020.

Chapter 16: A Tale of Two Impeachments

1. Ranier Bragon, Gustavo Uribe, and Valdo Cruz, "Cunha ameaça impeachment, e petistas discutem salvá-lo," *Folha de S.Paulo,* December 1, 2015.

2. Ricardo Mendonça, "Datafolha mostra pequena recuperação da presidente," *Folha de S.Paulo,* December 19, 2015.

3. Nathalia Passarinho, "Eduardo Cunha autoriza abrir processo de impeachment de Dilma," *G1/Globo,* December 2, 2015

4. "Para Ministério Público, pedaladas do governo Dilma não são crime," *Estadão,* July 14, 2016; "'O TCU nunca classificou a conduta da presidente Dilma como crime de responsabilidade,' diz Dantas," *UOL,* March 3, 2023.

5. "Há três anos, condução coercitiva de Lula foi 'confissão de medo' de seus perseguidores," *Rede Brasil Atual,* March 4, 2019.

6. "Maior manifestação da história do País aumenta pressão por saída de Dilma," *Estadão*, March 15, 2015. This would be the largest single protest, though counting all of June 2013 together would make that protest movement larger.

7. For an excellent academic overview of the interactions between competing Brazilian protest repertoires, see Angela Alonso, "A Política das Ruas: Protestos em São Paulo de Dilma a Temer," *Novos Estudos CEBRAP*, Especial: Volume Dinâmicas da Crise, June 2017.

8. Isabela Leite and Roney Domingos, "PSDB fecha posição a favor do impeachment após reunião em SP," *G1/Globo*, April 8, 2016.

9. "Marina Silva cobra novas eleições para presidente: quais as chances de isso ocorrer?" *El País*, April 6, 2016.

10. "Pesquisa Ibope mostra que 62% preferem novas eleições presidenciais," *G1/Globo*, March 25, 2016.

11. Author interviews with journalists active in 2016.

12. "Em diálogos gravados, Jucá fala em pacto para deter avanço da Lava Jato," *Folha de S. Paulo*, May 23, 2016.

13. Vincent Bevins, "Brazil clown will leave big shoes to fill in Congress," *Los Angeles Times*, March 28, 2013.

14. Vincent Bevins, "In post-impeachment Brazil, the new conservative Cabinet is 100% white men," *Los Angeles Times*, May 13, 2016.

15. Temer began to speak abruptly, and when the Brazilians in the crowd figured out who it was, they began to boo. Vincent Bevins, "As Rio Games open, Brazil downplays politics—including its interim president," *Los Angeles Times*, August 5, 2015.

16. Erik Mobrand, *Top-Down Democracy in South Korea* (Seattle: University of Washington Press, 2019), 7 and 25.

17. Vincent Bevins, "I went to the Olympics and all I got was this tentative sense of hope," *The Outline*, February 26, 2018.

Chapter 17: I Was in the 212

1. Cecilia Kang and Juliet Eilperin, "Why Silicon Valley is the new revolving door for Obama staffers," *Washington Post*, February 28, 2015; Hannah Kuchler, "Why Obama's West Wingers went west," *Financial Times*, January 10, 2018.

2. Max Fisher, *The Chaos Machine: The Inside Story of How Social Media Rewired Our Minds and Our World* (New York: Little, Brown, 2022), 133.

3. Julian Borger, Lauren Gambino, and Sabrina Siddiqui, "Tech Giants Face Congress as Showdown over Russia Election Meddling Looms," *The Guardian*, October 22, 2017.

4. Beissinger, *The Revolutionary City*, 99; Andreas Harsono, *Race, Islam and Power: Ethnic and Religious Violence in Post-Suharto Indonesia* (Clayton: Monash Publishing, 2019), 124–128.

5. "Pidato di Kepulauan Seribu dan hari-hari hingga Ahok menjadi tersangka," *BBC News Indonesia*, November 17, 2016.

6. Andreas Harsono, "The Human Cost of Indonesia's Blasphemy Law," Human Rights Watch, October 25, 2018.

7. Moses Ompusunggu, "MUI Chairman Testifies at Ahok Trial, Admits He Did Not Watch Video," *Jakarta Post*, January 31, 2017.

8. Author interview with Andreas Harsono, 2022; Adam Tyson and Nawawi, "Dictators Never Die: Political Transition, Dynastic Regime Recovery and the 2021 Suharto Commemoration in Indonesia," *Contemporary Southeast Asia* 44, no. 3, 2022.

9. Rodrigo Nunes, "It Takes Organizers to Make a Revolution," *Viewpoint Magazine*, November 9, 2017; Nunes traces the concept of "spontaneity" not to its concrete instantiation in the world (because in reality all actions are spontaneous, just as they are all influenced by prior stimuli), but rather an inside/outside distinction in the history of leftist thought. Everything inside the party was organized, while everything outside the party was "spontaneous"; Gerbaudo, *The Mask and the Flag*, 67.

10. Fisher, *The Chaos Machine*, 38.

Chapter 18: O Mito

1. Ricardo Balthazar, Felipe Bächtold, Bruna de Lara, Paula Bianchi, and Leandro Demori, "Conversas de Lula mantidas sob sigilo pela Lava Jato enfraquecem tese de Moro," *Folha de S.Paulo*, September 8, 2019.

2. "Al Capone, Lula e o preço dos menores pecados" *O Estado de São Paulo*, April 8, 2018.

3. Peter Prengaman and Marcelo Silva da Sousa, "Lula Conviction in Brazil Spotlight: Was It Sham or Solid?" Associated Press, August 30, 2018.

4. Fernando Morais, *Lula*, volume 1: *Biografia*, 29.

5. Ricardo Della Coletta and Carla Jiménez, "Censura a entrevista de Lula mostra parcialidade do STF no processo eleitoral, apontam juristas," *El País*, October 4, 2018.

6. Vincent Bevins, "Inquiry launched after mystery air crash kills Brazilian environmentalists," *The Guardian*, July 28, 2017.

7. Igor Gielow, "Lula chega a 39%, aponta Datafolha; sem ele, Bolsonaro lidera," *Folha de S.Paulo*, August 22, 2018.

8. For a detailed account of voter attitudes in 2018, see Maurício Moura e Juliano Corbellini, *A Eleição Disruptiva: Por Que Bolsonaro Venceu* (Rio de Janeiro: Editora Record, 2019).

9. On Moro's law-breaking that was already clear before 2018, see Pedro Canário and Marcos de Vasconcellos, "Sergio Moro divulgou grampos ilegais de autoridades com prerrogativa de foro," *Consultor Jurídico*, March 16, 2016. Moro himself asked the Supreme Court for "forgiveness" for the unauthorized wiretap and leak. See Renan Ramalho, "Moro pede desculpas ao STF por 'polêmicas' sobre grampos de Lula," *O Globo*, March 29, 2016; for the explanation of the logic that his ascendance to high office as a result of his legal judgments constitutes "corruption"—though not necessarily a distinct crime—see Janio de Feitas, "Moro num pais tropical," *Folha de S.Paulo*, November 29, 2018; in 2021, Brazil's Supreme Court (STF) ruled that Moro had failed to act as an impartial judge in his prosecution of Lula. "Brazil Supreme Court confirms ruling that judge was biased against Lula," Reuters, June 24, 2021.

10. Fabio de Sa e Silva, "From CarWash to Bolsonaro: Law and Lawyers in Brazil's Illiberal Turn (2014–2018)," *Journal of Law and Society* 47, no. S1, 2020.

11. Natalia Viana and Rafael Neves, "O FBI e a Lava Jato," *Agência Pública*, July 1, 2020; Andrew Fishman, Natalia Viana, and Maryam Saleh, "'Keep it Confidential': The Secret History of U.S. Involvement in Brazil's Scandal-Wracked Operation Car Wash," *The Intercept*, March 12, 2020; Natalia Viana, Andrew Fishman, and Maryam Saleh,

"Como a Lava Jato escondeu do governo federal visita do FBI e procuradores americanos," *Agência Pública*, March 12, 2020; for Lula's comments on the FBI and the Justice Department in relation to Brazilian industry, see "Lava Jato foi ideia dos EUA para destruir indústria nacional, afirma Lula," Partido dos Trabalhadores, July 9, 2020.

12. "Por que a Ucrânia, onde Sara Winter diz ter sido treinado, fascina bolsonaristas?" *BBC News Brasil*, June 15, 2020.

13. Ishchenko, Volodymyr. "The Communist Party of Ukraine." Forthcoming in: *The Palgrave Handbook of Radical Left Parties in Europe*, ed. L. March, F. Escalona, and M. Vieira, Palgrave Macmillan; the KPU routinely defended the pensions of aging Ukrainians; "КПУ и Батькивщина в полном составе не проголосовали за новый закон о пенсиях," o61.ua, July 8, 2011; "Святослав Хоменко, Красная партия в сине-желтом государстве," BBC News Ukraine, November 7, 2013.

14. Kateryna Choursina and Daryna Krasnolutska, "Macron and Bolsonaro Inspire Ukraine's Surprise Election Leader," Bloomberg, March 4, 2019.

15. Alexander J. Motyl, "Ukraine's TV President Is Dangerously Pro-Russian," *Foreign Policy*, April 1, 2019.

16. Paulo Toleda Piza, "Embaixador da Ucrânia explica bandeira usada em manifestação na Paulista," *CNN Brasil*, May 31, 2020.

Chapter 19: A Tale of Two Explosions

1. Dapiran, *City on Fire*, 17.

2. Alexandra Stevenson and Keith Bradsher, "As Hong Kong Erupted Over Extradition Bill, City's Tycoons Waited and Worried," *New York Times*, June 20, 2019; Dapiran, *City on Fire*, chap. 1.

3. Author interviews with Wong Yik Mo, 2022 and 2023.

4. Dapiran, *City on Fire*, 27.

5. Author interview with Derek Tai, 2022.

6. Au Loong-Yu, *Hong Kong in Revolt*, 17; Wasserstrom, *Vigil*, 74; Dapiran, *City on Fire*, 830.

7. A Reuters investigation cited an expert who guessed between five hundred thousand and eight hundred thousand. Simon Scarr, Manas Sharma, Marco Hernandez, and Vimvam Tong, "Measuring the Masses: The Contentious Issue of Crowd Counting in Hong Kong," Reuters, June 20, 2019.

8. Dapiran, *City on Fire*, 53.

9. All references to Finn Lau's experience draw on author interviews in London, 2021 and 2022.

10. Dapiran, *City on Fire*, 76; author interviews with Hong Kong protesters, 2022 and 2023.

11. Dapiran, *City on Fire*, 69.

12. *The Way of the Dragon*, Orange Sky Golden Harvest, 1972.

13. Dapiran, *City on Fire*, 71–72.

14. Daniel Vukovich, *After Autonomy: A Post-Mortem for Hong Kong's First Handover, 1997–2019* (Singapore: Palgrave Macmillan, 2022), 44 and 67–69; Billy Perrigo, "Trump Administration Freezes Funds Intended to Benefit Hong Kong Protesters," *Time*, June 27, 2020.

15. Dapiran, *City on Fire*, 81–83.

16. Au Loong-Yu, *Hong Kong in Revolt*, 85-87.

17. Francis L. F. Lee, Gary K. Y. Tang, Samson Yuen, Edmund W. Cheng, "Five Demands and (Not Quite) Beyond: Claim Making and Ideology in Hong Kong's Anti-Extradition Bill Movement," *Communist and Post-Communist Studies* 53, no. 4, December 2020, 29–35.

18. Au Loong-Yu, *Hong Kong in Revolt*, 129.

19. See Dapiran, *City on Fire*, 121, for his ruminations on this slogan as he watched Hong Kongers rip bricks out of the streets.

20. Author interview with Mung Siu-tat in London, 2022.

21. Au Loong-Yu, *Hong Kong in Revolt*, 116.

22. Dapiran, *City on Fire*, 126–138.

23. Author interviews with anonymous "braves," 2021; Dapiran, *City on Fire*, 136–137; Vukovich, *After Autonomy*, 65; Dapiran says that frontline protesters considered journalists to be "supporters." Vukovich, who is very critical of this phenomenon, writes that direct appeal to US and UK media was the "real action of the movement." Looking back, Hong Kongers described to me (in their own words) that both assertions were basically correct.

24. Dapiran, *City on Fire*, 140–141; author interviews with Hong Kong protesters. It should be noted that Yang Guang indicated that Beijing might offer economic, not political, concessions.

25. Chris Lau, Kinling Ho, and Sarah Zheng, "Hong Kong Media Mogul Jimmy Lai 'Unknowingly Funded' False Persona Report Discrediting Joe Biden," *South China Morning Post*, October 21, 2020.

26. The money came through the Solidarity Center, the nonprofit affiliated with the AFL-CIO. In retrospect, some protest organizers called it a "tactical error" to take money from the US government, as other funding sources were available, and this opened them up to accusations of collusion with a hostile foreign power. One remarked that if China funded Black Lives Matter protesters, Washington would probably respond very aggressively. In contrast, one labor leader said that the funding had no bearing on their decision-making in 2019, and it was their right to accept it. Author interviews, 2023.

27. The number supporting independence fluctuated between 14 percent and 22 percent in 2019 and 2020; Lee et al., "Five Demands," 36.

28. Au Loong-Yu, *Hong Kong in Revolt*, 92–96.

29. Author interview with Ronny Tong Ka-Wah, 2022. The member of the executive council said the tactics employed in the second half of 2019 would always be seen by many Chinese politicians as an attempt to undermine national sovereignty. He said the idea that enough trouble on the streets would cause the US or UK to arrive "like a knight in shining armor" was, tragically, "totally divorced from reality."

30. Au Loong-Yu, *Hong Kong in Revolt*, 40.

31. Daniel Vukovich, "A City and a SAR on Fire: As If Everything and Nothing Changes," *Critical Asian Studies* 52, 2020, 3–5; Wasserstrom, *Vigil*, 78; though it is outside of the chronology selected for this chapter, a particularly shocking media image was the recording of young Hong Kongers who literally set a middle-aged construction worker on fire, after he confronted the black-clad protesters. See Alex Lo, "Is Hong Kong

OK with Man Being Set on Fire?," *South China Morning Post*, November 12, 2019; in elections on November 24, the yellow camp did better than they did in 2015, receiving about 59 percent of the vote after a successful drive to increase turnout.

32. "Protestas en Chile: 'Estamos en guerra,' la frase de Piñera que se le volvió en contra en medio de las fuertes manifestaciones," *BBC News*, October 22, 2019.

33. Joshua Frens-String, Tanya Harmer, and Marian Schlotterbec, "Fifty years after Popular Unity: Chile's *estallido social* in historical context," *Radical Americas*, 2021.

34. Author interviews with Danitza Pérez Cáceres in Santiago, 2022.

35. Author interviews with Chilean protesters in Santiago, 2022.

36. Romina A. Green Rioja, "Collective trauma, feminism, and the threads of popular power: A personal and political account of Chile's 2019 social awakening," *Radical Americas*, 2021.

37. Author interviews with Chilean protesters in Santiago, 2022.

38. Sandra Cuffe, "Dockworkers in Chile paralyse ports ahead of broader strike," *Al Jazeera*, November 26, 2019.

39. Interview with Daniela Serrano in Santiago, 2022. The Party literature points out that "asambleísta" organizations quickly fell apart during the 1920s and 1930s.

40. Juan Pablo Luna, "La implosión de la política y la falta de legitimidad social," CIPER, November 11, 2019; author interview with Hernán Herrera, 2022.

41. Gerbaudo, *The Mask and the Flag*, 242, 243.

42. Taif Alkhudary, "'No to America . . . No to Iran': Iraq's Protest Movement in the Shadow of Geopolitics," London School of Economics Middle East Center, January 20, 2020.

43. On the use of the word "coup," see Oliver Stuenkel's comments to *Folha* on November 12, 2019. A military intervention into politics that forces the end of a government is a coup, despite the fact that Stuenkel had criticism of Morales as a president. Flávia Mantovani, "Evo Morales sofreu ou não golpe? Especialistas em política opinam," *Folha de S.Paulo*, November 12, 2019; see also Greg Grandin, "A Few Tips on How to Understand Latin American Coups," *Jacobin*, November 11, 2019; Jeanine Áñez was ultimately sentenced to prison for violating the constitution. Fernando Molina, "La Justicia boliviana condena a la expresidenta Jeanine Añez a 10 años de prisión," *El País*, June 11, 2022.

44. Dapiran, *City on Fire*, 254–255.

45. For skeptical analysis of the bill from the pro-protest dispora group, see *Lausan Collective*, "Hong Kong Human Rights and Democracy Act: A Critical Analysis," September 15, 2019.

Chapter 20: Reconstructing the Past

1. "The slave trade in Libya: What can development actors do?" Brookings Institution, January 25, 2018.

2. Author interview, 2022.

3. Rodrigo Nunes has characterized the turn to "self-organization" as "teleology without a revolutionary subject," and then notes that Lenin (unlike the tradition that now invokes Rosa Luxembourg, sometimes unfaithfully) was aware that an uprising could go in many different ways, and is therefore less deterministic. Rodrigo Nunes, *Neither Vertical nor Horizontal: A Theory of Political Organization* (London: Verso, 2021), 130–135.

4. Wang Hui, *China's Twentieth Century*, 302–303.

5. Though outside the scope of this study, it is nevertheless possible that the 2022 invasion may decrease the power of oligarchs. Mykhailo Minakov, "The War Has Helped Ukraine Rein in the Oligarchs," Focus Ukraine / Kennan Institute, November 15, 2022; even if that turns out to be the case, however, one must pay careful attention to who is likely to fill the power vacuum.

6. "За 11 років з України виїхали та не повернулися майже 3,3 млн громадян," Opendatabot Ukraine, December 16, 2021.

7. "23% украинцев считают события Майдана «антигосударственным переворотом—опрос," *Hromadske*, February 20, 2020.

8. Volodymyr Ishchenko and Oleg Zhuravlev, "How Maidan Revolutions Reproduce and Intensify the Post-Soviet Crisis of Political Representation," *PONARS*, October 18, 2021.

9. Author interview with Regina Ip, 2022.

10. Author interviews in Sidi Bouzid, 2021.

11. For an overview of recent literature that comes close to this supposition, see *Communization and Its Discontents*, ed. Benjamin Noys (New York: Autonomedia, 2012).

12. Mark Beissinger, *The Revolutionary City*, 175, 375–415; Beissinger discusses the original Gamson study, and responses to its thesis, on page 197.

13. Author interview, 2023. Mayara says she is just as committed to horizontalism as ever, but has an expanded view of the concept. She now works with struggling immigrants from Bolivia who are too busy to attend long meetings, so she believes the approach must allow people from every walk of life to participate. Others may object that this actually could be seen as a less "horizontalist" position, at least in relation to its 2013 definition, but I was happy to let her redefine as she pleases.

14. Tufekci, *Twitter and Tear Gas*, introduction.

15. In order: Yates, "Prefigurative Politics and Social Movement Strategy"; Tufekci, *Twitter and Tear Gas*, 89; Gordon, "Prefigurative Politics between Ethical Practice and Absent Promise"; Graeber, "The New Anarchists"; Gorz, "The Way Forward."

16. Bayat, *Revolution without Revolutionaries*, 11.

17. Author interviews with Paolo Gerbaudo, 2022 and 2023; Haddad, "Vivi na pele o que aprendi nos livros," *Piauí*. Free translation.

18. Cihan Tuğal, "Elusive revolt: The contradictory rise of middle-class politics," *Thesis Eleven* 130(I), 2015.

19. She sums up her position, in 2021, saying, "I think that hypothesis, of a hybrid war, and that the process that led to the coup had begun [in 2013], is correct." Interview with Diário do Centro do Mundo (DCM), "Dilma fala sobre o telefonema de Putin alertando sobre o golpe," *DCM TV*; the publishing house Expressão Popular, linked to Brazil's Landless Workers' Movement, published a book in 2021 that put the concept of "hybrid war" in the context of recent Latin American history. See Ana Penido and Miguel Enrique Stédile, *Ninguém regula a América* (São Paulo: Expressão Popular, 2021); in 2023 Rousseff wrote that the outbreak of the June 2013 uprising was "strongly spontaneous and localized" but that one political camp, representing "hegemonic factions of national elites and their international allies," began to act to influence the outcome, "with the goal of attracting capital flows, and the implementation of policies that would assure

high-profit, low-risk business conditions in the country." Conservative forces had "superior means of communications" at their disposal, she said. Dilma Rousseff, "Prólogo," in Ed. Breno Altman and Maria Carlotto, *Junho de 2013: A Rebelião Fantasma* (São Paulo: Boitempo, 2023).

20. In recent years, scholars have turned to the emotional components of revolt, but (in my experience at least) journalists are encouraged to make reference to states and economies. For the former, see *Passionate Politics: Emotions and Social Movements*, ed. Jeff Goodwin, James M. Jasper, and Francesca Polletta (Chicago: University of Chicago Press, 2001).

21. 37.6 percent said that "public transportation" brought them to the streets, while 29.9 percent said the "political environment" was their motivation for protesting. Subcategories "against the fare rise" and "corruption" got 28 percent and 24 percent from respondents, respectively. "Veja pesquisa completa do Ibope sobre os manifestantes," *G1/ Globo*, June 24, 2013.

22. Megan Brenan, "Americans' Trust in Media Remains Near Record Low," Gallup, October 18, 2022; Zacc Ritter, "How Much Does the World Trust Journalists," Gallup, December 27, 2019.

Chapter 21: Building the Future

1. Rodrigo Nunes, *Do Transe à Vertigem* (São Paulo: Ubu Editora, 2022), 200.

2. Nunes, *Neither Vertical nor Horizontal*, 15–39.

3. Vladimir Lenin, "Left-Wing Communism: An Infantile Disorder."

4. Author interview with Oliver Cauã Cauê in São Paulo, 2022.

Index

"A-20" (April 20) protest, 36
A Revolta do Buzu (documentary), 42
Abogados Feministas ("Feminist
    Lawyers"), 248
Adamovsky, Ezequiel, 43
Adbusters (magazine), 35, 79
Afghanistan war veterans, 160
Ahmed (Egyptian man), 94, 282
Al Jazeera, 57, 58
Alckmin, Geraldo, 117, 119, 120, 136,
    207, 226
Algeria, 254
Alicia (Chilean girl), 250, 253
Allende, Salvador, 83
alter-globalization movement.
    See anti-globalization movement
Amazon basin and forest, 99–101, 104,
    231
Americanization, as process, 29
Americas Quarterly, 198
anarchist politics, 37–38
anarchists, 2, 19, 34, 43, 69, 176, 271
"Anonymous," 82–83, 139–140, 146
anti-globalization movement, 34–36, 37,
    269–270
anti-politics, 192–194, 231, 233
Apple Daily (newspaper), 245
"April 6 Youth Movement,"
    63, 63n
Arab Socialism, 20, 23–24, 62

"Arab Spring"
    beginning, 3, 55–56
    conditions in, 271
    and Erdoğan, 109–110
    as inspiration, 79–80, 81
    outcomes, 70–71
    and social media, 58, 64, 92
    as term and concept, 3, 68, 70
Arabs, 22, 61
Argentina, 43–44
Aristotle, on teleology, 45
army, and revolutions, 21
Artem (fast food worker and protester)
    on outcome of protests, 167, 170, 265,
        272
    in protests, 151–152, 157, 159, 161–162,
        165
Assad, Bashar, 73–74, 109
assemblyism, as ideal, 43
Atala, Alex, 129
Atatürk, Mustafa Kemal, 108
Athens (Greece), 79–80
Atlas Network, 133, 178
Au Loong-Yu, 185–186, 187,
    242–243, 255
authoritarian governments, and
    internet, 92
Automaidan, 160, 164
autonomistas of Italy, 43
Avakov, Arsen, 169

Bachelet, Michelle, 84
Badr, Mahmoud, 110
Bahar (protester), 113–114
Bahgat, Hossam, 262, 264
Bahrain, 74–77, 262
Bandera, Stepan, 153, 156, 160–161
Baswedan, Anies, 221
Bayat, Asef, 270–271
Beissinger, Mark, 6, 265
Ben Ali, Zine El Abidine, 56, 57, 58,
    59–60, 65
Berlin Wall, 26–27, 28, 68
Bezos, Jeff, 218
Black Civil Rights Movement,
    13–14, 14n
Black Lives Matter movement, 186
Blair, Tony, 68
Bobrovska, Solomiia, 265–266
Bolivia, 254
Bolsa Familia program (Brazil), 50
Bolshevik Revolution, 17, 153
Bolsonarismo and Bolsonarista, 228, 229,
    231–232, 257
Bolsonaro, Eduardo, 177, 232
Bolsonaro, Jair
    description and as politician, 194
    election of 2018, 226, 227–230
    impeachment of Rousseff, 210, 212
    as president, 2–3, 230–231
    stabbing, 227–228, 229
Borguiba, Habib, 56
Boric, Gabriel, 84, 146, 201, 252, 253,
    261–262, 276–277
Bosnia, 46
Bouazizi, Mohamed, 55–56, 57–58,
    263
Bouteflika, Abdelaziz, 254
Brasília (city), 209, 210
Brazil
    anarcho-punk music, 34, 36–37
    anti-politics, 193–194
    antiterrorism law, 172
    ascent as country, 48, 49–50
    battle for Amazon and land, 99–101,
        104
    Congresso Nacional buildings,
        209

constitution, 85
corruption in government, 53, 139,
    194–198, 204–209, 230
cost of transportation as issue, 128, 131,
    134, 141
"de-communization," 232
deforestation, 100–101
and "development" model, 31n
economic structure, 39
election of 2010, 52–53
election of 2014, 174–177, 208
election of 2018, 223, 226–230
environmental defense, 231
"fiscal pedaling" practice, 205
foreign correspondents' life in,
    97–98
government to replace Rousseff,
    213, 214
immigration to, 190
impeachment stipulations, 205
inequalities in, 33–34, 49, 50, 97–98
law system in, 142
Lei (Law) 12.850/2013 and plea bargain
    deals, 142, 195
media in (see media in Brazil)
offshore oil reserves, 101
Olympics in, 49, 213–214
PEC 37 as issue, 132, 139, 141
police in, 117
post-dictatorship elections and
    policies, 40
protests in (see Brazil protests)
referendum to amend constitution,
    141–142
relationship with US, 101, 170
religion in, 102–103
and removal of Gaddafi,
    72–73
"right" as label, 174
social programs, 50
social revolution of 2010s, 98–99,
    100–101, 101n
split in young left, 41–42
Truth Commission, 101
and Ukraine, 231–232, 233
World Cup, 49, 139, 140, 171–174, 176,
    225

Brazil protests
    against bus rate hikes in São Paulo,
        1–2, 3, 53, 82, 115–117, 118–126,
        128–131, 134–135, 137, 173, 276,
        285–286
    of Bolsonarismo, 231
    bus rate hikes (generally), 41–42,
        132
    colors and flags (yellow and green), 114,
        130, 132, 206, 210, 231
    Congress' response, 142
    demands in 2013, 2
    diversity in participants and causes at
        protests, 129–130, 131, 132–133, 134,
        137, 147
    and "five causes" ("5 causas"), 139–142,
        146
    influences on, 82–83, 232, 271
    largest movement, 137
    and media, 35, 175
    national revolt from MPL, 132–133
    Ocupa Sampa, 82–83
    outcome of protests and unexpected
        consequences, 2–3, 257, 262–263,
        264, 284
    police in, 1–2, 118, 119, 120, 121, 122,
        123–126, 127–128
    removal or retreat of participants,
        137
    against Rousseff, 146–147, 177–178
    for Rousseff's impeachment, 205–206,
        210–211, 213
    on television, 128, 130, 131,
        132
    on World Cup, 171–172, 173
    See also Movimento Passe Livre
"Brazilian Spring," 133
Breines, Wini, 18–19, 270
Brexit, 191–192
Brezhnev, Leonid, 23, 27
BRICS, 47–48, 170
Britain, 12–13, 180–182, 191,
    242
    See also United Kingdom
Brown, Gordon, 91
Bush, George H. W., 154
Bush, George W., 47, 63, 91

C14 (militia), 162, 266
Cairo (Egypt)
    protests, 60–61, 64–68, 70–71
    repression today, 262
Calheiros, Renan, 139, 142
Camp David Accords, 61
Campeão, Nádia, 120
"canceled," in Chile, 253
Candlelight Demonstrations/Revolution,
    204, 259
capitalism, 62–63
Cappello, Nina, 124, 131
Cardoso, Fernando Henrique (FHC), 40,
    194, 207
Cariola, Karol, 146
Carr, David, 87, 88
"carry trade" strategy, 98
Carvalho, Olavo de, 177
Carvin, Andy, 87, 88
Cauã Cauê, Oliver, 285–286
Centro de Mídia Independente (CMI), 35
Channa, Jawaher, 57, 58–59
Chávez, Hugo, 34
Chile
    assemblies of protesters (cabildos), 250,
        253–254
    Brazilian community in, 226, 227, 230
    constitutional referendum, 251–252,
        256, 261–262
    dictatorship, 83
    diversity in participants and causes at
        protests, 250–251
    media in, 84–85
    neoliberalism in, 31, 225–226, 249
    outcome of protests, 261–262, 276–277
    protests, 226, 247–252, 253–254
    protests by students, 83–85, 247–248,
        251–252
    protests' solution from political class,
        251–253, 254, 276–277
    re-founding through assembly or
        convention, 252–253
    representation in, 199, 201, 276–277
    student leaders' move into politics, 146,
        201, 247, 253, 261
    "thirty years" period, 248–249
    transportation prices rise, 247

China
  coronavirus, 255
  Cultural Revolution, 23, 181
  economy, 182–183, 184
  and Hong Kong protests, 242–243,
    244–245, 246, 255
  Hong Kong reforms and laws, 179, 187,
    261
  in Hong Kong's history and present,
    181–184
  protests in, 182
  removal of Gaddafi, 72–73
  representation in, 199–200
Choi Soon-sil, 203, 215
Christian intellectual tradition, 19, 45
Chung Kwok-pan, Felix, 237
CIA, 20, 62, 68, 208
Civil Human Rights Front (CHRF), 237,
  242
Clarke, Nick, 193
Clinton, Hillary, 72, 91, 217
Cohen, Roger, 91
Cold War, 14, 17, 26–27, 44, 45, 46, 108,
  214, 218
Collor, Fernando, 40, 175
Comitê de Luta Marielle Franco
  ("Marielle Franco Struggle
  Committee"), 227
Communism, 20, 23, 26, 232
  See also Communist parties;
    Communist Party of China
Communist parties, 20, 21–23, 41–42
Communist Party of China (CPC), 183,
  199–200
consumer culture, 25–26, 270
contention (or contentious politics)
  definition, 12
  media in, 12, 15
  "occupation" as, 22
  practices in 1950s–60s, 12–15
  repertoire of, 12–13, 261–262, 264, 268
  structure today, 275–276
Cooper, Anderson, 68–69
Coptic Christian minority in Egypt,
  93–94
coronavirus and COVID-19, 255
corporations, and the internet, 88–90, 92

"coup" (golpe) in Brazil and Latin
  America, 208, 213, 213n
Crimea, 153–154, 168, 170, 260
Cuadros, Alex, 197
Cultural Revolution of Mao, 23, 181
Cunha, Eduardo, 204–205
Czechoslovakia, 23

Dapiran, Antony, 244, 254–255
Datena, José Luiz, 124–125
d'Ávila, Manuela, 227
de-Stalinization, 23
debt crisis in Latin America, 39
decade of protests
  approaches privileged, 4–5, 258,
    266–267
  beginning and cases chosen, 3–4, 6–7
  diversity at (see diversity in participants
    and causes at protests)
  and the future, 281–286
  global politics in, 272–273
  horizontalism in, 4–5, 266–267
  as illegible, 276–277
  impact globally, 255–256
  interviews and research by author, 5–6
  leaderless movements in, 4, 267
  media's role and impact, 11, 274–276,
    277–279
  outcomes (see decade of protests:
    outcomes)
  politics and political vacuum to fill,
    263–265, 272, 276–277, 283, 284
  spark from state repression and
    violence, 273–275
  strikes and boycotts in, 163
  See also mass protests
decade of protests: outcomes
  failures and backward results, 259–263
  reasons for outcome, 263–268
  result is different from goals, 2–3, 167,
    257–259
  unexpected consequences, 3–5, 257–259
¡Democracia Real Ya! ("Real Democracy
  Now!"), 80
democracy
  digital tools training for, 91
  in Egypt, 62–63

in Latin America, 51
   promotion by US, 46–47, 62
democratic centralism, 17–18
democratic government, and
   neoliberalism, 39
Deng Xiaoping, 181, 182
Derluguian, Georgi M., 6, 29
Diggers movement, 19
digital tools, 91–92, 267, 268
   See also internet; social media
direita envergonhada ("embarrassed
   right"), 98
diversity in participants and causes at
   protests
   in Brazil, 129–130, 131, 132–133, 134,
      137, 147
   in Chile, 250–251
   at Gezi Park, 110–112
   in Hong Kong, 187
   at Maidan, 160–162, 232
   and MPL, 129–134, 137
Donbas region (Ukraine), 168–169
Dorsey, Jack, 91
Dubček, Alexander, 23
Duterte, Rodrigo, 222
Dutschke, Rudi, 21–22

Egypt
   armed forces (SCAF), 70, 71, 93–94
   capitalist and democratic reforms,
      62–63
   change stalled, 93
   elections, 93–95, 143–144
   and Erdoğan, 109, 110, 144–145
   and Israel, 23, 24, 60–62
   Morsi presidency, 94–95, 109, 110, 143,
      144
   Nasserism, 20, 56, 108
   Old Left in, 20
   outcome of protests, 70–71, 262, 270,
      273, 282
   police violence, 64, 65, 66
   protests at Tahrir Square, 60–61, 62,
      63–68, 70–71, 93
   protests post-Tahrir Square, 93, 94
   rebellion of 2013 (Tamarod), 110,
      143–144

representation, 202
   and Tunis revolt of 2010, 60, 64
   uprising in 1968, 23, 24
"El Derecho de Vivir en Paz" (song),
   249–250
Eltahawy, Mona, 68
ends. See means and ends
Ennahda (party in Tunisia), 57
equality of opportunity globally, 191
Erdoğan, Recep Tayyip
   and Arab Spring, 109–110
   call to Rousseff, 135, 272–273
   and Egypt, 109, 110, 144–145
   opposition to, 111
   response to Gezi protests, 142–143
   rule and politics of, 106, 108–110,
      144–145
   support for, 113, 142–143
Estadão (newspaper), 118, 214
   and MPL protest, 119, 121,
      127–128
Estudantes Pela Liberdade, 133–134
Euromaidan, 159, 200, 259–260
   See also "Maidan" protest of 2013–2014
Euromaidan SOS, 159–160, 265
Europe, impact of protests, 80–81

Facebook and Facebook pages
   abandon of, 248
   in Arab Spring, 58, 64, 92
   in Arabic, 64
   description and creation, 90
   in Greece, 80
   in Indonesia, 218, 220
   "like" button, 90
   MPL on/use of, 118, 119
   in Ukraine, 158, 159–160
"fake news," in Brazil, 228–229
Fanfarra do Movimento Autônomo
   Libertário ("Autonomous Liberation
   Movement Fanfare Band"), 122
fast food, unionization of, 151
Fatherland (party), 160
Ferguson, James, 200n
financial crisis (2008), 47–48, 98
Firas (Syrian man), 189–190
"Five Pacts with Brazil," 141–142

Florianópolis (city), bus rate hike, 42, 119, 132

Folha de S.Paulo (newspaper)
blog of, 87, 132, 197–198
on corruption, 197–198
and election of 2014, 175, 176
as employer of author, 7, 87, 97–98, 99
at MPL protest and crackdown, 121, 122, 127, 132
talk from *NYT* journalists, 87–88
football hooligans, 111–112, 161
See also ultras
Fotouh, Abdel, 94
France, 4, 12, 21, 22–23, 24–25, 56, 233n
Franco, Marielle, 224, 227
Free Syrian Army, 109
Freedom House (NGO), 63, 63n
Freeman, Jo, 25, 201, 267
Freitas, Frederico, 36, 132
From Brazil (blog), 87, 132, 197–198
Fukuyama, Francis, 44
Furkan (student), 106, 107

Gaddafi, Muammar, 71–72
Gafsa mining region (Tunisia), 57
Galvão, Olavo Perin, 99–100, 225
Gamson, William, 265
Gehad (Egyptian woman), 61, 65, 67, 70, 94, 95, 144, 262, 282
"Geneva School," and neoliberalism, 30
Georgia (republic), 46–47
Gerbaudo, Paolo, 253, 271
Germany, 21–22, 26–27, 28, 190
Gezi Park (Istanbul)//demands, 143n
diversity in participants and causes at protests, 110–112
leaders and representation, 111, 114, 143
location and tree removal, 105, 106
protests, 3, 106–107, 110–114
response of Erdoğan, 142–143
Ghonim, Wael, 64, 69
Gitlin, Todd, 15, 16, 79, 202
Global South, 39, 191, 265, 270, 277
globalization, 29, 31, 269
Globo network (TV), 128, 130, 132, 140
Gmail, 90
Goodman, Amy, 68

Google, and advertising, 90
Gorbachev, Mikhail, 27–28, 154
Gorz, André, 24
Gove, Michael, 192
Graeber, David, 37–38, 79, 268
Greece, 79–80, 259
Green Rioja, Romina A., 251
Guarani-Kaiowá community, 104
Guarujá (Brazil), 223–224
Guimarães, Daniel, 132, 267
Gulf Cooperation Council (GCC), 76

Haddad, Fernando
background and description, 38, 40–41
bus fare hike and MPL, 115–116, 119–120, 121, 134–135, 136
election of 2018, 226–227, 228, 229, 230
interactions with social movements, 116–117, 119, 120
as mayor of São Paulo, 102–103
and media in politics, 103
as minister of education, 50, 99
on outcome of mass protests, 263, 271
and police, 117
writings on class, 38–40
Haddad, Habib, 38
Hadi, Abdrabbuh Mansour, 95
Haiti and United Nations Stabilization Mission in Haiti (MINUSTAH), 101
el-Hamalawy, Hossam (aka "3arabawy"), 60, 64, 65, 66, 70, 94, 262, 270
Hazar (shopkeeper), 107, 145
Henshaw-Plath, Evan, 90–91
history
going somewhere *vs.* end of, 44–47, 164
push to reach end of, 91–92, 258–259, 268
short term in, 6
Hitler, 153
Holodomor, as genocide, 156
Hong Kong
central area, 179
demands of protesters, 241–242
diversity in participants and causes at protests, 187
extradition legislation, 236–239, 241, 242, 246

handover of 1997, 180, 181–182, 241
historical background, 180–184
"If we burn, you burn with us" phrase,
    239, 241, 246, 256
legislative council (LegCo), 182, 183–184,
    188, 236, 238–239, 241, 242, 261
and media, 186–187, 245, 246
outcome of protests, 261
police in, 180, 184, 238–239, 242, 244
protests, 179–180, 181, 182, 184, 185–188,
    237–239, 240–246, 254–255, 256
"the stage" in, 185, 187, 238, 243
Hong Kong Federation of Students, 180,
    187–188
Hong Kong Federation of Trade Unions
    (HKFTU), 181, 185, 243, 245
"Hong Kong Human Rights and
    Democracy Act of 2019" (USA), 255
horizontalidad (or horizontality), in
    Argentina, 43–44
horizontalism
    in decade of protests, 4–5, 266–267
    description and as ideology, 43, 116,
        201, 267, 271
    in Hong Kong, 185
    vs. organization and structure, 266, 283
    in outcome of protests, 267–268
Hotimsky, Marcelo, 141
House of Khalifa, 74
Hu Jintao, 72–73
The Hunger Games (movie series), 186, 240
Hussein, Saddam, 47

"ideology of progress," 45, 46
"If we burn, you burn with us" phrase,
    239, 241, 246, 256
IMF (International Monetary Fund), 62
immigration, views on, 190–191
In Defense of Socialism (Haddad), 38–40
indigenous people, in Brazil, 104
indignados, 80, 82–83
Indonesia
    anti-leftist regime of 1965 and mass
        killings, 29, 218, 221–222, 232
    digital warfare, 221–222
    historical background, 218–219
    outcome of protests, 259

as posting for author, 218
    protests, 218–219, 220–222
    recent politics, 219–220, 221, 222
Indymedia website, 35, 41, 42, 90–91
injustice, responses to, 269
Instagram, 248
Institute of Environment and Renewable
    Natural Resources (IBAMA), 99–101
Instituto Nacional de Santiago, 247
internet
    advertising on, 90
    and coordination of mass protests, 267
    creation and control, 88–90, 92
    in election of 2016 in US, 217–218
    fake personalities on, 95
    influence, 89, 218
    See also digital tools; social media
Ip, Regina, 261
Iran, 21, 91
Iraq, 254
Iraq invasion, 34, 47
Ishchenko, Volodymyr, 162, 260
Ishii, Newton (Japonês da Federal), 196,
    214
Islamic Defenders Front (FPI, or Front
    Pembela Islam), 221
Israel, 23–24, 60–62
Istanbul (Turkey)
    description, 105
    development in, 106–107
    protests, 105, 106–107, 110–114

Jackson, Giorgio, 84, 85, 146
Jakarta (Indonesia), 218, 219–221
Jara, Víctor, 249
Jennings, Will, 193
journalists
    explanations for mass protests, 274, 277,
        278–279
    foreign correspondents, 51, 97
    funds for jobs, 87n
    misunderstanding of mass protests,
        277–278
    in São Paulo protest of 2013, 2
    and Tahrir Square, 68–69
Jribi, Maya, 95
Jucá, Romero, 209

Juliana (photographer), 122, 129, 276
Justice and Development Party (AKP) and
     AKP movement, 108–109

"Kasbah II," 70
"Kasbah" protests (Tunisia), 65, 70
Kassab, Gilberto, 53
Kataguiri, Kim, 177
Kefaya ("Enough") news organization,
     61, 63
Al Khalifa, Hamad bin Isa, 74, 75
Al Khalifa, Salman bin Hamad, 76
Khrushchev, Nikita, 154
King, Martin Luther, Jr., 45
Kissinger, Henry, 62
Klitschko, Vitali, 160, 164
Kmara (group), 47
Kristof, Nicholas, 91
Kurdish movement, 109
Kurdistan Workers' Party (PKK), 109
Kyiv
     media in, 159
     protests, 151–152, 158–166, 167,
          169–170
     See also Maidan

labor unions. See unions
Lake, Eli, 92
Lam, Carrie
     and extradition bill, 237, 239, 242, 246
     and protests, 188, 236, 241, 244–245
Lao Tse, 240
Latin America
     debt crisis, 39
     and economy of China, 183
     interventions by US, 34
     meaning of "coup," 208, 213n
     Old Left in, 20
     pink tide of democracy, 51
Lau, Finn, 239, 245, 246, 256
Lava Jato ("Car Wash") (Operação Lava
     Jato or "Operation Car Wash"),
     195–197, 204–206, 207, 209, 223–224,
     230, 231n
Law Society of Hong Kong, 237
lawyers, protest in Tunisia, 58
leaderless movements and protests

     in Chile, 253–254
     and collective decisions, 253–254
     in decade of protests, 4, 267
     emergence of leaders, 25, 267
     in Hong Kong, 185, 240, 241–242, 243
     in Indonesia, 221
     as model, 42–43
     MPL as, 42, 116
     in OWS, 81
     SDS example, 15–16
     in Tahrir Square, 66–67, 68, 71
     See also Brazil protests
leaders in protests, 271–272
Left21 (group), 186
"left pricks" or "plastic leftists" in Hong
     Kong, 187, 237, 246
left's tactics taken by right, 178
Lenin, Vladimir, 6, 17, 18, 272, 285
Leninism, 17–18, 284, 285
"Lennon Wall," 186, 240
Leung, C. Y., 180
Leung, Edward, 243
Leung Ling-kit, Marco, 241
Lewis, John, 81
liberal era (first), 30
liberal teleology, 44–46, 258–259
liberalism, 44–45
Libya, 70, 71–73, 257, 259
LIHKG online forum, 239, 241
Lo, Stephen, 238–239
"localist" movement in Hong Kong, 187,
     246
Locatelli, Piero, 118, 119, 122, 124,
     270, 274
Los Angeles Times (LA Times)
     author as correspondent, 7, 85, 87, 218
     funds for jobs, 87n
     impeachment article, 208–209
     MPL protest and crackdown, 127, 130
Löwith, Karl, 46
"Lula" da Silva, Luiz Inácio
     and BRICS, 47–48
     in elections, 40, 50, 52, 226–227
     on "five causes," 141
     gains in Brazil, 49–50
     imprisonment, 224, 226
     and Iraq war, 34

joining Rousseff government, 207, 209, 212, 223
in Lava Jato, 206, 207, 223–224, 231n
and power of media, 40
as president, 34, 49–51, 204
Luna, Juan Pablo, 198–199, 201
Lviv (Ukraine), 162
Lyashko, Oleh, 166n

Machado, Sergio, 209
Macron, Emmanuel, 233n
"Maidan" protest of 1990s, 154
"Maidan" protest of 2013–2014 (Euromaidan)
  anti-Maidan movement, 167–170
  crackdown on, 164–166
  diversity in participants and causes at protests, 160–162, 232
  "hundreds" in, 161–162
  outcome of protests, 259–260, 265–266
  police at, 152, 165
  protests, 151–152, 158–166, 167, 169–170
  and Western powers, 163–164
  See also Euromaidan
Mallet, Victor, 236
Mani Pulite (Clean Hands), 196
Mao Zedong, 21, 23, 181, 259
Mapuche people, 84, 250
Marcha da Maconha (the Marijuana March), 82
"Mario" of "Five Causes" video, 146
Marx, Karl, 46, 143, 276
Marxism, and history, 44
Marxist-Leninist parties, 20, 23, 42
Marxist-Leninist system, 18
mass protests
  approach in 2010s, 258
  burst of 2019, 235, 254
  collective euphoria in, 286
  as coordinated by West, 135
  diversity in tactics, 163
  diversity participants and causes (see diversity in participants and causes at protests)
  "ecology" of organizations, 284
  foreign involvement in, 272–273
  form of, 268, 271

impact in Europe, 80–81
influence of West, 269–270
influences and symbols within, 186
language used, 113
left's tactics taken by right, 178
organization in, 265–268, 283–285
outcomes (see decade of protests: outcomes)
pattern in, 167, 258
practices in history, 12–15
repertoire of responses, 268–272
and representation, 265, 276–277, 283
repressive practices' history, 181
as response to social injustice, 11, 274
retreat in, 285–286
strategy for after, 259
See also decade of protests
May 1968 in France, 22–23, 24–25
Mayara Vivian
  impeachment connection, 178, 224
  life in São Paulo, 33, 34, 36–37, 224–225
  move to and protests in Chile, 225–226, 227, 230, 249
  in MPL, 42, 44, 53, 115, 121, 124, 134, 136, 141, 145, 202, 224–225
  on outcome of mass protests, 263
  post-MPL events and issues, 173, 178
  in protests, 34, 82, 121, 122, 124, 135, 249
Mayo Feminista ("Feminist May"), 226
McCain, John, 163
McFoxy, 151
McLaren, Malcolm, 25
means and ends (in left and protests)
  as concept, 18, 37, 113, 268
  and representation, 143
media (global)
  cheap information in, 40
  in contention practices, 12, 15
  impact on organizations, 15–16
  and May 1968, 25
  and OWS, 81–82
  power and reach, 15, 39–40
  response to Tahrir Square, 68–69
  role in and impact on mass protests, 11, 274–276, 277–279
  view of US, 88

media in Brazil
and corruption, 196, 197–198
depiction of politicians, 193
and focus of protests, 131–133
impeachment of Rousseff, 210–211,
212
and MPL, 116–117, 118, 119, 120–121,
122, 127–128, 130–132, 141
in politics, 103–104
position of, 88
power of, 40
Merkel, Angela, 190
Middle East, democratization
efforts, 63
Milanovic, Branko, 191
military-industrial complex, and internet,
88–89
Monteiro, Lucas "Vegetable"
background, 42
in MPL, 116, 128, 131, 136, 173, 178,
201–202, 266, 276
on outcome of protests, 258, 266
post-victory decisions and role, 145,
146, 258
in protests, 118–119, 121, 128,
274–275
on tactics of MBL, 178
Moon Jae-in, 215
Morales, Evo, 254
Moro, Sergio
in government of Bolsonaro,
230–231
and Lavo Jato, 195–197, 198, 206–207,
230–231
and Lula, 207, 212, 223, 224
Morozov, Evgeny, 92
Morsi, Mohamed, and presidency, 93,
94–95, 109, 110, 143, 144
Moss, Jonathan, 193
Movimento Brasil Livre (MBL)
description, goals and tactics, 134, 177,
178
election of 2018, 229–230
impeachment of Rousseff, 204,
205–206, 210, 212–213
in protests, 177–178

Movimento Passe Livre (MPL or The Free
Fare Movement)
autonomy and horizontalism, 43–44,
53, 116, 201
and Chile protests, 85
description and principles, 42–43, 115,
136, 176, 194, 201–202, 266
diversity in participants and causes at
protests, 129–134, 137
and media, 116–117, 118, 119, 120–121,
122, 127–128, 130–132, 141
meeting with Rousseff, 141
police crackdown at protest, 1–2, 121,
123–126, 127–128, 131
post-victory events and issues, 145–146,
172, 173, 178, 258
protests in São Paulo, 1–2, 3, 53, 82,
115–117, 118–126, 128–131, 134–135,
137, 173, 276, 285–286
victory over fare hike and street
celebration, 136–137
See also Mayara Vivian; Monteiro,
Lucas
MPL. See Movimento Passe Livre
Mubarak, Gamal, 63
Mubarak, Hosni
fall of, 70–71, 258
as president, 62, 63, 68, 70
protests against, 60–61, 67–68, 70
and state violence, 64
Mung Siu Tat, 243
Muslim Brotherhood, 62, 63, 93–95,
109–110, 144, 200–201
Muslim Cyber Army, 222
Myanmar, 222

Nasser, Gamal, and government, 20, 23,
24, 29, 108
Nasser, Isamel Awled, 263
National Endowment for Democracy
(NED), 47, 62
NATO (North Atlantic Treaty
Organization), 71–73
Nayyem, Mustafa, 158
neo-Nazis, in Ukraine, 160–161,
162

neoliberalism and neoliberal era
and anti-politics, 192–193
in Chile, 31, 225–226, 249
class analysis in, 38–40
description and workings,
30–31, 46
fight against, 37
politics in, 39
Neves, Aécio, 174, 176, 207
New International Economic Order
(NIEO), 30
"New Left"
failures in, 18–19
formation and history, 17, 18–20, 25
ideology in rebellion, 26, 37
means and ends in, 18, 37
organizational forms, 18, 25, 37
and outcome of protests, 270
New York Dolls, 25–26
New York Times, 85, 87–88, 127
news, influence on organizations, 16
NGOs (nongovernmental organizations),
46–47, 200–201
Niemeyer, Oscar, 209
"no-fly zone" in Libya, 72–73
nomenklatura of USSR, 23, 27–28, 29
North Korea, 215
Nuland, Victoria, 163, 168
Nunes, Rodrigo, 38, 266, 273, 284–285

Obama, Barack, 68, 69, 95, 192–193,
258n
"occupation," as practice, 22
Occupy Central with Love and Peace, 179,
180
"Occupy Taiwan Legislature" ("Sunflower
Revolution"), 238
Occupy Wall Street (OWS), 81–82, 179,
259
Ocupa Sampa ("Occupy São Paulo"),
82–83
Odessa (city), 159, 169
oil economies and prices, 74, 170
Old Left
disappearance in US, 17, 25–26
life outside US, 20–25

oligarchs (of Russia), 29
Oliveira, Adélio Bispo de, 228
"Operation Car Wash." See Lava Jato
"Operation Gandhi," 12–13
"Orange Revolution," 155, 159
organization, in mass protests, 265–268,
283–285
Organization of Ukrainian Nationalists
(OUN), 153
Orsal, Osman, 107
Ostermann, Fábio, 133–134, 177
Otpor ("Resistance") (group), 46
Ottoman Empire, 107–108

Paes, Eduardo, 135
Palestinians, 60–61
Park Chung Hee, 203, 214
Park Geun-hye, impeachment of,
203–204, 215
Parti Communiste Français (PCF), 21,
22, 24
Parti Démocratique Progressiste (PDP),
57, 95
"participatory democracy," 14, 34, 80, 113
Partido Comunista de Chile (PCCh), 85
Partido Comunista do Brasil (PCdoB),
41–42, 227
Partido Social Liberal, 228
Parubiy, Andriy, 161–162, 166, 169
Penguin Revolution, 83–84
People's Republic of China (PRC). See
China
perestroika ("reconstruction"), 27–28
Pérez Cáceres, Danitza, 248, 251,
253, 256
Perspectives (journal), 56, 57
Petrobras, 196
Pfeifle, Mark, 91
Philippines, 222
Phillips, Dom, 127, 132, 263
Piñera, Sebastián
as president, 84, 253, 254, 261
and protests, 85, 226, 247, 249
"pink tide," 50–51
Pinochet, Augusto and dictatorship, 83,
249, 251

police
  goal of attacks, 1
  repressive practices, 181, 274–275
  See also specific countries, cities, and
    protests
political struggle, set of actions in, 4–5
politics
  anarchist politics, 37–38
  anti-politics, 192–194, 231, 233
  attitudes to in 2010s, 192–193
  as marketing, 40
  media in, 103–104
  in neoliberalism, 39
  and representation, 198–199
  social media in, 222, 228
  vacuum to fill from mass protests,
    263–265, 272, 276–277, 283, 284
Ponte Estaiada ("cable bridge") in São
    Paulo, 129–130
Poroshenko, Petro, 200, 232, 233
"Port Huron Statement" of SDS, 14
"Prague Spring" of 1968, 23
prefiguration, 19, 24–25, 267–268
"prefigurative politics," 18
Pro-Uni program (Brazil), 50
Project for the New American
    Century, 47
Pronzato, Carlos, 42
protests. See decade of protests; mass
    protests; see under individual
    countries, cities, and places
PT (Partido dos Trabalhadores) (Workers'
    Party)
  achievements, 2
  in bus fare celebration, 136–137
  and corruption, 132, 205
  election of 2010, 52
  election of 2018, 226–227, 228–229
  foundation and rise, 39
  ideology, 34
  and media, 40
  and MPL, 224
  paradox of anti-government sentiment,
    140–141
punk music, 25–26, 36–37, 130
Purnama, Basuki Tjahaja ("Ahok"),
    219–220, 221, 222

Putin, Vladimir
  annexation of Crimea, 168, 170, 260
  on "color revolutions," 135
  doctrine, 73
  problem with US, 164
  and Ukraine politics, 155, 157–158, 166,
    167
Pyatt, Geoffrey, 168

Rabaa Square and Massacre, 144
Radio Free Europe, 68
Reagan, Ronald, 192
Reddit, 239
Rede Globo conglomerate, 40
representation
  crisis in, 198–202
  definition, 199
  and means and ends, 143
  as solution to mass protests, 265,
    276–277, 283
Republic of Korea, 214
"responsibility to protect" doctrine,
    72, 73
revolutions, spread and truisms, 21
Rhee, Syngman, 214
rich anglophone world, triumph and
    opportunity, 44–45
Rigby, Claire, 127
Right Sector (Pravyi Sektor), 161, 163,
    164–165, 169, 232
Rocha, Camila, 133
Roda Viva ("Live Wheel") (interview
    show), 131
Ross, Alec, 92–93
Rousseff, Dilma
  antiterrorism law, 172
  background and work, 52
  bus fare hikes and protests, 115, 134
  call from Erdoğan, 135, 272–273
  economic policies, 104, 115, 174, 176,
    205
  election of 2010, 52
  election of 2014, 174–176
  and "five causes" ("5 causas"), 140,
    141–142, 146
  impeachment and removal, 177, 178,
    193–194, 204, 205–213

in media, 103–104, 135, 210–211, 212
meeting with MPL, 141
phone call with Lula, 207, 209, 212, 223
as president, 53, 101, 146–147, 172, 204
protests against, 146–147, 177–178, 205–206, 210–211, 213
and Putin, 135, 170
and removal of Gaddafi, 73
social revolution of 2010s, 98–99, 100–101, 101n
and Truth Commission, 101
Roy, Arundhati, 200
Rubio, Marco, 245–246, 255
Ruffalo, Mark, 175
ruling class, and revolutions, 21
Russell, Bertrand, 19–20
Russia
as enemy of US, 164
and removal of Gaddafi, 72–73
in Ukraine, 159, 165, 168, 170
in US election of 2016, 217–218
See also USSR
Russomanno, Celso, 102

Sabahi, Hamdeen, 93–94
Sadat, Anwar, 29, 61–62
Said, Khaled, 64, 274
Sakwa, Richard, 161, 164
Saleh, Ali Abdullah, 95
Salem, Mahmoud (aka "Sandmonkey"), 69, 71, 94, 258, 262, 282
Salvador (city), protest for bus fares, 41–42
São Paulo (city)
anti-globalization movement, 35–36
bus and metro fare hike, 115, 136
City Hall attack, 134–135
description, 51
F. Haddad as mayor, 102–103
inequalities in, 97–98
life in 1990s and early 2000s, 33–34, 38
media in politics, 103
police at protests, 1–2, 118, 119, 120, 122, 123–126, 127–128
police-less events, 117, 134–135

protests, 1–2, 3, 34, 53, 82, 114, 115–117, 118–126, 128–131, 134–135, 137, 173, 276, 285–286
World Cup and Itaquera stadium, 171
See also Movimento Passe Livre
Saudi Arabia, 23–24, 75, 76, 77, 95, 109–110, 202
SCAF (Supreme Council of the Armed Forces), 70, 71, 93–94
Scholarism (group), 180, 185
Seattle protests (1999), 35, 271
Second Intifada, 60–61
self-immolation, 56
Senkardes, Eren, 112
Sex Pistols, 26
Shafik, Ahmed, 93
Sharif, Ebrahim, 75–77, 262
Sharp, Gene, 163
Shenker, Jack, 69
Shevardnadze, Eduard, 47
Shihab, Rizieq, 221
Sidi Bouzid (Tunisia), 55–56
Silicon Valley and companies, 89–90, 217
Silva, Marina, 174–175
Silva, Orlando, 120–121
Simon, Mark, 245
Sisi, Abdel Fattah, 144, 202, 262, 277
Sitrin, Marina, 43, 267
Situationist International, 22–23, 26
"Six-Day" War, 23–24
1968, as year of revolutions, 20, 22–25
Slobodian, Quinn, 30–31
social democracy, on global scale, 38–39
social media
and Arab Spring, 58, 64, 92
in Brazilian politics, 228
content on, 90
control of, 81
digital warfare for politics, 222
early examples, 90–91
as emerging issue, 88
followers on, 88, 91
in Hong Kong, 239–240, 241–242
in Indonesia, 220, 221
in Philippines, 222
police crackdown at MPL protest, 127

social media *(continued)*
  power of, 88, 125–126, 279
  seen as force for good, 91–93, 268
  and Tahrir Square, 69
  in Taksim Square, 107
  in Ukraine, 158
  in US election of 2016, 217–218
  use in/for protests, 91, 158, 268
  See also individual platforms
social network, as online model, 90
socialism, 18, 38–39
Sorbonne university, 22
Soros Foundation, 46–47
South Korea, 203–204, 214–215, 259
Southern Europe, 79–81
Soviet Union. *See* USSR
Spain, 80, 259
spontaneity in protests, 266–267
"spring," as concept for protests, 68
"Springtime of Nations" ("Springtime of
    the Peoples") (1848), 21, 68, 74
Stalin, 108, 153, 156
Stoker, Gerry, 193
Strelkov, Igor "Shooter," 169
student union of Salvador, 41–42
Students for a Democratic Society (SDS),
    13–16, 18–19
Students For Liberty, 133
Suharto, Tommy, 221
Suharto, 218–219
Sukarno, 29, 219
Sullivan, Andrew, 91
"Sunflower Revolution" ("Occupy Taiwan
    Legislature"), 238
Suplicy, Eduardo, 121, 136
Svoboda ("Freedom") party, 160, 162, 166
Sylvain, Sylvain, 26
Syria
  protests, 70, 73–74, 95, 259
  representation, 202
  and Turkey, 109
  war in, 95, 109, 188
Syrians, in Brazil, 189–190

Tahrir Square (Egypt)
  description, 64
  as inspiration or model, 79, 80, 82, 269

  and media, 68–69
  monument of uprising, 277
  protests, 60–61, 62, 63–68, 70–71, 93
Tai, Benny, 179, 180
Tai, Derek, 238
Taksim Solidarity umbrella organization,
    111, 143n
Taksim Square (Turkey), 105, 107,
    110–114, 143
Tamarod ("Rebellion") movement, 110,
    143–144
technology, and progress, 88–89
Telegram app, 238, 239–240, 241
teleology, view of liberals, 44–46,
    258–259
television
  content and power of, 40
  and MPL protests, 128, 130, 131, 132
  in Ukraine, 158–159
Temer, Michel, 142, 208, 209, 213, 214, 225
Terena tribe, 104
Thatcher, Margaret, 181–182
Theo (Hong Konger), 258, 266, 269
theology, 46
Third World, 20, 29, 30, 31
Tiananmen Square, 182
Tidva, Artem. *See* Artem
Tilly, Charles, 12
Tiririca (performer) (Francisco Everardo
    Oliveira Silva), 52–53, 211, 257
Tomak, Maria, 158, 159–160, 165,
    166, 200
torture, 52, 59, 77, 212
Trump, Donald, 190–191, 217
Tufekci, Zeynep, 113, 267
Tuğal, Cihan, 143, 271, 276
Tunis (Tunisia), 58–60, 65, 70
Tunisia
  change stalled, 93, 95
  description and recent events, 56–57
  new constitution, 70, 95
  outcome of protests, 70, 263
  protests of 2010, 56–60, 65, 70, 95
  representation, 202
  as trigger Arab Spring, 3, 55–56
Tunisian Communist Workers' Party
    (PCOT), 57–58

Turkey
  crackdown on protesters, 107
  geopolitical issues, 109–110, 144–145
  historical background, 107–108
  and Kurds, 109
  as model for Muslim world, 106
  protests, 3, 105, 106–107, 110–114
  recent politics, 108–109
  state media, 107
Turkish Model of governmentality,
    109–110, 144
Twitter
  description and use, 88
  and MPL protest, 125–126, 127, 131
  roots and launch, 90–91
  use in/for protests, 91, 92, 114
212 protest, 220–221
Tymoshenko, Yulia, 155
"Tyranny of Structurelessness," 25

UGTT mega-union (Tunisian umbrella
    union), 57, 59
Ukraine
  annexation of Crimea, 168, 170, 260
  anti-terrorist operation (ATO), 169
  and Brazil, 231–232, 233
  crackdown on Maidan, 164–165
  "de-communization," 232
  election of 2014, 200
  election of 2019, 232–233
  EU and "Association Agreement," 152,
    157–158
  far-right nationalist militants, 160–161,
    162, 163, 165
  historical background, 152–154
  independence and as nation-state, 154,
    155
  "Independence Square" of 2004 (see
    Maidan)
  militarization of protests, 162–163
  "national unity" government, 165–166
  nationalism in, 153, 155–156, 157, 167,
    260
  outcome of protests, 259–260, 265–266
  politics and oligarchs, 154–158, 167
  post-Maidan administration, 166–168,
    169–170
  protests, 151–152, 154, 158–162
  sovereignty, 154
  split in "blue" and "orange" camps,
    156–157
  television, 158–159
  unionization, 151
Ukrainian, as official language, 156
ultras, 111–112, 140, 161, 165, 169, 250
Ulyanov, Vladimir Ilyich, 17
umbrella, as symbol, 184
"umbrella" campaign in UK, 13
"Umbrella Movement" in Hong Kong,
    180, 184, 185, 187–188, 236
UN Security Council, Resolution
    1973, 73
unions
  in May 1968 events, 22, 24
  in Tunisia, 56–57
United Kingdom (UK), 67–68, 191–192
  See also Britain
United Nations (UN), and Third World
    movement, 30
United States
  anti-American protests, 21–23
  in Bahrain, 76
  in Brazil and Latin America, 34, 231
  citizenship for nonwhites, 14
  as destination for refugees, 189–190
  in financial crisis (2008), 98
  "Hong Kong Human Rights and
    Democracy Act of 2019," 255
  immigrants, 190–191
  interest rates rise and ensuing crisis, 39,
    62, 98
  and Maidan 3.0, 163, 164
  promotion of democracy, 46–47, 62
  protests from Arab Spring, 79, 81
  and protests in Hong Kong, 245–246,
    255, 273
  protests in 1960s, 13–14
  relationship with Brazil, 101, 170
  and Russia, 164, 217–218
  Tahrir Square response, 68
uprisings. See mass protests
US Federal Reserve, 62, 98
US State Department, digital tools
    training, 91

USSR (or Soviet Union)
  de-Stalinization, 23
  in Egypt, 61
  fall of Soviet Union, 26–29, 154,
    156–157
  Leninism, 17–18
  See also Russia

Vallejo, Camila, 84–85, 146, 201,
  261
Vallone, Giuliana, 122, 123–124, 127, 128,
  131, 274
"Vamos Bien" *ultras,* 111–112
Vande-Hei, Jim, 218
Vanguard Organization, 20
Veja (magazine), 103
Vem Pra Rua ("Come to the streets"),
  177–178, 205–206
Verdurada parties ("Veggiefest" punk
  night), 36, 132
"verticalism," 266
Vietnam war, 15, 16, 25
Volcker, Paul, 39

Wa'ad ("Promise") party, 75
Wall Street, protests, 79
  See also Occupy Wall Street
Wang Hui, 199–200, 259
Washington Post, author as
  correspondent, 218
Wasserstrom, Jeff, 185
Watad (Struggle), 57–58

"We Are All Khaled Said" (Facebook
  page), 64
Weber, Isabella, 31
Westad, Odd Arne, 29
Western Europe, Old Left in, 20, 24
WhatsApp, 221, 228, 248
Widodo, Joko "Jokowi," 219, 222
Winter, Sarah, 232
Wisner, Frank, Jr., 68
Wong, Joshua, 180, 184–185, 246
Wong Yik Mo, 240–241, 273
Workers' Party (Brazil). *See* PT (Partido
  dos Trabalhadores)
World Social Forum in Porto Alegre, 42
Wyllys, Jean, 211

Xiao Jianhua, 236

Yanukovych, Viktor
  flight, 166
  and Maidan 3.0, 165–166, 168
  in Maidan (2004), 155–156, 157–158
  protests against, 152
Yatsenyuk, Arseniy, 160, 164, 168
Yeltsin, Boris, 28
Yemen, 95, 202
Yushchenko, Viktor, 155–156

Zelensky, Volodymyr, 232–233
Zhuravlev, Oleg, 260
Zubok, Vladislav, 28
Zuckerberg, Mark, 90, 218

Cassia Tabatini

Vincent Bevins is an award-winning journalist. He reported for the *Financial Times* in London, then served as the Brazil correspondent for the *Los Angeles Times* before covering Southeast Asia for the *Washington Post*.

His first book, *The Jakarta Method*, was named one of the best books of 2020 by NPR, *GQ*, the *Financial Times*, and *CounterPunch*, and has been translated into fifteen languages. Bevins lives in São Paulo.

PublicAffairs is a publishing house founded in 1997. It is a tribute to the standards, values, and flair of three persons who have served as mentors to countless reporters, writers, editors, and book people of all kinds, including me.

I. F. Stone, proprietor of *I. F. Stone's Weekly*, combined a commitment to the First Amendment with entrepreneurial zeal and reporting skill and became one of the great independent journalists in American history. At the age of eighty, Izzy published *The Trial of Socrates*, which was a national bestseller. He wrote the book after he taught himself ancient Greek.

Benjamin C. Bradlee was for nearly thirty years the charismatic editorial leader of *The Washington Post*. It was Ben who gave the *Post* the range and courage to pursue such historic issues as Watergate. He supported his reporters with a tenacity that made them fearless and it is no accident that so many became authors of influential, best-selling books.

Robert L. Bernstein, the chief executive of Random House for more than a quarter century, guided one of the nation's premier publishing houses. Bob was personally responsible for many books of political dissent and argument that challenged tyranny around the globe. He is also the founder and longtime chair of Human Rights Watch, one of the most respected human rights organizations in the world.

·   ·   ·

For fifty years, the banner of Public Affairs Press was carried by its owner Morris B. Schnapper, who published Gandhi, Nasser, Toynbee, Truman, and about 1,500 other authors. In 1983, Schnapper was described by *The Washington Post* as "a redoubtable gadfly." His legacy will endure in the books to come.

Peter Osnos, *Founder*